Project Director: J. J. Thompson, CBE

BIOCHEMISTRY AND MOLECULAR BIOLOGY

Nelson

Thomas Nelson and Sons Ltd
Nelson House   Mayfield Road
Walton-on-Thames   Surrey
KT12 5PL UK

51 York Place
Edinburgh
EH1 3JD   UK

Thomas Nelson (Hong Kong) Ltd
Toppan Building 10/F
22A Westlands Road
Quarry Bay   Hong Kong

Thomas Nelson Australia
102 Dodds Street
South Melbourne
Victoria 3205   Australia

Nelson Canada
1120 Birchmount Road
Scarborough, Ontario
M1K 5G4   Canada

First published by Thomas Nelson and Sons Ltd 1994

ISBN 0-17-448207-8
NPN 9 8 7 6 5 4 3 2 1

Prited in China

Contents

Theme 3: The Molecular Machine

The Project: an introduction

The **University of Bath · Science 16–19 Science Project,** grew out of reappraisal of how far sixth form science had travelled during a period of unprecedented curriculum reform and an attempt to evaluate future development. Changes were occurring both within the constitution of 16–19 syllabuses themselves and as a result of external pressures from 16+ and below: syllabus redefinition (starting with the common cores), the introduction of AS-level and its academic recognition, the originally optimistic outcome to the Higginson enquiry; new emphasis on skills and processes, and the balance of continuous and final assessment at GCSE level.

This activity offered fertile ground for the School of Education at the University of Bath to join forces with a team of science teachers, drawn from a wide spectrum of educational experience, to create a flexible curriculum model and then develop resources to fit it. The group addressed the task of satisfying these requirements:

- the new syllabus and examination demands of A- and AS-level courses;
- the provision of materials suitable for both the core and options parts of syllabuses;
- the striking of an appropriate balance of opportunities for students to acquire knowledge and understanding, develop skills and concepts, and to appreciate the applications and implications of science;
- the encouragement of a degree of independent learning through highly interactive texts;
- the satisfaction of the needs of a wide ability range of students at this level.

Some of these objectives were easier to achieve than others. Relationships to still evolving syllabuses demand the most rigorous analysis and a sense of vision – and optimism – regarding their eventual destination. Original assumptions about AS-level, for example, as a distinct though complementary sibling to A-level, needed to be revised.

The Project, though, always regarded itself as more than a provider of materials, important as this is, and concerned itself equally with the process of provision – how material can best be written and shaped to meet the requirements of the educational market-place. This aim found expression in two principal forms: the idea of secondment at the University and the extensive trialling of early material in schools and colleges.

Most authors enjoyed a period of secondment from teaching, which allowed them to reflect and write more strategically (and, particularly so, in a supportive academic environment) but, equally, to engage with each other in wrestling with the issues in question.

The Project saw in the trialling a crucial test for the acceptance of its ideas and their execution. Over one hundred institutions and one thousand students participated, and responses were invited from teachers and pupils alike. The reactions generally confirmed the soundness of the model and allowed for more scrupulous textual housekeeping, as details of confusion, ambiguity or plain misunderstanding were revised and reordered.

The test of all teaching must be in the quality of the learning, and the proof of these resources will be in the understanding and ease of accessibility which they generate. The Project, ultimately, is both a collection of materials and a message of faith in the science curriculum of the future.

J.J. Thompson

How to use this book

Biochemistry and molecular biology is a field of scientific research that has grown and developed tremendously over the last 40 years. Its discoveries have affected almost every area of our lives. This book gives an introduction to some of the basic processes that take place in living cells, without which life would not exist.

Biochemistry and Molecular Biology is written for A- or AS-level courses in biology and chemistry. It assumes an understanding of biology and chemistry up to GCSE level. The prerequisites at the beginning of each theme tell you what you should know before you study that theme.

The book is divided into three themes, which should be worked through in order. Theme 1 begins with the small, simple molecules found in living cells, and shows how these are built up into more complex molecules and then into biological structures. Theme 2 deals with the way in which genetic information is stored in cells, and how that information is used as a blueprint for the construction of the complex molecules necessary for life. Theme 3 considers the cell as a molecular 'machine' and describes some of the complex cycles of reactions that take place within it.

The best way to study any subject is to take some responsibility for your own learning. This means, for example, ensuring that you make a good set of notes and answer the questions as you come to them so that you can assess your progress. The book is designed to help you organise your studies and on the page opposite you will find information about the book which will help you get the best out of it.

Reading is, on its own, usually too passive to promote effective thinking and learning and the questions within the chapters are, therefore, an important feature of this book. They are intended to help you understand what you have just read. You should write down the answers to the questions as you come to them and then check the answers either with those at the back of the book or with your teacher. If you do not understand a question or an answer, make a note of it and discuss it with your teacher at the earliest opportunity.

Practical work in biochemistry in schools and colleges is difficult because of the time and the expensive equipment needed. Consequently, this book contains no suggestions for practical work, though some may be possible in some situations. Instead the book contains a number of data handling exercises, which will give you a feel for the kind of experiments biochemists carry out and how conclusions can be drawn from the data they obtain.

Biochemistry and molecular biology are very exciting areas of research, with many career openings. This book is intended not only to help you pass an exam, but also to give you some idea of what the subject is all about and whether you would like to work in this field.

Learning objectives

These are given at the beginning of each chapter and they outline what you should gain from the chapter. They are statements of attainment and often link closely to statements in a course syllabus. Learning objectives can help you make notes for revision, especially if used in conjunction with the review of crucial points at the end of the chapter, as well as for checking progress.

Questions

In-text questions occur at points when you should consolidate what you have just learned, or prepare for what is to follow, by thinking along the lines required by the question. Some questions can, therefore, be answered from the material covered in the previous section, others may require additional thought or information. Answers to questions are given in Appendix B at the end of the book.

Data handling

The data handling exercises are intended to provide more thought-provoking questions, and to give you practice in using the knowledge you have acquired in studying the text. Some of them also give an insight into the way in which scientists have devised ingenious experiments to unlock the mysteries of biochemical processes. Answers are given in Appendix A at the end of the book.

Tutorials

These provide background information on some basic biological and chemical topics.

Review of crucial points

These sum up the key points in the chapter which you should remember. They can be used to help you compile your own revision notes.

Margin notes

These give additional information or reminders of things you may have forgotten.

Acknowledgements

Allsport: p. 208; Biofotos/Heather Angel: p. 6; Biophoto Associates: p. 64, 73, 75, 79, 127; Anthony Blake Photo Library: p. 36; British Museum: p. 107; J. Allan Cash: p. 76, 82, 142, 201; Camera Press: p. 94; Ronald Grant Archive: p. 3; S & R Greenhill: p. 40; The Image Bank: p. 110; Kings College: p. 92; Massey University/David A D Parry: p. 144; The Mustograph Agency: p. 28; Science Photo Library: p. 73, 128, 138, 145 (2); Vision Bank: p. 139; C James Webb: p. 154, 173, 181

Theme 1

MOLECULES AND THEIR INTERACTIONS

Each cell is made up of billions of molecules and it is the nature of these molecules and the chemical reactions that occur between them that give rise to the phenomenon that we call life. Studying each type of molecule in isolation is like studying the pieces of an intricate and fiendishly complex jigsaw puzzle: every fact that is unearthed guides scientists along the path towards a goal where the puzzle is finally understood and the secrets of the cell are fully revealed.

PREREQUISITES

- GCSE Science or GCSE Chemistry and Biology.

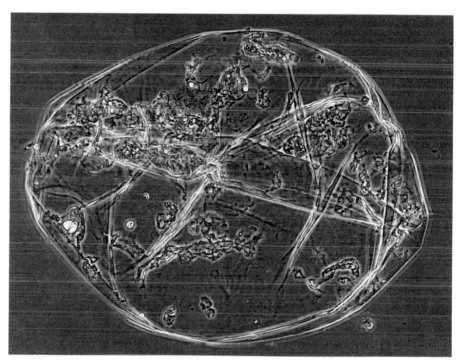

A cell from a tomato plant (*Lycopersicon esculentum*) showing some of the complex subcellular structures where chemical reactions are carried out.

Chapter 1

SMALL MOLECULES

Molecules are groups of atoms held together by covalent bonds. The way the molecule behaves depends on the type of atoms in the molecule, the number of atoms present and the way the molecule interacts with its surroundings.

There are many thousands of different substances in a single cell and each of those substances has its own, unique molecular formula. Learning the properties of every one of these different molecules would be an impossible task but luckily this is not necessary because similar molecules behave in a similar manner: the molecules fall into groups. We can learn about a group of molecules, then concentrate on the small differences within the group.

LEARNING OBJECTIVES

After studying this chapter you should:

1. appreciate that the structure of a molecule determines its function in the organism;

2. realise that an organism contains a huge number of different organic molecules;

3. be familiar with the general features of monosaccharides and disaccharides;

4. be familiar with the general features of amino acids;

5. be familiar with the general features of nucleotides;

6. be familiar with the general features of fatty acids, glycerides and phospholipids;

7. have some idea of the functions of organic and inorganic ions in organisms.

1.1 MOLECULES

Atoms make molecules and molecules make life possible

Atoms join together to make molecules by forming covalent bonds. Some molecules contain only a few atoms, for example the water molecule (H_2O), carbon dioxide (CO_2) and oxygen (O_2), while others contain many atoms, for example the protein insulin contains over five hundred atoms and a molecule of DNA running the length of a chromosome contains over seven thousand million atoms. Biologically important molecules contain only a limited number of different atoms, carbon, hydrogen, oxygen, nitrogen, phosphorus and sulphur, but those atoms can be joined together to make an unimaginably large number of different molecules. It is this huge range of molecules that makes life possible. A cell is a collection of different molecules that come together to make the structures in the cell and interact so that the cell functions: the cell can be thought of as a complicated machine where both structural and moving components are made up of molecules.

A molecule's properties depend on its atoms

It is possible to predict a molecule's properties from the atoms that it contains and the way that those atoms are joined together. Obviously, it is easier to predict the properties of a small molecule than a large molecule because there are fewer atoms to consider. Once the properties of the molecule have been established it is possible to predict how that molecule will interact with other molecules of the same substance, or with different substances. The principle that the behaviour of a substance can be predicted from the atoms and bonds within a molecule can be illustrated by studying the water molecule.

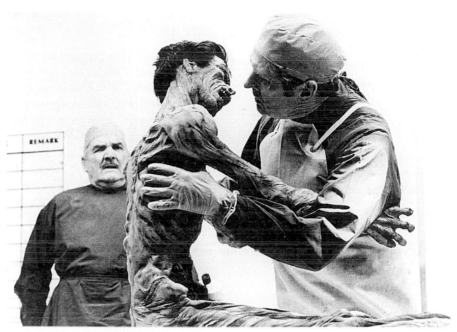

Fig 1.1 A dehydrated humanoid attacks a human being in a science fiction film. Water makes up about 70% of the human body and 60–95% of every living organism. Water is the solvent in which life evolved and every living cell is a droplet of the precious fluid in which the molecules of life are dissolved. Humans, like all land-living organisms, are a pool of the precious solvent enclosed in a protective outer layer so that our cells can survive in the alien environment of the air.

Water: a molecule that makes life possible

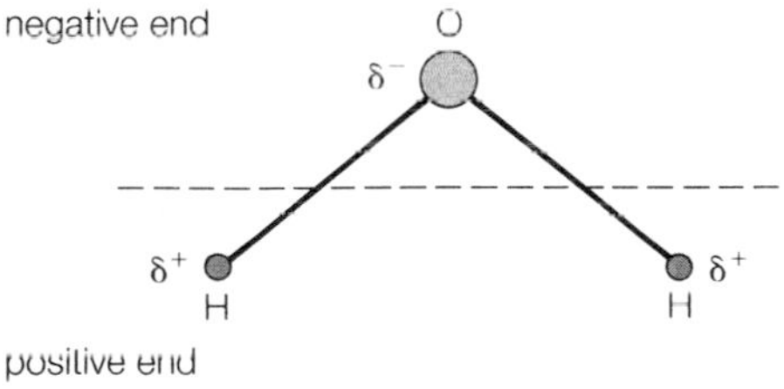

Water is the solvent of life. Every cell is 70% water and almost all the chemical reactions that occur within a cell are happening in aqueous solution, a solution in which water is the solvent. Life is thought to have evolved in water, and every cell can be thought of as a tiny bag of water with all the molecules needed for life dissolved in that water. The way that one oxygen joins with two hydrogen atoms makes life as we know it possible.

One oxygen atom joins to two hydrogen atoms to make a water molecule, H_2O, a bent molecule containing two covalent bonds (Fig 1.2). The electrons are not evenly distributed across a water molecule, the oxygen atom in the molecule having a small negative charge ($\delta-$) and the hydrogen atoms each having a small positive charge ($\delta+$). Exactly why an oxygen atom and two hydrogen atoms form a molecule with this particular shape and this charge distribution is explained in Tutorial 1.1 on page 7.

As the water molecule is bent, and the charge distribution across the molecule is uneven, there is a positive end to the molecule and a negative end (Fig 1.2). A molecule with a positive end and a negative end is a **polar** molecule.

Having determined that the shape and charge distribution of the water molecule are due to the atoms involved, it is possible to examine how the

negative end

$\delta-$ O

$\delta+$ H   H $\delta+$

positive end

Fig 1.2 A water molecule, H_2O, is crooked and polar.

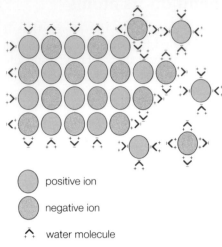

○ positive ion

○ negative ion

∧ water molecule

Fig 1.3 Water dissolves an ionic substance because the polar water molecules are attracted to the ions.

Ions are atoms or molecules that have an overall negative charge, because they have extra electron(s) or an overall positive charge because they have lost electron(s).

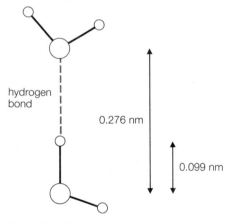

hydrogen bond

0.276 nm

0.099 nm

Fig 1.4 Weak bonds, called hydrogen bonds, form between water molecules.

A hydrogen bond can also form between a nitrogen atom in a molecule and a hydrogen atom in another molecule.

properties of water are due to the shape and charge distribution of the individual molecules. The biologically important properties of water are:

- it is a very efficient solvent, i.e. many substances will dissolve in water;
- it has a very high specific heat capacity, i.e. it takes a lot of energy to raise the temperture of 1 kg of water by 1 °C, and a lot of energy is given out when the temperature of 1 kg of water falls by 1 °C;
- it is a liquid across a very large temperature range, 0–100 °C;
- it is very cohesive, i.e. the water molecules stick together.

Water is an excellent solvent because the molecules are polar

The first of these properties, the fact that water is a very efficient solvent, is because water molecules are polar. A solvent dissolves a substance because the molecules of the solvent are attracted to the molecules of the substance to be dissolved. The molecules of the solvent get between the molecules of the substance, breaking up the solid or liquid and surrounding each molecule with a shell of solvent molecules, so distributing the molecules of the substance throughout the solvent (Fig 1.3).

The negative end of the water molecules will be attracted to positively charged ions, or to the positively charged parts of molecules, and the positive end of the water molecule will be attracted to negatively charged ions, or to the negatively charged parts of molecules (Fig 1.3). This means that water will dissolve substances that are made up of ions and substances that are made up of polar molecules. However, water will not dissolve non-polar molecules, molecules which have a completely even charge distribution. This is because non-polar substances do not have regions of charge to attract the water molecule. Substances which attract water are called **hydrophilic** ('water-loving') while those substances which are not attracted to water are called **hydrophobic** ('water-hating').

Water molecules form hydrogen bonds

The other three properties of water mentioned above are all due to the fact that the forces of attraction between the water molecules are very strong. These unusually strong forces of attraction are also due to the uneven charge distribution of water molecules. The positively charged end of one water molecule is attracted to the negatively charged end of another water molecule (Fig 1.4). This force of attraction is called a **hydrogen bond** and the attraction is at its strongest when an oxygen, a hydrogen and an oxygen are in a straight line as shown in Fig 1.4. Hydrogen bonds are about twenty times weaker than most covalent bonds but are ten times stronger than the normal forces of attraction between molecules.

Water has a high melting point and boiling point

Water melts at 0 °C and boils at 100 °C. These are very unusual melting and boiling points for a substance made up of small molecules. Table 1.1 shows the melting points and boiling points of various substances made up of molecules that are a similar size to water. As can be seen from the table all the substances except water would be gases at 0 °C, so none of them would make a very good solvent for biologically important molecules, at least not on Earth!

Table 1.1

Substance	Relative molecular mass	M.p. (°C)	B.p. (°C)	Liquid over
water (H$_2$O)	18	0	100	100°
methane (CH$_4$)	16	−182	−164	18°
ammonia (NH$_3$)	17	−78	−33	45°
hydrogen sulphide (H$_2$S)	34	−85	−152	67°
carbon monoxide (CO)	28	−199	−19	18°
nitrogen (N$_2$)	28	−210	−196	14°
nitrogen(II) oxide (NO)	30	−163	−152	11°
oxygen (O$_2$)	32	−218	−183	35°

The reason that water has a high boiling point and a high melting point is because of the strong forces of attraction between the molecules, the hydrogen bonds. Substances with weak forces of attraction between the molecules melt and boil at much lower temperatures because a lot less energy is needed to overcome the forces of attraction between the molecules, allowing the molecule to move more and change from a solid to a liquid or from a liquid to a gas.

Water is liquid over a large temperature range

Water also remains a liquid over a very wide temperature range, a much larger range than any other substance made from such small molecules (Table 1.1, final column). The forces of attraction between the molecules of liquid water are very strong, so a lot of energy is needed to overcome them and allow the molecules to escape to form a gas.

Water can act as a temperature buffer

Liquid water does not heat up or cool down quickly. It takes a lot of energy to raise the temperature of 1 kg of water by 1°C, and a lot of energy is given out before the temperature of 1 kg of water falls by 1°C: liquid water has a high specific heat capacity.

If energy is supplied to a substance the molecules will have more kinetic energy, and the temperature of the substance will rise. In liquid water some of the energy goes into breaking the hydrogen bonds that are holding the molecules together, and only part of the energy goes into increasing the temperature of the liquid. This is why it takes a lot of energy to raise the temperature of 1 kg of water by 1°C.

As liquids lose heat energy, usually all the energy comes from decreasing the kinetic energy of the molecules, so the temperature of the liquid falls quickly. In water, energy can be given out by the liquid through the forming of hydrogen bonds. When a hydrogen bond forms, the molecules of water become more stable and so energy is released. When energy is taken away from water, some will come from forming hydrogen bonds, and only some from decreasing the kinetic energy of the molecules, so the temperature of the water will only fall by a small amount.

The ability of the molecules in liquid water to form hydrogen bonds means that water acts as a temperature buffer. The hydrogen bonds release energy when energy is removed from the water and soak up energy when energy is given to the water. Only a fraction of any incoming energy goes to increase the kinetic energy of the molecules, and only a fraction of any outgoing energy comes from decreasing the kinetic energy of the molecules: the temperature of the water does not vary much.

This means that water acts as a **homeostatic medium**. Organisms living in water are protected from changes in the air temperature by the water

around them. A land-living organism carries about water that bathes every cell in its body. This water can absorb a lot of energy before the body temperature rises and give out a lot of energy before the body temperature falls. This is very important for land-living organisms that do not have sophisticated mechanisms for controlling their body temperature.

Water can act as a coolant

The most successful land-living organisms have evolved mechanisms for controlling their body temperature. One mechanism for lowering the body temperature is to evaporate water from the body surface, for example sweating in mammals. Water works as an efficient coolant because the forces of attraction between water molecules are so strong. This means that a lot of energy is needed to change liquid water into water vapour. The energy needed to evaporate the water is taken from the surface of the organism, cooling it.

Water is very cohesive

The presence of hydrogen bonds between the molecules in liquid water make water very cohesive. The cohesive properties of water have very important biological consequences, for example they allow blood to flow in blood vessels and allow trees to transport water from their roots to their leaves.

So the properties of the biologically important substance water are due to the shape and charge distribution of the water molecule. The same is true of every biologically important substance: an examination of the molecule indicates the properties of that molecule and the way in which it will behave inside the cell.

Fig 1.5 Water has many unusual properties on which life depends. It is an excellent solvent, it acts as a temperature buffer and it remains a liquid over a remarkably wide range of temperature. Water is also unusual in that it expands when it freezes, so that ice floats on water. As ice is a good thermal insulator this means that the water beneath the floating layer of ice rarely freezes, allowing aquatic organisms to survive when the air temperature falls below zero degrees Celsius.

QUESTIONS

Na^+Cl^-
sodium chloride

CH_3CH_2OH
ethanol

$CH_3CH_2CH_2CH_2CH_2CH_3$
hexane

CH_2OH
|
$CHOH$
|
CH_2OH
glycerol

CH_3
|
$CH_3CCH_2CH_3$
|
CH_3
2,2-dimethylbutane

Fig 1.6

1.1 (a) Look at the molecules in Fig 1.6. Divide the molecules into two groups, those you think would dissolve in water, and those you think would be insoluble in water.
(b) Petrol is a non-polar solvent. The molecules present are not attracted to charged or polar substances. However, the forces of attraction between the molecules in the petrol are the same as those between the molecules in uncharged and non-polar substances. Which of the substances in Fig 1.6 would be soluble in petrol and which would be insoluble?

1.2 (a) Describe the structure and charge distribution of the water molecule.
(b) Explain how the charge distribution of the water molecule leads to hydrogen bonds forming between water molecules.
(c) Explain the role of hydrogen bonds in the following:
  (i) water is a liquid across the temperature range 0–100°C;
  (ii) liquid water has a very high specific heat capacity;
  (iii) a lot of energy is needed to turn liquid water at any temperature into water vapour at that temperature;
  (iv) water is very cohesive.
(d) Give one biological consequence of each of the properties of water listed in (c).

1.3 (a) What percentage of each cell is water?
(b) Explain why the water molecule is polar.
(c) What types of substances are soluble in water and why?
(d) What types of substances are not soluble in water and why?

SMALL MOLECULES

The electron distribution in atoms

An atom consists of a tiny **nucleus** at the centre and **electrons** that are found outside the nucleus. Almost all the mass of the atom is concentrated in the nucleus and the nucleus is positively charged. The electrons have almost no mass and are negatively charged. In an isolated atom the positive charge in the nucleus is exactly balanced by the negative charge of the electrons and the atom is neutrally charged.

The electrons move around the nucleus in certain patterns depending on the amount of energy each electron has. One of the simplest ways of understanding these patterns is to imagine that there are shells around the nucleus. These shells are the positions where the electrons are most likely to be found.

Electrons fill up the lowest energy level shells first (Table 1.2), so a hydrogen atom, which has only one electron, will have its one electron in the lowest energy shell, while an oxygen atom, which has eight electrons, will have two electrons in the first shell and six in the second shell. Atoms are at their most stable if the shells are filled with electrons. One way in which each atom can obtain a full shell is by 'sharing' electrons. It is this sharing of electrons that makes a covalent bond. The electron sharing that occurs in a water molecule is shown in Fig 1.7.

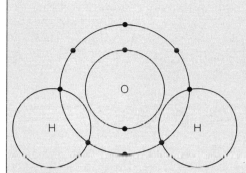

Fig 1.7 Covalent bonds can be thought of as 'sharing' electrons in order to gain a full outer shell.

Table 1.2

	Shell	Stable arrangement of electrons in shell
lowest energy	1	2
	2	8
	3	8
highest energy	4	2

Understanding the shape of the water molecule requires a more sophisticated understanding of how the electrons are arranged around the nucleus. The second electron shell is not arranged as a simple, spherical shell but contains four orbitals, each of which can hold a maximum of two electrons. One of the ways in which the electrons can be arranged in the second electron shell is shown in Fig 1.8(a).

The oxygen atom in water is arranged as shown in Fig 1.8(a) while the two hydrogens only have one electron in their first electron shell (Fig 1.8(b)). Two of the orbitals contain two electrons and two of the orbitals contain only one. The two orbitals with one electron overlap with the first electron shell of the hydrogen atoms, each with its one electron (Fig 1.8(c)). This means that all four orbitals around the oxygen atom now contain two electrons, the oxygen atom has a full outer shell and each hydrogen has a full outer shell: the molecule is stable.

The two covalent bonds are where the orbitals from two atoms overlap. If the two covalent bonds are represented by lines, and the orbitals are not drawn, the water molecule looks as it is drawn in Fig 1.2. The water molecule is bent because of the arrangement of the orbitals around the nucleus of the oxygen atom.

The electrons in a covalent bond are not always shared equally by the two atoms involved, particularly if the two atoms are different. In a water molecule, the electrons are attracted more by the oxygen nucleus than by the hydrogen nuclei so the shared electrons spend more of the time close to the oxygen nucleus than close to the hydrogen nuclei. This

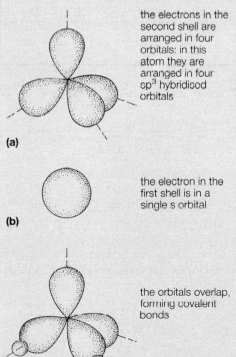

the electrons in the second shell are arranged in four orbitals: in this atom they are arranged in four sp^3 hybridised orbitals

(a)

the electron in the first shell is in a single s orbital

(b)

the orbitals overlap, forming covalent bonds

(c)

Fig 1.8

leads to the oxygen atom within the water molecule having a slight negative charge, because at any one time it has more electrons than are needed to neutralise the positive nucleus, and each hydrogen atom in the molecule having a slight positive charge, because at any one time it has fewer electrons than are needed to neutralise the positive nucleus.

The tendency for an atom or a molecule to attract electrons is called **electronegativity**. The more electronegative an atom is, the more inclined it is to attract the shared electrons in a covalent bond. The atoms which are commonly found in biologically important molecules, carbon (C), hydrogen (H), nitrogen (N), oxygen (O), sulphur (S) and phosphorus (P), can be arranged in this order according to their electronegativity: $O > N > S = C > P > H$.

1.2 ORGANIC MOLECULES

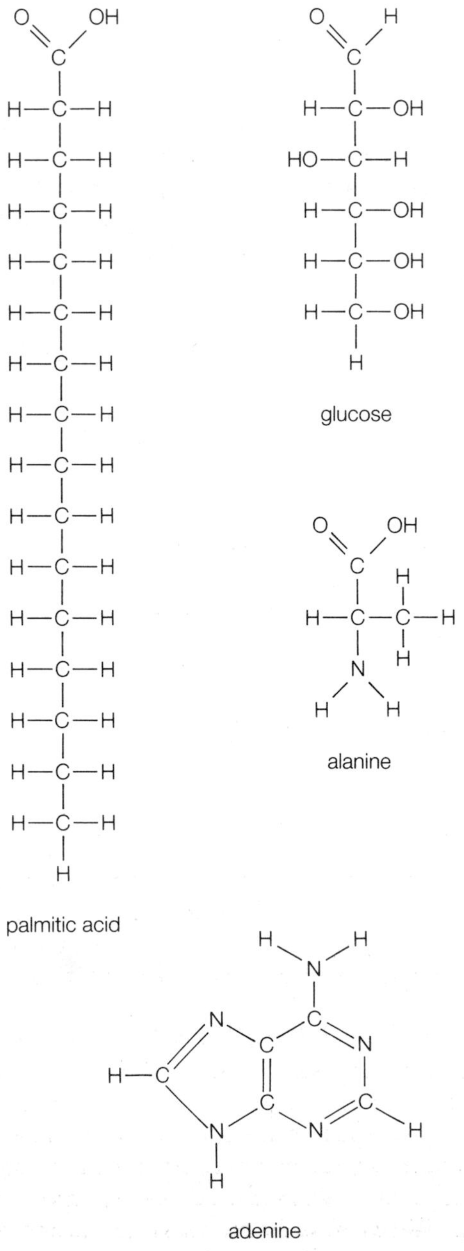

glucose

alanine

palmitic acid

adenine

Fig 1.9 Four organic molecules.

A cell is a collection of molecules: molecules put together to give solid structures; molecules that store the genetic code; molecules that are used as an energy store; molecules that act as catalysts in chemical reactions; thousands of different molecules each with a different role. All these molecules have something in common: they all contain carbon. Molecules that contain carbon are called **organic** molecules.

Carbon atoms form chains

If you study Fig 1.9 you will see that each molecule contains more than one carbon atom. Most of the molecules have many carbon atoms arranged in straight chains, branched chains, or rings. It is this ability of a carbon atom to bond to other carbon atoms that makes a large range of different carbon-containing molecules possible.

Organic molecules have stable, unreactive regions

Molecules that are made up of only carbon and hydrogen atoms are called **hydrocarbons**. There are very few molecules in cells which are hydrocarbons, but a large number contain hydrocarbon regions, parts of the molecule that contain only carbon and hydrogen. Hydrocarbons are very stable, unreactive molecules, and the hydrocarbon regions of other molecules have the same properties.

Organic molecules have reactive regions

Life is a series of chemical reactions, so the molecules making up cells cannot be completely stable and unreactive! Most organic molecules have regions which are much more reactive than hydrocarbons. These regions are called **reactive groups** and they often contain atoms such as nitrogen, oxygen, sulphur and/or phosphorus. It is important to know a little about some of these reactive groups because they have such an important part to play in the chemical reactions in cells. Some common reactive groups are listed in Table 1.3.

Each organic molecule has a specific shape

Molecules are three-dimensional structures. The bonds around each atom occur in certain positions and this means that the molecule as a whole has a typical three-dimensional shape. The shapes that the bonds form around carbon, nitrogen and oxygen atoms are summarised in Fig 1.10. These shapes form because of the way that electrons are distributed around the

Table 1.3   Five common reactive groups found in organic molecules.

—CH$_3$	methyl group
—OH	hydroxyl group
—NH$_2$	amine group
—C=O	carbonyl group
—C$\underset{OH}{\overset{O}{\diagup}}$	carboxylic acid group

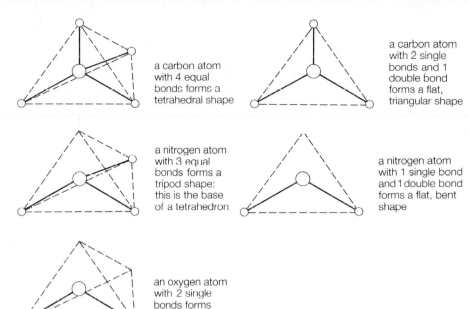

a carbon atom with 4 equal bonds forms a tetrahedral shape

a carbon atom with 2 single bonds and 1 double bond forms a flat, triangular shape

a nitrogen atom with 3 equal bonds forms a tripod shape: this is the base of a tetrahedron

a nitrogen atom with 1 single bond and 1 double bond forms a flat, bent shape

an oxygen atom with 2 single bonds forms a flat, bent shape

Fig 1.10

Table 1.4

Bond	Bond length (nm*)
C—C	0.154
C—C	0.134
C—H	0.108
C—O	0.143
C=O	0.122
O—H	0.096
hydrogen bond	
O- - -H	0.277

*1 nm is 0.000 000 001 m

nuclei of the atoms (Tutorial 1.1). As the bonds occur in certain positions it is possible to define bond angles, the angles between the bonds (Fig 1.10).

However, it is important to realise that organic molecules are not entirely rigid. Atoms joined by a single bond can twist; the single bond can rotate about its long axis. Atoms joined by a double bond cannot twist because the extra bond prevents rotation. This means that some sections of organic molecules are flexible while others are rigid.

Covalent bonds also have specific lengths, called the **bond length**. The bond length for a specific type of bond depends on the two atoms involved and whether the bond is a double bond or a single bond. The lengths of some bonds that are common in organic molecules are listed in Table 1.4.

So bonds are specific lengths, form at specific angles to each other and some bonds can be twisted and others cannot. This means that each organic molecule has a certain shape, and this shape can be flexible, or not, depending on whether double bonds are present in the molecule. As you read this book you will see that the three-dimensional shape of carbon-containing molecules is crucial to their biological activity.

Molecules can contain the same atoms arranged differently

As the shape of an organic molecule is crucial, the way the atoms are arranged in a molecule is as important as the type and number of atoms present. Molecules with the same atoms but with those atoms arranged in different ways are called **isomers**. For example, all simple sugars containing six carbon atoms have the same formula, $C_6H_{12}O_6$, but the atoms are arranged in different ways (Fig 1.11). The sugar molecules are all isomers of each other.

There are two main types of isomerism: **structural isomerism** and **stereoisomerism**. Structural isomers have the same number and type of atoms in the molecule, like all isomers, but the atoms are connected differently. One example of this is two molecules with the formula C_3H_6O in which the carbonyl group (C=O) is at a different place in the two molecules (Fig 1.12). Molecules with the carbonyl group at the end are called **aldehydes** and they react differently to molecules with the carbonyl group away from the ends of the molecule, which are called **ketones**.

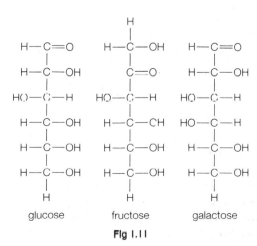

glucose   fructose   galactose

Fig 1.11

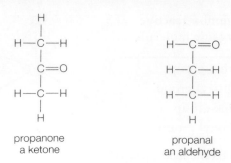

propanone
a ketone

propanal
an aldehyde

Fig 1.12 A molecule with the carbonyl group on the end carbon is an aldehyde. A molecule with the carbonyl group not on an end carbon is a ketone.

Stereoisomers have the same number and type of atoms in the molecule and all the atoms are connected in the same way but the two molecules cannot be superimposed. This happens when a carbon atom is connected to four different groups (Fig 1.13).

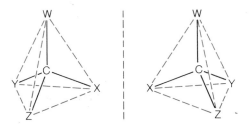

Fig 1.13 Both carbon atoms have four groups around them arranged as a tetrahedron.

Representing a three-dimensional molecule on paper

It is impossible to show a three-dimensional molecule accurately in a two-dimensional diagram, so certain conventions have become established in order that each scientist will understand what another scientist means. An **empirical formula** is used to represent the ratio of the different atoms present in the molecule. For an unsaturated fatty acid molecule, such as the molecule shown in Fig 1.14, the empirical formula would be $C_nH_{2n-2}O_2$. A **simple formula** is used to show which atoms are present and how many of each type of atom are present in the molecule. The simple formula for the molecule shown in Fig 1.14 is $C_{18}H_{34}O_2$. However, a simple formula does not give any information on how those atoms are arranged.

Structural formulae give much more information about the molecule. A structural formula is a two-dimensional diagram of the molecule showing which atoms are attached to which other atoms. A structural formula for oleic acid (a fatty acid with simple formula $C_{18}H_{34}O_2$) is given in Fig 1.14(a).

A structural formula like this still takes a long time to draw. Certain short cuts are used to make it easier to draw, and as the same 'abbreviations' are always used one scientist knows what another scientist means. The abbreviated form of the structural formula for oleic acid is given in Fig 1.14(b). The first abbreviation is that most of the hydrogens are left out. If a carbon atom looks like it is only forming two bonds, you can assume that the other two bonds are C—H bonds. The second abbreviation is that most of the carbon atoms are represented by bends in the lines rather than 'C'. These two abbreviations mean that the structural formula is easy to draw and less muddling to look at. Only the reactive group of the molecule is drawn out in full, because it is this part of the molecule that it likely to react and change.

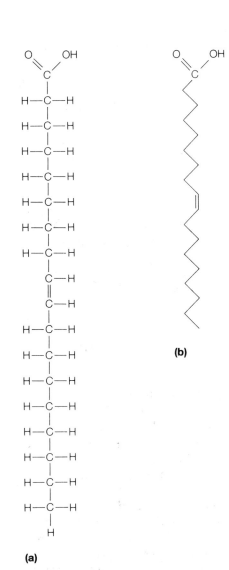

(b)

(a)

Fig 1.14 **(a)** The full structural formula of a fatty acid.
  (b) The abbreviated structural formula for the fatty acid shown in (a).

SMALL MOLECULES

1.4 (a) Write out a 'full' structural formula for each of the 'abbreviated' structural formulae shown in Fig 1.15(a).
(b) Write out an 'abbreviated' structural formula for each of the 'full' structural formulae shown in Fig 1.15(b).

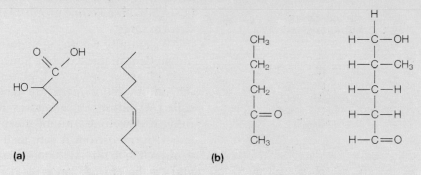

(a)   (b)

Fig 1.15

1.5 (a) Why does the element carbon form such a huge range of molecules?
(b) Why is it important that some regions of the organic molecules found in cells should be unreactive?
(c) Why is it important that some regions of the organic molecules found in cells should be reactive?

1.6 (a) Why is a C—O bond polar? (Refer to Tutorial 1.1.)
(b) Why is a —C—OH group reactive in a molecule while a —CH_2CH_3 group is unreactive?
(c) How many isomers exist with the simple formula C_3H_6O?

1.3 SUGARS

Solid sugars form crystals and dissolve in water to form a sweet-tasting solution. Sugars fall into two groups, **monosaccharides** (e.g. glucose) and **disaccharides** (e.g. sucrose). Disaccharides are formed from two mono-saccharide molecules by a condensation reaction (the elimination of water). Sugars are one form of **carbohydrate**, the other form is **polysaccharides**, the macromolecules formed by the joining of many monosaccharides.

Monosaccharides have the same empirical formula and the same reactive groups

Monosaccharides contain only carbon, hydrogen and oxygen in the ratio of 1C:2H:1O, therefore the empirical formula is $(CH_2O)_n$. As well as having a C:H:O ratio of of 1:2:1, monosaccharides also have certain reactive groups present. To be a monosaccharide the molecule must contain a **carbonyl** group (C=O) and at least two hydroxyl groups (O—H). All mono-saccharides have names ending in **-ose**.

The carbons in a monosaccharide are always numbered. This means that a certain carbon can be referred to without drawing out the whole structural formula. The end carbon nearest the carbonyl group is always carbon 1 (Figs 1.16 and 1.19(a)).

The larger monosaccharides can exist as chains or rings

The simplest form of monosaccharide is a **triose**. A triose contains three carbons (tri = 3). Trioses have a backbone of three carbons, a carbonyl group

H—$\overset{1}{C}$=O
|
H—$\overset{2}{C}$—OH
|
H—$\overset{3}{C}$—OH
|
H

glyceraldehyde
2,3-dihydroxypropanal

H
|
H—$\overset{1}{C}$—OH
|
$\overset{2}{C}$=O
|
H—$\overset{3}{C}$—OH
|
H

dihydroxyacetone
1,3-dihydroxypropanone

Fig 1.16

CH$_2$OH
|
C=O
|
CH$_2$OH

dihydroxyacetone

CH$_2$OH   CH$_2$OH
| |
C=O   C=O

L-erythrulose   D-erythrulose

all D-ketoses

Fig 1.18

and two hydroxyl groups. Figure 1.16 shows two important trioses, glyceraldehyde and dihydroxyacetone. Glyceraldehyde and dihydroxyacetone are structural isomers of each other. As can be seen from Fig 1.16 glyceraldehyde has a carbonyl group at the end of the molecule, this makes it an **aldose** (a sugar with an aldehyde group), while dihydroxyacetone has a carbonyl group away from the ends of the molecule, this makes it a **ketose** (a sugar with a ketone group). Trioses exist only as chains; they are too short to form rings.

All naturally occurring sugars are originally made from trioses. Glyceraldehyde contains a carbon joined to four different groups and can therefore form two stereoisomers, L-glyceraldehyde and D-glyceraldehyde (Fig 1.17). All aldoses in organisms are made from D-glyceraldehyde and are therefore called D-aldoses. All ketoses are made from dihydroxyacetone. While dihydroxyacetone cannot form stereoisomers, the tetrose (four-carbon sugar) formed from it can, as it contains a carbon joined to four different groups (Fig 1.18). All ketoses are formed from the D version of this sugar, and are therefore D-ketoses.

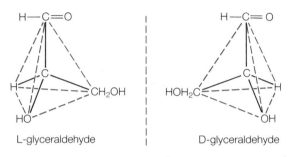

L-glyceraldehyde   D-glyceraldehyde

Fig 1.17

Hexoses, monosaccharides with six carbon atoms (hex = 6), all have the same simple formula, C$_6$H$_{12}$O$_6$. As all hexoses have the same simple formula they are all isomers of each other. Figure 1.19(a) shows some common hexoses, including glucose and fructose. Each hexose has a backbone of six carbons in a chain, a carbonyl group and at least two alcohol groups. Some of the hexoses, for example glucose, have the carbonyl group at the end of the molecule and are therefore aldoses, while other hexoses, for example fructose, have the carbonyl group on carbon 2, away from the end of the molecule, and are therefore ketoses.

Hexoses exist in two forms, a straight chain form (Fig 1.19(a)) and a ring form (Fig 1.19(b)). To form a ring the carbonyl group reacts with one of the hydroxyl groups elsewhere in the chain. The carbons are still numbered as they were in the straight chain form, and carbon 1 is always drawn on the right hand side (Fig 1.19(b)). Two types of rings can be formed: a ring of six atoms called a **pyranose** ring and a ring of five atoms called a **furanose** ring. The pyranose ring is the more stable ring form for aldoses, for example glucose and galactose, while the furanose ring form is more stable for ketoses, for example fructose and sorbose (Fig 1.19(b)).

Once a ring has formed the hydroxyl groups attached to the carbons in the ring will point up from the plane of the ring, or down from the plane of the ring. This is one way in which stereoisomers are formed. Glucose forms isomers of this type: the ring can form with the hydroxyl group on carbon 1 pointing down (this is α-glucose), or pointing up (this is β-glucose) (Fig 1.20).

Pentoses, monosaccharides with five carbon atoms (pent = 5), have the simple formula C$_5$H$_{10}$O$_5$, a carbonyl group and at least two hydroxyl groups. Pentoses exist in a chain form and a ring form. Figure 1.21 shows the structural formulae of two important pentoses, ribose and deoxyribose, in both the straight chain and the ring form. Both deoxyribose and ribose are stable in the furanose ring form.

SMALL MOLECULES

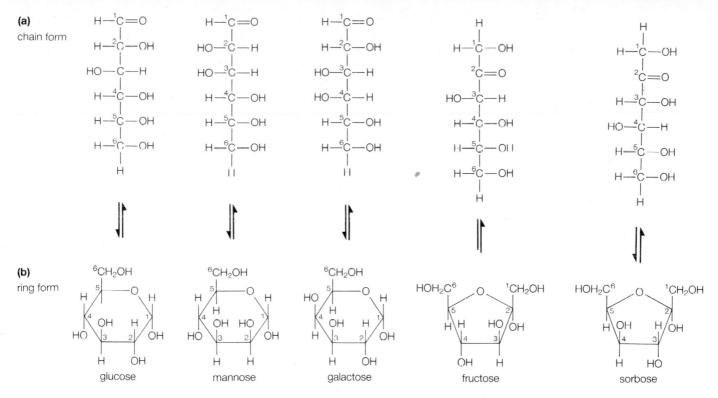

Fig 1.19 Five common hexoses in straight chain and ring forms.

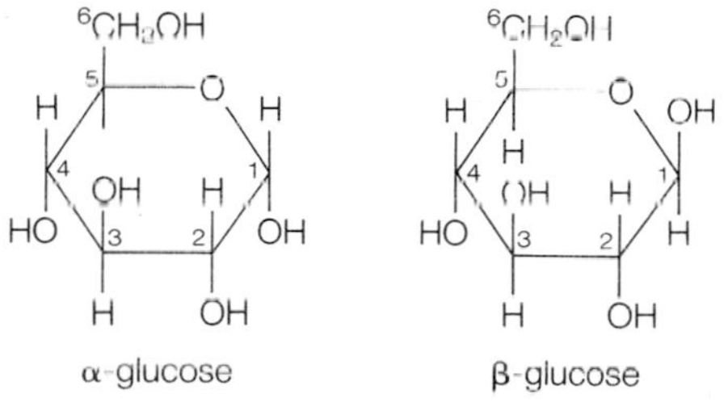

Fig 1.20 Glucose in the ring form can form two stereoisomers, one with the hydroxyl group on carbon 1 below the ring (α-glucose) and one with the hydroxyl group above the ring (β-glucose).

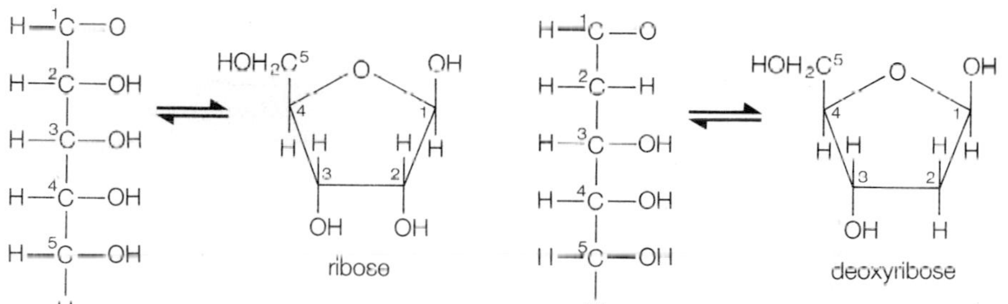

Fig 1.21 The structure of two common pentoses in both the linear and the ring forms.

Two monosaccharide molecules can be joined to make a disaccharide molecule

Monosaccharides react to make disaccharides, forming a bond between two monosaccharide molecules by eliminating a molecule of water

$$C_6H_{12}O_6 + C_6H_{12}O_6 \longrightarrow C_{12}H_{22}O_{11} + H_2O$$

This type of reaction, where a bond is formed by the elimination of a water molecule, is called a **condensation** reaction. The bond formed during the condensation reaction between monosaccharide molecules is called a **glycosidic bond**. This bond is formed between the carbonyl group on one monosaccharide and a hydroxyl group on the other monosaccharide. A 1→4 glycosidic bond is from carbon 1 of one monosaccharide to carbon 4 of the second monosaccharide (Fig 1.22(a)), while a 1→2 glycosidic bond is from the carbon 1 of one monosaccharide to carbon 2 of the second monosaccharide (Fig 1.22(b)). Three common disaccharides and the types of glycosidic bonds found in those molecules are listed in Table 1.5.

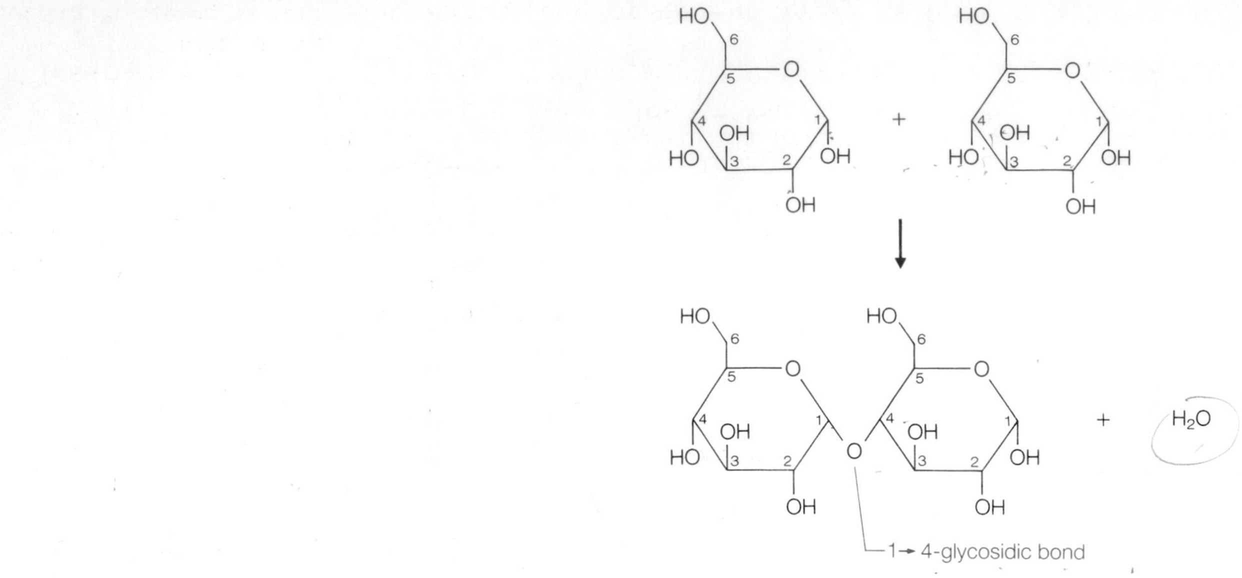

(a) glucose + glucose ⟶ maltose

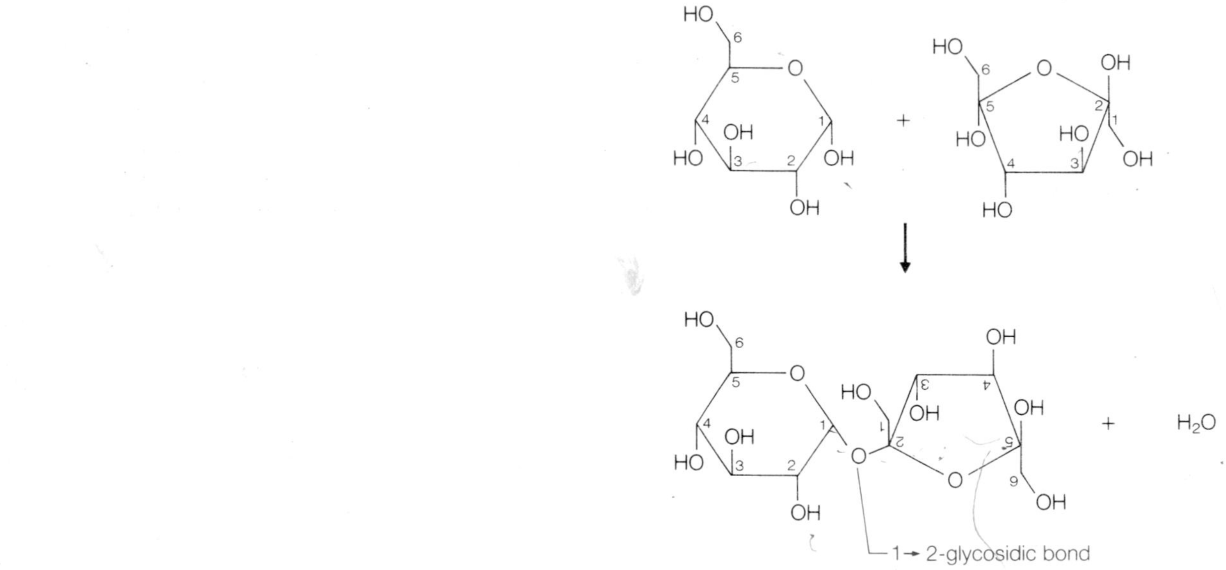

(b) glucose + fructose ⟶ sucrose

Fig 1.22 Monosaccharides react together in a hydrolysis reaction to form a disaccharide.

Table 1.5

Disaccharide	Monosaccharides	Type of bond
maltose	glucose & glucose	1→4 glycosidic
lactose	glucose & galactose	1→4 glycosidic
sucrose	glucose & fructose	1→2 glycosidic

Sugars have many roles in organisms

Sugars are an important source of energy for all organisms. Plants use the energy of the sun to synthesise hexoses which can be transported to other cells and oxidised to release energy. Animals and fungi obtain sugars from other organisms and oxidise them to release energy. The trioses glyceraldehyde and dihydroxyacetone are important intermediates in the process by which cells release energy from hexoses. You can read more about the processes by which organisms release the energy in sugars in Chapter 8.

SMALL MOLECULES

Polysaccharides and nucleic acids are polymers. A polymer is a long macromolecule formed by linking many small molecules, the monomers, in a chain.

Monosaccharides and disaccharides are also used as the starting material for the synthesis of other biologically important molecules in cells. Monosaccharides are the monomers from which polysaccharides are made, for example α-glucose forms starch while β-glucose forms cellulose. Some polysaccharides, such as starch, act as energy storage molecules while others, such as cellulose, are structural materials. The pentoses ribose and deoxyribose form part of the monomers that are joined together to form nucleic acids. Nucleic acids are used to store and express the genetic information in cells. You can read more about polysaccharides and nucleic acids in Chapter 2.

DATA HANDLING 1.1

Sugars contain a carbonyl group, C=O. A carbonyl group at the end of a molecule is called an aldehyde group and an aldehyde group can be oxidised to a carboxylic group, COOH. This means that an aldehyde group can act as a reducing agent. Sugars containing an aldehyde group can act as reducing agents and are therefore called reducing sugars. As can be seen in Fig 1.23 glucose contains an aldehyde group and is thus a reducing sugar.

Sugars that do not, at first sight, contain an aldehyde group can also act as reducing sugars. This is because a carbonyl group on carbon 2, one away from the end, can change places with a hydroxyl group on the end carbon, giving an aldehyde group that can act as a reducing agent. This is shown for fructose in Fig 1.23. Most hexoses have their carbonyl group on carbon 1 or a carbonyl group on carbon 2 and a hydroxyl group on carbon 1, and are therefore reducing sugars.

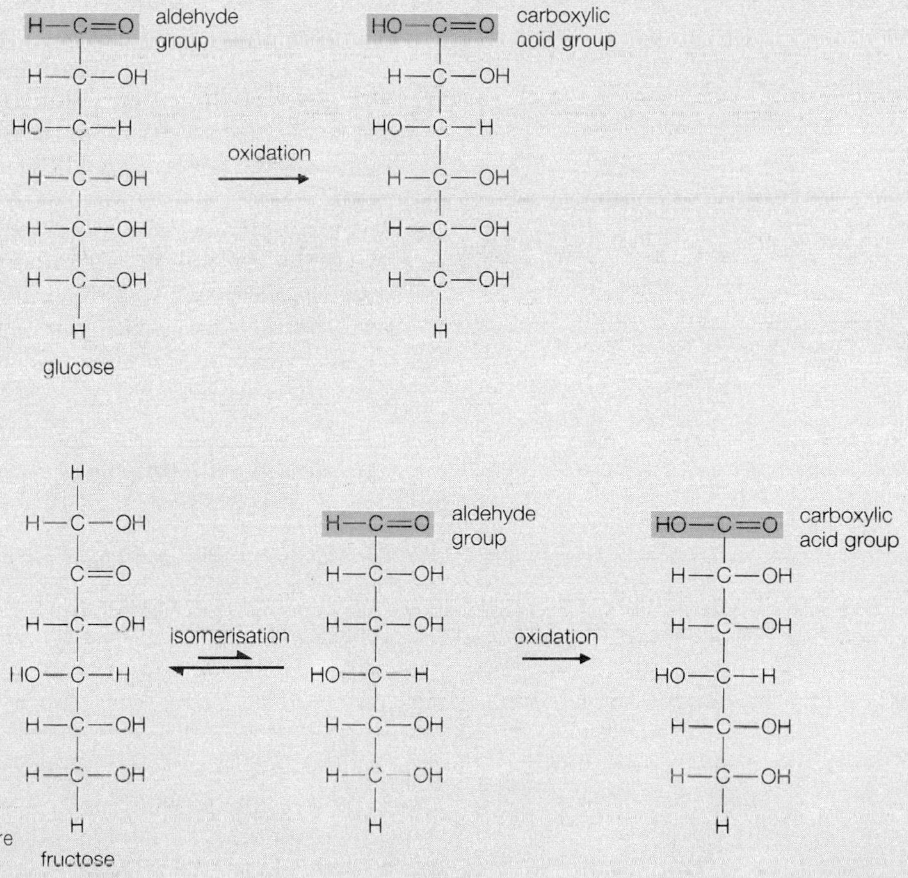

Fig 1.23 Monosaccharides that can be oxidised are called reducing sugars.

There are three common laboratory tests for reducing sugars:

- Benedict's reagent, in which blue copper(II) ions are reduced to a red-brown precipitate containing copper(I) ions;
- Fehling's reagent, in which blue copper(II) ions are reduced to brown copper(I) ions;
- the silver mirror test, in which silver nitrate is reduced to give silver metal.

Figure 1.24 shows glucose and fructose in ring form with the reducing groups shaded. The structures of maltose and sucrose are also shown in Fig 1.24.

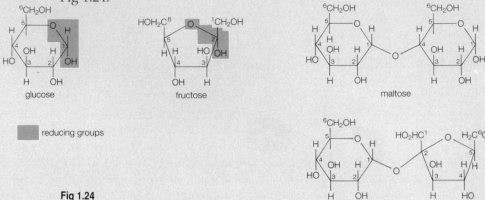

Fig 1.24

(a) When a silver mirror test is performed on a solution of maltose a layer of silver forms on the sides of the test tube but when a silver mirror test is performed on a solution of sucrose no silver forms. Explain this result with reference to the structure of the molecules shown in Fig 1.24.

(b) Sucrose can be hydrolysed to give glucose and fructose by adding acid to catalyse the hydrolysis reaction. How could you test for the presence of sucrose in a solution?

(c) Trehalose is a disaccharide found in the haemolymph of many insects. Trehalose is formed from two α-glucose molecules by a 1,1-glycosidic bond. Is trehalose a reducing sugar or a non-reducing sugar?

(d) A student obtained the following results using unlabelled solutions containing 0.1 mol dm^{-3} of either sucrose, lactose or glucose. The student tested each sugar solution with Benedict's reagent before and after the sugar solution had been subjected to a treatment that would hydrolyse any glycosidic bonds present. bl = a blue solution, g = a green suspension, br = red-brown precipitate

Results with different dilutions of the sugar solutions					
Solution	Undiluted	1 in 10	1 in 100	1 in 1000	1 in 10 000
A (before)	br	br	g	g	bl
A (after)	br	br	g	g	bl
B (before)	br	br	g	g	bl
B (after)	br	br	br	g	g
C (before)	bl	bl	bl	bl	bl
C (after)	br	br	br	g	g

Interpret these results, assigning the correct name to each solution and relating the results to the structures of the saccharides involved. The structure of galactose is shown in Fig 1.19 and the structure of lactose can be deduced from Table 1.5.

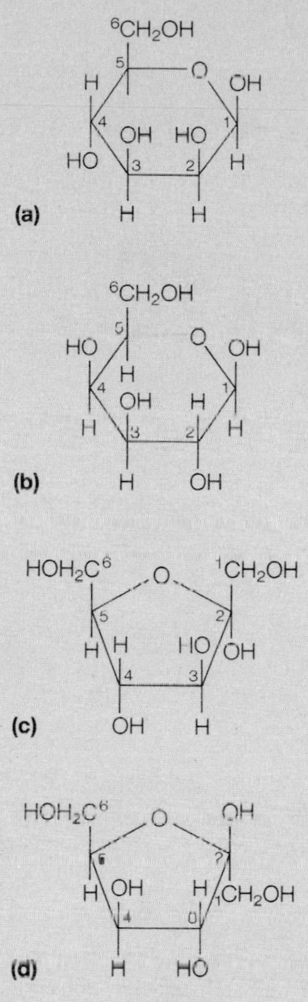

Fig 1.25

1.7
(a) What is the difference between a hexose and a pentose?
(b) What is the difference between ribose and deoxyribose?
(c) Look at the monosaccharides in Fig 1.25. Which of these monosaccharides have α-hydroxyl groups and which have β-hydroxyl groups?

1.8
(a) What three elements do sugars contain?
(b) What class of compounds do sugars belong to?
(c) What two reactive groups do all sugars contain?
(d) What is the difference between a monosaccharide and a disaccharide? Describe in detail, using a diagram, what happens when a named disaccharide is formed from two named monosaccharides.

1.9
(a) What is the simple formula of glucose?
(b) What is the structural formula of:
(i) linear glucose;
(ii) α-glucose;
(iii) β glucose?
(c) List three different functions of glucose in plants.

1.10
(a) Name two different trioses and give one function of trioses in cells.
(b) Name two different pentoses and give one function of pentoses in cells.
(c) Name two different hexoses and give one function of hexoses in cells.
(d) Of the three pairs you have named in (a), (b) and (c), which are isomers of each other and which are not? Explain your answer.

1.4 AMINO ACIDS

Amino acids are crystalline solids that are soluble in water. All amino acids contain two reactive groups, an amine group and a carboxylic group. In α-amino acids, the type found in most organisms, the carboxyl group is on carbon 1 and the amine group is on carbon 2 (Fig 1.26). There are twenty common amino acids found in organisms and these amino acids differ from one another by the composition of the other group attached to carbon 2, the R group (Fig 1.26). The R group varies in structure from a simple hydrogen atom, as found in glycine, to a complex ring structure as found in tryptophan. The 20 common amino acids are shown in Table 1.6.

Carbon 2 is joined to four different groups in every α-amino acid except glycine. This means that α-amino acids can form stereoisomers (Fig 1.27). All common amino acids in organisms are L-amino acids rather than D-amino acids but some D-amino acids do occur naturally, for example D-glutamic acid, found in the cell walls of many bacteria.

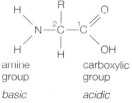

amine group — basic

carboxylic group — acidic

Fig 1.26 The general formula of an amino acid. R stands for one of a variety of reactive groups.

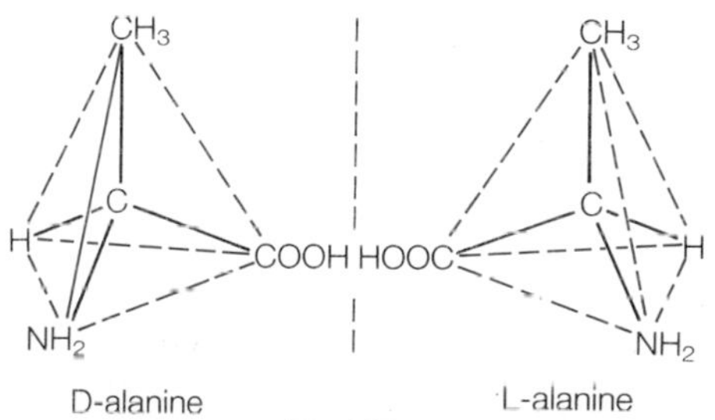

D-alanine   L-alanine

Fig 1.27

Table 1.6   The 20 common amino acids, showing the form of the R group that occurs at pH 7.

Name	Abbreviation	Structure	Name	Abbreviation	Structure
Alanine	Ala	CH_3	Leucine	Leu	$CH_2-CH{<}^{CH_3}_{CH_3}$
Arginine	Arg	$CH_2-CH_2-CH_2-NH-C{<}^{\overset{+}{N}H_2}_{NH_2}$	Lysine	Lys	$CH_2-CH_2-CH_2-CH_2-\overset{+}{N}H_3$
Asparagine	Asn	$CH_2-C{<}^{O}_{NH_2}$	Methionine	Met	$CH_2-CH_2-S-CH_3$
Aspartic acid	Asp	CH_2-COO^-	Phenylalanine	Phe	$CH_2-C_6H_5$
Cysteine	Cys	CH_2-SH	Proline	Pro	$CH_2{<}^{CH_2}_{\quad}CH_2$
Glutamic acid	Glu	$CH_2-CH_2-COO^-$	Serine	Ser	CH_2-OH
Glutamine	Gln	$CH_2-CH_2-C{<}^{O}_{NH_2}$	Threonine	Thr	$CH{<}^{CH_3}_{OH}$
Glycine	Gly	H	Tryptophan	Trp	CH_2 (indole)
Histidine	His	CH_2 (imidazolium)	Tyrosine	Tyr	$CH_2-C_6H_4-OH$
Isoleucine	Ile	$CH{<}^{CH_3}_{CH_2-CH_3}$	Valine	Val	$CH{<}^{CH_3}_{CH_3}$

$$\boxed{} = H-\overset{+}{\underset{H}{\overset{H}{N}}}-\overset{H}{\underset{H}{C}}-C{<}^{O}_{O^-}$$

All twenty amino acids have many properties in common

Each amino acid molecule contains an acidic group (COOH) and a basic group (NH_2). This means that amino acids have the properties of an acid and the properties of a base; such substances are called **amphoteric**. At the pH of the cell, about neutral, both the amino group and the carboxylic group are ionised.

$$-COOH \longrightarrow -COO^- + H^+$$

$$-NH_2 + H^+ \longrightarrow -NH_3^+$$

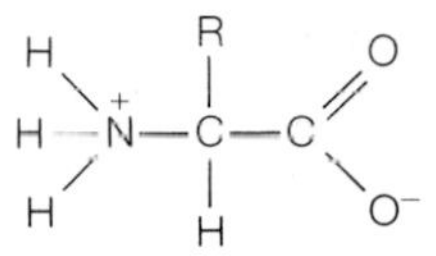

Fig 1.28 A zwitterion is a molecule with a positive group and a negative group: a double ion.

A residue is the part of the monomer molecule that is present in the polymer.

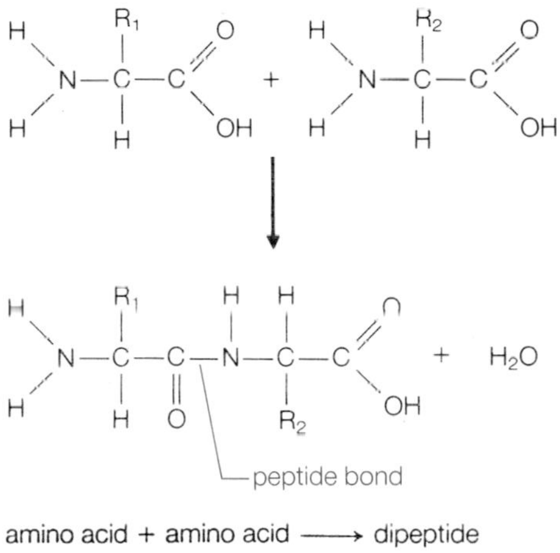

amino acid + amino acid ⟶ dipeptide

Fig 1.29 Two amino acid molecules react together in a condensation reaction to form a dipeptide.

This means that each amino acid molecule is positively charged at one end and negatively charged at the other end, a strange type of ion called a **zwitterion** (Fig 1.28).

Two amino acid molecules can join together in a condensation reaction in which a molecule of water is eliminated (Fig 1.29). A **dipeptide** is formed, and the bond between the two amino acid residues is called a **peptide bond**. Additional amino acids can react with the dipeptide to form first a tripeptide and then a polypeptide. Polypeptides are discussed in more detail in Chapter 2.

Each of the twenty amino acids is different

The different R groups give each amino acid slightly different properties. These R groups are very important because they are unaffected when the amino acids join to make a polypeptide and contribute towards the properties of the polypeptide. Table 1.6 shows the different R groups of the twenty common amino acids. The different R groups can be classified according to whether they are charged or neutral, uncharged polar or uncharged non-polar, at the pH of the cell.

Some of the R groups will have a positive or negative charge at the pH of the cell. These are called **charged** R groups. **Acidic amino acids** have an R group which is negatively charged at the pH of the cell, e.g. glutamic acid. **Basic amino acids** have an R group which is positively charged at the pH of the cell, e.g. lysine. The other amino acids all have uncharged R groups. However, those uncharged groups can be **polar** or **non-polar (hydrophobic)**. An example of an amino acid with a polar R group is serine, which has a hydroxyl group within its R group. An example of an amino acid with a non-polar R group is alanine, the R group of which is a simple methyl group.

Amino acids in organisms

The most important role of amino acids is as the monomers which are polymerised to make proteins. Proteins fulfil a vast number of different functions within the cell and are discussed throughout the later chapters. Some hormones and neurotransmitters are short peptides formed from amino acids. Amino acids from the diet can be used as intermediates for the synthesis of other molecules and they can be used as a source of energy if there is no other source available. This is discussed in Chapter 8.

Plants synthesise all the amino acids they need from the carbohydrate they make by photosynthesis and the nitrate ions they absorb from the soil. Animals take in most amino acids as part of their diet but humans can synthesise all but eight of the amino acids they require. The eight amino acids that must be in the diet are called **essential amino acids**.

Rare amino acids

Not all amino acids are α-amino acids; any molecule containing both a carboxylic group and an amine group is an amino acid. α-amino acids have the amine group on carbon 2 but other amino acids have the amine group further away from carbon 1 (Fig 1.30). A β-amino acid has the amine group on carbon 3, a γ-amino acid has the amine group on carbon 4 and a δ-amino acid has the amine group on carbon 5. These amino acids do not join together to make proteins but some of them have important functions in organisms, for example β-alanine is a building block for vitamin B5 and γ-aminobutyric acid is one of the chemicals used by cells as a neurotransmitter.

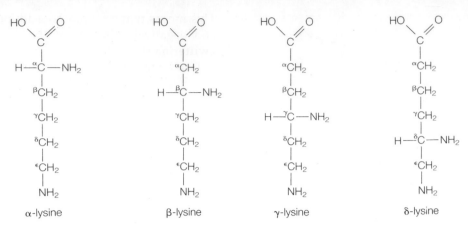

α-lysine   β-lysine   γ-lysine   δ-lysine

Fig 1.30 Common amino acids are all α-amino acids, but other isomers occur.

DATA HANDLING 1.2

Figure 1.31 shows what happens to three different amino acids when they are dissolved in water and the pH of the solution is varied. On the right of Fig 1.31 are three titration curves showing how the pH of the amino acid solutions varies as the concentration of hydroxyl ions is increased. At one point in the titration all the amino acid molecules in the solution will have a neutral charge overall and the pH of the solution when all the amino acid molecules are neutral is called the **isoelectric point**. The isoelectric point of each amino acid is marked C.

(a) Study the titration graph for alanine. What will be the overall charge on the majority of the alanine molecules:
   (i) at pH 1;
   (ii) at pH 6;
   (iii) at pH 11?

(b) Study the titration graph for glutamic acid. What will be the overall charge on the majority of the glutamic acid molecules:
   (i) at pH 1;
   (ii) at pH 6;
   (iii) at pH 11?

(c) Study the titration graph for lysine. What will be the overall charge on the majority of the lysine molecules:
   (i) at pH 1;
   (ii) at pH 6;
   (iii) at pH 11?

Electrophoresis is a method of separating similarly sized molecules on the basis of their charge and is an excellent way of separating amino acids. A sheet of paper is soaked in a solution of a certain pH and the paper is then placed in an electric field with the positive electrode at one end and the negative electrode at the other end. The mixture of amino acids is dissolved in a little distilled water to make a very concentrated solution and the mixture is applied to the middle of the paper, half way between the positive and the negative electrodes. If the molecules have a positive charge they will be attracted towards the negative electrode and if the molecules have a positive charge they will move towards the negative electrode.

In a way electrophoresis is like electrolysis, only with a piece of paper soaked with solution rather than in a container of solution.

(d) A solution contains alanine, glutamic acid and lysine at pH 1. Which way will the three different amino acids move: toward the positive electrode or towards the negative electrode?

SMALL MOLECULES

(e) If the same amino acids are dissolved in a solution at pH 11, which way will the three different amino acids move?

(f) If the same amino acids are dissolved in a solution at pH 6, which way will the three different amino acids move?

(g) At which pH should the electrophoresis be done in order to ensure a good separation of all three amino acids?

Alanine

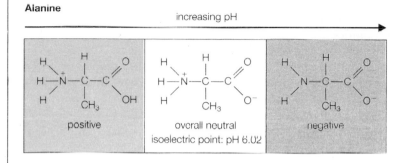

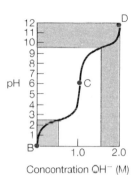

Glutamic acid

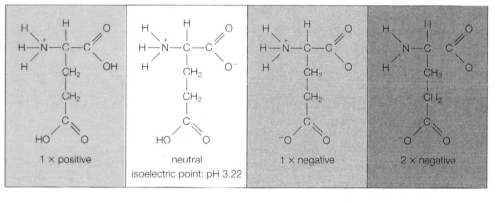

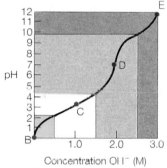

Lysine

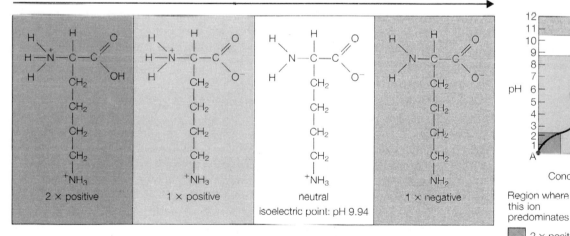

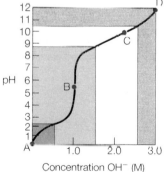

Region where this ion predominates	Point where this ion should be pure
2 × positive	A
1 × positive	B
neutral	C
1 × negative	D
2 × negative	E

Fig 1.31 Amino acids change when the pH is varied. Increasing the concentration of OH⁻ causes H⁺ to be removed from the amino acid molecules. Typical titration curves for three common amino acids are shown on the right-hand side of the diagram.

1.11 **(a)** What elements are present in amino acids?
(b) What two reactive groups are present in all amino acids?
(c) What is the general formula for an amino acid?
(d) What is the structural formula for glycine?
(e) Describe the reaction by which two amino acids join together to make a dipeptide.

1.12 **(a)** What is the meaning of the term amphoteric?
(b) What are the features of an amino acid molecule that make it amphoteric?
(c) Carboxylic groups (—COOH) are usually negatively charged in the cell, while amine groups (—NH_2) are usually positively charged in the cell. What is the overall charge on the following:
  (i) a glycine molecule in the cell;
  (ii) a lysine molecule in the cell;
  (iii) a glutamic acid molecule in the cell?

1.13 **(a)** What is the meaning of the term isomer?
(b) Name two different types of isomerism that occur in amino acids. Explain the difference between these two types of isomerism using amino acids as examples.

1.5 NUCLEOTIDES

A whole range of different nucleotides exist within a cell. Nucleotides are complicated molecules made from three components: a sugar, phosphate groups, and a base (Fig 1.32).

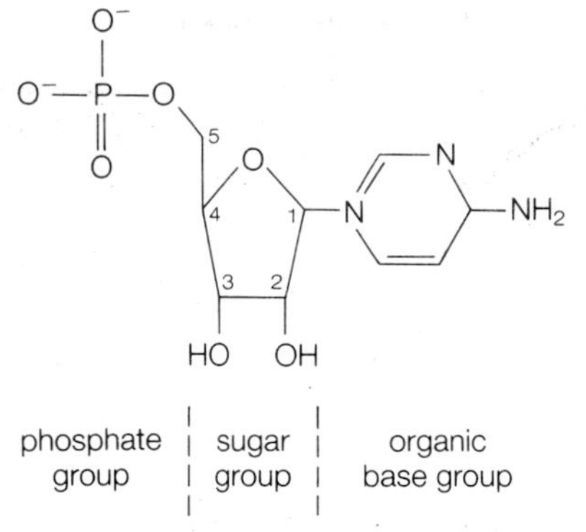

Fig 1.32 A nucleotide molecule contains a phosphate group, a pentose sugar group and an organic base group.

Nucleotides contain one of two alternative sugar components

Nucleotides fall into two groups, those that contain a ribose sugar group and those that contain a deoxyribose sugar group. The base component of the nucleotide is connected to carbon 1 of the sugar and the phosphate group of the nucleotide is joined to carbon 5 of the sugar (Fig 1.32). Figure 1.21 shows the small difference in structure between a ribose molecule and a deoxyribose molecule; the deoxyribose molecule has one less oxygen on carbon 2. This very small difference has far reaching consequences in the cell: ribonucleotides (nucleotides containing a ribose residue) form RNA and deoxyribonucleotides (nucleotides containing a deoxyribose residue) form DNA. RNA and DNA have very different functions in the cell, functions that are discussed in Theme 2.

Nucleotides contain one of five alternative base components

The five organic bases found in nucleotides are adenine, guanine, cytosine, thymine and uracil, which are usually abbreviated to A, G, C, T and U (Fig 1.33). Adenine and guanine are purines, which means that they have a double ring structure, while cytosine, thymine and uracil are pyrimidines, which means that they have a single ring structure. The base is connected to carbon 1 of the sugar (Fig 1.32).

Nucleotides contain one, two or three phosphate groups

Phosphate is an inorganic ion carrying three negative charges. Either one, two or three phosphates can be joined to the sugar molecule through the hydroxyl group on carbon 5 (Fig 1.32). The monophosphate form of the nucleotide has two negative charges, the diphosphate form has three and the triphosphate form has four.

There are a lot of variables involved in building a nucleotide. There are two possible sugars, five possible bases and the option of one, two and three phosphate groups. This means that there is a large number of possible nucleotides and conventions have grown up for naming them. Table 1.7 explains the naming of nucleotides (for reference only).

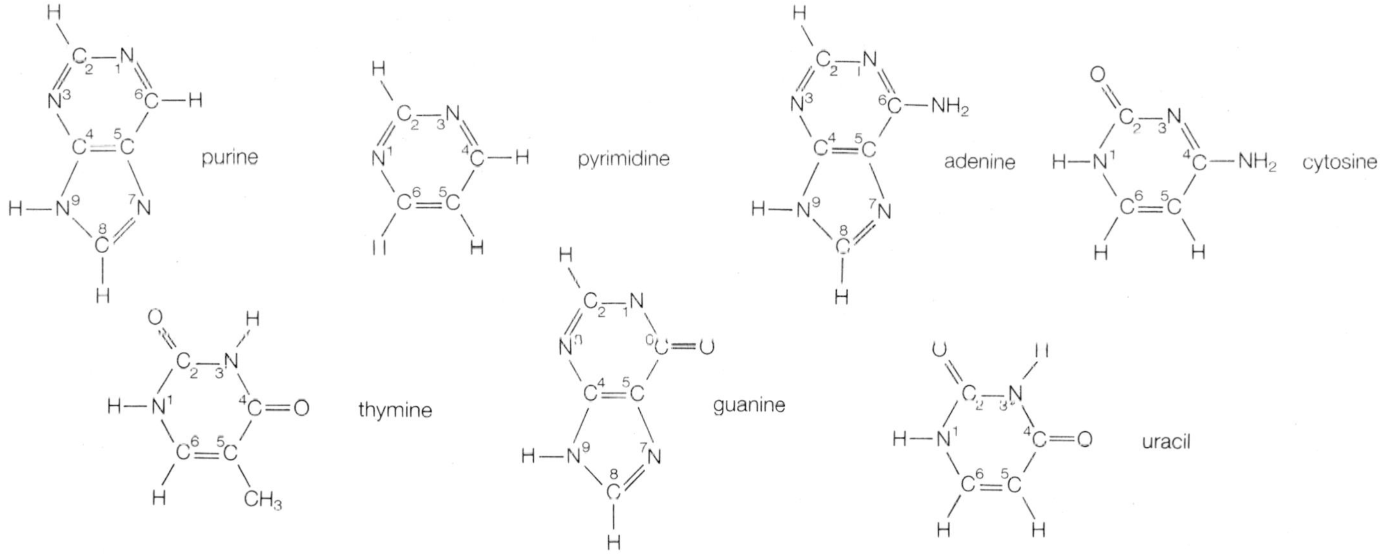

Fig 1.33 There are two common purine bases found in nucleotides, adenine and guanine, and three common pyrimidine bases found in nucleotides, cytosine, thymine and uracil.

Table 1.7

Sugar	Base	Sugar + base	+1 phosphate	+2 phosphates	+3 phosphates
ribose	adenine	adenosine	adenosine monophosphate (AMP)	adenosine diphosphate (ADP)	adenosine triphosphate (ATP)
deoxyribose	adenine	deoxyadenosine	deoxyadenosine monophosphate (dAMP)	deoxyadenosine diphosphate (dADP)	deoxyadenosine triphosphate (dATP)
ribose	guanine	guanosine	guanosine monophosphate (GMP)	guanosine diphosphate (GDP)	guanosine triphosphate (GTP)
deoxyribose	guanine	deoxyguanosine	deoxyguanosine monophosphate (dGMP)	deoxyguanosine diphosphate (dGDP)	deoxyguanosine triphosphate (dGTP)
ribose	cytosine	cytodine	cytodine monophosphate (CMP)	cytodine diphosphate (CDP)	cytodine triphosphate (CTP)
deoxyribose	cytosine	deoxycytodine	deoxycytodine monophosphate (dCMP)	deoxycytodine diphosphate (dCDP)	deoxycytodine triphosphate (dCTP)
deoxyribose	thymine	deoxythymidine	deoxythymidine monophosphate (dTMP)	deoxythymidine diphosphate (dTDP)	deoxythymidine triphosphate (dTTP)
ribose	uracil	uridine	uridine monophosphate (UMP)	uridine diphosphate (UDP)	uridine triphosphate (UTP)

Nucleotides have a variety of roles in organisms

Nucleotides react together in a condensation reaction to form nucleic acids (Fig 1.34). Ribonucleotides join together to give **ribonucleic acid (RNA)** and deoxyribonucleotides join together to give **deoxyribonucleic acid (DNA)**. The nucleotide residues are linked together by phosphodiester bonds between carbon 3 of the sugar in one nucleotide and the phosphate group of another nucleotide. This process is described in more detail in Chapters 2, 4 and 5. Nucleic acids are essential for the storage of the genetic information, the passing of that genetic information to the next generation and the expression of that genetic information in the organism. These processes are discussed in Theme 2.

The ribonucleotide **adenosine triphosphate (ATP)** (Fig 1.35) acts as an energy storage molecule in cells. When the end phosphate group is removed by hydrolysis, energy is released. Energy is stored by converting **adenosine diphosphate (ADP)** to ATP by the addition of a phosphate group. These reactions are discussed in more detail in Chapter 8.

Modified nucleotides also fulfil many important roles in cells. Coenzyme A has an important role in the TCA (Krebs) cycle, NAD and NADP are hydrogen carriers and cyclic AMP regulates events within the cell. Some of these processes are discussed in Theme 3.

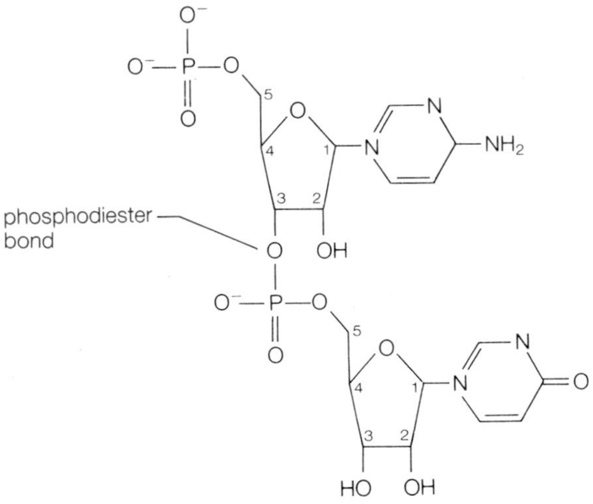

Fig 1.34 Two ribonucleotides have reacted together in a condensation reaction to form a dinucleotide.

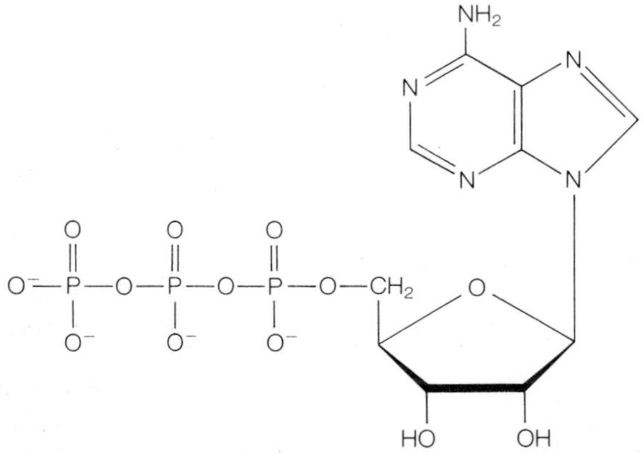

Fig 1.35 Adenosine triphosphate, ATP, is an energy storage molecule found in all cells.

SMALL MOLECULES

QUESTIONS

1.14 **(a)** What are the two different sugar groups that are found in nucleotides?
(b) What are the five different bases that are found in nucleotides?
(c) What is the name of the third group found in nucleotides?
(d) Draw a simple diagram to show the way that the three different groups are linked to make a nucleotide.

1.15 **(a)** What are ribonucleotides used to make?
(b) What are deoxyribonucleotides used to make?
(c) Name a nucleotide that has a different function to those mentioned in (a) and (b). What is this nucleotide's function?

1.6 FATTY ACIDS

Fatty acids have a carboxylic group and a long hydrocarbon chain

Fatty acids are long hydrocarbon chains with a carboxyl group at one end (Fig 1.36). The carboxyl group (COOH) gives fatty acids their acidic properties. The long hydrocarbon chain is uncharged and non-polar.

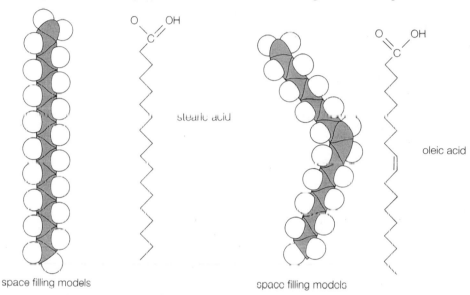

stearic acid

oleic acid

space filling models   space filling models

Fig 1.36   A double bond in the hydrocarbon tail of an unsaturated fatty acid introduces a kink.

Fatty acids can be saturated or unsaturated

There is a large range of fatty acids present in organisms. The length of the hydrocarbon chain varies, and some fatty acids have double bonds in the chain while others do not. Fatty acids with double bonds in the chain are called **unsaturated** fatty acids, while those with only single bonds are called **saturated** fatty acids.

Two common fatty acids are stearic acid ($C_{17}H_{35}COOH$) and oleic acid ($C_{17}H_{33}COOH$). The difference between these two molecules is the presence of one double bond in the hydrocarbon chain. As can be seen in Fig 1.36, the double bond introduces a 'kink' into the hydrocarbon chain.

Fatty acids react to form glycerides and phospholipids

Glycerol is a simple three-carbon molecule with a hydroxyl group on each carbon (Fig 1.37). These hydroxyl groups can react with carboxyl groups (Fig 1.38). The bond formed between the two molecules is called an **ester** bond.

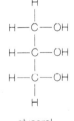

glycerol
2,3-dihydroxypropanol

Fig 1.37

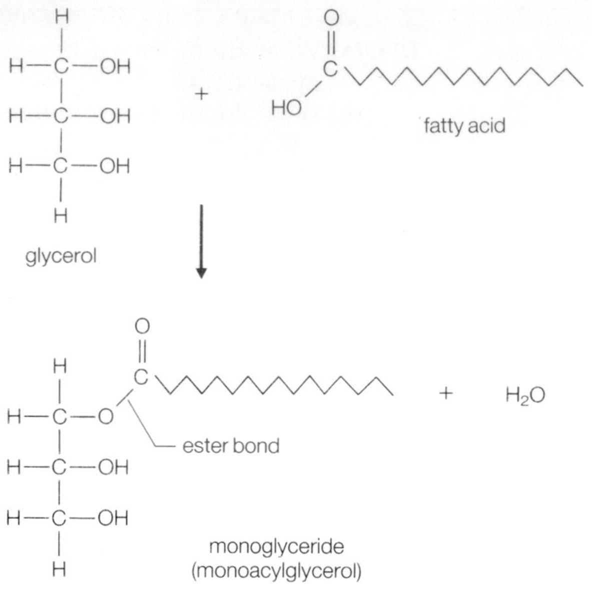

Fig 1.38 Glycerol reacts with fatty acids in a condensation reaction leading to the formation of a monoglyceride.

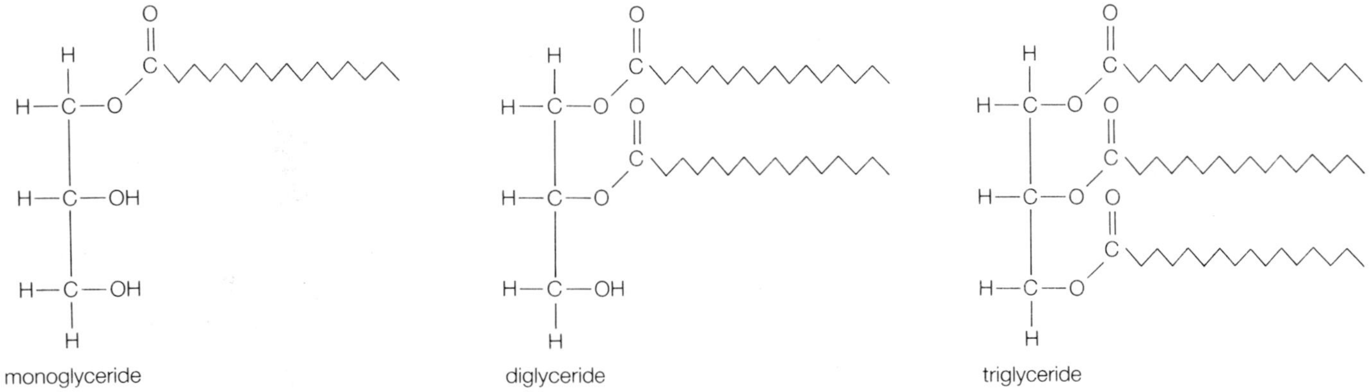

glycerol

fatty acid

ester bond

monoglyceride
(monoacylglycerol)

H_2O

monoglyceride

diglyceride

triglyceride

Fig 1.39 A monoglyceride, diglyceride or triglyceride is formed depending on how many fatty acid molecules react with each glycerol molecule.

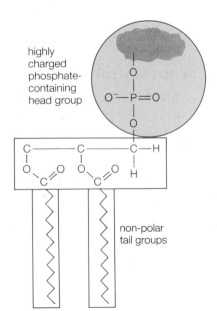

highly charged phosphate-containing head group

non-polar tail groups

Fig 1.40 Phospholipids contain a highly charged polar 'head' group and two hydrophobic hydrocarbon 'tail' groups, all linked to the glycerol residue.

Each of the hydroxyl groups on the glycerol molecule can react with the carboxyl group of a fatty acid (Fig 1.39). If only one reacts with a fatty acid a **monoglyceride** is formed, if two of the hydroxyl groups react with a fatty acid a **diglyceride** is formed and if all three react a **triglyceride** is formed. Glycerides are also referred to as **acylglycerols**. **Glycerides** are one type of **lipid**. Lipids are substances which are soluble in organic solvents such as ether and 1,1,1-trichloroethane but insoluble in water.

Fatty acids contain a lot of chemical energy. Excess fatty acids are converted into glycerides which can then be stored. You can read more about energy storage molecules in Chapter 8.

Phospholipids are complicated molecules made from four parts: two fatty acid groups, a glycerol group, a phosphate group and a large polar group (Fig 1.40). The fatty acids are joined to the glycerol by ester bonds and then the third hydroxyl group on the glycerol is linked via the phosphate group to the polar group. Phospholipids form the basis of all cellular membranes. The structure of cellular membranes is discussed more fully in Chapter 3.

The roles of fatty acids in organisms

Fatty acids can be broken down by the chemical machinery in a cell to release energy or converted into glycerides to act as a store of chemical energy in the form of fats or oils. Fatty acids can be converted into phospholipids which are the basic components of all cellular membranes. They can also be reacted with long-chain alcohols to form **waxes**. Waxes are found as waterproofing compounds in many organisms.

In plants fatty acids are synthesised from the carbohydrate made by photosynthesis. In other organisms fatty acids are usually obtained from the diet. Humans can make most fatty acids if necessary but a few cannot be synthesised and must be present in the diet. These are called **essential fatty acids**.

DATA HANDLING 1.3

The empirical formula for a saturated fatty acid, one with no double bonds, is $C_nH_{2n}O_2$. The empirical formula for an unsaturated fatty acid with one double bond is $C_nH_{2n-2}O_2$. The empirical formula for an unsaturated fatty acid with two double bonds is $C_nH_{2n-4}O_2$. The empirical formula for an unsaturated fatty acid with three double bonds is $C_nH_{2n-6}O_2$. Table 1.8 shows the melting points for a number of common fatty acids.

Table 1.8

Formula of fatty acid	Melting point (°C)
A $C_{18}H_{34}O_2$	13.4
B $C_{24}H_{48}O_2$	86.0
C $C_{18}H_{32}O_2$	−5.0
D $C_{16}H_{32}O_2$	63.1
E $C_{20}H_{40}O_2$	76.5
F $C_{18}H_{30}O_2$	−11.0
G $C_{16}H_{30}O_2$	−0.5
H $C_{20}H_{32}O_2$	−49.5

(a) Which of the fatty acids in Table 1.8 are saturated fats?

(b) Which of the fatty acids in Table 1.8 are unsaturated fats with one double bond?

(c) Which of the fatty acids in Table 1.8 are unsaturated fats with two double bonds?

(d) Which of the fatty acids in Table 1.8 are unsaturated fats with three double bonds?

(e) How many double bonds are there in fatty acid H?

(f) Comment on the melting points of the unsaturated fats as compared to the melting points of the saturated fats.

(g) Which of the fatty acids shown in Table 1.8 would be solids at room temperature (20 °C) and which would be liquids?

(h) Which of the fatty acids in Table 1.8 would be liquids at −10 °C?

QUESTIONS

1.16 (a) What two groups are present in a fatty acid?

(b) What charge will be on the two groups you have named in (a)?

(c) Which of these two groups would you expect to be attracted to water (hydrophilic) and which of the two groups would you expect not to be attracted to water (to be hydrophobic)?

(d) List three uses of fatty acids in organisms.

1.17 (a) What is the structure of glycerol?

(b) Explain how a triglyceride is formed.

(c) Would you expect a triglyceride to be soluble in water? Explain your answer.

1.18 (a) What is a phospholipid?

(b) Would you expect a phospholipid to be soluble in water? Explain your answer.

1.7 OTHER SMALL ORGANIC MOLECULES

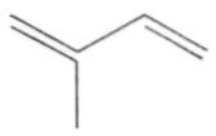

isoprene

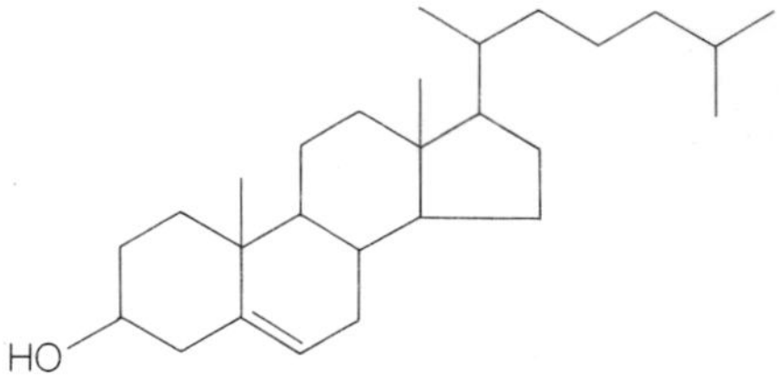

cholesterol,
a steroid

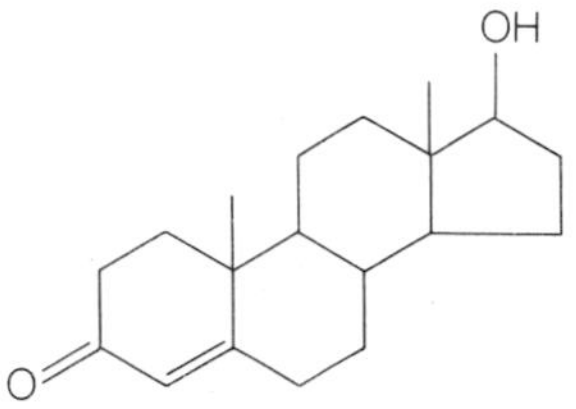

OH

testosterone,
a steroid

Fig 1.41 Isoprene is a simple hydrocarbon from which many important molecules, including steroids, are synthesised.

Most of the carbon-containing molecules in organisms are sugars, amino acids, nucleotides, fatty acids or molecules made from one of these four types. However, there are still hundreds of substances in living organisms that do not fall into one of these groups.

Steroids and terpenes are fat-soluble organic molecules

Steroids and terpenes are fat-soluble organic molecules derived from **isoprene**, a simple hydrocarbon containing two double bonds (Fig 1.41). **Steroids** have many important roles in organisms, for example testosterone is a hormone, vitamin D is needed for the development of strong bones and cholesterol is found in the cell membrane. The structures of testosterone and cholesterol are shown in Fig 1.41. **Terpenes** are particularly important in plants: the terpene gibberellin is a plant hormone, menthol is the terpene that gives mint its flavour and rubber is a commercially important terpene. Terpenes are also found in animals, e.g. vitamin A, vitamin K and vitamin E. Other molecules are also produced from isoprene, including coenzyme Q, a very important hydrogen carrier that is found in mitochondria and has an important role in respiration (section 8.5).

Waxes are formed from fatty acids and alcohols

Waxes are formed when fatty acids react with long-chain alcohols. Waxes are important in organisms because they are an excellent waterproofing material and they are found on the surfaces of leaves, on the skin, fur and feathers of animals, on the exoskeleton of insects as well as being used as a building material by bees (beeswax).

Fig 1.42 Organisms with very different evolutionary histories have evolved to use the same compounds for the same function. All land-living organisms have had to overcome the problem of losing vital water by evaporation. This problem has been solved in a similar way by flowering plants and insects, both of which produce waxes as waterproofing. The flowering plant has a waxy cuticle outside the epidermis and the insect covers its chitin exoskeleton with wax.

Porphin is modified to produce many small, important organic molecules

Many important molecules in cells contain a **porphyrin ring** and the synthesis of these molecules begins with the starting material porphin (Fig 1.43). Molecules with a porphyrin ring include chlorophyll, the cytochromes that have an important role in respiration and the haem group found in haemoglobin (Fig 1.43).

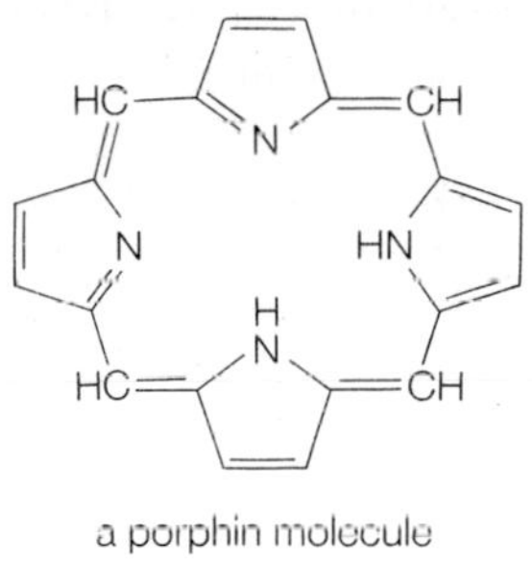

a porphin molecule

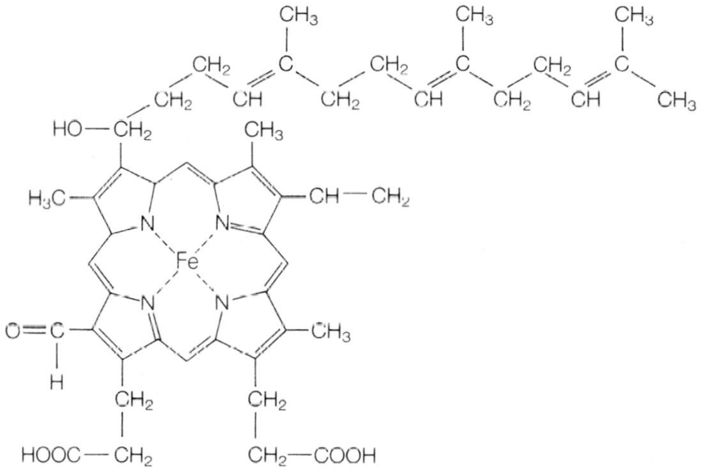

the haem group from
cytochrome oxidase

Fig 1.43 Porphin is a starting material for many biologically important molecules such as haem and chlorophyll.

QUESTION

1.19 (a) Look at the structure of cholesterol as shown in Fig 1.41. Would you expect cholesterol to be soluble in water? Explain your answer. Would you expect cholesterol to be soluble in oil?
(b) Look at the structure of the haem group shown in Fig 1.43. What is at the centre of this group? Find the diagram of a chlorophyll molecule on page 193. What is at the centre of this group?

1.8 IONS

Many organic molecules are ionised within the cell

Ions are atoms or molecules that carry a positive or negative charge. Many organic molecules form ions when they are dissolved in the intracellular solution. Carboxylic acids form negative ions in the cell: pyruvic acid forms pyruvate ions, citric acid forms citrate ions and oxaloacetic acid forms oxaloacetate ions. Many other molecules are phosphorylated, for example nucleotides, phospholipids and phosphorylated sugars; all these phosphate groups are negatively charged in the cell. This means that cells contain a lot of negatively charged organic ions or **organic anions**.

There are also some positively charged organic ions, **organic cations**, in the cell but these are much less common than organic anions. Amino acids are actually an organic anion and an organic cation within one molecule (section 1.4).

Inorganic ions also have many roles in organisms

Solutions in organisms are not just organic molecules dissolved in water. They also contain a large range of inorganic ions such as sodium ions (Na^+), potassium ions (K^+), magnesium ions (Mg^{2+}), calcium ions (Ca^{2+}) and chloride ions (Cl^-).

Table 1.9

Inorganic ion	Concentration inside the cell (mM)	Concentration in the body fluids (mM)
Na^+	5–15	145
K^+	140	5
Mg^{2+}	30	1
Ca^{2+}	1–2	2–3
Cl^-	4	103

As can be seen from Table 1.9 there is about a 180 mM concentration of positive inorganic ions (cations) and very few negative inorganic ions (anions) inside cells. The cations neutralise the many organic anions in cells. Overall the cell is neutral, the positive and negative charges balance.

The concentrations of different ions do not vary much from cell to cell, even between different species. This is because the concentrations of inorganic ions inside the cell are carefully controlled. You can read more about how this is achieved in Chapter 3 and Chapter 8.

Organisms absorb inorganic ions from their food or dissolved in the water they take in. Inorganic ions have many different roles in organisms:

- inorganic cations balance the many organic anions in the cell;
- differences in inorganic ion concentrations across membranes inside cells are often used as a temporary energy store, e.g in mitochondria, chloroplasts and nerve cells;
- cations such a Zn^{2+} and Mg^{2+} often act as cofactors for enzymes (see Chapter 7);
- cations which can exist in more than one oxidation state, e.g. iron (Fe^{2+} and Fe^{3+}) and copper (Cu^+ and Cu^{2+}), form an important part of molecules which act as electron carriers, e.g. cytochromes, and oxygen carriers, e.g. haemoglobin;
- cations form an important part of some pigments, e.g. Mg^{2+} in chlorophyll;
- salts of inorganic cations and organic anions are often used as a structural material, e.g. calcium pectate in plant cell walls and calcium salts in bone, enamel and shells (Chapter 3);
- certain cations, especially calcium, act as signalling molecules inside cells.

QUESTION

1.20 Table 1.9 shows the concentrations of various inorganic ions inside cells and in the fluid surrounding them, for the human body.
   (a) Which inorganic cations are at a greater concentration inside the cell than outside the cell?
   (b) The environment inside the cell is actually neutral. What balances the inorganic cations inside the cell?
   (c) What does Table 1.9 tell you about the cell membrane?

REVIEW OF CRUCIAL POINTS

- The atoms in a molecule determine the shape of a molecule and its charge distribution which, in turn, determine the properties of the molecules and finally the properties of the substance. This can be illustrated by studying the shape and charge distribution of the water molecule and relating them to the properties of water.

SMALL MOLECULES

- Water dissolves a large range of charged and polar molecules because the water molecule is polar, a useful property as water is the solvent within the cell and the organism. Water molecules form intermolecular hydrogen bonds so the forces of attraction between water molecules are unusually strong: this leads to water having a high specific heat capacity, water being a liquid across a wide temperature range, water acting as an excellent coolant and water being a very cohesive substance. All in all, water's biological importance should not be underestimated.

- Organic molecules come in a wide range of sizes and shapes because carbon atoms form stable chains of carbon atoms linked by covalent bonds. As well as stable, unreactive hydrocarbon regions organic molecules contain less stable, reactive regions. These reactive groups often contain oxygen or nitrogen.

- The most important small organic molecules in organisms are sugars, amino acids, nucleotides and fatty acids. Many of these small organic molecules are actually ions at the the pH of the cell (pH 7), including fatty acids and nucleotides which are negatively charged and amino acids that have both a positively and a negatively charged group within the molecule. There are also a number of inorganic ions in the cell, including K^+, Mg^{2+}, Ca^{2+} and PO_4^{3-}. Overall the positive ions and the negative ions balance each other, making the cell neutral.

- Sugars contain carbonyl groups and hydroxyl groups and can exist as single units, monosaccharides (e.g. glucose) or double units, disaccharides (e.g. sucrose). The larger sugars, pentoses and hexoses, can exist as chains or as rings. Monosaccharides are oxidised in cells to release energy, or joined up to make polysaccharides that can act as energy stores. In plants monosaccharides are linked together to make the important structural polysaccharide, cellulose.

- Amino acids contain an amine group and a carboxylic group spaced by a single carbon. The carbon between the amino group and the carboxylic is joined to one of twenty reactive groups, called the R group, making the twenty common amino acids. The simplest of these is glycine, where the R group is hydrogen. All amino acids are ions at the pH of the cell (pH 7) because the basic amine group is positively charged and the carboxylic acid group is negatively charged. The R group may be neutral, negative or positive. Amino acids are linked together to make proteins.

- Fatty acids are long hydrocarbon chains with a carboxylic group at one end. They are oxidised in the cell to release energy or they can be reacted with glycerol to make triglycerides, one form of energy storage molecule. Fatty acids can also react to form phospholipids, one component of cell membranes. The melting point of fatty acids increases with the length of the hydrocarbon chain, but unsaturated fatty acids, those with double bonds in the hydrocarbon chain, have lower melting points than saturated fatty acids.

- Nucleotides are complex molecules formed of a sugar group (ribose or deoxyribose), a base (adenine, guanine, cytosine, thymine or uracil) and one, two or three phosphate groups. Deoxyribonucleotides (those containing deoxyribose) are joined together to make DNA while ribonucleotides (those containing ribose) are joined together to make RNA. Nucleotides also have other roles in the cell, including energy storage in the form of ATP (adenosine triphosphate).

Chapter 2

MACROMOLECULES

Many molecules in organisms are very large, with a relative molecular mass of over 10 000. These very large molecules are referred to as **macromolecules**. Proteins, starch, cellulose, RNA and DNA are all macromolecules and these macromolecules fufil a vast range of functions within the organism. This chapter concentrates on the structure of the different types of macromolecule but only touches on their functions. You will learn more about their functions in the later chapters of the book.

LEARNING OBJECTIVES

After studying this chapter you should:

1. understand the processes of condensation polymerisation and hydrolysis;

2. know the structure of starch, glycogen and cellulose;

3. understand the terms primary, secondary, tertiary and quaternary structure as applied to proteins;

4. understand the difference between fibrous and globular proteins;

5. know the basic structure of RNA and DNA;

6. appreciate some of the methods by which biologically important macromolecules are purified.

2.1 POLYMERS

Joining many similar molecules is called polymerisation

Most macromolecules are polymers. A **polymer** is a molecule formed from small repeating units called **monomers** joined together by covalent bonds. When a monomer has been added to a polymer the part of the polymer molecule that was originally the monomer is called a **residue**. The common polymers that are found in organisms are listed in Table 2.1.

Table 2.1

Macromolecule	Polymer	Monomer
starch	a polysaccharide	α-glucose
glycogen	a polysaccharide	α-glucose
cellulose	a polysaccharide	β-glucose
proteins	polypeptides	α-amino acids
DNA[1]	a polynucleotide	deoxyribonucleotides
RNA[2]	a polynucleotide	ribonucleotides

[1]deoxyribonucleic acid
[2]ribonucleic acid

The process by which monomers are joined to make polymers is called **polymerisation**. Most polymers in organisms are made by a similar

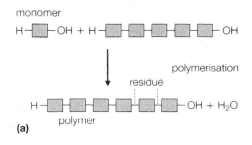

monomer

polymerisation

residue

polymer

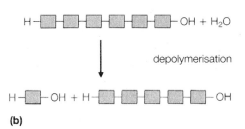

depolymerisation

(b)

Fig 2.1 **(a)** Most biologically important macromolecules are formed by condensation polymerisation.
(b) Depolymerisation occurs by an addition reaction.

chemical reaction in which two of the monomer molecules are joined with the removal of a molecule of water (Fig 2.1(a)). This is an elimination reaction because atoms in each of the monomer molecules are eliminated and it is also a condensation reaction because the atoms that are removed join up to make a water molecule. The overall reaction is therefore an **elimination polymerisation**, or more precisely, a **condensation polymerisation**. Almost all macromolecules in organisms are formed by condensation polymerisation reactions.

Depolymerisation occurs by hydrolysis

When a polymer is split into its monomers it is **depolymerised**. Most polymers in organisms are depolymerised by reversing the condensation polymerisation reaction shown in Fig 2.1(a). The reverse reaction is an addition reaction, because a molecule is added when the bond between the monomer residues is broken. As it is a water molecule that is added, the reaction is called hydrolysis. Figure 2.1(b) shows the **addition depolymerisation**, or more precisely, the **hydrolysis** of a polymer.

Polymerisation allows large, complex structures to be formed

A cell takes in, or synthesises, small organic molecules such as sugars, amino acids and nucleotides. Polymerising these small organic molecules to form polysaccharides, proteins or nucleic acids means that the cell can make complicated structures that can carry out a range of functions. Solid structures in organisms are constructed from polymers. For example, the polysaccharide cellulose makes up cell walls in plants and the protein collagen is found in animal tendons and the matrix from which bones are made. Other polymers are found within the cell: polynucleotides in the form of DNA act as the genetic material and polypeptides coil to form enzymes that catalyse all the chemical reactions within the cell. Polymers are nature's way of making a huge number of different materials for a vast number of functions from a limited number of starting materials: sugars, amino acids and nucleotides.

Some macromolecules are soluble, some form colloids and some are insoluble

(a) The weak bonds between the ions and the water molecules are stronger than the forces of attraction between the ions in the solid. The substance **dissolves.**

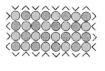

(b) The forces of attraction between the ions are greater than the weak bonds between the ions and the water molecules. The substance is **insoluble.**

Solids dissolve in water because the molecules in the solid are attracted to the molecules of water more than they are attracted to each other. The water molecules surround each molecule of the substance, forming a shell, and then the water molecules in this shell are attracted to the other water molecules that are moving freely in the liquid (Fig 2.2(a)). If the molecules in the solid attract each other more than they are attracted to water, then the water molecules will not come between the molecules in the solid and the solid is insoluble (Fig 2.2(b)).

What types of groups within a molecule attract water?

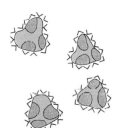

(c) The surface of the macromolecule attracts many water molecules. The macromolecules separate but each is too large to dissolve properly. This is a **colloidal suspension.**

Fig 2.2

If a big molecule, for example a large macromolecule, is attracted to water the molecules can end up suspended in the water rather than actually dissolved in it. Water molecules bind to the surface of the macromolecule and then the bound water molecules form hydrogen bonds with the free moving water molecules in the liquid. However, the water does not penetrate into the macromolecule itself so each molecule is like a tiny particle of solid suspended in the liquid (Fig 2.2(c)). Such particles are called **colloids** and the mixture of the particles and water is called a **colloidal suspension**. The colloid particles never settle out of the liquid because the surface of the particle is attracted to the water. The particles are large enough to scatter light, so a colloidal suspension always looks slightly cloudy.

QUESTIONS

2.1 (a) Name three different types of monomers found in cells and the polymers that are formed from these monomers. What macromolecules do these polymers form?

(b) What is meant by condensation polymerisation? Why is condensation polymerisation an elimination reaction?

(c) What is the name of the reaction by which biological polymers are depolymerised? Describe what happens in this reaction.

2.2 (a) The simple formula for glucose is $C_6H_{12}O_6$. Write an equation, using simple formulae, for the formation of a polysaccharide containing 300 residues.

(b) Write an equation, using simple formulae, for the hydrolysis of a polypeptide that contains one hundred glycine residues and no other amino acid residues. The simple formula for glycine is $C_2H_5O_2N$.

2.3 There are four solids, A, B, C and D. A contains macromolecules held together by strong forces of attraction between them. B contains small, polar molecules. C contains small, uncharged, non-polar molecules. D contains large macromolecules with weak forces of attraction between them and polar groups on their surface.

What will happen when you put A, B, C and D in water and why?

2.2 POLYSACCHARIDES

Polysaccharides are formed by the polymerisation of monosaccharides

The common polysaccharides (starch, glycogen and cellulose) are all formed from glucose. The glucose monomers are covalently linked together in a condensation polymerisation reaction (Fig 2.3) and the bonds between the glucose residues are called **glycosidic** bonds. The position of the glycosidic bonds is given by numbers in front of the word glycosidic, for example 1→4 glycosidic means that the bond goes from the carbon 1 of one sugar residue, via an oxygen, to the carbon 4 of the next sugar residue (Fig 2.3). The characteristics of the common polysaccharides are summed up in Table 2.2.

Table 2.2

Polysaccharide	Monomer	Position of bonds	Shape of polymer
starch (amylose)	α-glucose	1→4	helical
starch (amylopectin)	α-glucose	1→4 & 1→6	branched
glycogen	α-glucose	1→4 & 1→6	highly branched
cellulose	β-glucose	1→4	straight

Starch is found in two forms, both formed from α-glucose residues

Starch is a polymer formed from α-glucose monomers. Starch can exist in two forms: a coiled polymer without branches called **amylose** and a branched polymer called **amylopectin**.

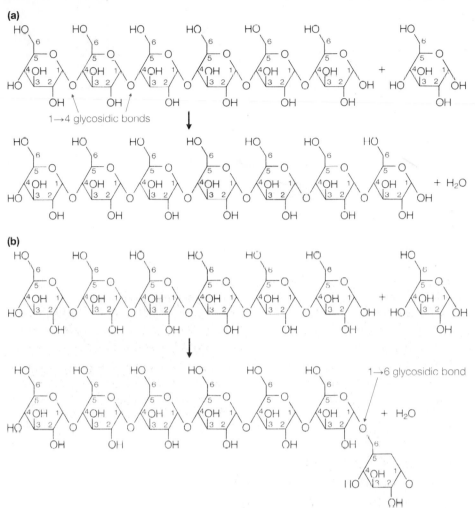

Fig 2.3 Starch is made from α-glucose monomers joined in a condensation polymerisation reaction. The monomers can be joined in two ways, one way forms 1→4 glycosidic bonds **(a)** and the other forms 1→6 glycosidic bonds **(b)**.

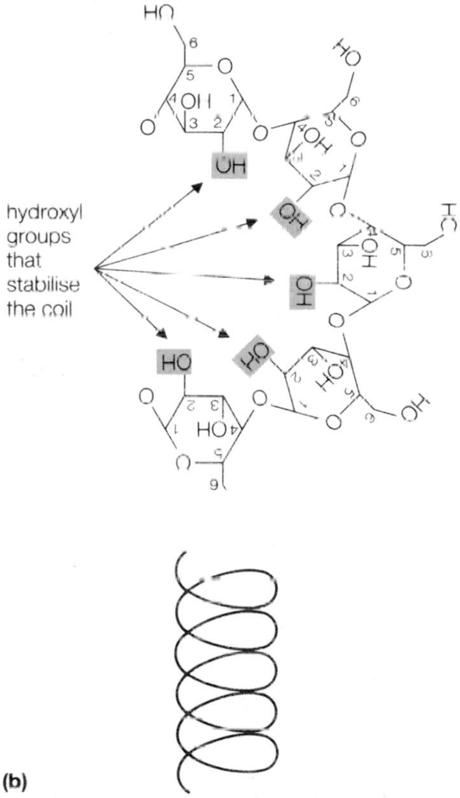

hydroxyl
groups
that
stabilise
the coil

(b)

Fig 2.4 The amylose polymer coils into a helical, compact structure that is stabilised by hydrogen bonds between different parts of the polymer.

Osmosis is the movement of water across a membrane from a region where the solution is less concentrated to a region where the solution is more concentrated.

In amylose the α-glucose residues are joined by 1→4 glycosidic bonds (Fig 2.4(a)). The angle made between the two C—O bonds between the rings is similar to the angle of the water molecule, about 109° (Fig 2.4(a)). This angle means that the polymer is twisted into a helix (a shape like a spiral staircase). The hydroxyl group on the carbon-2 of each glucose residue projects into the middle of the spiral. These hydroxyl groups form hydrogen bonds with each other which stabilise the shape of the amylose polymer, holding it in its helical shape (Fig 2.4(b)).

In amylopectin the α-glucose monomers are joined by either 1→4 glycosidic bonds or 1→6 glycosidic bonds (Fig 2.5(a)). Each time a 1→6 glycosidic bond is made a branch point is put into the polymer. The branch points occur every 24–30 residues, making a multi-branched, compact polymer (Fig 2.5(b)).

Both forms of starch, amylose and amylopectin, are very compact. Amylose is coiled up into a compact helical shape and amylopectin is branched to form a closely packed brush shape. The function of starch is to act as an energy storage molecule in plant cells and the compact shape means that many glucose residues can be stored in a small volume within the cell. As well as saving space, converting the glucose molecules into a polysaccharide reduces the number of small molecules in the cell. This is important because water enters the cell by osmosis and the more molecules

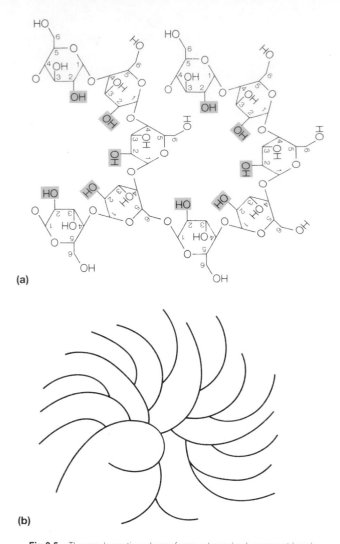

(a)

(b)

Fig 2.5 The amylopectin polymer forms a branched, compact brush.

inside the cell, the more concentrated the solution inside the cell and the more water that will enter by osmosis. Storing the glucose as starch means that the solution inside the cell is less concentrated and so less water will enter by osmosis.

Glycogen is also formed from α-glucose residues

Glycogen is a polymer of α-glucose monomers in which the residues are joined by either 1→4 glycosidic bonds or 1→6 glycosidic bonds. The glycogen polymer is branched like amylopectin but the branch points in glycogen occur every 8–12 residues, so the macromolecule is even more brush-like and compact. As with amylose and amylopectin, this means that many glucose molecules can be stored in a single macromolecule and it prevents there being too high a concentration of glucose within the cell.

Cellulose is formed from β-glucose residues

Cellulose is a polymer of β-glucose monomers joined by 1→4 glycosidic bonds. In order to make the 1→4 glycosidic bonds, every second β-glucose residue must be turned 'upside down' (Fig 2.7(a)). As every second residue is 'upside down', every kink that bends the polymer one way is cancelled out by the next kink, which is in the opposite direction. This means that the polymer forms a straight chain. As there are only 1→4 glycosidic bonds there are no branches in the polymer.

Fig 2.6 The staple food in every part of the world is starch. The Sun's energy is trapped by photosynthesis and transferred into the chemical energy of α-glucose. Polymers of α-glucose are coiled into tight helices that are held in place by hydrogen bonds to form the perfect energy storage macromolecule.

MACROMOLECULES

(a)

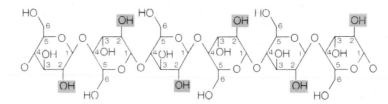

hydroxyl groups stick out both above
and below and will hydrogen bond to
adjacent molecules

(b)

Fig 2.7   Cellulose polymers are straight and unbranched. Separate polymers lie close together and are held together by hydrogen bonds between the molecules.

These straight, unbranched polymers pack closely together to form microfibrils (Fig 2.7(b)). The polymers making up the microfibril are held together by hydrogen bonds between adjacent chains. The cellulose microfibrils are very strong when subjected to a pulling force along their length and this strength makes them an excellent building material. You can read more about cellulose in Chapter 3.

DATA HANDLING 2.1

Plants contain many different forms of carbohydrate. They contain various monosaccharides, disaccharides and polysaccharides. Monosaccharides are synthesised in the leaves by photosynthesis and temporarily stored in the leaf as starch, usually in the amylose form. Later the starch is converted into sucrose so that it can be transported to all parts of the plant as a sugar solution in the phloem, one of the types of transport vessels that run the length of the stems and roots of the plant. Once it arrives in the cells the sucrose can be broken down to give monosaccharides that can be oxided to release energy, or converted back into starch, or used to synthesise cellulose.

(a) Why is glucose soluble in water? (The structure of glucose is given in Fig 1.19.)

(b) What other monosaccharide must be synthesised in the leaf so that sucrose can be made? (Refer to section 1.3 if you are unsure.)

(c) By what reaction is glucose converted into starch?

(d) The structure of a macromolecule of amylose is shown in Fig 2.4. The hydroxyl groups that project into the centre of the helix form intramolecular hydrogen bonds while those that project on the outside of the helix are available to form hydrogen bonds with water. Would you expect amylose to be soluble, insoluble or form a colloidal suspension? Explain your answer. (Refer to section 2.1 if you are stuck.)

(e) All cells are surrounded by a membrane. Suggest why carbohydrate is transported around the plant as sucrose rather than starch.

(f) By what reaction is sucrose broken down to give monosaccharides?

(g) Cellulose is used as a building material in plants. In particular, it is used to build a cell wall outside the cell membrane in plant cells. Explain why cellulose microfibrils are insoluble in water, and therefore make a good building material. (Refer to Fig 2.7 and section 2.1 if you need help.)

Intramolecular bonds are bonds between different parts of the same molecule.

2.4 **(a)** From what monomer is starch made?
(b) What terms are used to describe the reaction in which the starch is made?
(c) What type of bond is formed when starch is made?
(d) What are the characteristics of starch that make it a good energy storage macromolecule?

2.5 **(a)** Describe the structure of a single cellulose polymer.
(b) Explain why cellulose polymers are straight rather than curved.
(c) Explain how cellulose polymers form microfibrils.

2.6 Amylose, amylopectin and glycogen are all energy storage polysaccharides while cellulose is a structural polysaccharide, yet all four polysaccharides are made from glucose monomers. Discuss how such chemically similar substances can fulfil two such different functions.

2.3 POLYPEPTIDES

A chain of amino acid residues linked together to form a polymer is referred to as a **polypeptide**. **Proteins** are polypeptides in their final form: some proteins are just a single polypeptide chain folded into a certain shape, while others contain more than one polypeptide, or have been chemically modified, or contain groups other than amino acid residues. This section concentrates on the structure of the polypeptides themselves; the other aspects of protein structure are discussed in Chapter 6.

Most polypeptides have a similar backbone

Polypeptides are formed when α-amino acids react together in a condensation polymerisation reaction forming **peptide bonds** between the amino acid residues (Fig 2.8). The polypeptide has a backbone that runs the length of the macromolecule (Fig 2.9). As the only differences between the α-amino acids are the R groups, this backbone does not vary much from polypeptide to polypeptide.

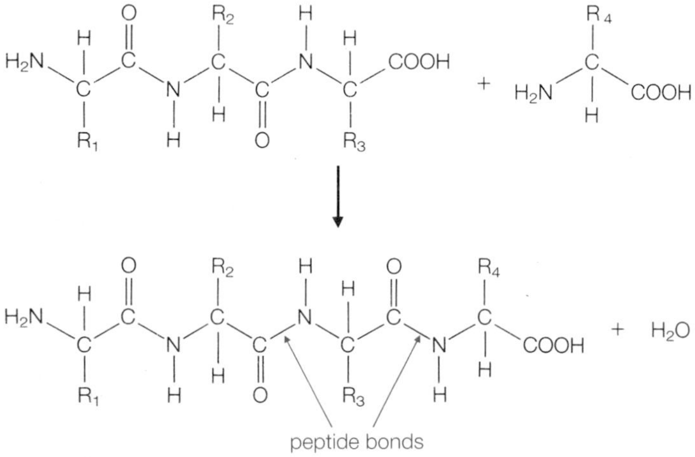

Fig 2.8 Polypeptides are formed from amino acids by a condensation polymerisation reaction in which peptide bonds are formed.

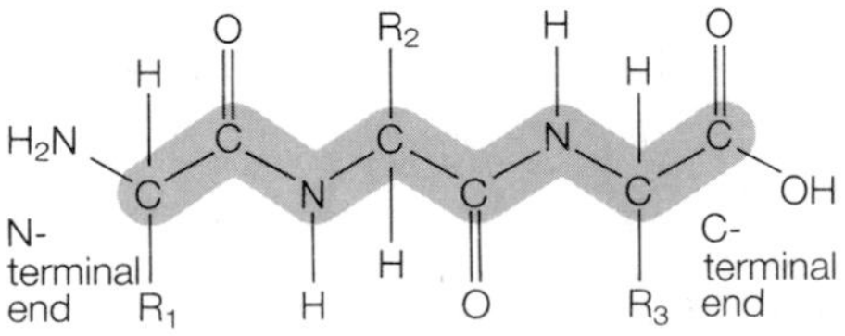

Fig 2.9 All polypeptides have a similar backbone and R groups that vary depending on the amino acid residues present.

Polypeptides fold into three-dimensional structures

The polypeptide backbone is flexible and can fold into a variety of shapes. In some of these shapes hydrogen bonds can form between different parts of the polypeptide backbone. Every time a hydrogen bond forms, the polypeptide becomes a little more stable and the most stable shapes are those which contain the most hydrogen bonds.

Two of the most stable shapes that polypeptides can form are the α-helix (Fig 2.10) and the β-pleated sheet (Fig 2.11). Both these structures have many hydrogen bonds between different parts of the backbone and are therefore very stable. In the α-helix the polypeptide forms a coil or helix with 3.6 amino acid residues per turn. In the β-pleated sheet the polypeptide backbones are side by side, with hydrogen bonds between the adjacent sections of the polypeptide.

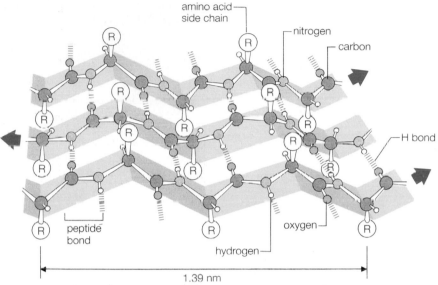

Fig 2.11 The polypeptide folds into sections that lie side by side, forming a sheet. The sheet is held together by hydrogen bonds between adjacent parts of the polypeptide.

Some polypeptides form fibrous proteins, others form globular proteins

An uninterrupted α-helix forms a long, elongated structure. Polypeptides with long, elongated structures form fibrous proteins. Fibrous proteins usually have a structural role in organisms because they can pack side by side in bundles that are quite strong when they are pulled. α-keratins, the proteins that form hair, nails and hooves, consist almost entirely of polypeptides coiled into α-helices. An uninterrupted β-pleated sheet also forms fibrous proteins. Silk fibroin, the protein that makes up the silk secreted by silkworms, is made almost entirely of β-pleated sheet.

However, not all polypeptides form perfect α-helices or β-pleated sheets. Sometimes the R groups projecting from the backbone interfere with the folding pattern. Table 2.3 shows those amino acid residues that allow an α-helix to form, those that reduce the stability of an α-helix and those that break an α-helix by introducing a sharp kink.

Table 2.3

Allow a stable α-helix	Destabilise an α-helix	Break an α-helix
alanine	tyrosine, cysteine	proline
leucine	asparagine, serine,	hydroxyproline
phenylalanine	isoleucine, threonine,	
tryptophan	glutamic acid,	
methionine	aspartic acid,	
histidine	lysine, arginine,	
glutamine	glycine	
valine		

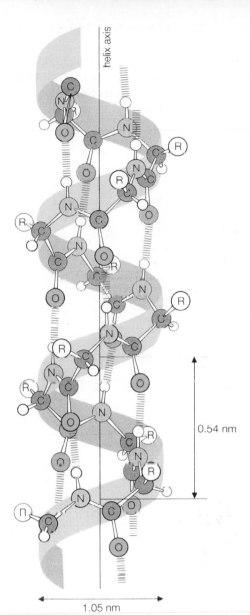

Fig 2.10 The polypeptide is coiled into a helix and the helix is held in position by hydrogen bonds between different groups in the backbone.

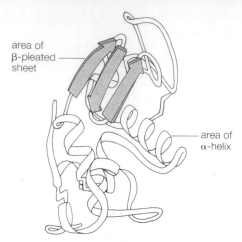

area of
β-pleated
sheet

area of
α-helix

Fig 2.12 A polypeptide can fold into a compact, globular shape.

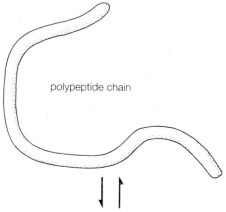

polypeptide chain

in water the chain folds up on itself

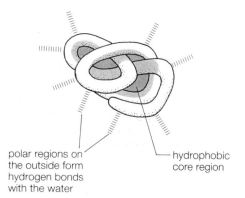

polar regions on
the outside form
hydrogen bonds
with the water

hydrophobic
core region

Fig 2.14 The most stable folding patterns leave the hydrophilic amino acid residues on the outer surface, where they form hydrogen bonds with water; and the hydrophobic amino acid residues on the inner surface, away from the water.

The presence of certain amino acid residues can introduce a kink into the polypeptide. This can cause the polypeptide to fold up into a compact structure, rather than forming an elongated, fibrous structure. Folded, compact polypeptides form **globular proteins**. The structure of a globular protein is shown in Fig 2.12. It consists of regions of α-helix and regions of β-pleated sheets joined by lengths of polypeptide containing kinks.

Fig 2.13 Humans use the structural proteins produced by animals in many ways. Silk fibroin is a fibrous protein consisting of β-pleated sheet that is produced as a thread by silk worms, *Bombyx mori*, to make their cocoons. The R groups of the amino acid residues in silk fibroin are small, allowing the polypeptide chains to be tightly packed together to form sheets. The chains are held together by numerous hydrogen bonds, producing a very thin but very strong thread that can be woven into a fabric that has been prized for thousands of years for its hard wearing properties as well as its shine.

R groups affect the folding of a polypeptide

In a globular protein there will be some R groups that are charged or polar, and therefore attracted to water, and other R groups that are both uncharged and non-polar and are therefore hydrophobic. A folding pattern that has most of the charged or polar R groups on the outer surface and most of the hydrophobic R groups on the inside, away from the surface, will be more stable than a folding pattern that leaves hydrophobic R groups on the surface. A globular protein will be inclined to fold so that its hydrophilic R groups are on the outside surface and the hydrophobic R groups are hidden away from the water (Fig 2.14).

Yet another consideration is the possibility of interactions between the R groups. A very few R groups can form covalent bonds with each other. The most common of these covalent bonds is the **disulphide bridge** that forms between two cysteine residues (Fig 2.15). The other, weaker, interactions that occur between R groups are also shown in Fig 2.15. Some R groups can form hydrogen bonds, positively charged R groups will attract negatively charged R groups and hydrophobic R groups are more stable close together than when separated by water. Again, the greater the number of bonds that form between the R groups the more stable the folded polypeptide will be.

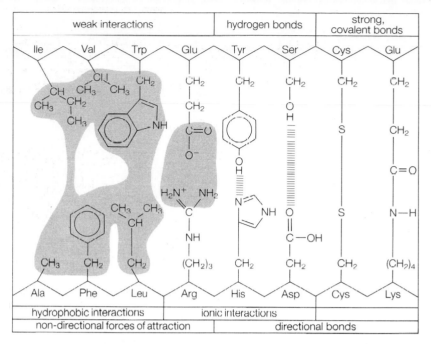

Fig 2.15 Interactions that occur between R groups.

Protein structure can be thought of as a series of levels

Describing the exact three-dimensional structure of a polypeptide requires you to give quite a lot of information. You must state which amino acid residues are present and in what order: this is called the **primary structure** of the polypeptide. You would also have to describe the interactions between the different parts of the polypeptide backbone, for example sections of α-helix or β-pleated sheet: this is called the **secondary structure** of the polypeptide. You would then have to describe the interactions between the R groups of the amino acid residues: this is called the **tertiary structure** of the polypeptide.

Finally, there might be more than one polypeptide chain present in the mature protein. Some proteins contain many polypeptide chains of the same type while other proteins contain polypeptide chains of different types. The protein haemoglobin contains two α-globin chains and two β-globin chains (Fig 2.16). To describe the structure of haemoglobin you would have to describe the interactions between the different polypeptides present in the protein: this is called the **quaternary structure** of the protein.

Proteins are a very diverse group of macromolecules

Proteins fulfil a vast range of functions in organisms. For example, in a human just a few of the functions that proteins perform are to form tendons, the lens of the eye, nails, hair, muscle, some hormones, hormone receptors and to make up thousands of enzymes each catalysing a specific reaction. Compared to polysaccharides or nucleic acids, proteins are very versatile macromolecules. This versatility arises because every protein is different from every other protein. The amino acids used to make the polypeptide, the number of each amino acid used and the order in which they are polymerised together is different for every protein. Every molecule of a certain protein is the same as every other molecule of that protein, but it is different from every other protein. You can read more about how the order of amino acid residues is determined in Chapter 5.

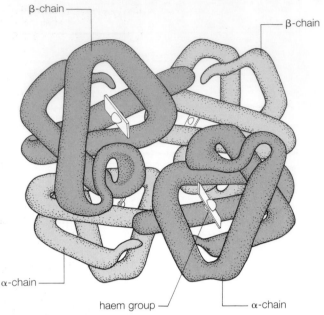

Fig 2.16 Haemoglobin contains four polypeptide chains. It is an example of a protein that has a quaternary structure.

In other words, the primary structure of a protein is different from the primary structure of every other protein. As the primary structure is different the secondary structure is different, because some amino acid residues will form α-helices, some will form β-sheets and some will introduce kinks into the backbone. Likewise, if the primary structure is different the tertiary structure is different because the tertiary structure depends on the R groups and the primary structure determines which R groups are present and their position in the polypeptide. This means that the folding pattern is unique for each polypeptide and therefore the three-dimensional shape of each protein is unique to that protein. Throughout this book there are examples of how the functions of macromolecules depend on their three-dimensional shape. The huge variety of shapes that proteins can make accounts for the large number of functions those proteins can fulfil.

The 3D shape of a protein is sensitive to both temperature and pH

The peptide bonds in a polypeptide are strong, covalent bonds. However, most of the bonds that hold together the secondary and tertiary structures are weak bonds such as hydrogen bonds. Increasing the temperature can provide enough energy to break these weak bonds, allowing the protein to unfold and destroying its three-dimensional shape. One everyday example of this is cooking egg white. Egg white is a solution of the protein egg albumen. When the egg is cooked the temperature of the egg albumen increases, providing enough energy to break the weak bonds that hold the egg albumen molecule in a compact, globular shape. The egg albumen polypeptides unfold, making them less soluble, and form other weak bonds between the different egg albumen polypeptides, making the egg white rigid. A protein that loses its unique three-dimensional shape is said to be **denatured**.

A change in pH can also destroy the three-dimensional shape of a protein. Many of the bonds that hold together the tertiary structure of a protein depend on the charge of the R groups involved. Changing the pH of the environment can change the charge on the R group, breaking some weak bonds and causing others to form. This alters the three-dimensional shape of the protein and can make the protein non-functional.

MACROMOLECULES

Scientists analyse the structure of proteins in a variety of ways

As the structure of proteins is so vital to their function, scientists have spent much time and effort developing techniques for studying it. One of the big breakthroughs in analysing protein structure was the development of **protein sequencing**. Protein sequencing is a method of determining the primary structure of a protein (the nature and order of the amino acid residues in the polymer). To do this the end amino acid residue must be hydrolysed away from the rest of the polypeptide and then identified by chromatography.

The most efficient method of protein sequencing is the **Edman degradation**. The protein is cut into manageable polypeptide sections and each polypeptide analysed separately. The polypeptide is treated with a chemical which reacts with the terminal amino acid residue in the peptide chain (Fig 2.17). The modified amino acid residue is hydrolysed from the peptide by treatment with mild acid, and is identified by chromatography. The reaction is repeated, removing one amino acid residue at a time, until the whole polypeptide has been analysed. Finally the sequences of the polypeptides are put together to give the sequence of the whole protein.

Having obtained the primary structure of the polypeptide the scientist must then proceed to determine its secondary, tertiary and possibly quaternary structure. As explained above, the secondary and tertiary structure of the protein depend on the nature of the amino acid residues and their position in the polymer, in other words on the primary structure of the polypeptide. Nowadays computer programs exist which can predict the secondary and tertiary structure of a polypeptide from its primary structure. The scientist can 'fold up' the polypeptide within the computer.

However, predicting the three-dimensional structure is not hard evidence. **X-ray diffraction** is used to provide direct evidence of the three-dimensional shape of the polypeptide. A beam of X-rays is fired through a crystal of the protein. The pattern that the X-rays make once they have been scattered by the crystal gives us information about the arrangement of the atoms in the crystal and therefore about the spatial arrangement of the atoms in the protein. Experienced scientists using computers can use the X-ray diffraction data to calculate the exact three-dimensional shape of a protein molecule to an accuracy of 0.7 nm.

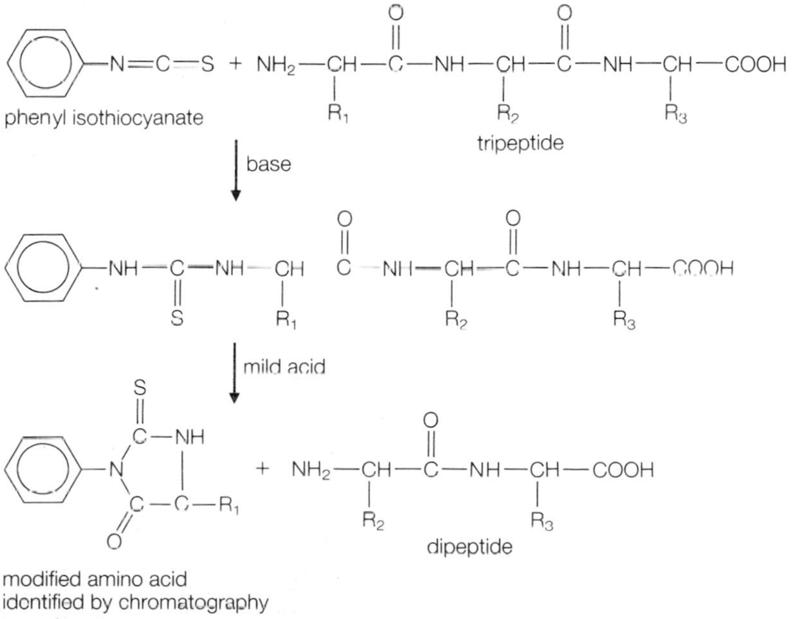

Fig 2.17 The Edman degradation is a series of chemical reactions that splits off the N-terminal amino acid residue of a polypeptide so that it can be identified by chromatography.

Scientists trying to determine the primary structure of bovine ribonuclease, an enzyme from cattle, first hydrolysed the protein into its constituent amino acids by treating with strong, concentrated acid at 60 °C and then analysed these amino acids using an amino acid analyser (a machine that identifies the nature and amount of an amino acid).

The amino acid composition of bovine ribonuclease

Non-polar residues
Ala 12, Val 9, Leu 2, Ile 3, Pro 4, Met 4, Phe 3, Trp 0

Polar residues
Gly 3, Ser 15, Thr 10, Cys 8, Tyr 6, Asn 10, Gln 7

Negatively charged residues at pH 7
Asp 5, Glu 5

Positively charged residues at pH 7
Lys 10, Arg 4, His 4

(a) What is the total number of amino acid residues present in bovine ribonuclease?
(b) What was the most abundant amino acid residue in bovine ribonuclease?
(c) Would the bovine ribonuclease macromolecule have a net positive charge at pH 7 or a net negative charge at pH 7? Explain your answer.

The scientists then treated a sample of the protein to remove the terminal amino acid residue at the end with a free amine group (the N-terminus). This amino acid was identified as lysine (Lys). The scientists then treated a sample of the protein to remove the terminal amino acid from the end with a free carboxylic group (the C-terminus). This amino acid was identified as valine (Val).

A fresh sample of the protein was then broken up by treating with a chemical called cyanogen bromide. Cyanogen bromide breaks the polymer after a methionine (Met) residue. Four long polypeptides were obtained and sequenced using the Edman degradation technique. A large amount of methionine was also obtained.

The four long polypeptides

Polypeptide A (49 residues)
Lys–Ser–Arg–Asn–Leu–Thr–Lys–Asp–Arg–Cys–Lys–Pro–Val–Asn–Thr–Phe–Val–His–Glu–Ser–Leu–Ala–Asp–Val–Gln–Ala–Val–Cys–Ser–Gln–Lys–Asn–Val–Ala–Cys–Lys–Asn–Gly–Gln–Thr–Asn–Cys–Tyr–Gln–Ser–Tyr–Ser–Thr–Met

Polypeptide B (16 residues)
Asp–Ser–Ser–Thr–Ser–Ala–Ala–Ser–Ser–Ser–Asn–Tyr–Cys–Asn–Gln–Met

Polypeptide C (45 residues)
Ser–Ile–Thr–Asp–Cys–Arg–Glu–Thr–Gly–Ser–Ser–Lys–Tyr–Pro–Asn–Cys–Ala–Tyr–Lys–Thr–Thr–Gln–Ala–Asn–Lys–His–Ile–Ile–Val–Ala–Cys–Glu–Gly–Asn–Pro–Tyr–Val–Pro–Val–His–Phe–Asp–Ala–Ser–Val

Polypeptide D (13 residues)
Lys–Glu–Thr–Ala–Ala–Ala–Lys–Phe–Glu–Arg–Gln–His–Met

(d) Which polypeptide, A, B , C or D, occurs at the end of the original polypeptide with a free carboxylic group (the C-terminus)? Give reasons for your choice.

(e) Which two polypeptides could occur at the N-terminus of bovine ribonuclease? Explain your answer.

(f) There are 123 amino acid residues in the four polypeptides shown above, yet there are 124 amino acid residues in bovine ribonuclease. What is the 124th amino acid residue? Explain your answer.

Another sample of the bovine ribonuclease protein was taken and broken into polypeptides using the protease trypsin. Trypsin breaks the polymer after a lysine (Lys) or an arginine (Arg) residue. Many polypeptides resulted from this treatment. The scientists only sequenced those polypeptides with a methionine residue (Met).

Sequence of polypeptides from the trypsin treatment containing methionine

Asn–Gly–Gln–Thr–Asn–Cys–Tyr–Gln–Ser–Tyr–Ser–Thr–Met–Ser–Ile–Thr–Asp–Cys–Arg

Gln–His–Met–Asp–Ser–Ser–Thr–Ser–Ala–Ala–Ser–Ser–Ser–Asn–Tyr–Cys–Asn–Gln–Met–Met–Lys

(g) Using this extra information the scientists were able to determine the actual order of polypeptides A, B, C and D in bovine ribonuclease. What is the order? Explain how you deduced your answer.

QUESTIONS

2.7 (a) What type of reaction occurs when two amino acids join together to make a dipeptide?

(b) Write out the chemical equation for two glycine residues reacting together to make a dipeptide.

(c) A polypeptide is heated to 60 °C with 6M hydrochloric acid in order to break it down into its constituent amino acids. What type of reaction has occurred?

2.8 (a) What is meant by the primary structure of a protein?

(b) What is meant by the secondary structure of a protein? List two examples of common secondary structures.

(c) What is meant by the tertiary structure of a protein? List three different types of interaction that can contribute towards the tertiary structure of a protein.

(d) What is meant by the quaternary structure of a protein? Give one example of a protein that has a quaternary structure.

2.9 (a) What is the difference between a fibrous protein and a globular protein?

(b) Collagen is a structural protein from which tendons are made. Would you expect collagen to be a fibrous protein or a globular protein?

(c) Catalase is an enzyme that is found in many cells. It is a soluble protein found in the cytoplasm of the cell. Would you expect catalase to be a fibrous protein or a globular protein?

2.10 (a) What do scientists mean when they say that a protein has denatured?

(b) Explain how raising the temperature of a solution of a protein can cause that protein to denature.

(c) Explain why placing a protein from a neutral environment into a high or low pH environment can change its three-dimensional structure.

Polynucleotides are formed by the polymerisation of nucleotides

Nucleotides are molecules which have three components: a sugar, one or more phosphate groups and a base (see section 1.5). They are joined together in a condensation polymerisation reaction to form polynucleotides. The nucleotides are joined when a covalent bond forms between carbon-3 of the pentose sugar group and the phosphate group of the next nucleotide. As can be seen in Fig 2.18, the polynucleotide has a **sugar–phosphate backbone** (the shaded area) with the bases projecting from one side of this backbone. The sugar–phosphate backbone of the polynucleotide has two distinct ends, the **5' end** ('five prime' end) and the **3' end** ('three prime' end) (Fig 2.18). This sugar–phosphate backbone is negatively charged because of the negative charges on each of the phosphate groups.

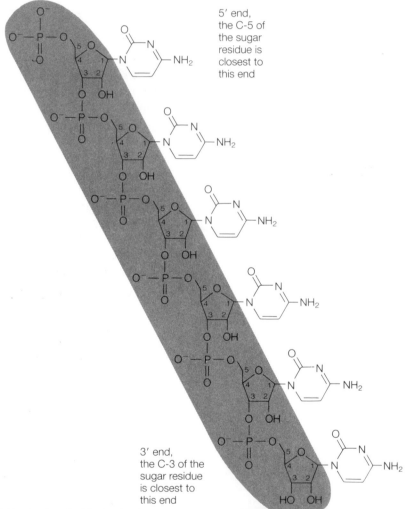

5' end, the C-5 of the sugar residue is closest to this end

3' end, the C-3 of the sugar residue is closest to this end

Fig 2.18   A polynucleotide showing the sugar–phosphate backbone (the shaded area) and the base groups that project from the backbone.

Deoxyribonucleotides polymerise to form DNA

There are two main types of nucleotides in a cell, deoxyribonucleotides and ribonucleotides (section 1.5). Deoxyribonucleotides contain a deoxyribose sugar group, one of the four bases adenine (A), guanine (G), cytosine (C) or thymine (T) and at least one phosphate group. They polymerise to form **deoxyribonucleic acid, DNA**.

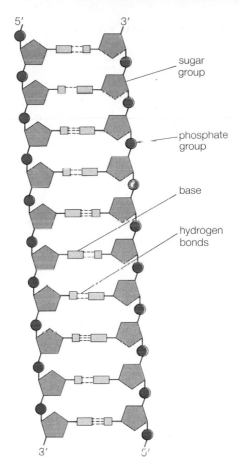

Fig 2.19 DNA is double stranded, containing two polynucleotides made from deoxyribonucleotide residues.

DNA is usually **double stranded**. This means that there are two polynucleotides side by side held together by weak bonds (Fig 2.19). The weak bonds are hydrogen bonds between the bases of the two polynucleotides, forming **base pairs** (Fig 2.20). Only certain bases can hydrogen bond together: adenine base pairs with thymine and cytosine base pairs with guanine. We say that adenine is **complementary** to thymine and that cytosine is complementary to guanine.

In order for the base pairs to form, the polynucleotides have to run in opposite directions. Figure 2.21 shows that one polynucleotide runs 5′ to 3′ while the other polynucleotide runs 3′ to 5′. We say that the two polynucleotide strands are **antiparallel**. Finally, when the base pairs form they twist the polynucleotides into a helix in which there are 10 base pairs for every one turn of the helix: double-stranded DNA is a **double helix**.

Double-stranded DNA is a very stable structure: it has to be because it stores the genetic information of the organism. A double-stranded DNA macromolecule can be very long. Each human chromosome contains one, long, double-stranded DNA macromolecule. The largest human chromosomes contain about 10 cm of double-stranded DNA.

Working out the structure of DNA revolutionised biology. This was because DNA is the genetic material of almost all organisms. All the information to build a human and to make him or her function is stored in the DNA of the single cell that was formed when the sperm fertilised the egg. Exactly how the genetic information is stored in the DNA and how that information is used to make an organism is discussed in Theme 2 of this book.

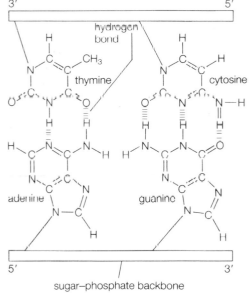

Fig 2.20 Thymine forms two hydrogen bonds with adenine and cytosine forms three hydrogen bonds with guanine. The two polynucleotides are complementary, the bases forming base pairs.

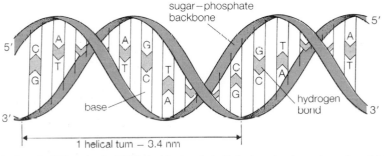

Fig 2.21 Part of a DNA molecule. DNA is double stranded with the two strands running antiparallel. The strands are held together by hydrogen bonds between them. The double-stranded structure twists into a helix.

Ribonucleotides polymerise to form RNA

Ribonucleotides contain the ribose sugar group, one of the four bases adenine (A), cytosine (C), guanine (G) or uracil (U) and at least one phosphate group (section 1.5). Ribonucleotides polymerise to form ribonucleic acid, RNA. Again, the polynucleotide has a sugar–phosphate backbone with the bases projecting from it. RNA is usually single stranded but the single polynucleotide has a flexible sugar–phosphate backbone that can fold. Base pairs form between complementary bases, A with U and C with G, and these base pairs hold the RNA into complex three-dimensional shapes (Fig 2.22).

RNA molecules are very short as compared to DNA molecules. A DNA polynucleotide in a chromosome may contain 300 000 000 nucleotide residues while an RNA polynucleotide is more likely to contain about 400 nucleotide residues. RNA is also much less stable than DNA. RNA needs to be less stable as it acts as a short term functional molecule in the cell, while DNA needs to be extremely stable because it is the store for the genetic information.

RNA is present in all cells and fulfils a number of very important functions. There are several different types of RNA in cells and they all have essential roles in taking the genetic information from the DNA and using it to build the molecules that make up the cell. The roles of RNA in cells are discussed in Chapters 5 and 6.

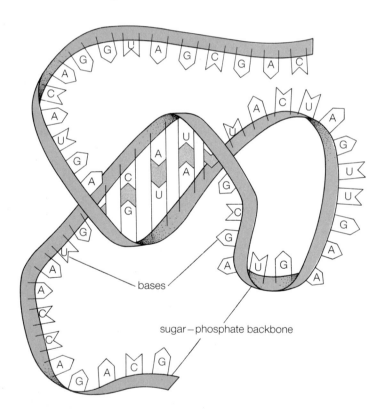

Fig 2.22 Part of an RNA molecule. RNA is a single-stranded polynucleotide. It often folds, forming small areas that are double stranded.

QUESTIONS

2.11 **(a)** Describe the structure of a generalised polynucleotide.
(b) List the differences between RNA and DNA.

2.12 The following terms are used to describe the structure of nucleic acids. Briefly explain their meaning.
(a) sugar–phosphate backbone
(b) complementary bases
(c) double helix
(d) antiparallel strands.

MACROMOLECULES

2.5 MANIPULATING MACROMOLECULES

In order to study a certain macromolecule we must be able to isolate a considerable amount of that substance in a pure form. This task is much easier for some substances than for others. If we want to study cellulose there is an almost unlimited supply available: all we have to do is obtain a chunk of wood. Other substances are in much smaller supply and are much more difficult to isolate in a pure form.

We must be able to follow the macromolecule

Before we can begin to purify a substance there must be an **assay** for that substance. An assay is a test for the substance under study; if the test is positive the substance is still present and we know that the substance that we are trying to purify has not been put down the sink by mistake. A good assay also allows us to calculate the amount of the substance that is present.

The assay used is different for each substance under study. For example, if we are purifying starch then we are likely to use the standard test for starch: we would add iodine solution and if starch was present the iodine would stain the starch blue-black. Likewise if we were purifying all the proteins from a mixture we would perform a standard protein test, for example the biuret test where a purple colour indicates the presence of peptide bonds.

A good assay is simple, cheap and effective

If we wish to isolate a single pure substance we need an assay which will only be positive for that particular substance. The assay would have to depend on some unique property of the substance under study. Some assays are easier to develop than others. The iodine solution test for starch is a good example of an easy but effective assay: it is positive for starch, it is negative for all other substances and it is quick, easy to perform and cheap. Finding an assay for the protein haemoglobin was also easy: haemoglobin is red, unlike almost all other proteins, therefore we can follow the presence of haemoglobin by its red colour.

Some assays for a particular substance depend on the substance's boiling point, or melting point, or its relative molecular mass or its chemical reactivity. A scientist will seize on any unique property that a molecule possesses in order to develop a usable assay.

Antibodies are used to assay proteins

Every protein has a unique three-dimensional shape. This provides us with the unique property needed to develop an assay for that particular protein. Mammals produce **antibodies** when a foreign macromolecule is introduced into their bodies. If foreign proteins are injected into an animal the animal will produce antibodies that will stick to that particular protein and to no other.

We can now grow the cells that produce the antibodies outside the animals in sterile bottles containing a nutrient solution. Every culture of cells can produce an unlimited supply of one particular antibody to one particular protein. These are called **monoclonal antibodies** and the method by which they are produced is outlined in Fig 2.23.

Nucleic acids are assayed by their unique sequence of bases

All polynucleotides are chemically similar, just as all polypeptides are chemically similar. The scientist seeking to develop an assay for one particular section of DNA must use a unique property of that section of DNA. The only property that varies from one section of DNA to another is the exact order of the bases A, T, C and G.

We use this property by making a **probe** to that unique sequence of bases. A probe is a polynucleotide in which some of the nucleotide residues

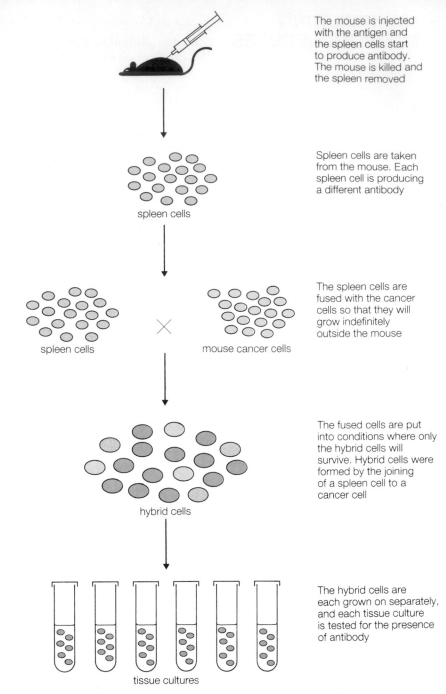

The mouse is injected with the antigen and the spleen cells start to produce antibody. The mouse is killed and the spleen removed

Spleen cells are taken from the mouse. Each spleen cell is producing a different antibody

spleen cells

The spleen cells are fused with the cancer cells so that they will grow indefinitely outside the mouse

spleen cells

mouse cancer cells

The fused cells are put into conditions where only the hybrid cells will survive. Hybrid cells were formed by the joining of a spleen cell to a cancer cell

hybrid cells

The hybrid cells are each grown on separately, and each tissue culture is tested for the presence of antibody

tissue cultures

Fig 2.23 How monoclonal antibodies are produced.

The DNA is cut in short lengths The DNA is put into a high pH solution so that the hydrogen bonds break, producing single-stranded DNA

The single-stranded DNA is stuck to a special type of filter paper

The filter paper is then treated so no more DNA will stick to it

The radiolabelled DNA probe is added and the pH is made neutral so that it will base pair to the complementary piece of DNA

Fig 2.24 The presence of a specific section of DNA can be detected using a probe that is complementary to this section of DNA.

are radioactive and which is complementary to the section of DNA that we want to study. If the probe is added to a mixture of DNA, it will hydrogen bond to the section of DNA under study. This means that the section of DNA under study can be followed using a radiation detector. An outline of how a probe can be used is shown in Fig 2.24.

We can use the properties of a macromolecule to isolate it

Once we have a usable assay we can proceed to isolate the macromolecule we are studying. It is relatively easy to isolate all the proteins from a mixture, or all the polysaccharides, or all the lipids or all the nucleic acids: proteins have different properties from polysaccharides or nucleic acids. It

MACROMOLECULES

is once we have our mixture of proteins that the task becomes more challenging. All proteins have very similar chemical and physical properties and it is therefore very difficult to separate one protein from all the others. There are two methods of approaching the problem: we can concentrate on methods that differentiate between very small differences in the physical properties of the proteins or we can develop a separation method that exploits a unique property of the protein under study.

Traditional separation methods exploit small differences in the physical properties of proteins

Ion exchange chromatography is a good example of a traditional method of separating proteins that relies on small differences between proteins. Each protein has a unique primary structure. This means that the combination of R groups projecting from the backbone of the polypeptide is different for each protein. The R groups can be uncharged or charged, so each protein has a net charge due to its R groups. **Ion exchange resins** are positively or negatively charged. A positively charged resin will bind all proteins with a net negative charge and a negatively charged resin will bind all proteins with a net positive charge. We select the correct resin by trial and error and then use the resin to fill a column. The mixture of proteins is then poured down the column and all the proteins with a charge opposite to that on the resin will stick.

We then **elute** (remove by washing) the proteins that have stuck to the resin. This can be done by reducing the charge on the proteins so that they stick to the resin less tightly. The charge on the proteins can be altered by changing the pH of the surrounding solution. Decreasing the pH of the solution means an increase in the concentration of hydrogen ions. These extra hydrogen ions neutralise negative charges on the R groups and may cause other R groups to become positively charged. This would make a protein stick less strongly to a positively charged resin. Similarly, increasing the pH of the solution would decrease the concentration of hydrogen ions. This would cause neutral R groups to become negatively charged and neutralise some of the positively charge R groups. This would make a protein stick less strongly to a negatively charged resin.

Another way of eluting a protein from a resin is to wash the resin with a high concentration of a salt. The positive ions in the salt solution compete for the charged groups on a negatively charged resin, washing off the positively charged protein. Similarly, the negatively charged ions in the salt solution compete for the charged groups on a positively charged resin, washing off the negatively charged protein.

By gradually changing the pH of the solution being fed through the column, or by gradually increasing the salt concentration, or both, we can cause the proteins to come away from the resin one by one and collect them separately.

Modern methods exploit the unique 3D shape of proteins

The most effective, modern separation techniques are based on the fact that each protein is shaped slightly differently. Monoclonal antibodies can be used to prepare a pure sample of a certain protein by **affinity chromatography** because each monoclonal antibody fits a particular protein perfectly. The antibody is linked to a resin and the resin is used to fill a column. When the mixture of proteins is poured down the column the protein that sticks to the antibody, and no other protein, will stick to the column. The protein is eluted once all the other proteins have been washed away. Purification of a protein using a monoclonal antibody is shown in Fig 2.25.

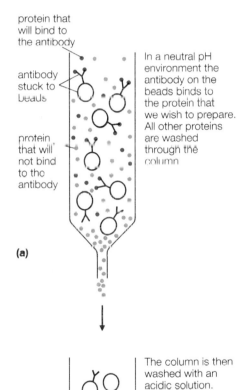

protein that will bind to the antibody

antibody stuck to beads

protein that will not bind to the antibody

In a neutral pH environment the antibody on the beads binds to the protein that we wish to prepare. All other proteins are washed through the column

(a)

The column is then washed with an acidic solution. At a low pH the interaction between the antibody and the protein weakens, and the protein is eluted from the column

(b)

Fig 2.25 Proteins can be purified by affinity chromatography.

Nucleic acids can also be prepared by affinity chromatography.

Affinity chromatography can also be used to purify nucleic acids. Every section of nucleic acid has a unique sequence of nucleotide residues and this property can be used to purify both RNA and single-stranded DNA. A short polynucleotide that is complementary to part of required RNA is linked to a resin and the resin is used to fill a column. The mixture of nucleic acids is poured down the column and only the correct RNA will form hydrogen bonds with the polynucleotide on the resin. After the other nucleic acids have been washed away the RNA can be eluted from the column. An outline of the method used to purify nucleic acids by affinity chromatography is shown in Fig 2.26.

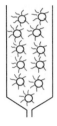 A column is prepared. The column contains beads that have a probe attached to them. The probe is complementary to part of the sequence of the polynucleotide that we wish to isolate

 A mixture of single-stranded polynucleotides is put down the column under conditions in which double-stranded polynucleotides will form if a complementary base sequence is present. The polynucleotides that do not bind are washed through the column

 The polynucleotide that we wish to isolate is left on the column

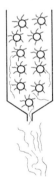 The polynucleotide is eluted by changing the conditions so that hydrogen bonds no longer form between complementary bases. A preparation of pure polynucleotide is eluted from the column

Fig 2.26   Affinity chromatography can be used to purify nucleic acids.

There are many strategies used to purify macromolecules, only a few of which have been outlined in this section. Scientific research is always unearthing previously undiscovered substances that may have a crucial role in an essential cellular process or may be the faulty link that leads to a particular disease developing. Scientists use their knowledge of biochemistry in general, and what little they know of the new substance, to develop a method for purifying that new substance. Only then can the work of studying the substance and of researching its role in the organism begin.

DATA HANDLING 2.3

Figure 2.27 shows a standard procedure for detecting the presence of a protein in solution. The procedure requires there to be an antibody available that binds to the protein. This type of assay can be used to detect the presence of a protein such as insulin in a blood sample. Table 2.4 shows the results that a scientist obtains when testing a number of blood samples for insulin.

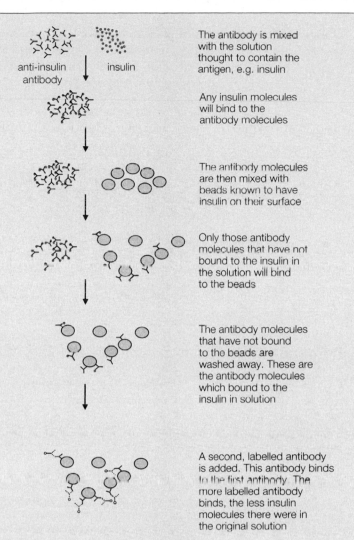

The antibody is mixed with the solution thought to contain the antigen, e.g. insulin

anti-insulin antibody   insulin

Any insulin molecules will bind to the antibody molecules

The antibody molecules are then mixed with beads known to have insulin on their surface

Only those antibody molecules that have not bound to the insulin in the solution will bind to the beads

The antibody molecules that have not bound to the beads are washed away. These are the antibody molecules which bound to the insulin in solution

A second, labelled antibody is added. This antibody binds to the first antibody. The more labelled antibody binds, the less insulin molecules there were in the original solution

Fig 2.27

Table 2.4

Sample	Number of radioactive counts using a detector
Control 1 (no insulin present)	123 863 963
Control 2 (insulin present)	7 528
Control 3 (no anti-insulin antibody present)	725
Patient A (no food for 12 hours)	113 484 239
Patient A (20 minutes after meal)	116 674 349
Patient B (no food for 12 hours)	111 236 349
Patient B (20 minutes after meal)	8 582

(a) Why were each of the controls included?
(b) Which of the four blood samples from the patients contained the most insulin?
(c) Which patient might be suffering from diabetes? Explain your reasoning.

DATA HANDLING 2.4

A scientist is trying to purify the protein bovine ribonuclease. Bovine ribonuclease is an enzyme that catalyses the hydrolysis of RNA in cattle. The scientist starts by putting an extract of bovine cells through a procedure that should separate the proteins in the mixture from all the other substances. This procedure gives a preparation that contains only proteins, which is good, but about 22% of the protein is lost during the procedure. The scientist ends up with 15 cm^3 of the protein preparation.

(a) What assay could the scientist use to show the presence of this particular enzyme?

The scientist then uses 1 cm^3 of the preparation of protein to test whether bovine ribonuclease binds to DEAE-cellulose, a positively charged resin, or CM-cellulose, a negatively charged resin. When the mixture of proteins is poured down a tiny column filled with the CM-cellulose the solution that flows straight through the column is negative in the assay for bovine ribonuclease.

(b) Does the bovine ribonuclease protein have a net positive charge or a net negative charge? Explain your answer.

The scientist then makes a large column containing CM-cellulose and pours through the rest of the protein preparation containing the bovine ribonuclease. She then has to elute the proteins from the column. After considering the alternatives, she decides to use a pH gradient to elute the proteins from the column.

(c) Starting with pH 7, the pH of the original solution, should the scientist increase or decrease the pH in order to elute the proteins from the column? Explain your answer.

(d) What other method could the scientist have used to remove the proteins from the CM-cellulose resin? How does this alternative method work?

The scientist collects the elute from the column in 150 fractions, each of 1 cm^3. She considers that the elution procedure is very efficient and that 100% of the protein is eluted from the column.

As a first step towards finding which fraction the bovine ribonuclease is in, the scientist tests 0.1 cm^3 of each sample for protein.

(e) Name a simple test for protein that the scientist could use.

(f) Why did the scientist only use 0.1 cm^3 of each fraction for the protein test?

Fifteen of the fractions contain protein. The scientist then tests another 0.1 cm^3 of these fractions for the presence of bovine ribonuclease. Bovine ribonuclease is found in three adjacent samples.

(g) If the initial bovine cell extract contained 100 mg of bovine ribonuclease, what is the maximum mass of bovine ribonuclease that the scientist could have in the three fractions?

The scientist uses the purified protein to make a monoclonal antibody to bovine ribonuclease.

(h) Why might the scientist want a monoclonal antibody to the bovine ribonuclease protein?

2.13 (a) What is an assay?
   (b) Name a simple assay for:
      (i) reducing sugars;
     (ii) proteins;
    (iii) starch.
   (c) Why is an antibody a good method of testing for the presence of a specific protein?
   (d) Why is a polynucleotide probe a good way of assaying for a specific RNA?

2.14 (a) What is ion exchange chromatography?
   (b) CM-cellulose is a negatively charged ion exchange resin. DEAE-cellulose is a positively charged ion exchange resin. Which of the following proteins would you expect to stick to a CM-cellulose column and which would you expect to stick to a DEAE-cellulose column?

Table 2.5

Protein	Number of amino acid residues		
	Uncharged	Negatively charged	Positively charged
lysozyme	101	10	18
cytochrome c	68	8	24
α-casein	172	32	25
silk fibroin	188	8	10
alcohol dehydrogenase	287	38	49

   (c) Which of the five proteins in Table 2.5 has the lowest percentage of charged amino acid residues?

2.15 (a) What is meant by affinity chromatography?
   (b) What is the advantage of affinity chromatography over ion exchange chromatography for purifying a protein?

   A scientist is trying to purify an RNA molecule with the base sequence
   AUUAGCGAAGCUAGGCAACGUGUGUCAAAAGUACGCA
   GCAGCCCUGGCUGUGUGUG. Experience tells the scientist that a polynucleotide probe has to be at least fifteen nucleotides long to be effective in affinity chromatography. The scientist synthesises the polynucleotide CACACACAGCCAGGG, covalently links this polynucleotide to a resin and packs the resin into a column.

   (c) To what part of the RNA molecule will the synthetic polynucleotide bind?
   (d) Why is the synthetic polynucleotide covalently linked to a resin?
   (e) Suggest a reason why a shorter synthetic polynucleotide is not as effective when used for affinity chromatography.

REVIEW OF CRUCIAL POINTS

- Most biologically important macromolecules are polymers. Polymers are large molecules made by covalently linking small monomer units together. Most biologically important polymers are made by condensation polymerisation reactions, where a molecule of water is eliminated each time a monomer is added to the polymer.

Depolymerisation of these biologically important polymers is by the reverse reaction: hydrolysis.

- Polypeptides are polymers made from amino acids. All polypeptides are similar, possessing a chemically identical backbone, but differ according to the R groups that project from the amino acid residues. Polypeptides fold up into three-dimensional shapes that are stabilised by weak bonds such as hydrogen bonds. The precise three-dimensional shape of the polypeptide depends on interactions between different parts of the backbone, the secondary structure, and interactions between R groups, the tertiary structure. Occasionally the polypeptide will interact with other polypeptides to form a larger structure, this is called the quaternary structure. In its final, mature form a polypeptide is referred to as a protein.

- Polypeptides whose R groups do not influence the folding pattern form long, elongated secondary structures and are called fibrous proteins. α-keratin is one such protein, made from long α-helices, and silk fibroin is another, formed from β-pleated sheets. Polypeptides whose folding pattern is interrupted because of interactions between the R groups are more inclined to form compact structures and are called globular proteins. Most soluble proteins are globular proteins.

- It is the presence or absence of influential R groups, and their position in the polypeptide, that determine the three-dimensional structure of the protein. This depends on the primary structure of the polypeptide, the nature and order of the amino acid residues in the polypeptide chain. As every protein has a unique primary structure, every protein has a unique three-dimensional shape. It is this unique three-dimensional shape that allows each protein to fulfil a precise role in the organism.

- Polynucleotides do not have a unique three-dimensional shape. Instead they have a unique sequence of nucleotide residues. DNA is a polymer made of deoxyribonucleotide residues that contain one of four bases, adenine (A), cytosine (C), guanine (G) or thymine (T). It is the order of the nucleotides in the DNA polynucleotide that contains the genetic information. DNA is usually found as a very large, double-stranded macromolecule. In contrast RNA is a much smaller, single-stranded macromolecule made from ribonucleotide monomers containing one of the four bases A, C, G or U (uracil).

- Polysaccharides are much less varied than either proteins or nucleic acids. Some polysaccharides, like cellulose, form long, straight chains that pack together in bundles and make excellent structural materials. Other polysaccharides, like starch and glycogen, form compact structures and make excellent energy storage macromolecules.

- Much is known about biologically important macromolecules because they have been isolated and studied. Polysaccharides are usually very abundant and can be isolated because of their particular chemical and physical properties. However, all proteins are chemically and physically similar, as are all nucleic acids. The most effective methods of isolating proteins are based on each protein's unique three-dimensional shape. The most effective methods of purifying nucleic acids are based on their unique sequence of nucleotide residues.

Chapter 3

STRUCTURES MADE FROM MOLECULES

Organisms are made up of cells and cells are made up of molecules. However, these molecules are not randomly gathered together and surrounded by a cell membrane, instead they are arranged in stunningly beautiful structures that are perfectly adapted to fulfil their functions. This chapter examines a very few of the structures found in organisms and discusses how the molecules that make up each structure come together and interact.

LEARNING OBJECTIVES

After studying this chapter you should:

1. understand that molecules associate together to form structures and be familiar with the weak interactions that hold the molecules together;

2. have revised the structure of the eukaryotic cell;

3. be able to describe the fluid mosaic model of the plasma membrane and to discuss the evidence that this model reflects the true situation;

4. be able to relate the fluid mosaic model to the functions and properties of the plasma membrane;

5. be able to discuss the structure and function of skeletal muscle in terms of the sliding filament model of muscle contraction;

6. be able to describe the structure of the plant cell wall and discuss how it is modified to fulfil its various functions.

3.1 STRUCTURES IN CELLS

Living organisms are made up of cells. Some organisms consist of only a single cell, while others are made up of billions of cells that co-operate to make a complex multicellular organism. To understand the phenomenon of life it is essential to understand the cell. Cells are complex structures but essentially they contain three things:

- the genetic information
- the cell membrane
- the cellular machinery.

The genetic information is the DNA molecule or molecules that contain the instructions for how the organism is to be built and operated. The structure and function of the genetic information is discussed in Chapters 4 and 5.

The cell membrane, or **plasma membrane**, separates the cell from the external environment. The cell membrane acts as a barrier so that the environment inside the cell can be different from the environment outside the cell. As well as operating as a barrier, the cell membrane is the cell's interface through which it interacts with other cells or with the external environment.

The cellular machinery is the collection of individual molecules and subcellular structures that make up the rest of the cell. This machinery replicates the genetic information, reads the information and carries out the instructions in it. It builds the cell itself, maintains the cell and carries out the role of that cell within the organism as a whole. It is this cellular machinery that varies most from cell to cell, because it reflects the instructions contained in the genetic material of that organism. The cellular machinery is discussed in detail in Theme 3.

The generalised structure of a cell is shown in Fig 3.1. This is a **eukaryotic** cell, a cell where the genetic information is contained within a nucleus. All multicellular organisms and many unicellular organisms consist of eukaryotic cells. Bacteria are **prokaryotic** cells, cells that do not contain a true nucleus. In bacteria the DNA molecule, the genetic information, is not separated from the rest of the cell within a nucleus.

As can be seen from Fig 3.1 the cell is a complicated structure. There are many subcellular structures within a eukaryotic cell: these are called **organelles**. Organelles are membrane bags, often with very complicated shapes, that separate one part of the cell from the rest. Within these bags specific functions are carried out. There are also structures in the cell without membranes, for example **ribosomes** and **cytoskeletal** fibres. If you are unfamiliar with the structure of a eukaryotic cell you should refer to a general biology text.

Subcellular structures are made from molecules

Understanding how molecules make up the subcellular structures is a stepping stone to understanding how molecules interact to make a cell. One of the first questions to ask when studying structures made from molecules is why the molecules should gather together to make larger structures rather than stay as single molecules. Another way of asking this same question is to ask whether the molecules are more stable dissolved in solution or gathered together in groups.

Take the example of a single phospholipid molecule (Fig 3.2(a)). When this single molecule is placed in water, the negatively charged phosphate-containing head group forms weak electrostatic interactions with the water because it attracts the positive parts of the polar water molecules. When these weak interactions occur some energy is released, and the molecule is made alittle more stable. However, the long hydrocarbon tail regions of the molecule do not interact with the water molecules and contribute nothing towards the stability of the molecule.

When many phospholipid molecules are present, hydrophobic interactions can occur between the long hydrocarbon tail regions of one phospholipid molecule and the next. Hydrophobic interactions are weak forces of attraction that occur between neutral molecules or neutral parts of molecules. Each individual attraction is weak, but the force of attraction becomes significant when many weak interactions occur, for example between large neutral molecules or between the long hydrocarbon chains of the phospholipid molecules. Energy is released when these hydrophobic interactions occur, so the phospholipid molecules are more stable when grouped together than when separated by water molecules. The phospholipid molecules form groups with the hydrophobic tail regions grouped together and the hydrophilic heads pointing outwards. Arranged in this way, the tails can form weak hydrophobic interactions with each other and

Fig 3.1 What's in a cell? An artist's impression of an animal cell from data collected by electron microscopy.

MACROMOLECULES

Plasma membrane

The plasma membrane surrounds the cell.

The plasma membrane separates the cell contents from the solution outside. It controls the import and export of many different types of molecule and therefore has a role in controlling the environment inside the cell. It is the surface for communication with other cells.

Cilia

Cilia are mobile projections from the cell surface containing parallel microtubules.

Cilia are used to move the cell, or move the solution outside the cell relative to the cell.

Lysosome

Lysosomes are small membrane bags.

Lysosomes are the waste disposal system of the cell.

Endoplasmic reticulum

rough endoplasmic reticulum
smooth endoplasmic reticulum

The endoplasmic reticulum (ER) is a series of interconnected channels bounded by membrane. If the cytoplasmic surface of these membranes is coated with ribosomes it is referred to as rough ER, if not it is the smooth ER.

Lipid synthesis occurs throughout the ER. The ribosomes on the rough ER are the sites of synthesis of proteins that will be either embedded in the cell membranes or secreted from the cell.

The nucleus

The nucleus is the control centre of the cell. The nuclear envelope separates the nucleus from the rest of the cell, and consists of a double layer of membrane studded with nuclear pores. Inside this envelope is the nucleolus and the chromatin.

nuclear envelope { **nuclear membrane**
nuclear pore
nucleolus
chromatin

The nucleus has the main role in storage, replication and decoding the genetic information.

The nuclear membrane separates the chromatin from the rest of the cell. The nuclear pores control import and export of large molecules to and from the nucleus.

The nucleolus is the site of ribosomal RNA synthesis and of ribosome assembly.

The chromatin contains DNA and proteins. The DNA is the genetic information that codes for the cell and all its activities. The proteins provide the means by which this information is maintained, replicated and decoded.

Mitochondrion

Mitochondria have two layers of membrane separating their contents from the rest of the cell. The inner membrane is folded.

The mitochondria are the sites of ATP (adenosine triphosphate) synthesis. Each molecule of ATP is a store of chemical energy for the cell to use.

Golgi body

The Golgi body is a collection of flattened membrane bags which can be distinguished by its characteristic shape.

The Golgi body is the site of carbohydrate synthesis. Some proteins and lipids are 'processed' in the Golgi body; carbohydrate groups are added making the molecules into glycoproteins or glycolipids.

The cytoplasm

The contents of the cell, other than the membrane-bound organelles, are called the cytoplasm. The cytoplasm contains a vast range of biologically important molecules in solution plus a variety of structures, including the cytoskeleton, a complicated arrangement of microtubules and other filaments, and the ribosomes.

Thousands of biologically important chemical reactions occur in the cytoplasm.

The cytoskeleton gives the cell its shape and plays an important role in moving both the whole cell and individual organelles.

The ribosomes are the site of protein synthesis. Cytoplasmic proteins are synthesised on free ribosomes in the cytoplasm.

Centrioles

Centrioles are short cylinders of microtubules found in animal cells. There are two centrioles per cell.

Centrioles appear to have a role in cell division in animal cells.

Not all cells are the same.

All organisms (except viruses!) are made up of cells. The cell illustrated here is a **eukaryotic** cell (a cell with a nucleus). Bacteria do not have a nucleus and are examples of **prokaryotic** cells. Prokaryotic cells are smaller and simpler than eukaryotic cells: their chromatin is not separated from the cytoplasm and there are no membranous organelles other than the plasma membrane. In certain prokaryotes (organisms made of prokaryotic cells) the plasma membrane is folded inwards to make specialised structures with specific functions.

Eukaryotic cells also come in a wide range of shapes and fulfil many different functions. Plant cells differ from animal cells in a number of ways: they do not have centrioles, they have a cellulose cell wall outside the plasma membrane, they often have a large membrane-bound vesicle containing the 'cell sap' and they may contain chloroplasts. Chloroplasts have two membranes separating their contents from the rest of the cell and also contain a complicated arrangement of flattened membrane bags. Chloroplasts absorb light energy and convert it into chemical energy.

hydrophilic head group containing negatively charged phosphate group

hydrophobic 'tails' consisting of hydrocarbon chains

(a)

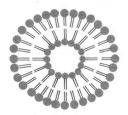

(b) micelle

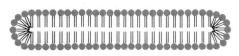

(c) liposome

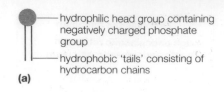

(d) bilayer

Fig 3.2 When phospholipid molecules are placed in water, structures form that keep the hydrophobic tails away from the water.

the head regions can form weak electrostatic interactions with the water molecules. Phospholipids spontaneously form these spherical structures, which are called **micelles**, when they are mixed with water (Fig 3.2(b)). Under certain conditions other arrangements of phospholipids occur, in which the hydrophilic 'heads' are in contact with water while the hydrophobic 'tails' are only in contact with each other. These structures include the liposome (c) and the bilayer (d).

It was possible to predict the structure that the phospholipid molecule would form when mixed with water from knowing the chemical nature of the phospholipid molecule and the chemical nature of water. This knowledge allows us to predict the weak interactions that will occur between the phospholipid molecules, between the water molecules and between phospholipid and water molecules. The structure that allows the formation of the maximum number of favourable weak interactions will be the most stable structure. In the case of the phospholipids the micelle structure is the most stable because it allows both the hydrophobic interactions between the tail regions of the phospholipid molecules and the weak electrostatic interactions between the phospholipid head groups and the water molecules.

Weak interactions between molecules are much weaker than covalent bonds. As a rule of thumb, weak interactions between molecules are about 10–100 times weaker than a covalent bond. Common types of weak interactions are listed in Table 3.1.

Table 3.1

Type of weak interaction	Where formed
Hydrophobic interactions	Occurs between uncharged, non-polar regions, e.g. hydrocarbon groups
Electrovalent (ionic)	Occurs between negatively charged and positively charged groups or between the negatively and positively charged regions of polar groups
Hydrogen bonds	A specific type of electrovalent attraction that forms a very stable interaction. Occurs between the positively charged hydrogen in a polar hydroxyl or amine group and a negatively charged oxygen or nitrogen

Studying subcellular components

The present understanding of the structure and function of a subcellular structure comes from integrating all the information from thousands of different investigations carried out over the last hundred years in hundreds of laboratories all over the world. Most of the studies on subcellular structures can be placed in one of three categories:

- breaking the structure up and analysing what molecules are present;
- observing the whole structure;
- studying how the structure works.

Scientists use the information from these three types of investigations to propose a **model** of the subcellular structure and how it operates. A model is the scientists' best guess based on all the information available at the time. If the information is thin on the ground the model may be based more on imagination than on fact. If the information is inaccurate the model may be completely wrong. A good scientist never thinks that the current model is 'right'; it is merely a way of thinking about the problem that the scientist is studying.

STRUCTURES MADE FROM MOLECULES

The reason that a model is so important is that it gives us something to test. Once there is a model we can make predictions and test them. If a prediction based on the model turns out to be true, then the model becomes a little firmer, a little more believable. If a prediction based on the model turns out to be false, then we should be willing to modify the model and maybe to abandon it entirely.

In this chapter, models for four subcellular structures are discussed. In each case the evidence that supports or challenges the model is reviewed. Obviously these models are considered to be sound representations of the 'real' situation or they would not be included in a book of this nature. However, the principle of forming a model and then testing it would be the same for any scientific investigation.

QUESTIONS

3.1 Where in a eukaryotic cell do the following processes occur?
   (a) protein synthesis
   (b) DNA replication
   (c) ATP synthesis
   (d) waste disposal
   (e) addition of carbohydrate side chains to proteins.

3.2 (a) Why is a bacterial cell referred to as a prokaryotic cell while animal and plant cells are referred to as eukaryotic cells?
   (b) List four differences between a plant cell and an animal cell.
   (c) List the membrane-bound cell organelles in a eukaryotic cell.

3.3 (a) What is the difference between a covalent bond and a weak interaction?
   (b) Describe three different types of weak interaction.
   (c) Imagine a container containing an equal volume of water and oil. Three substances are added to the container and the container is then shaken before the contents are allowed to separate out as two layers. The three added substances are a monosaccharide, a phospholipid and a triglyceride. Where in the container would each of these three substances end up and why?

3.2 THE PLASMA MEMBRANE

The plasma membrane is an obvious candidate for scientists to study. It is an important structure: it separates the cell from the external environment; it acts as an interface between the cell and its surroundings; it controls the import and export of molecules to and from the cell.

Plasma membranes are relatively easy to isolate in large amounts. Any source of animal cells can be used as a source of plasma membranes and blood cells are often used because they are easy to collect. The cells are burst open by placing them in a hypotonic solution (one with a higher concentration of water than is present within the cell) so that water enters the cells, making them swell until the plasma membrane breaks. The membranes can be separated from the rest of the cell contents because the plasma membrane is the least dense structure in the cell. When a preparation of plasma membranes is analysed it is found to contain about 50% phospholipids and 50% proteins.

Early models of membrane structure: a phospholipid bilayer

Knowing that the plasma membrane is 50% phospholipid gave scientists an insight into the structure of the membrane. Phospholipids have a hydrophilic head region and a hydrophobic tail region (Fig 3.2(a)). When placed in an aqueous (water-based) solution the phospholipids group together to form structures in which the hydrophilic heads are in contact with the water and the hydrophobic tails are protected from the water. One such structure is the micelle structure discussed in section 3.1 (Fig 3.2(b)). Another such structure is a **phospholipid bilayer** (Fig 3.2(d)). It is easy to imagine the phospholipid bilayer structure extended to form a sphere lined on both inside and outside by hydrophilic heads. This sphere would form a barrier between the solution within the sphere and the solution outside the sphere, very like the barrier that the plasma membrane forms around the cytoplasm. The first model of plasma membrane structure had the phospholipid component of the membrane arranged as a bilayer.

In 1925 two scientists, Gorter and Grendel, extracted the phospholipids from red blood cells using propanone and spread these phospholipids on the surface of a water-based solution. The scientists then compared the area covered by the phospholipid with the estimated surface area of a red blood cell and came to the conclusion that their data supported the model of the plasma membrane as a phospholipid bilayer. In fact, Gorter and Grendel had made two mistakes in their calculations. They had underestimated the surface area of a red blood cell and they had overestimated the amount of phospholipid extracted by the propanone. Luckily these two errors cancelled out in their calculation so that they reached an essentially correct conclusion. Later the model of the plasma membrane as a phospholipid bilayer was supported by evidence from many other sources.

However, no amount of analysis of the phospholipid and protein components of the plasma membrane separately would yield information about how the protein component of the plasma membranes was arranged relative to the phospholipid bilayer. In order to collect such evidence it was necessary to observe whole plasma membranes.

Observing whole membranes: electron microscopy

Living cells can be observed using the light microscope but even the very best light microscope cannot separate two structures less than 175 nm apart. This limitation is imposed by nature rather than by technology: the wavelength of light is too long. Many structures within cells are smaller than 175 nm, including the plasma membrane, so the light microscope can yield very little relevant data about the structure of the plasma membrane.

Biological scientists turned to the electron microscope. This microscope uses electrons rather than light. The wavelength of electrons is much smaller than the wavelength of light, therefore it should be possible to use electrons to 'see' subcellular structures. Figure 3.3 shows the basic components of an electron microscope as compared to those of a light microscope.

However, using the electron microscope to study biological structures has its problems. Electrons are not reflected or scattered by the elements found in biological material: they would simply punch through the material as if it was not there. Another problem is that an electron beam can only be used in a vacuum: if a biological sample is placed in a vacuum the water in the sample will boil away leaving a dry powder.

This means that electron microscopy cannot be used to observe living cells, or even freshly prepared material. Instead, a **replica** of the cell must be made. The early replicas of cells were made by fixing the cell and then staining it with the salts of heavy metals such as osmium. The fixation process uses chemicals to kill the cell and crosslink all the macromolecules in the cell, 'fixing' all the structures within the cell. The fixed specimen is then soaked in a solution of osmium salts. Some structures in the cell bind many heavy metal ions and are 'stained' heavily, while other structures in the cell bind few heavy metal ions and are 'stained' lightly. The specimen is then cut into ultra-thin sections using a specialised instrument. These ultra-

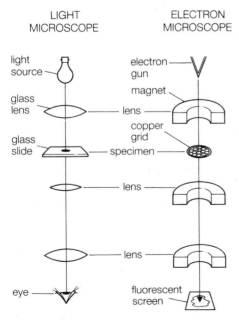

Fig 3.3 The electron microscope can be compared to the light microscope.

STRUCTURES MADE FROM MOLECULES

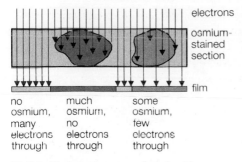

no osmium, many electrons through

much osmium, no electrons through

some osmium, few electrons through

Fig 3.4 Electron microscopy of an ultra-thin, osmium-stained section. An image is formed on the film that depends on how many electrons can pass through the specimen.

thin sections are placed on tiny copper grids and inserted in the electron microscope (Fig 3.3).

The beam of electrons hits the ultra-thin section (Fig 3.4). If the electrons hit a structure that is heavily stained with osmium ions they will be stopped by the osmium. If the electrons hit a lightly stained structure the electrons will pass through the section and will be detected by the fluorescent screen or photographic film below the specimen. The images of the plasma membrane obtained by this technique are lacking in detail. The plasma membrane is seen as a structure about 8 nm wide that appears to have three layers, two dark outer layers with a lighter layer between them.

Models of the plasma membrane based on electron microscopy

These vague images of the plasma membrane tempted two scientists, H. Davson and J.F. Danielli, to propose a new model of plasma membrane structure in 1935. The model was based around the phospholipid bilayer that was already accepted. The novel aspect of the model was that it suggested that the protein component of the plasma membrane was arranged as a network of protein around the phospholipid bilayer, forming a protein–lipid–protein sandwich. The three-layer structure of the plasma membrane as seen using the electron microscope was cited as supporting evidence for this protein–lipid–protein sandwich.

This model of plasma membrane structure was taken up by J.D. Robertson who made the bold statement that all the membranes in cells had a similar structure and that this structure was the protein–lipid–protein sandwich proposed by Davson and Danielli. This was the **unit membrane theory** and it dominated scientists' ideas about cell membranes for forty years.

It is easy to expose the faults in the unit membrane theory using hindsight, but it was many years before enough contradictory experimental evidence mounted up to convince scientists that it was an inaccurate representation of the true situation. The nails were finally hammered into the coffin of the Davson–Danielli model by two main lines of evidence: studies of the dynamic nature of the plasma membrane and data about the structure of the plasma membrane obtained by using a new method of making replicas for viewing in the electron microscope.

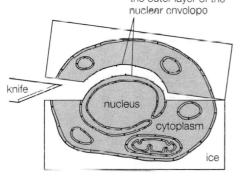

the cell splits along a line of weakness, in this case through the outer layer of the nuclear envelope

knife

nucleus

cytoplasm

ice

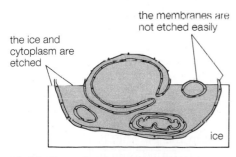

the membranes are not etched easily

the ice and cytoplasm are etched

ice

Fig 3.5 Preparation of a specimen by freeze fracture.

Studies of living cells indicated that membranes were dynamic structures

One problem with the Davson–Danielli model was that it proposed that the flexible phospholipid bilayer was enclosed in a rigid protein coat. Living cells are flexible structures that change shape easily. Liquid-filled spheres of membrane called **vesicles** are always fusing with the plasma membrane or being created by pinching off small parts of the plasma membrane. Certain membrane proteins, such as hormone receptors, are known to move over the surface of the cell. All these processes indicate that the plasma membrane is dynamic, or mobile. It is very difficult to reconcile the dynamic properties of the plasma membrane with the rigid protein framework proposed in the Davson–Danielli model of plasma membrane structure.

The best direct evidence for the structure of the plasma membrane came from a revolutionary method of preparing replicas of cells for study in the electron microscope. The living cells are frozen in liquid nitrogen and then cracked open using an extremely sharp knife: this technique is referred to as **freeze fracture**. The broken surface is then 'etched' to emphasise the structures that have been exposed (Fig 3.5).

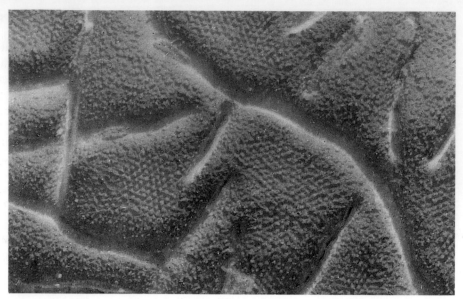

Fig 3.6 The plasma membrane of an animal cell, visualised by using the freeze fracture and etching technique and then viewing the platinum shadowed replica in an electron microscope. The 'knobs' are thought to be proteins. (Magnification × 100 500)

Still frozen, the surface is then covered in a thin layer of platinum. The platinum is deposited at an angle so that the thickness of the layer of platinum emphasises the exposed structures still further. The biological material is allowed to defrost and is removed by chemical treatments. The platinum replica is then viewed in the electron microscope.

Platinum replicas of cells that had been fractured through the plasma membrane showed some very interesting features: 'knobs' and 'holes' (Fig 3.6). There was no place for these 'knobs' and 'holes' in the Davson–Danielli model of the plasma membrane. S.J. Singer and G. Nicholson proposed that the frozen cells split along the junction between the two layers of the phospholipid bilayer and that the 'knobs' and 'holes' showed the distribution of protein in the phospholipid bilayer.

A new model for plasma membrane structure: the fluid mosaic model

In 1972 S.J. Singer and G. Nicholson proposed the fluid mosaic model of membrane structure. This model is illustrated in Fig 3.7. The fluid mosaic model is the currently accepted model for the structure of membranes throughout the cell.

In the fluid mosaic model the membrane is a continuous phospholipid bilayer studded with proteins. The phospholipid molecules move freely in the plane of the membrane. In this phospholipid sea float proteins which are also free to move in the plane of the membrane. However, the proteins are not free to bob up and down at right angles to the plane of the phospholipid bilayer: they are held in place by hydrophobic interactions between the surface of the protein and the hydrophobic region of the bilayer.

The main components of the fluid mosaic model of the plasma membrane are the phospholipid bilayer and the proteins that float within it. However, as can be seen from Fig 3.7, some additional features are also typical of the plasma membrane. The membranes of most animal cells contain **cholesterol**, a small lipid-soluble molecule that makes the phospholipid bilayer more fluid. The proteins within the phospholipid bilayer are found in different positions. Some proteins are found only in the inner face of the bilayer, some proteins are found only in the outer layer of the bilayer

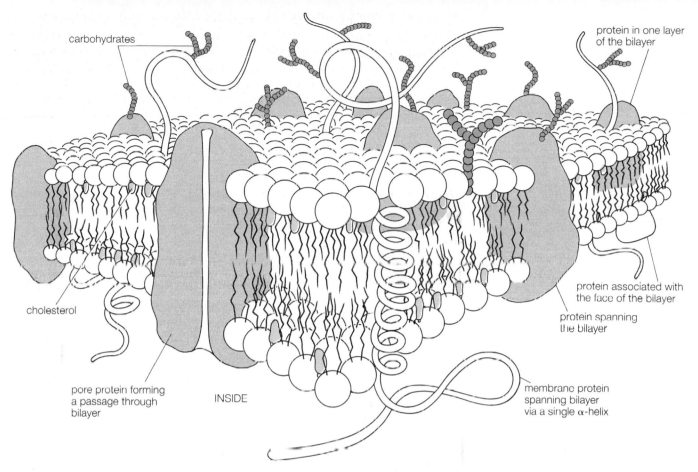

labels on figure:
carbohydrates

protein in one layer
of the bilayer

cholesterol

protein associated with
the face of the bilayer

protein spanning
the bilayer

pore protein forming
a passage through
bilayer

INSIDE

membrane protein
spanning bilayer
via a single α-helix

Fig 3.7 The Singer–Nicholson model of the plasma membrane, showing the 'fluid mosaic'.

and other proteins span the entire bilayer. Some of the proteins that span the entire bilayer have a pore though the centre of the protein: this pore provides a channel for substances to enter the cell. Those proteins that project from the outer surface of the bilayer often have covalently linked carbohydrate groups: these proteins are called **glycoproteins**.

Testing the fluid mosaic model

The fluid mosaic model suggests that the membrane is made of phospholipid and protein. This agrees with the data. The amount of protein present in a membrane varies according to the type of membrane and the fluid mosaic model allows for this, as the model does not demand a set amount of protein to be present.

The fluid mosaic model is based on a phospholipid bilayer. Evidence that membranes contain a phospholipid bilayer comes from the line of weakness observed in freeze fracture studies: this line of weakness appears to correspond to the junction between the two phospholipid layers. X-ray diffraction studies have shown that membranes contain a highly ordered arrangement of phospholipid molecules: a bilayer would give rise to this type of X-ray diffraction data. Finally, phospholipid molecules spontaneously form bilayers in aqueous solution: this is strong indirect evidence for a phospholipid bilayer.

The membrane as described in the fluid mosaic model would have the correct overall dimensions. The phospholipid bilayer would be about 6 nm across and then the projecting proteins would add another few nanometres, making the total width about 8 nm. This is indeed the width of the plasma membrane as seen using transmission electron microscopy through thin sections.

The fluid mosaic model has the proteins floating in a phospholipid sea. Electron microscopy of freeze fractured membranes shows 'knobs' and 'holes' that indicate that the proteins are within the phospholipid bilayer rather than outside it. When membranes are washed some proteins are washed away from the membrane easily while others cannot be removed without disrupting the membrane with detergents: this is in keeping with the model where some proteins are **peripheral**, associated with the outside of the bilayer, and others are **integral**, actually embedded in the bilayer. Treating membranes with water-soluble chemicals that 'label' the surface of proteins shows that some parts of the proteins are labelled while others are not: the model has some parts of the protein embedded within the phospholipid bilayer where they would be protected from the chemicals. Analysis of membrane proteins shows that they have regions rich in hydrophobic amino acid residues: these regions would anchor the proteins in the phospholipid bilayer, as suggested by the fluid mosaic model.

The unique feature of the fluid mosaic model is that it allows for a dynamic membrane. It is possible to label proteins with fluorescent markers and then observe those proteins in living cells. These proteins can be shown to move across the surface of the cell: the fluid mosaic model allows the proteins to move in the plane of the phospholipid bilayer. Electron spin resonance (e.s.r.), an advanced spectroscopic technique, can be used to show that phospholipid molecules move freely in the plane of the membrane but almost never move from one face of the bilayer to the other: again this supports the fluid mosaic model where movement is restricted to the plane of the membrane.

The permeability of the plasma membrane can also be related to the fluid mosaic model. The plasma membrane is **selectively permeable**, that is, it allows small uncharged molecules and lipid-soluble molecules to pass freely: such molecules could pass through the phospholipid bilayer. Charged molecules and large molecules also pass through the plasma membrane under the appropriate conditions: in the fluid mosaic model these molecules could pass through **protein pores**, proteins that span the lipid bilayer and contain a channel through which the molecules could pass.

The plasma membrane also contains receptors. The fluid mosaic model suggests that surface proteins could act as receptors, binding to the signal molecules outside the cell and then transmitting the signal through the phospholipid bilayer to the inner surface of the membrane. The signal could be transmitted across the membrane through one protein spanning the bilayer or via a number of different proteins.

The fluid mosaic model is an excellent model of membrane structure. It incorporates all the information that scientists have collected and it is a powerful aid to thinking about the cell membrane and its functions.

DATA HANDLING 3.1

Glycophorin A is a protein found in the membrane of red blood cells. Figure 3.8 shows how the glycophorin A molecule spans the plasma membrane.

(a) Consider the part of the glycophorin A molecule that is within the bilayer, between the two fine dotted lines. Calculate what percentage of the amino acid residues are:
  (i) hydrophobic;
  (ii) polar;
  (iii) charged.
(b) Consider the part of the glycophorin A molecule that lies outside the cell, above the fine dotted line. Calculate what percentage of the amino acid residues are:
  (i) hydrophobic;
  (ii) polar;
  (iii) charged.

STRUCTURES MADE FROM MOLECULES

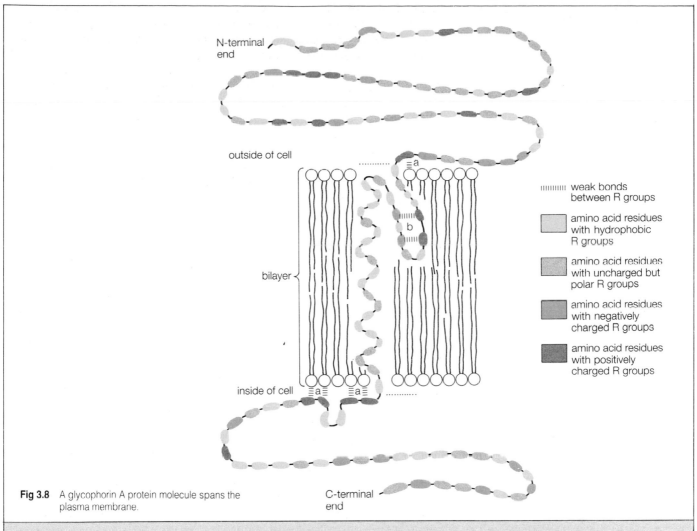

Fig 3.8 A glycophorin A protein molecule spans the plasma membrane.

(c) Consider the parts of the glycophorin A molecule that lies inside the cell, below the fine dotted line. Calculate what percentage of the amino acid residues are:

(i) hydrophobic;

(ii) polar;

(iii) charged.

(d) Compare your answers to (a), (b) and (c). Can you relate the differences between the three regions to their positions relative to the bilayer?

(e) Account for the weak bonds formed at 'a'.

(f) Account for the weak bonds formed at 'b'.

(g) The portion of the protein that actually spans the bilayer forms a common secondary structure. What is this structure? How is this structure stabilised?

(h) Imagine that red blood cells that contained glycophorin A in their plasma membranes were treated with a chemical that reacted with polar amino acid residues, labelling each residue with a fluorescent group. The chemical is soluble in water but insoluble in lipids.

(i) Which parts of the protein would you expect to be labelled in the intact cells?

(ii) Which parts of the protein would you expect to be labelled in isolated membrane fragments?

(iii) Which parts of the protein would you expect to be labelled if the entire lipid bilayer had been disrupted using detergents and the mixture treated with the chemical?

Read this passage and then answer the questions below. Some of the questions refer to the passage and others to the information you have read in this chapter.

Cells often maintain very different concentrations of inorganic ions on either side of the plasma membrane. Mammals have a much higher concentration of potassium ions (K^+) inside the cell than outside, and a much lower concentration of sodium ions (Na^+) inside the cell than outside.

Figure 3.9 shows a protein found in the plasma membrane of cells, the Na^+ pump. This protein transports Na^+ out of the cell and K^+ into the cell. The transport is against *concentration gradients* so energy is required. This energy is provided by the hydrolysis of ATP (section 1.5). This is one example of *active transport*, transport across a membrane that requires the input of energy.

The protein has three sites where Na^+ can bind and two sites where K^+ can bind. The protein can exist in two stable shapes or configurations. In one shape the sites where the ions can bind are exposed to the cytoplasm inside the cell. When in this shape the protein has a high affinity for Na^+ and a low affinity for K^+; this means that Na^+ bind but K^+ do not. When the protein is *phosphorylated* the shape of the protein changes. The sites where the ions can bind are now exposed to the extracellular solution. When in this second shape the protein has a low affinity for Na^+ and a high affinity for K^+; this means that K^+ bind and Na^+ do not.

Step 1 shows the protein in the first configuration. The ion binding sites are exposed to the cytoplasm. In this shape the protein has a high affinity for Na^+ and a low affinity for K^+ so any of K^+ ions bound to the protein are released into the cytoplasm and Na^+ ions from the cytoplasm bind to the protein (step 2). The protein is now *phosphorylated* and changes shape (steps 3 and 4). The ion binding sites are now exposed to the extracellular solution. In this shape the protein has a high affinity for K^+ and a low affinity for Na^+ so the Na^+ ions are released into the extracellular solution and K^+ from the extracellular solution bind to the protein (steps 5 and 6). The protein is then *dephosphorylated* (step 6), and the protein reverts to its original shape (steps 7 and 8). The process then begins again.

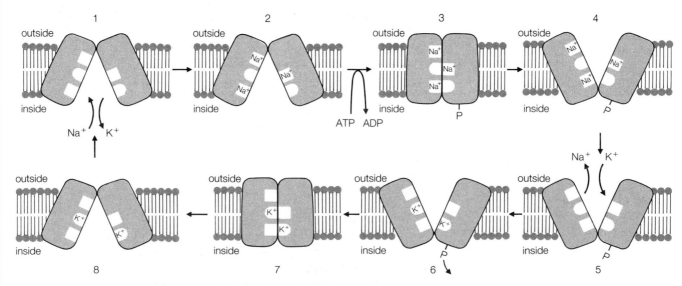

Fig 3.9 Active transport of K^+ into the cell and Na^+ out of the cell is via a protein channel called the Na^+K^+ ATPase. The energy for the process comes from ATP.

1 (a) What is the name of the process by which a substance moves from an area with a high concentration of that substance to an area with a low concentration of that substance?

(b) There is a higher concentration of K^+ inside the cell than outside. K^+ ions do not move out of the cell by the process you named in (a). Why not?

(c) What do you think is meant by the term *concentration gradient*?

(d) How does the passage define the term *active transport*?

(e) What is the energy source for the process described in the passage?

(f) At what point in the cycle shown in Fig 3.9 is the energy put into the process?

(g) What do you think is meant by *phosphorylated* and *dephosphorylated*?

2 (a) What determines the shape of a protein? (If you cannot remember, refer to section 2.3.)

(b) The Na^+ pump can exist in two different shapes. The change in shape is caused by a phosphate group being covalently bonded to a hydroxyl group on the R group of one of the amino acid residues.

$$X\!-\!CH_2\!-\!OH \rightarrow X\!-\!CH_2\!-\!\overset{\displaystyle O^-}{\underset{\displaystyle O^-}{\overset{|}{\underset{|}{P}}}}\!=\!O$$

(i) What effect has this reaction had on the nature of the R group of this amino acid residue?

(ii) How might this affect the three-dimensional shape of the protein?

(c) The chemical reaction described in (b) is catalysed by an enzyme called a **phosphorylase**. What name do you think is given to the enzyme that catalyses the reverse reaction?

3 (a) Make a sketch of the Na^+ pump protein as shown in Fig 3.9, step 2. Which surfaces of the protein would you expect to be rich in hydrophobic amino acid residues and which surfaces would you expect to be rich in charged and polar amino acid residues? Show these on your sketch and then write a few sentences explaining your argument.

(b) How would you expect the Na^+ pump to move within the membrane?

4 Although the cycle is shown in Fig 3.9 as going around in one direction, all the reactions shown are reversible.

(a) What is meant by a reversible reaction?

(b) If all the reactions were reversed what would be produced?

QUESTIONS

3.4 List all the substances that you can think of that are imported into a cell and all the substances that you can think of that are exported from a cell. How would these lists vary if you were considering:

(a) a red blood cell;

(b) a white blood cell (a lymphocyte);

(c) a cell in the islet of Langerhans of the pancreas?

3.5 Study Fig 3.7 carefully.

(a) Comment on the distribution of carbohydrate in the membrane. To what component of the membrane is this carbohydrate attached?
What is the name for this type of molecule?

(b) Where is the cholesterol in the membrane? Look up the structure of cholesterol (p.28). Why is cholesterol located in this position in the membrane?

(c) The proteins shown in Fig 3.7 can be put into three categories according to their location in the membrane. Describe these three categories. Which of these categories would contain proteins with the highest percentage of hydrophobic amino acid residues on their surface?

(d) One of the proteins shown in Fig 3.7 has a channel through the molecule that is lined with hydrophilic residues. What role do you think this protein would have in the cell?

(e) What would be the advantage of having protein pores that could be opened and closed over protein pores that were open at all times?

3.6 Figure 3.10(a) shows the Singer–Nicholson model of the plasma membrane and Fig 3.10(b) shows the Davson–Danielli model of the plasma membrane. Discuss this list of the properties of the plasma membrane with reference to the two models:

• small, lipid-soluble molecules can pass through the plasma membrane freely;
• large, polar or charged molecules can pass through the plasma membrane under certain conditions;
• membrane proteins that act as receptors can move freely in the plasma membrane;

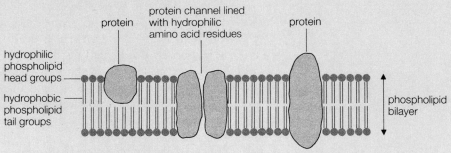

(a) The Singer–Nicholson model of the plasma membrane

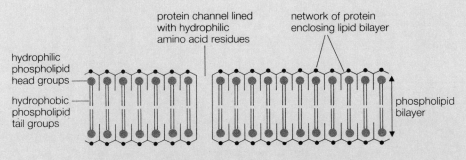

(b) The Davson–Danielli model of the plasma membrane

Fig 3.10

- the plasma membrane appears to be 8 nm thick when observed in ultra-thin sections by transmission electron microscopy;
- the plasma membrane appears to contain 'knobs' and 'holes' when platinum replicas of freeze fracture specimens are observed using electron microscopy.

3.7 Human cells and mouse cells were fused together. Before the fusion and at time intervals after the fusion, samples were taken, 'fixed' to keep the proteins in place, labelled with fluorescent antibodies and then observed using a microscope illuminated with ultraviolet light. Figure 3.11 shows the results from such an experiment.

(a) Why are cells from two different species used?

(b) One fused cell was labelled only with the green fluorescent antibody and not with the red fluorescent antibody: what does this mean?

(c) How does this experiment support the fluid mosaic model of membrane structure?

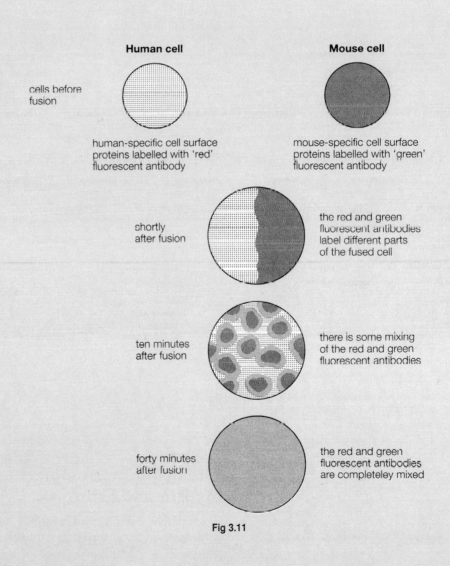

Fig 3.11

3.3 THE SARCOMERE OF SKELETAL MUSCLE

Another extensively studied and well understood subcellular structure is the **sarcomere** of skeletal muscle. Unlike the plasma membrane that occurs in all cells, the sarcomere only occurs in one specialised type of cell: the muscle fibres that make up the muscles that move the bones of animals.

Each sarcomere is about 2 μm long and they are repeated end to end to make up a **myofibril**. The myofibrils are bundled together to make **muscle fibres**. Each muscle fibre is the skeletal muscle equivalent of a cell: it is surrounded by a plasma membrane but contains many nuclei. This rather odd structure means that the myofibrils can run the whole length of the muscle. Each sarcomere can contract. This reduces the length of the individual sarcomere by a very small amount, but when all the sarcomeres contract together the overall length of the myofibril is reduced by a considerable amount and the whole muscle contracts lengthways. Figure 3.12 shows the structural relationship of the sarcomere to the skeletal muscle of which it is a small part.

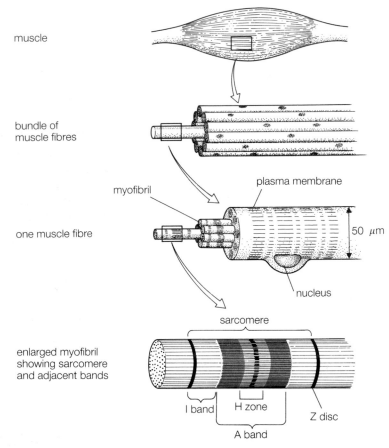

muscle

bundle of muscle fibres

myofibril

plasma membrane

one muscle fibre

50 μm

nucleus

sarcomere

enlarged myofibril showing sarcomere and adjacent bands

I band   H zone   Z disc

A band

Fig 3.12   A sarcomere is a small part of a myofibril, which is a small part of a muscle fibre, which is a small part of a muscle.

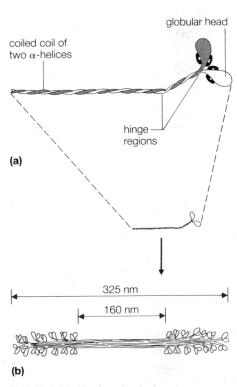

coiled coil of two α-helices

globular head

hinge regions

(a)

325 nm

160 nm

(b)

Fig 3.13   **(a)** Myosin molecules have two polypeptide chains.
(b) Thick filaments are made up of several myosin molecules.

The major macromolecules in the sarcomere are myosin and actin

Biochemical analysis of skeletal muscle indicates that the sarcomere contains two major proteins: myosin and actin. **Myosin** is an oddly shaped protein (Fig 3.13(a)) with two polypeptide chains. One end of the polypeptide chains is folded up into two globular head groups while the other ends of the polypeptides form a fibrous tail. These myosin molecules then associate to form myosin fibres as shown in Fig 3.13(b). Myosin fibres are about 11 nm in diameter and are sometimes referred to as **thick filaments**.

STRUCTURES MADE FROM MOLECULES

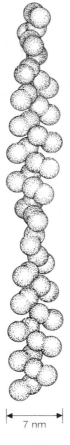

(a) a single actin macromolecule

|← 7 nm →|

(b) an actin filament

Fig 3.14 Actin is a dumbbell shaped globular protein **(a)**. Actin molecules associate together to form filaments called F-actin or actin filaments **(b)**.

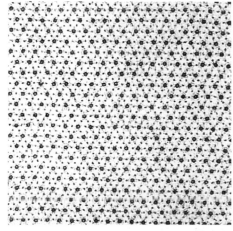

Fig 3.16 A cross section through a myofibril of insect flight muscle showing the overlap of thick and thin filaments. (Magnification × 11 960)

Actin is a globular protein, often referred to as G-actin (Fig 3.14(a)) that associates with other actin molecules to form a long filament that is called F-actin (Fig 3.14(b)). F-actin filaments are about 7 nm in diameter and are sometimes referred to as **microfilaments** or **thin filaments**.

Observing the whole structure

When myofibrils are observed using the electron microscope a series of bands are seen (Fig 3.15). There is a black line, called the **Z disc**, that marks the beginning and the end of each sarcomere. Around each Z disc is a light band called the **I band**. In the centre of each sarcomere there is a dark band called the **A band**. In the centre of the A band is a paler region called the **H zone**. Cross sections through the sarcomere can be observed using the electron microscope. A cross section through the I band shows a series of small dots, about 7 nm in diameter. A cross section through the H zone shows a series of larger dots, about 11 nm in diameter. A cross section through the A band outside the H zone shows both large dots, about 11 nm in diameter, and small dots, about 7 nm in diameter (Fig 3.16).

Fig 3.15 Low magnification electron micrograph of skeletal muscle showing the bands on the myofibrils. (magnification × 32 725)

These observations led two scientists, Hugh Huxley and Jean Hanson, to propose that the sarcomere is constructed from overlapping thick and thin filaments (Fig 3.17). The thin filaments, the actin filaments, are anchored at the Z discs by a number of actin binding proteins. The thick filaments, the myosin filaments, are found in the centre of the sarcomere. The thick filaments and the thin filaments overlap to form the dark A band. The I band is the region of the sarcomere that contains only actin filaments and the H zone is the region of the sarcomere that contains only the myosin filaments.

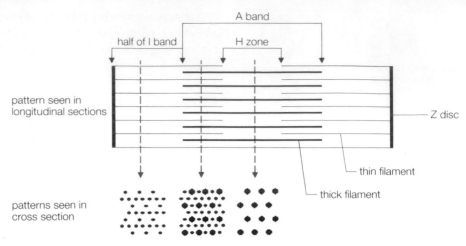

Fig 3.17   Structure of the sarcomere as suggested by Huxley and Hanson.

The sliding filament model

When a muscle contracts the sarcomere decreases in length by 20–50%. In 1953 Hugh Huxley and Jean Hanson proposed the **sliding filament model** of muscle contraction based on their observations of myofibril structure using the electron microscope.

In its initial form the sliding filament model of muscle contraction was very simple. Huxley and Hanson suggested that the myosin filaments moved across the actin filaments when the sarcomere contracted, increasing the region of overlap. They presented microscopic evidence that supported their model. They also made a suggestion that the myosin filaments contained an enzyme that hydrolysed ATP to release energy and that this energy was used to move the myosin filament across the actin filaments.

Testing the sliding filament model

If the sliding filament model of muscle contraction is correct then there should be a change in the appearance of the sarcomere when the muscle contracts. By studying Fig 3.17 carefully some predictions can be made: if the model is correct the width of the I band and the width of the H zone should decrease when the muscle contracts because the region of overlap of the filament should increase. However, the width of the A band should remain constant because the A band is the whole length of the myosin filaments, which does not change.

These predictions turn out to be true, providing supporting evidence for the sliding filament model. Figure 3.18 shows the structure of a sarcomere from a relaxed myofibril (a) and a contracted myofibril (b) from the same muscle tissue. As can be seen, the width of the A band remains constant while the width of the I band and the H zone decreases.

Studies of isolated myosin filaments also support the Huxley and Hanson model. Treatment of myosin proteins with a proteolytic enzyme splits the myosin molecules into three, the two head groups and the tail region. The isolated myosin head groups show two properties that are consistent with the sliding filament model: the head groups hydrolyse ATP (they are an ATPase) and they have the amazing property of crawling along actin filaments in the presence of ATP. This latter property can be demonstrated in a simple experiment in which small beads are coated with isolated myosin heads and then added to purified actin filaments in the presence of ATP: the small beads can be seen to move along the actin filaments.

The contact points between the thick myosin filaments and the thin actin filaments can be observed if insect flight muscle is freeze fractured, deeply

STRUCTURES MADE FROM MOLECULES

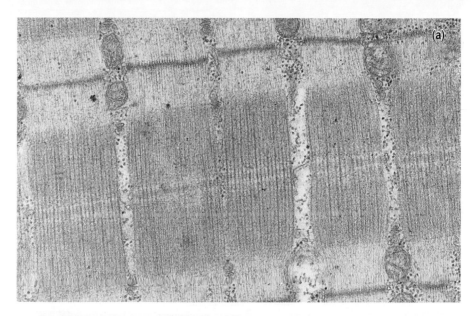

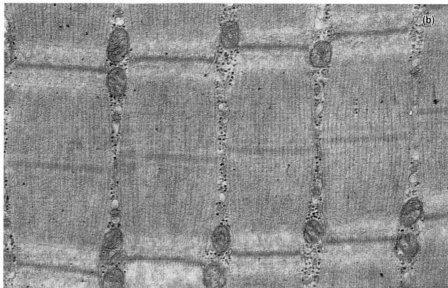

Fig 3.18 A sarcomere from a relaxed myofibril **(a)** and a contracted myofibril **(b)** showing that the A band remains constant, the H zone decreases and the I band decreases. This is consistent with the sliding filament model of muscular contraction. (Magnification × 40 000)

etched, shadowed with platinum and then observed in the electron microscope (Fig 3.19). This image is consistent with the idea that the myosin heads act as cross links between the myosin filaments and actin filaments.

There is therefore evidence to support the suggestion that myosin contains an ATPase and that the myosin heads are responsible for movement observed when the muscle contracts. These were both suggestions that Huxley made in the original sliding filament model.

The sliding filament model is still thought to be correct but has been elaborated

Scientists now understand the mechanism of muscle contraction in great detail. An outline of the interaction between the myosin and actin filaments is given in Fig 3.20. The myosin heads are usually locked to the actin filaments (a). When ATP binds to the myosin head the head detaches from the actin filament (b). The myosin then hydrolyses the ATP to ADP and P_i (inorganic phosphate ion) and the myosin head pivots relative to the myosin tail (c). The ADP molecule remains attached to the myosin head. The myosin head then re-attaches to the actin filament and the ADP is

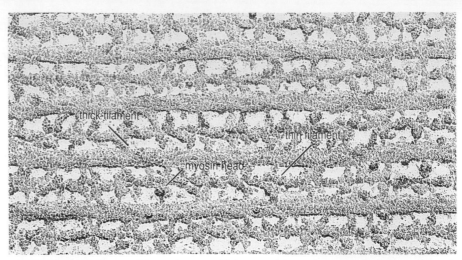

Fig 3.19 Myofibrils from crayfish muscle were quick-frozen and then etched, shadowed with platinum and observed in the electron microscope.

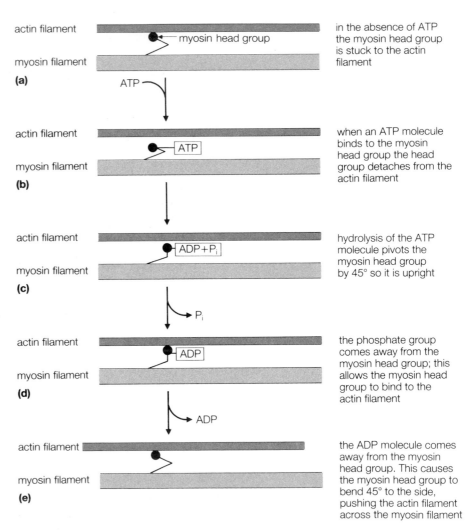

Fig 3.20 The mechanism by which actin filaments slide.

Fig 3.21 The heart must beat every minute of life. The heart of a seventy-year-old person will have contracted approximately three thousand three hundred million (3.3×10^9) times. Each one of these contractions involves a complex molecular mechanism in which millions of myosin head groups bind ATP, detach from an actin filament, hydrolyse the bound ATP, change three-dimensional shape and then rebind to the actin filament, sliding the myosin filament along.

released from the myosin head (d). As the ADP is released the myosin head pivots, moving the actin filament with respect to the myosin filament (e).

Huxley and Hanson's model has been an extremely powerful tool for studying the mechanism of muscle contraction, allowing us to imagine interactions between the myosin and actin filaments. The model has been developed by many scientists in the field over the years and has been extended to include the way in which muscle contraction is controlled.

STRUCTURES MADE FROM MOLECULES

When a muscle contracts, all the sarcomeres within the muscle contract simultaneously. This simultaneous contraction is possible because calcium ions are released from the sarcoplasmic reticulum (Fig 3.22). The sarcoplasmic reticulum is a complex of membrane-bound tubules wrapped around the myofibrils.

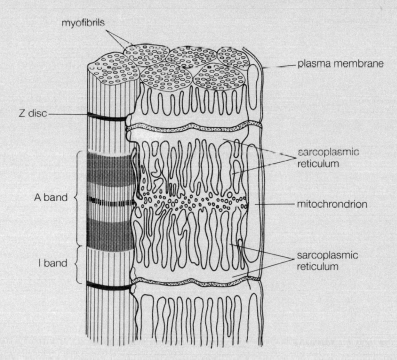

Fig 3.22 Bundles of myofibrils are wrapped in the sarcoplasmic reticulum, a complex of connected membrane tubules that release Ca^{2+} simultaneously throughout the muscle fibre.

How do these calcium ions (Ca^{2+}) influence contraction? To answer this question it is necessary to investigate the proteins present at the region of filament overlap in the sarcomere. In this region there are thick filaments made of myosin, thin filaments made of actin, tropomyosin and the troponins. The tropomyosin forms rod-like molecules of about 40 nm in length that lie along the actin filament, making the actin filament more rigid. Each tropomyosin molecule has seven actin binding sites and therefore can bind to the actin filament at seven different points. To each tropomyosin molecule are bound three troponin peptides, the most important of which is troponin C.

A mixture of myosin filaments and purified actin filaments hydrolyses ATP at the maximum rate. When tropomyosin and the troponins are present ATP hydrolysis is inhibited. However, when Ca^{2+} ions are added to myosin and actin filaments in the presence of tropomyosin and the troponins the rate of ATP hydrolysis increases again.

Scientists believe that the tropomyosin molecule comes between the actin filament and the myosin head. The ATPase in the myosin head is only activated when the head can bind to the actin filament. When Ca^{2+} is present the Ca^{2+} binds to the troponin C peptide, which alters the shape of both the troponin C itself and the tropomyosin molecule. This change in shape moves the tropomyosin molecule so that it no longer interferes between the myosin head and the actin filament. The myosin head binds to the actin filament and the ATPase can hydrolyse ATP. Evidence for this complicated mechanism comes from X-ray diffraction studies of the protein complex. The X-ray diffraction data are summed up in Fig 3.23.

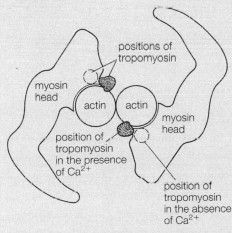

Fig 3.23 The myosin–actin interaction, from X-ray diffraction data. When the tropomyosin is in the dotted position the actin cannot bind to the myosin head. When Ca^{2+} is bound to the tropomyosin the tropomyosin moves to the side, allowing the myosin to interact with the actin.

1 (a) Why is it important that all the sarcomeres in the myofibril contract at exactly the same time?
   (b) Study Fig 3.22. Why is the sarcoplasmic reticulum wrapped around the myofibril?
   (c) There is a store of Ca^{2+} in the sarcoplasmic reticulum. Why do these Ca^{2+} stay in the sarcoplasmic reticulum and not diffuse throughout the myofibril? Speculate on how these Ca^{2+} are released.

2 (a) A mixture of myosin filaments and purified actin hydrolyses ATP at the maximum rate as long as ATP is available. What would happen if the sarcomere was made just of myosin filaments and actin filaments?
   (b) What effect does the presence of tropomyosin and the troponins have on the rate of ATP hydrolysis? What explanation do scientists have for this effect?
   (c) ATP is present in the myofibril. The muscle does not contract all the time: why not?
   (d) What effect does the addition of Ca^{2+} have on the ATP hydrolysis rate of complete sarcomeres? What explanation do scientists have for this effect?
   (e) When the nervous impulse reaches the end of the nerve a chemical messenger crosses the gap between the nerve and the muscle, causing the Ca^{2+} to be released from the sarcoplasmic reticulum. List the events that occur after Ca^{2+} release up to and including the muscle contraction.

QUESTIONS

3.8 (a) Describe the structure of a single myosin protein. What common secondary structure is present in the myosin molecule? What part of the myosin protein can be described as globular?
   (b) How do myosin proteins associate to form myosin filaments?
   (c) Describe the structure of an actin protein subunit.
   (d) How do actin proteins come together to form F-actin filaments?

3.9 (a) Describe the structure of a sarcomere in terms of the proteins present.
   (b) What is meant by the I band, the A band and the H zone?
   (c) Compare the structure of a sarcomere in a relaxed myofibril with the structure of a sarcomere in a contracted myofibril.

3.10 (a) Describe the original sliding filament model of myofibril contraction as proposed by Huxley and Hanson.
   (b) Discuss how the appearance of the sarcomere in the light microscope and the electron microscope supports the sliding filament model.

3.4 THE PLANT CELL WALL

Plant cells, unlike animal cells, have a rigid cell wall outside the plasma membrane. Plant cells have a higher concentration of solutes (and hence a lower concentration of water) than the solution between the cells. This means that the cells would take in water by osmosis from their surroundings, swell and burst if it were not for the rigid cell wall pushing back against the expanding plasma membrane. In plants the cell wall also provides the strength to maintain the shape of the plant and is often modified to provide specialised structures like xylem and phloem.

STRUCTURES MADE FROM MOLECULES

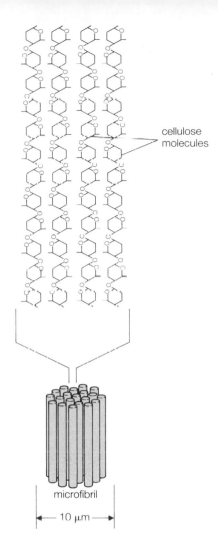

cellulose molecules

microfibril

|← 10 μm →|

Fig 3.24 The cellulose molecules pack into bundles that together form a microfibril.

The plant cell wall differs from the other structures discussed in this chapter because it is outside the cell. It also differs from both the plasma membrane and the sarcomere in that no scientist has published a definitive model of the plant cell wall for other scientists to challenge or support. Instead the current concept of the plant cell wall has grown and evolved in a rather haphazard manner. In fact the plant cell wall is a very elegant structure that is modified in subtle ways to adapt it to the function of the particular cell it surrounds.

Cellulose gives tensile strength to the plant cell wall

The most important component of the plant cell wall is **cellulose**. Cellulose is a polymer of β-glucose residues linked by $1 \rightarrow 4$ glycosidic bonds (section 2.2). Cellulose molecules are long and straight and hydrogen bond together to form bundles called cellulose **microfibrils** (Fig 3.24). These microfibrils can be many micrometres long (Fig 3.25).

The cellulose in the plant cell wall provides strength because the cellulose microfibrils have enormous tensile strength. However, it would not be a wall unless there were some 'cement' or **matrix** holding these microfibrils together. This matrix has been studied by investigating the cell walls of sycamore cells grown away from the tree in small, sterile containers. The matrix proves to be a mixture of the polysaccharides **hemicellulose** and **pectins**.

Hemicelluloses are connecting molecules in the plant cell wall

Hemicelluloses have a backbone of about 50 β-glucose residues linked by $1 \rightarrow 4$ glycosidic bonds, very much like a short stretch of cellulose. This backbone has numerous branches of other sugar residues (galactose, xylose and fucose). The hemicellulose molecules are hydrogen bonded tightly to the cellulose microfibrils with their branches sticking outwards. The structure of a hemicellulose molecule is shown in Fig 3.26.

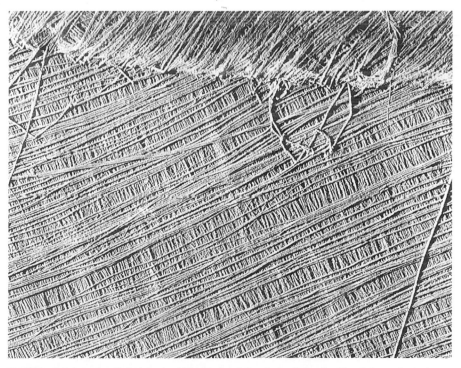

Fig 3.25 Cellulose microfibrils from the primary cell wall of a plant cell visualised by platinum shadowing and viewed in the electron microscope. (Magnification × 22 800)

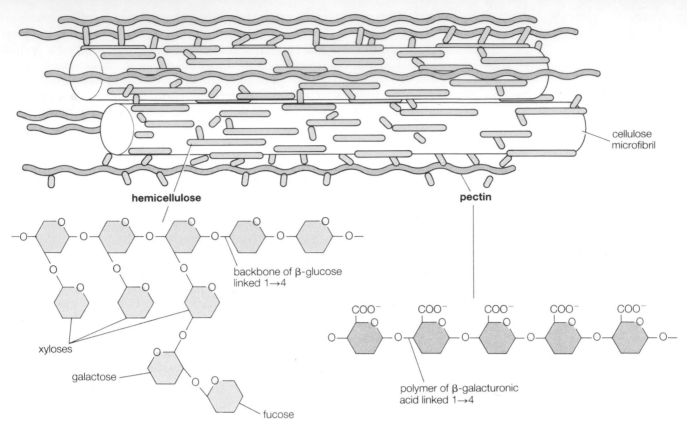

Fig 3.26 The cellulose microfibrils are embedded in a matrix of pectin. The cellulose microfibrils are linked to the pectin polymers by hemicellulose molecules.

cellulose
microfibril

hemicellulose

pectin

backbone of β-glucose
linked 1→4

xyloses

galactose

fucose

polymer of β-galacturonic
acid linked 1→4

Pectins act as the glue in the plant cell wall

Pectins are polysaccharides made from **galacturonic acid** that are cross linked by short polymers of other sugars (Fig 3.26). Galacturonic acid is a sugar with a carboxylic group on carbon-5 so when it is polymerised by forming 1→4 glycosidic bonds the polysaccharide bristles with negative charges. These negative charges attract Ca^{2+} ions, forming the salt **calcium pectate**.

Calcium pectate has a very high affinity for water. Water soaks into the calcium pectate, forming a gel. This gel is the matrix in which the cellulose microfibrils are embedded. Calcium pectate is very abundant at the middle lamella, the junction between adjacent plant cells. The pectin polymers may also be linked to the side branches of the hemicellulose molecules. If this is so, it means that the pectin is actually linked to the cellulose microfibrils via the hemicellulose molecules. The interactions between cellulose, hemicellulose and pectin molecules are summarised in Fig 3.26.

Extensins give the plant cell wall more strength

Some plant cell walls also contain a macromolecule called **extensin**. Extensin has a protein core of about 300 amino acid residues, most of which have carbohydrate residues linked to them. The protein core forms a rod-like helix with the carbohydrate projecting in all directions. Extensin is thought to bind to the polysaccharides making up the cell wall, increasing the strength of the matrix. Plant cell walls can contain up to 15% extensin.

The plant cell wall is added to in layers

A young plant cell, one that has recently been produced by cell division, has a thin cell wall that is referred to as a **primary cell wall**. The primary

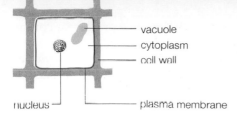

(a) A young plant cell

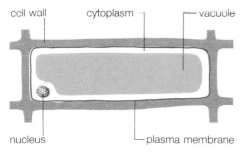

(b) A plant cell that has elongated

Fig 3.27 Plant growth is achieved by a combination of cell division and cell elongation. After cell division the cell is small **(a)** but further growth is achieved by cell elongation **(b)**. The cell wall must be loosened for cell elongation to occur.

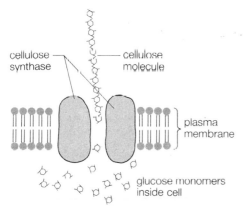

Fig 3.28 The cellulose polymer is produced outside the cell by a membrane protein called cellulose synthase. The glucose monomers are taken from inside the cell and the polymer is 'spun out' outside the cell.

cell wall is relatively thin and flexible. A mature plant cell is much longer than the young plant cell: the plant cell elongates as it grows (Fig 3.27). Plant growth is controlled by small, diffusible water-soluble substances that are sometimes called **plant hormones**. One class of plant hormones, the **auxins**, cause plant cell elongation. One hypothesis suggests that auxin causes the cell to pump hydrogen ions out into the cell wall at one end of the cell. This decrease in pH causes a weakening of the hydrogen bonds between the cellulose microfibrils and may activate certain enzymes in the cell wall that break down some of the polysaccharides in the wall.

Once the plant cell wall is loosened the cell takes in water and expands the size of the cell vacuole and therefore the size of the cell. The cell only elongates lengthways because only one end of the cell wall was softened and loosened. A new cell wall is laid down outside the plasma membrane as the cell elongates. The cellulose microfibrils of this new cell wall are laid down by a rather elegant process. Cellulose is synthesised on the outside of the plasma membrane by an enzyme called **cellulose synthase**. The cellulose synthase enzyme takes monomers from inside the cell and spins out polymers of cellulose on the outside of the membrane (Fig 3.28). The cellulose synthase is thought to move around the cell as it spins out the cellulose molecules, laying down the cellulose microfibrils at right angles to the direction of elongation.

Once the plant cell has reached its final size the secondary cell wall is formed. This is achieved by synthesising more layers of cellulose microfibrils beneath the first and cementing them together with the polysaccharide glue (Fig 3.29). The cellulose microfibrils are laid down in a different orientation to those in the primary cell wall, and the direction changes with each layer added. This makes the cell wall very strong as the cellulose microfibrils now lie in in every orientation, giving the cell wall tensile strength in all directions. This secondary cell wall is very strong but very rigid. Once the secondary cell wall has formed the cell can no longer enlarge.

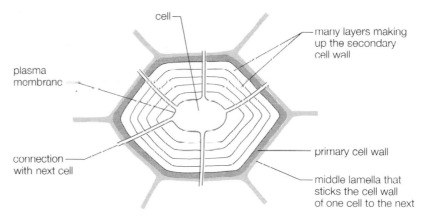

Fig 3.29 Multiple layers make the plant cell wall extremely strong. The cellulose microfibrils run in a different direction in each of the layers of the secondary cell wall, ensuring that the cell wall is strong in all directions.

The plant cell wall can be modified to provide specialised functions

The plant cell wall is often modified further as the plant cell develops. One example of this is the formation of **xylem vessels**, the system of tubes through which water is transported in many plants. Xylem vessels have to be very strong because the water is 'sucked' up the xylem under negative pressure and the xylem walls must not collapse. Xylem vessels are formed from cells, but for the xylem vessels to function the cells themselves must

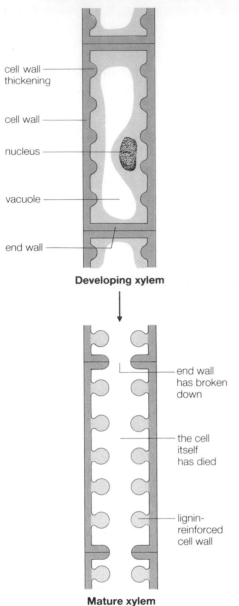

cell wall thickening

cell wall

nucleus

vacuole

end wall

Developing xylem

end wall has broken down

the cell itself has died

lignin-reinforced cell wall

Mature xylem

Fig 3.30 Lignin is added to the cellulose cell wall as the xylem vessel develops. This strengthens the cell wall but causes the cell to die.

die and the ends of the cell walls have to break down to produce a continuous tube (Fig 3.30).

Lignin is a substance produced by many plant cells to strengthen the cell wall. It is a complicated, crosslinked polymer made from monomers that are modified phenol residues. As well as making the cell wall much stronger, lignin makes it impermeable to water if it is present in large amounts. Cells that are becoming xylem vessels have a large amount of lignin laid down in their side walls (Fig 3.30). The end walls of the cells then break down and the cell itself dies. This leaves a tube of cellulose, hemicellulose, pectin and extensin which is lignified in a pattern that varies between xylem vessels. The xylem vessel is waterproof where it is lignified, but water can enter and leave it between the lignified sections.

Fig 3.31 For thousands of years humans used cellulose as their main structural material. This sailing ship was made by plant cells from the energy of the sun. The plant cells trapped the energy of the sun and transferred it, first to α-glucose and then into cellulose. Layer upon layer of cellulose fibres formed cell walls and millions upon millions of cell walls formed the tree that was felled to build the ship. The sails of the ship were also made of cellulose fibres from flax or hemp.

QUESTIONS	

3.11 Cellulose polymers are long and straight with hydroxyl groups projecting from both sides of the polymer.
(a) The cellulose molecules associate together to form microfibrils. What forces hold the cellulose molecules together?

Starch molecules are chemically very similar to cellulose molecules but starch polymers form compact, coiled structures that are soluble in water.

STRUCTURES MADE FROM MOLECULES

(b) Why do starch polymers coil while cellulose polymers are straight?

(c) Why are cellulose molecules insoluble while starch molecules are soluble?

3.12 Hemicellulose is made from lengths of β-glucose residues linked by 1→4 bonds, with short branches containing other sugars.

(a) What part of the hemicellulose molecule resembles cellulose?

(b) The hemicellulose molecule sticks very tightly to the surface of the cellulose microfibrils. What forces hold the hemicellulose molecules to the cellulose microfibrils?

(c) The short side chains of the hemicellulose molecules, the ones that contain sugars other than glucose, are thought to connect to another polysaccharide in the cell wall. What is the name of this other polysaccharide?

3.13 Pectin is a polysaccharide of galacturonic acid residues. Pectin forms the matrix that binds the cellulose microfibrils together in the cell wall.

(a) What charge is on each of the galacturonic acid residues?

Pectin binds calcium ions.

(b) Why does the pectin polymer bind calcium ions?

(c) What type of force holds the calcium ions to the pectin polymer?

The complex of pectin and calcium ions attracts water.

(d) Why does the calcium pectate attract water?

3.14 Extensin adds strength to the plant cell wall.

(a) Extensin contains two different types of polymers covalently linked together. What are these two types of polymers?

In some cells lignin is also used to strengthen the cell wall.

(b) Name one type of plant tissue that contains lignin.

(c) What property other than strength does lignin contribute to the cell wall?

3.15 When plant cells elongate, one end of the primary cell wall is loosened and may be partially digested by enzymes.

(a) Why must the cell wall be loosened and 'softened' before elongation can occur?

(b) How is this loosening and softening thought to come about?

3.16 A secondary cell wall is laid down once the cell reaches its final size.

(a) Why must the cell have reached its final size before the secondary cell wall is laid down?

(b) Is the secondary cell wall inside or outside the primary cell wall?

The secondary cell wall is multilayered, with the cellulose microfibrils running in different directions in each of the layers.

(c) Why is it an advantage to the cell to have the cellulose microfibrils running in different directions in each of the layers of the secondary cell wall?

(d) How is the orientation of the cellulose microfibrils thought to be controlled?

- Biologically important molecules are either soluble or come together to make structures in the organism. Molecules that form structures have forces of attraction between them. These forces of attraction are stronger than any weak bonds that the individual molecules would make with water: the molecules are more stable forming the structure than they would be dissolved in water.

- Phospholipid molecules form a bilayer. This bilayer structure allows the long hydrocarbon chains of the phospholipid molecules to form hydrophobic interactions while the negatively charged head groups can form weak electrostatic interactions with the polar water molecules. The phospholipid molecules are more stable as a bilayer than they would be dissolved in water.

- Myosin molecules come together to make myosin filaments (thick filaments). Again this is because the myosin molecules in the muscle cell are more stable as thick filaments than they would be as individual myosin molecules in the cytoplasm. In the muscle cell actin molecules are more stable as F-actin (thin filaments) than as individual, globular proteins (G-actin).

- Cellulose molecules form microfibrils, bundles of cellulose molecules held together by hydrogen bonds. Again the cellulose molecules are more stable as bundles than they would be as individual molecules in solution: the hydrogen bonds between the polymers are stronger and more numerous than the hydrogen bonds that each individual polymer would make when surrounded by water molecules.

- The phospholipid bilayer is the basis of all membrane structure. Proteins float laterally in the phospholipid bilayer, held in position vertically by hydrophobic interactions between the R groups on the protein surface and the hydrocarbon tails of the phospholipid molecules. These proteins can occupy only one face of the bilayer or span the entire bilayer. If it spans the entire bilayer the protein may act as a channel or pore. This concept of membranes being proteins floating in a phospholipid bilayer sea is referred to as the fluid mosaic model. The fluid mosaic model is well supported by studies of membrane structure and function.

- Myosin filaments and actin filaments overlap with each other in the sarcomere, the basic contractile unit in muscle. In the presence of ATP the myosin filaments move over the actin filaments, increasing the overlap and decreasing the length of each sarcomere, leading to a decrease in the overall length of the muscle. When the muscle relaxes the overlap between the myosin and actin filaments decreases and the sarcomere returns to its original length. This is the sliding filament model of muscle contraction, a model that is supported by evidence from investigations of the structure of the sarcomere and the behaviour of isolated myosin and actin filaments.

- Cellulose microfibrils are the main component of the plant cell wall. They have great tensile strength, allowing the cell wall to resist the force of a swollen cell pushing outwards. The cellulose microfibrils are embedded in a matrix of hydrated calcium pectate. Hemicellulose molecules link the cellulose microfibrils to the pectate polysaccharides. The cell wall is strengthened by adding more layers of cellulose microfibrils embedded in matrix, the microfibrils being at a different angle in each of the layers to provide strength in all directions. Extensin and lignin are other polymers found in the cell wall that add strength to the structure.

Theme 2

THE CODE OF LIFE

'We wish to suggest a structure for the salt of deoxyribose nucleic acid (D.N.A.). This structure has novel features which are of considerable biological interest.'

(From the article 'Molecular Structure of Nucleic Acids' by J.D. Watson and F.H.C. Crick published in *Nature*, April 25, 1953).

If any branch of science can be said to have a birthday it is molecular biology. Molecular biology was born on 25 April 1953 when Watson and Crick published their model for the three-dimensional structure of DNA. In the forty years since 1953 many of the secrets of the cell have been revealed: the transmission of the genetic information from one generation to another, the manner in which the genetic information is encoded in the DNA and the way in which the genetic information is decoded to build proteins. Understanding these processes has allowed scientists to persuade bacteria to produce human insulin, to identify a criminal from a flake of skin and to trace the prehistory of the human race. By studying the function of DNA scientists begin to understand how a collection of molecules can have led to the phenomenon of life.

PREREQUISITES

To understand the material covered in this theme you will need to have studied sections 1.4, 1.5, 2.3 and 2.4. In particular you will need to be familiar with the structure of the following molecules:

- nucleotides;
- amino acids;
- polynucleotides;
- polypeptides.

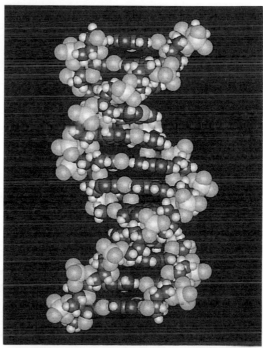

A computer graphics representation of part of a DNA molecule.

Chapter 4

STORING AND MAINTAINING THE GENETIC INFORMATION

Understanding how the genetic information is stored, replicated and transmitted is a problem which has inspired and enthralled generations of scientists. During the first half of this century scientists concentrated on the task of identifying which substance in the cell carried the genetic information. Having identified this substance as DNA, scientists were puzzled as to how this apparently simple, repetitive molecule could store the genetic information. They laboured to determine its exact structure in the hope of gaining some insight. Their hopes were fulfilled: the elegant double helix model of DNA immediately suggested a mechanism for DNA replication and pointed the way to deciphering the genetic code.

LEARNING OBJECTIVES

After studying this chapter you should:

1. be able to discuss the evidence that DNA is the genetic material;

2. understand and be able to describe the double helix model of DNA;

3. have some appreciation of the research that led to this model;

4. be able to explain what is meant by semiconservative replication of DNA and be able to discuss the evidence that this mechanism occurs in living cells;

5. appreciate that the eukaryotic chromosome is a complex structure of DNA, histones and other proteins;

6. be aware that DNA repair has an essential role in controlling the rate of mutation.

4.1 THE GENETIC MATERIAL

A prokaryotic cell has no nucleus, the genetic material is present in the cytoplasm (e.g. a bacterium), while a eukaryotic cell has a nucleus that contains the genetic material (e.g. a human cell).

Offspring resemble their parents: this is true of all species whether animal or plant, prokaryote or eukaryote. In the middle of the nineteenth century an Austrian monk, Gregor Mendel, investigated breeding patterns in pea plants. From his experiments he suggested that there were **factors** that determined the characteristics of an organism. These factors occurred in pairs; an organism inherited one factor of each pair from one parent and the other factor from the other parent. Each pair of factors determined one characteristic of the organism, for example in pea plants there was one pair of factors that determined if the pea plant was tall or short and another that determined whether the plant produced round peas or wrinkled peas. Later these factors became known as **genes**.

For many scientists, studying the way in which genes were passed from generation to generation was not enough. They wanted to know what genes were made of and how the genes influenced the structure of an organism. The elusive substance that the genes were made of was called the **genetic material** and its identification and the determination of its structure is one of the great stories of molecular biology.

DNA seemed an unlikely genetic material

Early biochemical research had established that cells contained a limited range of macromolecules: polysaccharides, lipids, proteins and nucleic acids. Of these four types of macromolecules proteins seemed the most interesting because the structure of proteins is so much more varied than the structure of carbohydrates or lipids. Nucleic acids were regarded as little more than a polysaccharide with a few uninteresting modifications. If someone had taken a poll of biochemists living in the 1930s asking them what type of macromolecule was likely to turn out to be the genetic material, there would have certainly been a majority for the proteins. Proteins were the macromolecule of the moment: proteins were varied; proteins were exciting; enzymes, the most fascinating area of biochemistry of the time, were made of protein.

However, proving that the genetic material was protein was a great deal more difficult than believing it to be. It was extremely difficult to conceive of an experiment that would test whether or not the genetic material was made of one substance or another.

Avery first showed that DNA was the genetic material

An American scientist, Oswald Avery, was one of those who wanted to identify the genetic material. An experiment described by another scientist, Fred Griffith, in 1928 caught Avery's attention in the early 1940s. Griffith was working with two types of bacteria, one which caused a lethal infection in mice and one that was harmless. When grown on agar in petri dishes the two types of bacterial colony looked different. The lethal bacteria made smooth colonies and the harmless bacteria made rough colonies. This was because the lethal bacteria had a capsule outside their cell walls while the harmless bacteria did not.

Griffith had heated a sample of the lethal bacteria to kill them, then mixed the heat-killed bacteria with live harmless bacteria and injected the mixture into mice (Fig 4.1). The mice died and when the bacteria were taken from the dead mice and grown on agar they made smooth colonies, like the original lethal bacteria, rather than rough colonies like the harmless bacteria.

Something had changed the harmless bacteria into lethal bacteria and the change was inherited through generation after generation of bacteria. Avery hypothesised that a substance from the dead, lethal bacteria had changed the harmless bacteria. He thought that this substance was the genetic material because it caused a change in the harmless bacteria, making them lethal and giving them a capsule outside the cell wall. With his colleagues Maclyn McCarty and Colin MacLeod, Avery set out to identify the substance that changed the bacteria.

The scientists proceeded in a very systematic fashion (Fig 4.2). They broke open the heat-killed, lethal bacteria and processed the mixture through a series of purification steps that removed one type of substance after another. Every time one type of substance was removed from the mixture the remainder was tested to see if it made the harmless bacteria into lethal bacteria. After many such experiments Avery and his colleagues came to an inescapable, if unexpected, conclusion. If DNA was present the

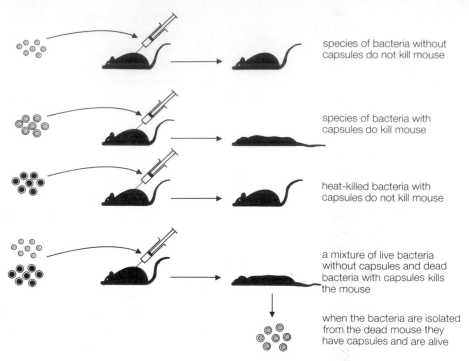

Fig 4.1 Griffith's experiment showed that a substance from one bacterium can transform another bacterium.

mixture would change harmless bacteria into lethal bacteria. If DNA was not present the mixture would not turn harmless bacteria into lethal bacteria. The DNA from the lethal bacteria was making a change in the harmless bacteria that was inherited. This strongly supported the hypothesis that DNA was the genetic material. Avery, McCarty and MacLeod published their experiments and their conclusions in 1944.

Many scientists remained unconvinced by Avery's experiments although others began investigating DNA with enthusiasm. Support for the notion that DNA is the genetic material came from another, very different, experiment.

Hershey and Chase confirmed that DNA was the genetic material

Alfred Hershey and Martha Chase were working with **bacteriophages**, viruses that infect bacteria. Once the virus had infected the bacterium the bacterium would start to produce viruses. This meant that a copy of the genetic information for the complete virus had to be passed from the bacteriophage to the bacterium on infection. The bacteriophage was made of only two substances, nucleic acid and protein. Hershey and Chase hypothesised that if only the nucleic acid was transferred from the virus to the bacteria on infection then this would provide evidence that DNA was the genetic material. If only protein was transferred, and no nucleic acid, then this would suggest that the genetic material was made of protein.

Hershey and Chase used radioactive isotopes to follow the nucleic acid and the protein. They grew the bacteriophage in a population of bacteria with ^{35}S-labelled sulphate present. When the bacteria made the amino acids methionine and cysteine the molecules of amino acid contained atoms of ^{35}S. The protein in the virus contained methionine residues, so the viral protein became labelled with radioactive ^{35}S atoms. The nucleic acid of the virus was not labelled with radioactivity because nucleic acids do not contain sulphur atoms.

Hershey and Chase used these ^{35}S-labelled bacteriophages to infect bacteria (Fig 4.3). The bacteria were then washed to remove any of the

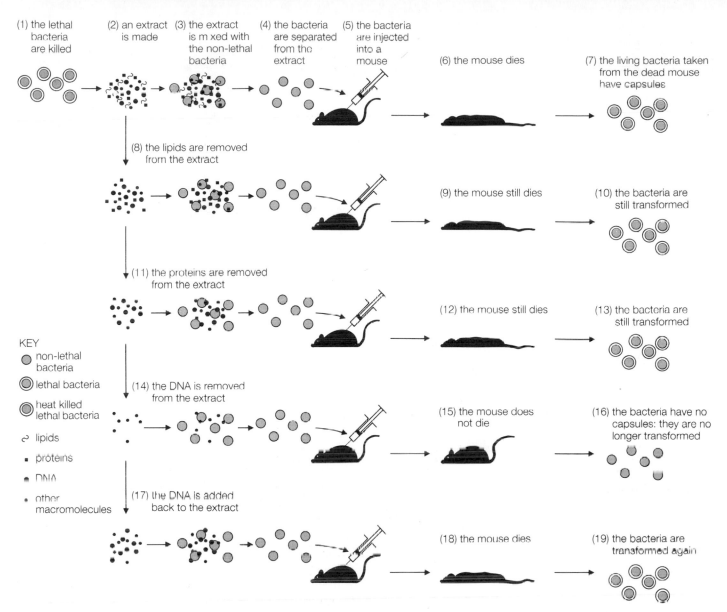

(1) the lethal bacteria are killed

(2) an extract is made

(3) the extract is mixed with the non-lethal bacteria

(4) the bacteria are separated from the extract

(5) the bacteria are injected into a mouse

(6) the mouse dies

(7) the living bacteria taken from the dead mouse have capsules

(8) the lipids are removed from the extract

(9) the mouse still dies

(10) the bacteria are still transformed

(11) the proteins are removed from the extract

(12) the mouse still dies

(13) the bacteria are still transformed

KEY

- non-lethal bacteria
- lethal bacteria
- heat killed lethal bacteria
- lipids
- proteins
- DNA
- other macromolecules

(14) the DNA is removed from the extract

(15) the mouse does not die

(16) the bacteria have no capsules: they are no longer transformed

(17) the DNA is added back to the extract

(18) the mouse dies

(19) the bacteria are transformed again

Fig 4.2 Avery designed a systematic approach to identify the substance that transformed bacteria. He hypothesised that this substance was the genetic material.

virus that had not gone into the cells and tested with a radiation counter. No radioactivity was detected in the bacteria, indicating that none of the proteins from the virus had entered the bacterial cells.

Another sample of virus was prepared, this time in a population of bacteria with ^{32}P-labelled phosphate present. This phosphate was incorporated into the nucleotides and then into the nucleic acid of the bacteriophage. The nucleic acid was now labelled with radioactive ^{32}P atoms but no radioactivity was present in the viral proteins as no amino acids contain phosphate atoms. Hershey and Chase then used these ^{32}P-labelled bacteriophages to infect bacteria (Fig 4.3). The bacteria were washed to remove virus that had not entered the cells and tested with a radiation counter. The bacteria contained ^{32}P, indicating that the nucleic acid from the virus had entered them.

This study showed that only the nucleic acid from the bacteriophages entered the bacteria yet these bacteria could then produce complete virus. All the information needed for a complete organism, the virus, was present in the nucleic acid alone. This was strong supporting evidence for the hypothesis that DNA was the genetic material. Hershey and Chase published their results in 1952.

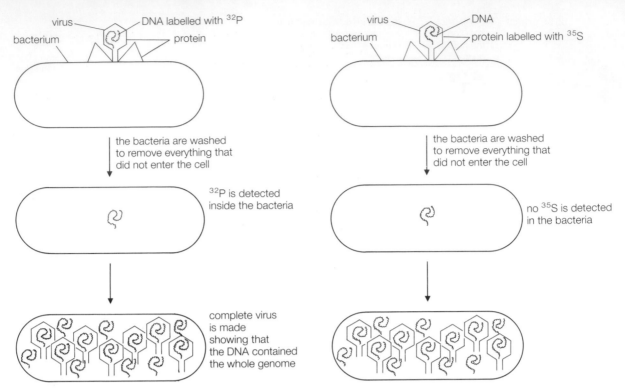

Fig 4.3 Hershey and Chase showed that only DNA from the bacteriophage entered the bacteria, yet this DNA alone contained the information for making complete virus particles.

QUESTIONS

4.1 DNA is hydrolysed by an enzyme called DNase. Proteins are hydrolysed by proteases. Study the outline of Avery's experiment given in Fig. 4.2.
   (a) What would happen if the initial extract from the lethal bacteria was treated with proteases before being mixed with the harmless bacteria?
   (b) What would happen if the initial extract from the lethal cells was treated with DNase before being mixed with the harmless bacteria?

4.2 In the Hershey and Chase experiment the viruses were labelled with radioactive isotopes. The protein in the virus coat was labelled with ^{35}S. The DNA was labelled with ^{32}P.
   (a) Why were the proteins and the DNA labelled with two different isotopes?
   (b) Viruses of this type are produced in bacteria. What radiolabelled amino acids could be supplied to the bacteria so that ^{35}S would be incorporated into the viral proteins?
   (c) What radiolabelled substances other than phosphate could be supplied to the bacteria so that ^{32}P would be incorporated into the viral DNA?

4.3 Listed below are five true statements about Avery's experiments. Which of these facts were crucial to supporting the hypothesis that DNA was the genetic material and which were just details of this particular experiment?
   A. One of the types of bacteria had a capsule outside the bacterial cell wall.
   B. The change in the bacteria produced by the transfer of the substance was inherited from generation to generation.

4.2 THE STRUCTURE OF DNA

Once DNA was identified as the genetic material, scientists surveyed all the literature to unearth some clue as to how this apparently simple macromolecule could carry the information for an entire organism.

Biochemical analysis identified the chemical groups present in DNA

Many scientists had worked on the chemical composition of DNA, identifying the atoms that are present in the molecule and how they are joined together. Biochemistry became a distinct branch of science in the latter half of the nineteenth century when the distinguished German chemist Felix Hoppe-Seyler set up the first exclusively biochemical laboratory at Strasbourg. One of Hoppe-Seyler's many outstanding contributions to the field of biochemistry was the description of a substance within the nucleus of cells that he called **nuclein**. Work on nuclein was continued by Hoppe-Seyler's student, Albrecht Kossel, who discovered that nuclein consisted of protein and a hitherto undescribed substance that Kossel called nucleic acid. Further investigation of nucleic acid by Kossel revealed that it contained organic bases and some carbohydrate.

Research into the chemical nature of nucleic acid continued throughout the first half of this century. Phoebus Levene identified two separate types of nucleic acid. He isolated one type and showed that it contained ribose in 1909: this nucleic acid therefore became known as ribonucleic acid, later abbreviated to RNA. In 1929, he showed that the other type contained deoxyribose, leading to the name deoxyribonucleic acid (DNA). Levene suggested likely formulae for the purine and pyrimidine bases in nucleic acids. These formulae were confirmed by Alexander Todd in the 1940s.

Through the work of these scientists, and others, the nucleotide was established as the basic unit of DNA structure and the structures of the four nucleotides present were worked out. DNA appeared to be a very simple molecule, and Avery's report that it was the long-sought genetic material was greeted with a certain amount of scepticism.

X-ray diffraction provided information about intact DNA

Only a certain amount can be learnt about a macromolecule by breaking it up but macromolecules are far too small to be studied using a microscope, even an electron microscope. Scientists studying the structure of protein used the technique of X-ray diffraction throughout the 1940s and 1950s to obtain accurate information about the positions of individual atoms in the intact macromolecule. In X-ray diffraction X-rays are directed at a crystal of the substance to be studied. The X-rays are diffracted by the crystal, and the patterns they make give a skilled scientist, armed with a computer, information about the positions of atoms in the molecule.

Once DNA had been identified as the genetic material scientists were keen to use the technique of X-ray diffraction that had been so successful with proteins to study DNA. However, this aim was not easily achieved.

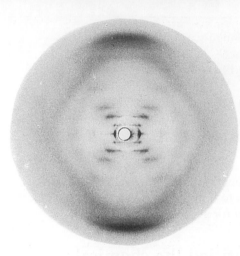

Fig 4.4 Photograph of Rosalind Franklin's X-ray diffraction data from the B form of DNA.

The X-ray diffraction techniques available at the time required excellent crystals of the substance being studied and, unlike proteins, DNA is not easily crystallised. Two of the scientists who succeeded in overcoming the technical difficulties were Maurice Wilkins and Rosalind Franklin. These two scientist were both members of the Biophysics Research Unit at King's College, London, but for reasons of their own Wilkins and Franklin always worked independently. Wilkins was the first to obtain crystals of pure DNA but these were crystals of the A form of DNA: this is the structure formed when little water is present. In contrast, Franklin worked on crystals of the B form: this is the structure that DNA forms when more water is present. It was the B form of DNA that proved to be the more biologically important.

Both Wilkins and Franklin obtained a great deal of information about the structure of the intact DNA molecule. Both scientists showed that DNA was a helix, with Franklin producing the most convincing evidence (Fig 4.4). Franklin also showed that the phosphate groups were on the outside of the macromolecule and her data clearly indicated that DNA contained more than one polynucleotide strand. The Franklin data also showed a 3.4 nm repeat in the macromolecule, suggesting that the helix turned every 3.4 nm, and a 0.34 nm repeat for which she had no explanation.

Patterns in DNA composition provided a vital clue

One scientist, Erwin Chargaff, set out to prove that DNA was a more complex molecule than had first been thought, a molecule that was worthy to be the genetic material. He used paper chromatography and other new techniques to analyse the DNA from a large number of different organisms. He found that the amount of each nucleotide in the DNA was the same for the individuals of any one species, but different when he compared different species. He concluded that every species had its own, unique type of DNA.

Chargaff realised that his data showed certain patterns and in the true spirit of science he described these patterns even though he did not know what they meant. He observed that the number of purine-containing nucleotides (A and G), always equalled the number of pyrimidine-containing nucleotides (C and T). He also observed that the number of A nucleotides equalled the number of T nucleotides and the number of G nucleotides equalled the number of C nucleotides. The patterns that Chargaff discovered are shown in the simple equations below. Chargaff published his results in 1950.

In this book A is used to represent a nucleotide containing adenine, G a nucleotide containing guanine, C a nucleotide containing cytosine, T a nucleotide containing thymine and U a nucleotide containing uracil.

$$A + G = C + T$$
$$A = T$$
$$G = C$$

All the available data was integrated using model building

By 1951 a model for the structure of DNA was one of those scientific advances that seem to be waiting to happen. All that was needed was some original thought, a little luck and a lot of determination. The original thought was provided by an unlikely partnership. Francis Crick was a talented physicist-turned-biophysicist working at the recently founded Molecular Biology Laboratory at Cambridge University when a young American biologist passed through on his way to study biochemistry in Germany. Instead of continuing to Germany James Watson stayed in

STORING AND MAINTAINING THE GENETIC INFORMATION

Cambridge and persuaded Crick that it was worth pursuing the prize of the moment, a model for the three-dimensional structure of DNA.

Crick and Watson's approach differed from that of other scientists who had worked on DNA. They did no careful biochemical analysis, nor did they wrestle with the technical difficulties of X-ray diffraction. Instead they decided to try to integrate all the information that they could collect about the structure of DNA. To obtain a scientific model for the structure of DNA they decided to build an actual model of a DNA molecule.

Crick and Watson knew that DNA was made from deoxyribonucleotides so they had scale models of the components of the four nucleotides made up in metal (Fig 4.5). The shapes of these metal models were based on all the information they could find in the scientific literature. The precise chemical formulae for the bases, sugars and phosphates were known and it was possible to calculate all the bond lengths and all the bond angles based on these formulae. Provided all the information was correct the metal shapes should be perfect scale models of the nucleotides and if they could be fitted together in exactly the correct fashion it would be possible to build a scale model of the entire DNA molecule.

There were two separate sources of information that gave Crick and Watson clues to how to fit the metal nucleotides together: the X-ray diffraction data and Chargaff's data. Wilkins agreed to supply X-ray diffraction data to Crick and Watson, but it was photographs of X-ray diffraction images of the B form of DNA shown by Franklin at a seminar that gave Watson one of the vital clues. From these photographs Watson realised not only that DNA was a helix but that it contained two polynucleotide strands.

Playing with the metal shapes provided the other clue. While fiddling with the scale models of the four organic bases Watson realised that an adenine and a thymine side by side had the same dimensions as a guanine and a cytosine side by side. This suggested an explanation for Chargaff's findings that A = T and G = C for any one DNA molecule. Further examination showed that adenine would bind to thymine with the formation of two hydrogen bonds and guanine would bind to cytosine with the

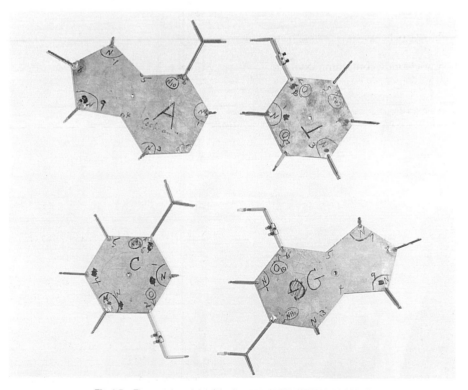

Fig 4.5 The metal models of the bases used by Watson and Crick.

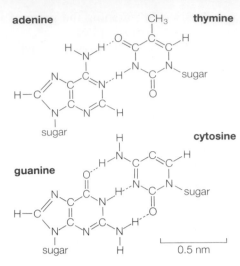

Fig 4.6 The pairing of the bases present in DNA.

formation of three hydrogen bonds (Fig 4.6). However, these hydrogen bonded pairs would only form if one of the bases in each pair was 'upside down'.

The hydrogen bonded bases, or **base pairs**, gave Crick and Watson the starting point for solving the rest of the puzzle. The crucial finding was that the two polynucleotide strands ran in opposite directions. This meant that all the bases in one of the strands were 'upside down' and the base pairs could form between the bases projecting from one strand and the bases projecting from the other strand.

The rest of the structure fell into place once the base pairs were formed (Fig 4.7). As the bases were paired they had to be on the inside of the double-stranded molecule and the phosphate groups had to project outwards, in keeping with Franklin's data. There was little problem forming a double helix with a 3.4 nm turn, again indicating that their structure agreed with the X-ray diffraction data. When the scale model of the double helix was assembled it proved to have ten base pairs per 3.4 nm turn, accounting for the 0.34 nm repeat in the Franklin data. The essential features of the Watson and Crick model for the three-dimensional structure of DNA are shown in Fig 4.8.

- There are two polynucleotide strands.
- The strands run in opposite directions; they are antiparallel.
- The sugar–phosphate backbones are on the outside.
- The bases are on the inside.
- The bases in one strand are hydrogen bonded to the bases in the other strand.

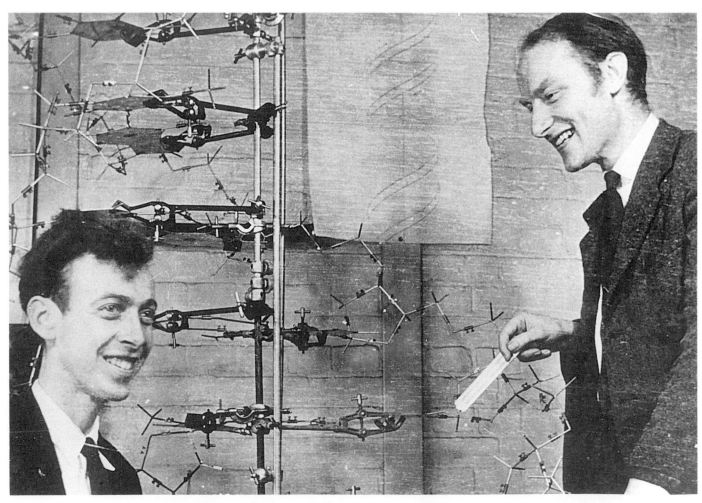

Fig 4.7 James Watson (left) and Francis Crick with their model of the DNA molecule.

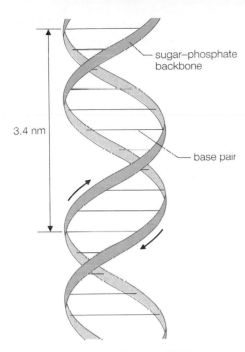

- A is hydrogen bonded to T and G is hydrogen bonded to C.
- The base pairs lie at right angles to the backbones.
- The double-stranded structure is twisted into a right-handed helix.
- There are ten base pairs in every full turn of the helix, a 3.4 nm length.

Once it had been assembled there was little doubt that the metal model was an accurate representation of the three-dimensional structure of the DNA molecule. Not only did it account for all the known data, but it indicated a possible mechanism by which the DNA could be replicated. As Watson and Crick wrote in the article describing the model that was published in the journal *Nature* in 1953: 'It has not escaped our notice that the specific pairing we have postulated immediately suggests a possible copying mechanism for the genetic material.'

The double helix structure for DNA was only a model: it was two scientists' best guess at the real situation based on all available evidence. Like all the best models, it was so simple and elegant that there was little doubt that it was accurate: but the model still had to be tested.

The double helix model of DNA structure has been tested in three ways. Firstly, more data about DNA structure has been collected and all this data has proved to be consistent with the model as proposed by Watson and Crick. Secondly, the model predicted a certain mechanism for DNA replication and experiments have shown that DNA does indeed replicate by this mechanism. Thirdly, the double helix model of DNA structure led Crick to propose a mechanism by which the information in the DNA was transcribed into RNA and then used to make proteins. The available evidence indicates that the mechanism Crick proposed was accurate, again suggesting that the double helix model is an accurate representation of the true situation.

Fig 4.8 The double helix model of DNA structure.

3.4 nm
sugar–phosphate backbone
base pair

QUESTIONS

4.4 (a) What elements are present in nucleic acids?
(b) Name the two sugars found in nucleic acids. To which family of sugars do these two sugars belong?
(c) Name the five organic bases found in nucleic acids. Which of these bases are pyrimidines and which of them are purines?
(d) What are the chemical differences between RNA and DNA?

4.5 RNA and DNA contain organic bases but they are nucleic acids. Which groups in nucleic acids are acidic and which are basic?

4.6 Rosalind Franklin's X-ray diffraction data showed that:
- the DNA was a helix;
- the DNA contained more than one strand;
- there was a 3.4 nm repeating structure in the DNA;
- there was a 0.34 nm repeating structure in the DNA;
- the phosphate groups were on the outside of the structure.
How does the Watson and Crick model for DNA structure account for these observations?

4.7 Erwin Chargaff showed that:
- the number of purine bases present in a preparation of DNA always equals the number of pyrimidine bases present (A + G = C + T);
- the number of adenine bases equals the number of thymine bases (A = T);
- the number of guanine bases equals the number of cytosine bases (G = C).
How does the Watson and Crick model for DNA structure account for these observations?

4.3 DNA REPLICATION

The genetic material of an organism must have a structure that can be copied accurately. The copy must be identical to the original so that the offspring cell or, even more importantly, the offspring organism receives all the information without any errors or **mutations**.

The double helix model suggests semiconservative replication of DNA

One of the most attractive features of the double helix model of DNA structure is that it immediately suggests a replication mechanism. The double helix consists of two polynucleotides joined by hydrogen bonds between the bases that project from each of the strands. These hydrogen bonds will only form if the correct bases are adjacent to each other, adenine opposite thymine and guanine opposite cytosine. If the correct bases are not present the hydrogen bonds will not form and the double helix will be unstable.

Crick and Watson suggested in a second paper that the hydrogen bonds between the bases could be broken and the two polynucleotide strands separated (Fig 4.9). Each polynucleotide could then act as a **template** for the formation of a new polynucleotide. Deoxyribonucleotides would bind to the exposed bases, the base in the deoxyribonucleotide forming hydrogen bonds with the deoxyribonucleotide residue in the polynucleotide (Fig 4.9). The formation of the hydrogen bonds, or **base pairing**, would ensure that the correct deoxyribonucleotide was placed in the correct position, A opposite T and G opposite C. Once the deoxyribonucleotides were in place they could be polymerised to form a new polynucleotide that was complementary to the original (Fig 4.9). In this way two double helices would be formed, each a perfect copy of the original.

The mechanism that Watson and Crick suggested was called **semiconservative** replication because each of the double helices formed contained one of the old strands and one newly synthesised strand. The other possibility was that DNA was replicated by a **conservative** mechanism. Conservative replication would result in the original double-stranded structure being left intact and a copy being made entirely of newly synthesized material. Whether DNA was replicated by a semiconservative or a conservative mechanism became one of the tests of the Watson and Crick model of DNA structure. If the replication mechanism was shown to be semiconservative this would lend support to the Watson and Crick model. If DNA was shown to be replicated by a conservative mechanism this would cast doubt on Watson and Crick's hypothesis because their model could not account for conservative replication.

Meselson and Stahl obtain evidence that supports a semiconservative mechanism

It was two other scientists who thought up an ingenious series of experiments to show that *E. coli*, a bacterium, replicated its DNA using a semiconservative mechanism. Matthew Meselson and Franklin Stahl published their results in 1957.

Meselson and Stahl grew bacteria for several generations in a solution where the only source of nitrogen was ammonium chloride (NH_4Cl). All the nitrogen in the ammonium chloride was the ^{15}N isotope rather than the common ^{14}N isotope. After many generations, all the nitrogen in the bacteria was the ^{15}N isotope. DNA isolated from such bacteria had a greater mass than DNA containing the common ^{14}N isotope. When centrifuged through a dense solution the heavy DNA travelled to near the base of the tube (Fig 4.10(a)). DNA containing only ^{14}N would only have travelled a short distance down the tube.

STORING AND MAINTAINING THE GENETIC INFORMATION

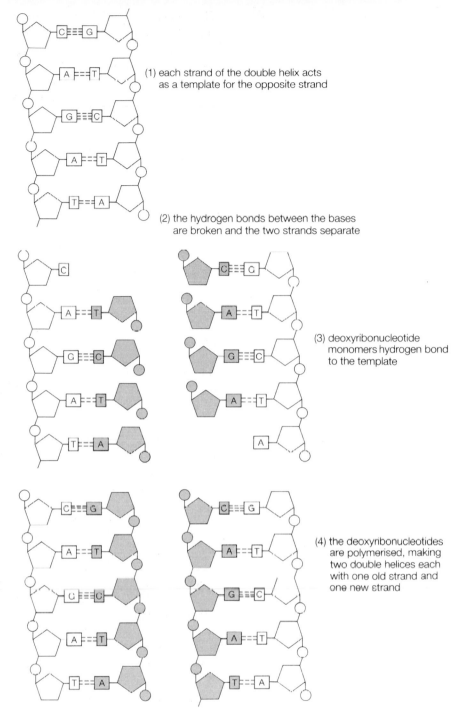

(1) each strand of the double helix acts as a template for the opposite strand

(2) the hydrogen bonds between the bases are broken and the two strands separate

(3) deoxyribonucleotide monomers hydrogen bond to the template

(4) the deoxyribonucleotides are polymerised, making two double helices each with one old strand and one new strand

Fig 4.9 Watson and Crick suggested a semiconservative replication mechanism based on their double helix model of DNA structure.

The scientists then transferred the bacteria to a solution containing ammonium chloride with ^{14}N ($^{14}NH_4Cl$) and allowed the bacteria to replicate their DNA once. The DNA was isolated from the bacterial cells and centrifuged in the same way as before. The DNA did not travel to the position of the DNA containing ^{15}N, nor to that of the DNA containing ^{14}N. It all travelled to a position between the two, showing that it had an intermediate mass (Fig 4.10(b)). Therefore, after one generation in the $^{14}NH_4Cl$ solution the DNA contained half ^{14}N and half ^{15}N. This was consistent with the semiconservative mechanism as each double helix would contain an original strand, with ^{15}N, and a new strand, with ^{14}N.

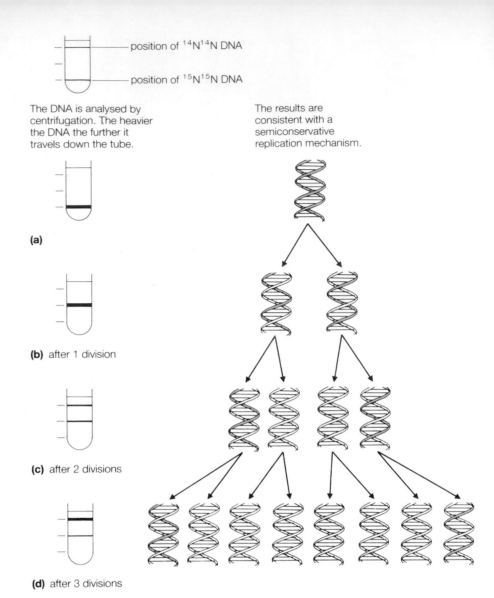

position of $^{14}N^{14}N$ DNA

position of $^{15}N^{15}N$ DNA

The DNA is analysed by centrifugation. The heavier the DNA the further it travels down the tube.

The results are consistent with a semiconservative replication mechanism.

(a)

(b) after 1 division

(c) after 2 divisions

(d) after 3 divisions

Fig 4.10   The data from Meselsohn and Stahl's experiment supported the hypothesis that DNA was replicated semiconservatively.

Meselson and Stahl then followed the DNA through another two cell divisions, while the cells grew in the $^{14}NH_4Cl$ solution. Every time the DNA replicated the new strand contained ^{14}N. The original DNA strands containing ^{15}N were still present, each paired with a ^{14}N strand, but these heavier molecules became diluted out every time the bacteria replicated their DNA (Fig 4.10(d)).

The results of the Meselson and Stahl experiment were consistent with a semiconservative mechanism for DNA replication. This was supporting evidence that DNA inside a living cell was in the form of a double helix.

Polynucleotide synthesis is catalysed by DNA polymerase

Like all chemical reactions in cells, the synthesis of new DNA is catalysed by enzymes. The enzyme responsible for the synthesis of DNA is called **DNA polymerase**. This enzyme was first purified from *E. coli* by Arthur Kornberg. He showed that this enzyme would synthesize a new DNA strand on a single-stranded DNA template in the presence of deoxyribonucleotides and ATP.

STORING AND MAINTAINING THE GENETIC INFORMATION

Later experiments showed that DNA synthesis required a **primer**, a small section of double-stranded nucleic acid, in order for the DNA polymerase to work efficiently. This is because there must be a hydroxyl group for the DNA polymerase to join the next nucleotide to. In the cell the synthesis of this primer is catalysed by an enzyme called **primase** that is associated with the DNA polymerase.

It was also discovered that DNA polymerase worked much faster if it was supplied with deoxyribonucleotide triphosphates (dATP, dTTP, dCTP, dGTP) rather than with the deoxyribonucleotide monophosphates (dAMP, dTMP, dCMP, dGMP). The extra two phosphate groups are released during the reaction.

See Table 1.7, p.23.

The genome is the total DNA content of a cell.

A huge number of other proteins are also involved in DNA replication

Synthesising a new polynucleotide strand on a single-stranded piece of DNA in a test tube is very different from replicating the whole genome of a living cell. Scientists are still working on the precise mechanism involved, forty years after Watson and Crick suggested their deceptively simple mechanism.

One complication is that a polynucleotide can only be polymerised in one direction. The phosphate group of the incoming nucleotide is joined to the sugar group of the end nucleotide of the growing polynucleotide. This means that any polynucleotide has a phosphate group at the start: this phosphate group is joined to carbon-5 of the sugar group of the first nucleotide, so this end of the polynucleotide is called the 5' end. The other end of the polynucleotide always has a hydroxyl group on the carbon-3 of the sugar group of the final nucleotide residue, so this end is called the 3' end (see Fig 2.18.) All polynucleotides are synthesized in the 5' to 3' direction (Fig 4.11).

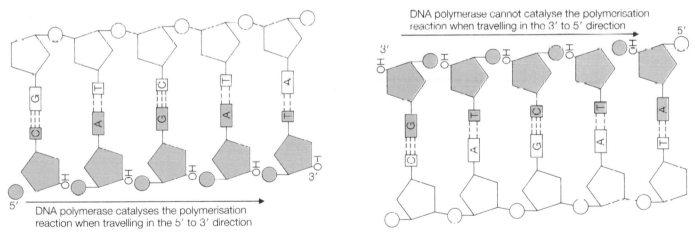

Fig 4.11 A polynucleotide can only be synthesised in the 5' to 3' direction.

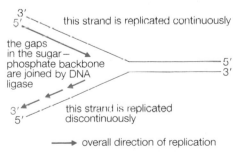

Fig 4.12 One strand is replicated continuously and the opposite strand is replicated in short sections.

However, the two strands of the double helix are antiparallel; if one scans the DNA, one strand runs 5' to 3' while the other strand runs 3' to 5'. This means that one of the two strands can be replicated without difficulty, as the copy will grow in the 5' to 3' direction. But the complementary strand has to be replicated in small sections, with the DNA polymerase 'jumping forward' and then synthesising the new polynucleotide in the 5' to 3' direction until it reaches the end of the double-stranded section. These short sections are joined by an enzyme called **DNA ligase** (Fig 4.12).

Another problem is that the double helix is a very stable structure. Once the hydrogen bonds between the two strands have been broken the strands have to be held apart or they will come back together spontaneously, reforming the double helix. Proteins called **single-stranded DNA binding proteins** bind to the polynucleotide strands once they have been separated. These stabilise the single strands of DNA until the DNA polymerase has done its job.

Yet another complication is that the DNA becomes tangled when the two strands are pulled apart, just like string gets tangled when the different strands are pulled apart. The cell contains unwinding proteins called **topoisomerases** that take extra twists out of the DNA molecule.

Ligases, single-stranded DNA binding proteins and topoisomerases are only a few of the proteins that cooperate with the DNA polymerase to replicate the genome of a cell. One of the fascinating aspects of molecular biology is that the closer we look the more we see of the intricate and complex machine that maintains and replicates the genetic information that is contained in the nucleus of every cell.

QUESTIONS

4.8 Study the Meselson and Stahl experiment shown in Fig 4.10. Imagine a slightly different experiment in which the bacteria had been grown in $^{14}NH_4Cl$ solution for several generations.

(a) What result would you expect if the DNA from these bacteria was isolated and analysed by centrifuging through a dense solution?

The bacteria were then transferred to a solution of $^{15}NH_4Cl$.

(b) What result would you predict if the DNA from these bacteria was isolated and analysed after one cell division?

(c) What result would you expect if DNA from these bacteria was isolated and analysed after four cell divisions?

4.9 What features of the double helix model for the structure of DNA suggested that DNA might be replicated by a semiconservative mechanism rather than a conservative mechanism?

4.10 Briefly describe the functions of the following proteins in DNA replication:
(a) DNA polymerase;
(b) DNA ligase;
(c) single-stranded DNA bonding proteins;
(d) topoisomerases.

DATA HANDLING 4.1

DNA sequencing is a technique used by scientists to determine the order of the nucleotides in a piece of DNA. The DNA that the scientist wishes to sequence is cut into fragments by enzymes and then each fragment is put into a virus. This virus makes a large number of single-stranded copies of one strand of the DNA. The single-stranded DNA is mixed with a primer. The primer is complementary to the first part of the fragment and forms a double-stranded region at the beginning of the molecule.

If DNA polymerase, dTTP, dATP, dGTP and dCTP were added to the primed DNA, the DNA polymerase would catalyse the synthesis of another polynucleotide that was complementary to the single-stranded DNA template, producing double-stranded DNA.

(a) dATP has three phosphate groups. Which of these three phosphate groups should contain a ^{32}P atom rather than a ^{31}P atom so that the newly synthesised DNA is radiolabelled?

The trick that the scientist uses is to stop the synthesis of the new strand randomly. This is done by mixing a very small amount of a dideoxyribonucleotide into the mixture.

STORING AND MAINTAINING THE GENETIC INFORMATION

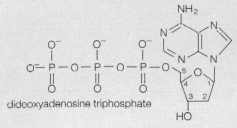

dideoxyadenosine triphosphate

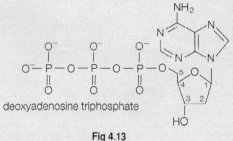

deoxyadenosine triphosphate

Fig 4.13

(b) Look at Fig 4.13. How does the dideoxyadenosine triphosphate (ddATP) differ from deoxyadenosine triphosphate (dATP)?

(c) Will this difference affect the ddATP being joined to a growing polynucleotide strand? Explain.

(d) Will this difference affect the next nucleotide being joined to the polynucleotide? Explain.

If ddATP is added to the mixture at a ratio of dATP:ddATP = 100:1, the synthesis will have a 100:1 chance of stopping after each A nucleotide.

(e) If there are ten million (10^7) single-stranded DNA molecules being replicated in the mixture, how many would you expect to stop polymerisation after the first A nucleotide inserted?

At the end of the synthesis the solution will contain a mixture of different DNA molecules, each with the second strand terminating after a different A nucleotide. The mixture of DNA molecules is then heated. This supplies enough energy to separate the two strands of the double helix.

(f) Why do the hydrogen bonds between the two strands break but not the covalent bonds in the polynucleotide?

The mixture of DNA molecules is then analysed using gel electrophoresis. Gel electrophoresis separates molecules according to their charge and their size. In this case the charge is all the same, negative, so the molecules are separated according to size. Large molecules find it difficult to move through the gel and therefore do not move far. Small molecules find it easy to move through the gel and travel a long way.

(g) Why is the DNA negatively charged?

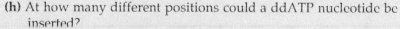

Imagine that a scientist begins with this primed DNA:

CGAT
GCTAATGCTTAGCATGCTCATC

ddATP is included in the mixture.

(h) At how many different positions could a ddATP nucleotide be inserted?

(i) Write out the different double-stranded molecules that would be produced.

(j) Write out the radiolabelled single-stranded DNA molecules that would be present once the DNA was heated, arranging them in order from the smallest to the longest.

(k) Figure 4.14 shows a series of radioactive bands on the DNA sequencing gel of the molecules you have identified in (j). Write out the sequences that correspond to bands X, Y and Z.

The procedure would be repeated using ddTTP, ddGTP and ddCTP as well as ddATP and the mixtures analysed using gel electrophoresis.

(l) Figure 4.15 shows the radioactive bands on a gel obtained by sequencing a 28-nucleotide long piece of DNA using a 6-residue long primer. Read the sequence of the polynucleotide, remembering that a band only occurs if a dideoxynucleotide has been inserted and that the primer will not be radioactive.

The procedure described here is a simplified version of the DNA sequencing technique developed by Fred Sanger and it gives some idea of the creativity and devious thinking that can be involved in developing a new technique. Sanger received a Nobel prize for his work sequencing proteins and DNA.

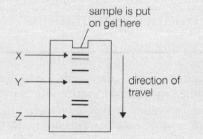

sample is put on gel here

X →
Y → direction of travel
Z →

Fig 4.14 Diagram of DNA sequencing gel showing position of radioactive bands.

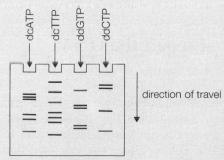

DNA synthesised in the presence of:

dcATP dcTTP ddGTP ddCTP

direction of travel

Fig 4.15 Diagram of DNA sequencing gel showing position of radioactive bands.

Fig 4.16 How alike are humans and their nearest relative? The technique of DNA hybridization can detect no difference between the DNA of humans and that of chimpanzees. Human DNA is separated into two unpaired strands and then allowed to reform into double helices in the presence of other DNA. Chimpanzee DNA and human DNA inhibit the reformation of the double helices by exactly the same amount, indicating that they are indistinguishable using this technique.

4.4 DNA REPAIR

Ionising radiations include alpha particles, beta particles, gamma rays, uv and some X-rays. These cause the bases in the DNA to form ions which then react with other substances present in the nucleus.

DNA can be damaged, introducing mutations

As well as having an accurate DNA replication mechanism, cells need a DNA repair mechanism. This is because DNA can become damaged, introducing errors into the genetic information by chemically changing the bases. These errors are called **mutations**. Mutations can be due to chemicals that react with the DNA, ionising radiation or mechanical damage.

When a polynucleotide containing a mutation is replicated, the DNA cannot insert the correct deoxyribonucleotide into the new strand because there is no base for the correct deoxyribonucleotide to base pair with. Instead, a random deoxyribonucleotide is put in, introducing a permanent change into the DNA which will be replicated in all future copies.

Cells contain enzymes that repair the DNA

To prevent this happening the cell has groups of enzymes that 'cruise' around the DNA looking for mutations. The mutations can be detected because they usually introduce a small alteration into the three-dimensional structure of the DNA. Once a mutation has been detected an **endonuclease** removes the altered deoxyribonucleotide residue and those around it (Fig 4.17(b)). A special type of DNA polymerase then synthesises a new section of polynucleotide, using the other strand as a template (Fig 4.17(c)). Finally, the new section of the polynucleotide is joined up to the old section by an enzyme called DNA ligase (Fig 4.17(d)).

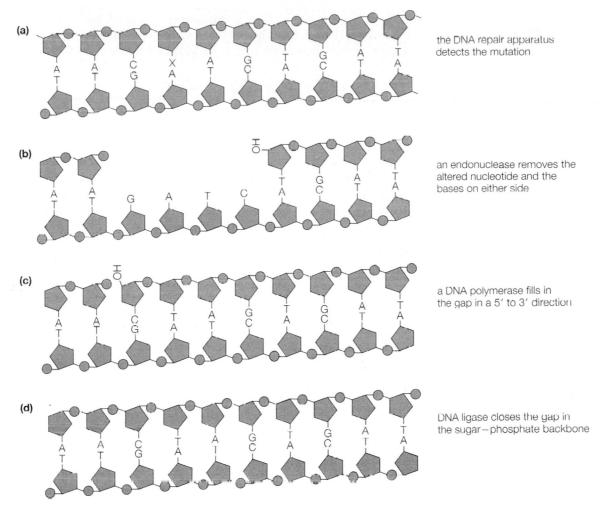

(a)   the DNA repair apparatus detects the mutation

(b)   an endonuclease removes the altered nucleotide and the bases on either side

(c)   a DNA polymerase fills in the gap in a 5' to 3' direction

(d)   DNA ligase closes the gap in the sugar–phosphate backbone

Fig 4.17   The DNA repair mechanism.

The importance of DNA repair is illustrated by a inherited disease called xeroderma pigmentosum. Individuals with xeroderma pigmentosum lack one of the enzymes needed to repair mutations in the DNA of their skin cells caused by ultraviolet radiation. One of the symptoms of the disease is a very high rate of skin cancer. Such cancers usually arise from a single mutant cell.

QUESTIONS

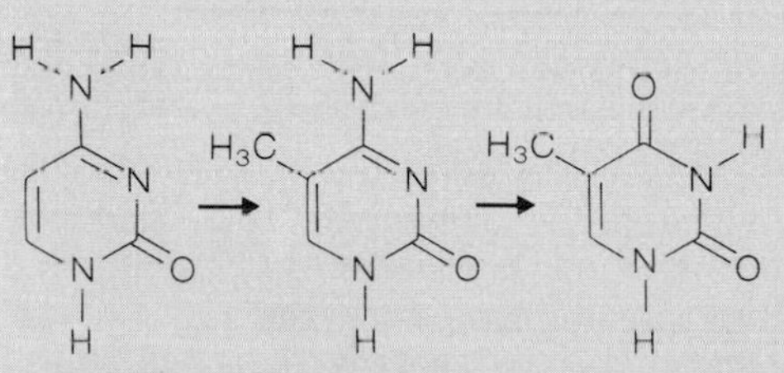

cytosine

Fig 4.18   A mutation of cytosine involving two chemical reactions.

4.11 DNA consists of two complementary polynucleotide strands. How does this ensure accurate repair of mutations?

4.12 Three different enzymes each play a role in DNA repair. What are these three enzymes and what functions does each perform?

4.13 Why must humans with xeroderma pigmentosum go to great lengths to protect their skin from exposure to sunlight?

4.14 Occasionally a cytosine base in the DNA will undergo two chemical modifications (Fig 4.18). In the first a methyl group is added, in the second an amine group is replaced by an oxygen. Why is this mutation not recognised and removed by the DNA repair mechanism? (*Clue*: look at Fig 1.33.)

4.5 CHROMOSOME STRUCTURE

Scientists agree that DNA is the genetic material and that pure DNA is in the form of a double helix. However, DNA in the cell is not pure, it is encrusted with proteins and coiled into structures called **chromosomes**.

There is a lot of DNA in a cell

Even a simple bacterial cell is a complex organism, filled with specialised structures and able to respond to a range of environmental factors. The genetic information for a bacterium requires a circle of DNA with a circumference of 1.36 mm that has to pack into a cell that is only 0.003 mm long. A human liver cell contains 46 DNA molecules whose total length adds up to 2.2 m, all packed into a nucleus only 10 μm (0.000 001 m) in diameter. The DNA in a cell must be very well organised in order to pack this huge length into such a small space.

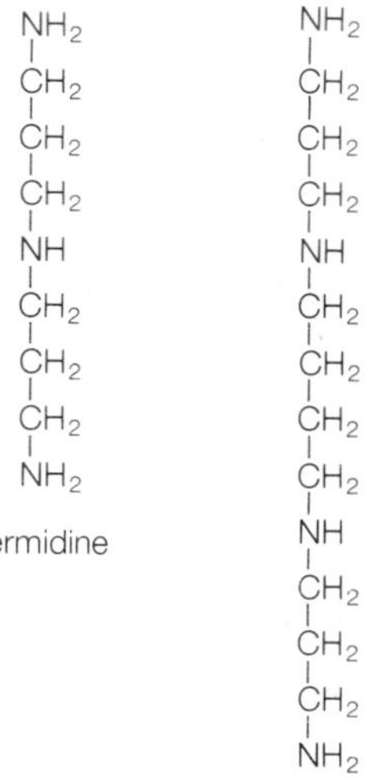

DNA is acidic and must be neutralised

DNA is a nucleic acid: every phosphate group in the DNA behaves as an acid. At the pH of the cell, around pH 7, all the phosphate groups have given up their hydrogen ions and are negatively charged. There are approximately 10^8 (100 000 000) phosphate groups in each of the DNA molecules in the nucleus of a human cell. If each of these were negatively charged there would be 46 rigid little rods, each about 5 cm long!

In fact the DNA in cells is neutralised. In bacterial cells the DNA is neutralised by positive cations such as Ca^{2+} and Mg^{2+} and two substances called **spermine** and **spermidine** (Fig 4.19). These substances contain many basic groups that gain hydrogen ions at the pH of the cell and are therefore positively charged. These positive charges neutralise the negative charges on the DNA.

Eukaryotic cells contain a family of proteins called **histones**. These histones contain many basic amino acid residues. The amino acid residues gain hydrogen ions at the cell pH and are therefore positively charged. These positive charges neutralise the negative charges on the DNA.

spermidine

spermine

Fig 4.19

The DNA is tightly packed

There is still the problem of understanding how a circle of DNA 1.36 mm in circumference fits into a bacterial cell and how 2.2 m of DNA fits into a nucleus. The DNA must be folded or coiled or looped but the packing must be done in such a way that the DNA does not tangle or break.

The circular bacterial DNA is thought to be **supercoiled**. The double helix is twisted and then the circle sealed so that the twists cannot fall out. The extra twists make the circle spring into a much more compact structure.

The problems associated with packing eukaryotic DNA are much greater. In eukaryotes the DNA is arranged as chromosomes. Each chromosome contains one long DNA molecule: in a human cell each chromosome contains an average of 5 cm (50 000 μm) of DNA. The chromosomes are only visible as separate structures during cell division. When the cell divides the nuclear membrane breaks down and the chromosomes are distributed between the two daughter cells. During cell division each chromosome is approximately 5 μm long. Somehow the 50 000 μm of DNA is packed down so that it is ten thousand times shorter.

Some packing occurs when the DNA is associated with the histones. Four different histones form a core around which the DNA is wound, forming a structure called the **nucleosome** (Fig 4.20). Nucleosomes look like beads on a string when observed under the electron microscope. This beaded structure is then wound to form a spring-like coil and fixed in

You can try this for yourself with a piece of string. Cut 10 cm of string, then roll one end of it between your thumb and finger to introduce about twenty twists into the string. Tie the ends together so that the twists do not fall out. The string circle should spring into a much more compact structure.

STORING AND MAINTAINING THE GENETIC INFORMATION

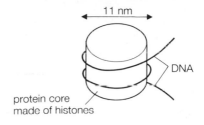

Fig 4.20 The structure of a nucleosome.

place by a fifth histone (Fig 4.21). This coil is 30 nm wide and is therefore called the **30 nm fibre**.

When the DNA is associated with the histones to form the 30 nm fibre the 50 000 μm of DNA is shortened to only 1000 μm, a reduction in length of fifty times. However, there is still a lot more packing required to reduce the length to 5 μm. Electron microscopy indicates that the 30 nm fibre is looped and the bases of the loops attached to a protein structure that is sometimes called a scaffold (Fig 4.21). This looping would reduce the 1000 μm length to about 100 μm. This reduction in length from 50 000 μm to 100 μm, by five hundred times, is probably the degree of packing or **chromosome condensation** that occurs when the cell is not dividing. However, when the cell divides the complex structure of DNA and proteins is packed even tighter. The protein structure at the base of the loops is thought to coil up, forming the very compact, 5 μm structure that can be seen during cell division (Fig 4.21).

One important question is why does a human cell need 2.2 m of DNA? Replicating, repairing and packing 2.2 m of DNA is a complicated process requiring a vast number of different proteins and using up a considerable supply of energy. How much genetic information is stored in 2.2 m of DNA? Is all this DNA really necessary? How is the genetic information used? All these questions are asked in the next chapter.

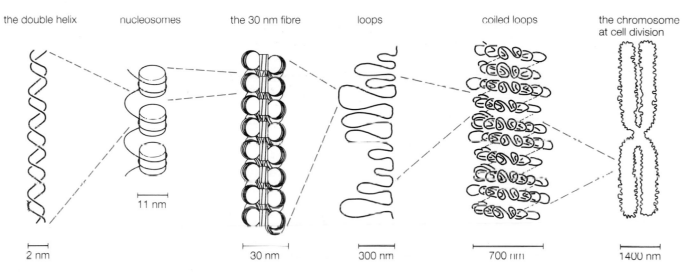

the double helix   nucleosomes   the 30 nm fibre   loops   coiled loops   the chromosome at cell division

2 nm   11 nm   30 nm   300 nm   700 nm   1400 nm

Fig 4.21 How 5 cm of DNA is packed into a chromosome only 5 μm long.

QUESTIONS

4.15 DNA is an acidic molecule that is negatively charged at the pH of the cell. How is this negative charge neutralised in:
(a) a bacterial cell;
(b) a eukaryotic cell?

4.16 Study the structures of the substances spermine and spermidine shown in Fig 4.19. What reactive groups do these molecules have in common? Explain how these substances neutralise the negative charges on the DNA.

4.17 Histones contain a large number of the basic amino acid residues lysine and arginine. What reactive group is common to the R group of lysine and the R group of arginine (Table 1.6, p. 18)? Explain how a protein rich in lysine and arginine residues can neutralise the negative charges on the DNA molecule.

4.18 The DNA molecule in a bacterium is large enough to form a circle over 400 μm in diameter yet it fits inside a bacterial cell that is only 3 μm long. Explain how this is made possible.

4.19 Each chromosome in a human cell contains a 5 cm length of DNA, yet 46 chromosomes fit inside a nucleus that is only 10 μm in diameter. In what way does the cell achieve this remarkable feat of packing?

DATA HANDLING 4.2

DNA analysis can be very useful: it can identify a murderer or a rapist, it can settle a paternity dispute, it can help untangle evolutionary relationships. However, all too often in the past there was too little DNA available for any useful analysis to begin and the scientist had to embark on the long and risky process of trying to copy the DNA without losing it. One day in 1983, while driving down a road in northern California, Kary Mullis thought of a technique that would make such situations a thing of the past. Using his technique a single molecule of DNA could be made into as many copies as were needed within a few hours in a single test tube.

The **polymerase chain reaction** or **PCR** is a very simple idea (Fig 4.22). The DNA is heated to between 60 and 98 °C so that the hydrogen bonds between the two strands of the double helix break (step 1). A lot of primer molecules are then added to the mixture. These are short, single-stranded DNA molecules that are complementary to part of the DNA that is to be amplified. The mixture is cooled and the primers hydrogen bond to the long, single-stranded polynucleotides (step 2). DNA polymerase, dATP, dGTP, dCTP and dTTP are then added. The DNA polymerase then synthesises the rest of the polynucleotide, starting at the primer (step 3).

(a) Why does heating the double-stranded DNA cause the double helix to separate?

(b) Why is a primer necessary?

The beauty of the PCR is that the mixture can then be re-heated and re-cooled. More of the primers bind to the long single-stranded molecules, and these primers are then extended to form more double-stranded DNA. The process can be repeated again and again until the necessary amount of DNA is made.

(c) If there was one copy of a DNA molecule at the start, how many copies would there be after the mixture had been put through 20 cycles?

(d) A huge number of primer molecules are added at the beginning of the process. There is only one molecule of the DNA present at this time so why are so many primer molecules necessary?

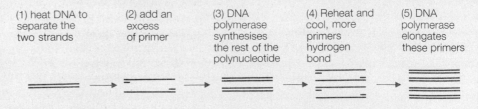

| (1) heat DNA to separate the two strands | (2) add an excess of primer | (3) DNA polymerase synthesises the rest of the polynucleotide | (4) Reheat and cool, more primers hydrogen bond | (5) DNA polymerase elongates these primers |

Fig 4.22   PCR allows a single molecule of DNA to be amplified by an unlimited amount.

STORING AND MAINTAINING THE GENETIC INFORMATION

(e) Other than primer molecules what other substances might be used up during the many cycles of the reaction?

One clever refinement of the PCR process was to use DNA polymerase from a bacterium called *Thermus aquaticus*. This species of bacteria lives in hot springs where the temperature of the water is close to boiling.

(f) The proteins in *Thermus aquaticus* are very resistant to denaturation by heat. Why is DNA polymerase from this type of bacteria particularly useful in the PCR?

(g) What would happen to normal DNA polymerase when it was heated to between 60 and 98° C?

PCR is so simple that it seems surprising that it was not thought of long before 1983. However, there are very good reasons why PCR was not possible before the 1980s. Firstly, the PCR needs primers. Primers are single-stranded polynucleotides 20–30 residues long that are complementary to part of the DNA that the PCR is to amplify. By the 1980s machines were available that would synthesise such short polynucleotides automatically; all the scientist needed to do was to type in the sequence of the polynucleotide required.

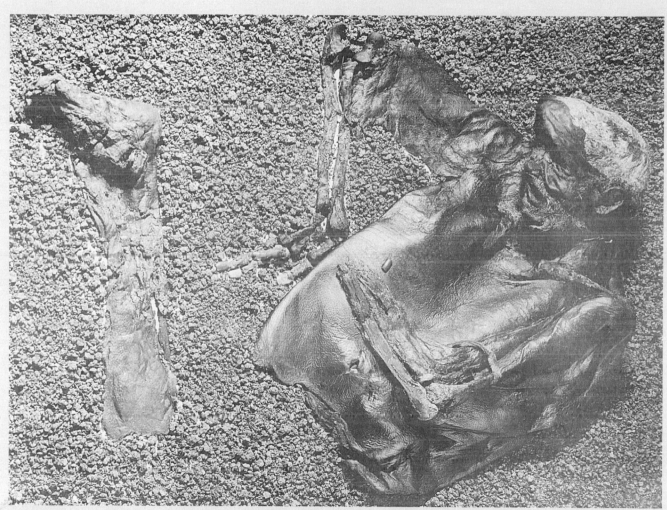

Fig 4.23 Lindow Man, the 2000-year old body of a man found preserved in a bog at Lindow, Germany. The developing techniques of DNA technology may soon allow the recreation of a person's genome from a single hair or scrap of skin or fragment of bone. The polymerase chain reaction will amplify a single copy of the DNA so that it can be cloned, analysed and sequenced. Soon scientists will be able to tell us just how different we are from our ancestors. Maybe in the future the techniques will be available to recreate an individual who has been dead for thousands of years from a single hair.

Secondly, the scientists needed to be able to make educated guesses as to what primers to use. This was only possible once many, many stretches of DNA had been sequenced. For example, if the DNA to be amplified was human a scientist could look in a data bank for a 20–30 nucleotide sequence that was common to all human DNA. They would then program the polynucleotide synthesiser to make the polynucleotide that was complementary to this sequence.

(h) What would be the sequence of the polynucleotide that was complementary to this stretch of DNA: $^{5'}$AGGTAACCTATATGC$^{3'}$?

The polymerase chain reaction is now widely used. In one case DNA from a woolly mammoth that had been frozen in a Siberian glacier for millions of years was amplified by PCR and then sequenced. This allowed scientists to investigate the evolutionary relationship between the extinct woolly mammoth and its living relations.

REVIEW OF CRUCIAL POINTS

- DNA was first identified as the genetic material in an experiment by Avery and his colleagues in 1944. They showed that one species of bacteria could be changed by treating it with DNA from another species of bacteria. This change was then inherited from one generation to the next. Their findings were confirmed by Hershey and Chase in 1952 who showed that only viral nucleic acid had to be introduced into a bacterium for that bacterium to start producing entire viruses. This showed that the nucleic acid alone carried the entire genetic information for the virus.

- The double helix model of DNA structure was proposed by Watson and Crick in 1953. The scientific model was worked out using a scale model of the molecular structure. This scale model was based on all available evidence about the molecular shape of the nucleotide residues, the X-ray diffraction data and information about the ratio of the different nucleotides present in DNA.

- The essential feature of the double helix model is that the two strands are complementary, an A opposite a T and a G opposite a C. This means that each strand can act as a template for the other in both replication and repair.

- Evidence supporting the semiconservative replication mechanism proposed by Watson and Crick from their double helix model was obtained by Meselson and Stahl in 1957. They showed that after replication each DNA molecule contained one of the original strands and one newly synthesised strand.

- Although a lot of information about DNA has been collected over the last forty years scientists still only know a limited amount about the way that it is stored, replicated and repaired in the eukaryotic nucleus. Many eukaryotic cells contain a vast quantity of DNA, more than two metres, that is wrapped around histones and then packed into a compact, ordered shape using other proteins. There are a huge number of proteins involved in DNA replication and repair, each fulfilling a particular function to ensure that the genetic information is preserved error-free and is replicated accurately before each cell division.

Chapter 5

ACCESSING THE GENETIC INFORMATION

The last chapter dealt with how the genetic information, DNA, is stored, how it is carefully maintained to prevent damage and how it is accurately replicated so that a copy can be handed down to the next generation. All these processes occur within a cell, and that cell exists because the DNA contains a plan of the structure of cell, and how to build it and how it should work once it is built. None of the cellular processes described in this book would exist if the information in the DNA was not decoded and put to work. This chapter deals with how the cell reads the information stored in the DNA and transfers that information to the cytoplasm where it will be used to build proteins.

LEARNING OBJECTIVES

After studying this chapter you should:

1. understand that genetic information is arranged as genes;

2. be able to discuss the evidence for the one gene–one polypeptide hypothesis;

3. know that DNA is transcribed to make RNA;

4. be able to describe the mechanism of transcription;

5. be able to discuss the *lac* operon as an example of the regulation of transcription;

6. know that cells contain messenger RNA, ribosomal RNA and transfer RNA.

5.1 GENES

The genetic information is in sections called genes

The last chapter discussed the scientific research that identified the genetic information as DNA and led to a workable model of DNA structure. Information about the genetic code can also be obtained by studying how the DNA functions. Genetics is the science of how the genetic information influences an organism. Gregor Mendel had said that the characteristics of an organism are governed by factors. The organism has two factors for each characteristic and the appearance of the characteristic depends on how these two factors interact. Most organisms inherit one of these factors from one parent and the other from the other parent. The factors do not merge or alter while in the organism and it will pass on one of its two factors to each of its offspring. Later these 'factors' were called **genes**.

Genes are passed on to the next generation in groups, as if they were physically joined together. Scientists observed the way that chromosomes were moved in the cell when it divided and deduced that chromosomes were groups of genes. Once the genetic material was shown to be DNA and

Fig 5.1 All organisms, however diverse, have the same genetic code and the same fundamental molecular mechanism for reading that genetic code and expressing it as proteins. This human's DNA and the macromolecules that read its message are little different to that of the fish, the coral and the tiny microscopic organisms that populate the sea.

the structure of DNA was understood, it became accepted that each chromosome was a long double helix of DNA containing thousands of genes. A gene is a small section of DNA.

The genetic information is coded in the sequence of nucleotides

DNA is a double helix consisting of two strands of polynucleotide held together by hydrogen bonds between the bases (section 4.2). The sugar–phosphate backbone is the same all the way along the polymer but the nature of the bases varies: adenine, guanine, cytosine or thymine. As the bases are the only part of the DNA that varies, the information in the DNA must be stored in the nature and order of the nucleotides.

A gene contains the information for a single polypeptide

Exactly how much information is in a single gene? This question was addressed by two scientists, George Beadle and Edward Tatum. Like all scientists who design an investigation to answer a specific question, Beadle and Tatum were building on the findings of many other scientists. As early as 1909, Archibald Garrod had realised that patients suffering from a rare inherited disorder, alkaptonuria, lacked a certain enzyme. The disease was inherited as a typical recessive gene and was therefore thought to be caused by a single defective, or mutant, gene. Garrod suggested that there was the link between a gene and an enzyme.

The link between genes and enzymes was strengthened by scientists working on the genetics of the fruit fly, *Drosophila*. Genetic studies of eye colour suggested that flies with a mutant gene lacked an enzyme responsible for pigment synthesis. Beadle was one of the scientists who worked on *Drosophila* and he joined up with Tatum to test the hypothesis that one gene coded for one protein. The organism they chose for the study was *Neurospora crassa*, a common bread mould. *Neurospora crassa* had two advantages for this study: its genetics were well understood and a single spore could be grown into a large amount of mould in a simple culture medium. Normal *Neurospora crassa* grows on a simple solution containing

ACCESSING THE GENETIC INFORMATION

water, a sugar (a source of carbon), ammonium ions (a source of nitrogen) and the vitamin biotin. This simple solution is called **minimum medium**. The fact that the mould can grow on the minimum medium implies that the mould contains all the enzymes it needs to synthesize all the amino acids it requires.

Occasionally a spore would be produced that would grow on a solution containing amino acids but not on minimum medium. This was a defect that was passed on to the offspring of that particular mould so it was a fault in the genetic material, a mutation. Standard genetic studies crossing the mutant mould with normal moulds confirmed that the defect was due to a single faulty gene.

Beadle and Tatum showed that a mutant mould of this type required a single amino acid to grow (Fig 5.2). They concluded that the mutant was missing the enzyme needed to synthesise that particular amino acid. As adding the amino acid to the solution allowed the mould to grow, Beadle and Tatum assumed that only one enzyme was missing from the mould. Beadle and Tatum already knew that the defect was due to a mutation in a single gene and their data indicated that the mould was missing a single enzyme. They therefore proposed the **one gene–one enzyme hypothesis** in 1940. This hypothesis suggested that one gene contained the genetic information for a single enzyme.

As enzymes are proteins, this hypothesis was broadened to the **one gene–one protein hypothesis**. Later, when it was realised that many proteins contained more than one polypeptide, the hypothesis was refined to the **one gene–one polypeptide hypothesis**. In modern terms, a single gene contains the information for a single polypeptide.

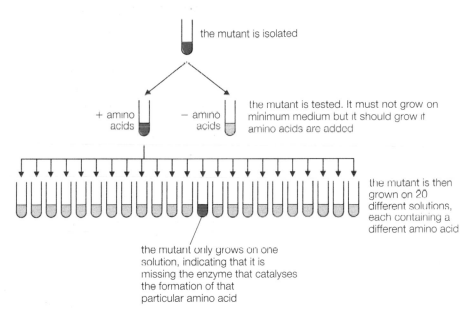

the mutant is isolated

+ amino acids

− amino acids

the mutant is tested. It must not grow on minimum medium but it should grow if amino acids are added

the mutant is then grown on 20 different solutions, each containing a different amino acid

the mutant only grows on one solution, indicating that it is missing the enzyme that catalyses the formation of that particular amino acid

Fig 5.2 The one gene–one enzyme hypothesis.

QUESTIONS

5.1 Human cells contain 46 chromosomes which have 6 000 000 000 base pairs of DNA. If the average sized gene is 1500 base pairs, and assuming that all chromosomes are the same size, what would be the maximum number of genes on each chromosome?

5.2 There are four different deoxyribonucleotide residues in DNA: A, C, G and T. If a stretch of DNA has ten nucleotide residues, how many possible combinations are there? (Most genes have about 1500 nucleotide residues!)

5.3 *Neurospora crassa* can grow on a solution containing only sugar, ammonium ions and the vitamin biotin.
  (a) Why does the mould need a source of nitrogen?
  (b) Why does the mould need a source of carbon?
  (c) Why does the mould need sugar?

5.4 A mutant *Neurospora crassa* does not grow on minimum medium. The mutant mould did grow if amino acids were added to the minimum medium.
  (a) What is meant by minimum medium?
  (b) Suggest why the mould grew on the second solution but not the first.
  (c) Suggest an experiment that would help identify the enzyme that was missing from the mould.

DATA HANDLING 5.1

Valine is an amino acid and is needed by all organisms for the synthesis of proteins. Valine is an essential amino acid in man but *Neurospora crassa* and many other organisms can synthesise it.

(a) What is meant by an essential amino acid?
(b) What type of organism is *Neurospora crassa*?

Valine is synthesised from pyruvic acid, one of the substances made from glucose during the chemical reactions of respiration. The synthesis of valine from pyruvic acid involves five enzyme-catalysed reactions. The enzymes catalysing the five steps will be referred to as 1, 2, 3, 4 and 5 and the four intermediate substances will be referred to as A, B, C and D.

$$\text{pyruvic acid} \xrightarrow{1} A \xrightarrow{2} B \xrightarrow{3} C \xrightarrow{4} D \xrightarrow{5} \text{valine}$$

Five different mutant strains of *Neurospora crassa* were isolated. None of these mutants could grow on a simple solution of sugar, ammonium ions and biotin but all five could grow on the simple solution if valine was added to it.

(c) Suggest why the mutants cannot grow on the simple solution.
(d) What might the mutants be missing?

Genetic analysis showed that each strain carried a single mutant gene. The five mutant strains will be referred to as strain V, strain W, strain X, strain Y and strain Z.
  Scientists tried adding one of six different substances to the simple solution and seeing if each of the mutant strains would grow. The following results were obtained. A plus sign (+) means that the strain grew and a minus sign (–) means that the strain did not grow.

Added substance	V	W	X	Y	Z	Wild type
none	–	–	–	–	–	+
valine (2-amino-3-methyl-butanoic acid)	+	+	+	+	+	+
pyruvic acid (2-keto-propanoic acid)	–	–	–	–	–	+
2,3-dihydroxy-3-methyl-butanoic acid	+	+	–	+	–	+
2-methyl-2-hydroxy-3-keto-butanoic acid	–	–	–	+	–	+
2-keto-3-methyl-butanoic acid	+	+	+	+	–	+
2-keto-3-methyl-3-hydroxy-butanoic acid	+	–	–	+	–	+

(e) What is meant by a wild type strain?

(f) Why was a wild type strain included in the experiment?

(g) Are any of the strains mutant in the same gene? Explain your answer.

(h) What was the only substance that would let strain Z grow when it was added to the solution?

(i) Which enzyme is strain Z missing: 1, 2, 3, 4 or 5?

(j) What substances would allow strain X to grow when added to the solution?

(k) Which enzyme is strain X missing: 1, 2, 3, 4 or 5?

(l) What substances would allow strain W to grow when added to the solution?

(m) Which enzyme is strain W missing: 1, 2, 3, 4 or 5?

(n) What substances would allow strain V to grow when added to the solution?

(o) Which enzyme is strain V missing: 1, 2, 3, 4 or 5?

(p) What substances would allow strain Y to grow when added to the solution?

(q) Which enzyme is strain Y missing: 1, 2, 3, 4 or 5?

(r) Based on these results, suggest a pathway (the reactions in order) by which pyruvic acid is converted into valine in *Neurospora crassa*.

5.2 TRANSCRIPTION

The information in a gene is transcribed

When the information stored in the DNA is needed for use in the cell, a copy of the information must be made. Scientists say that the information is **transcribed** and the process is called **transcription**. Transcription uses DNA as a **template** for the synthesis of an RNA molecule. The template determines the order of the ribonucleotide residues in the RNA. RNA that carries the genetic information from the DNA out into the cell is called **messenger RNA** or **mRNA**. Ribonucleic acid (RNA) is a polynucleotide of ribonucleotide residues. Each ribonucleotide consists of a ribose sugar group, a phosphate group and a base. There are four ribonucleotides: one containing the base adenine (A), one the base guanine (G), one the base cytosine (C) and one the base uracil (U).

The DNA double helix is separated into its two strands by breaking the hydrogen bonds between the bases (Fig 5.3(a)). This exposes the bases and it is these bases that act as the template or pattern for the sequence of ribonucleotides that will make the RNA molecule. An adenine ribonucleotide is exactly the right shape to hydrogen bond with a thymine deoxyribonucleotide, a guanine ribonucleotide with a cytosine deoxyribonucleotide, a cytosine ribonucleotide with a guanine deoxyribonucleotide and a uracil ribonucleotide with an adenine deoxyribonucleotide. This is summarised in Table 5.1.

Table 5.1

Base in DNA template	Base in complementary DNA	Base in transcribed RNA
A	T	U
T	A	A
G	C	C
C	G	G

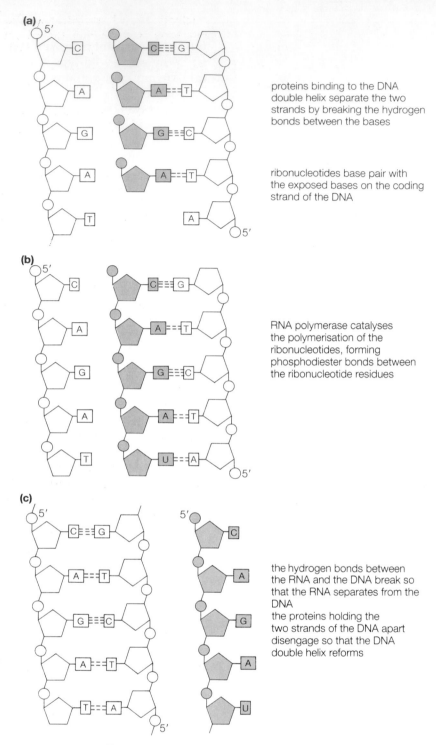

(a) proteins binding to the DNA double helix separate the two strands by breaking the hydrogen bonds between the bases

ribonucleotides base pair with the exposed bases on the coding strand of the DNA

(b) RNA polymerase catalyses the polymerisation of the ribonucleotides, forming phosphodiester bonds between the ribonucleotide residues

(c) the hydrogen bonds between the RNA and the DNA break so that the RNA separates from the DNA
the proteins holding the two strands of the DNA apart disengage so that the DNA double helix reforms

Fig 5.3   Transcription: RNA synthesis on a DNA template.

Once the ribonucleotides are in place they are polymerised to make the RNA molecule (Fig 5.3(b)). When the RNA molecule is complete it detaches from the DNA template and the DNA 'zips up' to form the double helix again (Fig 5.3(c)).

The enzyme that catalyses the polymerisation of the ribonucleotides is **RNA polymerase**. However, like DNA replication, the process is very complex and involves many different proteins. For example, the DNA double helix is a very stable structure so it does not 'unzip' spontaneously: proteins are needed to 'unzip' the DNA and to hold the two strands apart while transcription takes place.

In this way the information in the DNA that is stored in the order of the nucleotide residues, is transferred to the mRNA molecule. As the mRNA is made by base pairing the ribonucleotides to the bases in the DNA, the mRNA is not a copy of the DNA but is complementary. For example, if the sequence of nucleotide residues in the DNA was ^{3}TTAGACGTAGCC-CGA^5 the sequence of nucleotide residues in the mRNA will be ^{5}AAUCUGCAUCGGGCU^3.

Although genes can occur on either strand of the double helix, there are never two genes on the opposite strands of any one section of the DNA. If there is a gene on one strand of the double helix there is only a complementary version of the same gene on the other strand. This complementary version is a template so that the gene can be replicated and repaired.

RNA polymerase can find the beginning of a gene

RNA polymerase is like DNA polymerase in that it can only synthesise a polynucleotide in the 5' to 3' direction. It always starts transcribing at exactly the right position: the mRNA molecules produced all have exactly the same 5' end. Also, many RNA polymerase molecules start transcribing the gene in quick succession. The mechanism by which the RNA polymerase finds the beginning of the gene and starts transcribing must be very efficient.

One of the methods that scientists have used to investigate the transcription mechanism is to compare the sequence of many sections of DNA that contain genes. When scientists compared the sequences around many *E. coli* genes they discovered that there is a sequence TTGAC that lies 35 nucleotide residues before the beginning of many genes and a sequence TATAAT that lies 10 before the beginning of many genes (Fig 5.4). We say that these two regions are **upstream** of the gene. If mutations occur in either of these two upstream regions, transcription no longer starts in exactly the right place and the efficiency of transcription drops.

Scientists using the same approach to compare genes from eukaryotic organisms have found a sequence (TATA) 35 nucleotide residues upstream from the start of many genes. This sequence seems to work in a similar way to the sequences found in bacteria: if a mutation occurs in the TATA sequence the accuracy and the efficiency of transcription decreases.

Sequences upstream of the gene that contribute to the efficiency of transcription are called **promoters**. The TTGAC and TATAAT promoters in bacteria and the TATA promoter in eukaryotes are **non-specific** promoters because they have been found upstream of many different genes.

Promoters work by binding proteins

At first it is not obvious how a sequence only four to six nucleotide residues long can influence an event like transcription. Scientists have

The direction of transcription, 5' to 3', is thought of as a running stream, so sequences before the gene are upstream and sequences after the gene are downstream.

Eukaryotes are organisms whose cells have a true nucleus.

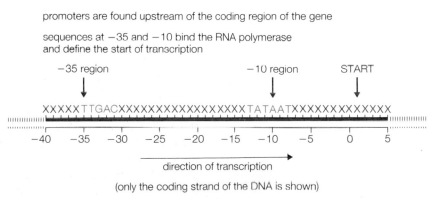

promoters are found upstream of the coding region of the gene

sequences at −35 and −10 bind the RNA polymerase and define the start of transcription

direction of transcription

(only the coding strand of the DNA is shown)

Fig 5.4 The bacterial promoter.

shown that promoters work by binding proteins. For example, the TTGAC promoter in bacteria binds a protein called σ (sigma) that is part of the RNA polymerase. In this way the σ protein guides the RNA polymerase to the correct place, safely upstream from the gene. The RNA polymerase can then 'slide' down the DNA and begin transcription. Proteins like σ that bind to promoter regions are called **transcription factors**.

A technique called **footprinting** can be used to show that proteins bind to DNA. Footprinting is based on the fact that proteins bound to the DNA will protect the DNA from chemical damage or attack by enzymes. By looking at the results of a footprinting experiment the scientist can tell which part of the DNA is bound to the protein.

The study of promoters established two important facts about transcription. The first is that transcription is controlled by sequences outside the gene itself. The second is that control is achieved by proteins called transcription factors binding to these promoter regions.

QUESTIONS

5.5 **(a)** What are the chemical differences between RNA and DNA?
(b) What are the main physical differences between RNA and DNA?

5.6 This is the sequence of deoxyribonucleotide residues in a DNA template: AATTCGCGTTGGCTATTACG. What is the sequence of ribonucleotide residues in the RNA molecule formed by transcription of this template?

5.7 **(a)** What is the monomer used to make DNA?
(b) What is the monomer used to make RNA?
(c) What is the name of the enzyme that catalyses DNA synthesis?
(d) What is the name of the enzyme that catalyses RNA synthesis?
(e) What type of chemical reaction is it when the ribonucleotides are joined together to make the RNA?

5.8 The word 'transcription' implies much more than the words 'RNA synthesis'. Define the term 'transcription'.

5.9 **(a)** What is a promoter?
(b) What is a transcription factor?

5.10 Figure 5.5 shows a section of DNA that is being transcribed by successive RNA polymerases.
(a) Are the RNA polymerases moving in the direction A to B or from B to A?
(b) Which is the 5′ end of the RNA being produced?
(c) Which strand is being transcribed: the upper strand or the lower strand?
(d) Will the promoter of the gene be at W, X, Y or Z?

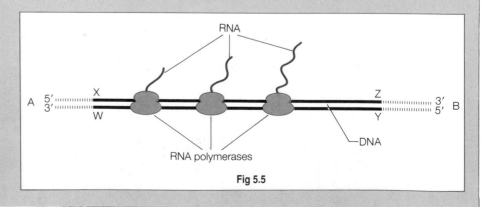

Fig 5.5

ACCESSING THE GENETIC INFORMATION

DATA HANDLING 5.2

DNA footprinting is a technique for showing that a protein binds to a specific sequence in the DNA. If the protein is bound to the specific sequence on the DNA then that part of the DNA will be protected from chemical treatments or enzymes that would cut the DNA molecule.

The technique requires a sample of the DNA to be investigated that has been labelled at one end with radioactive ^{32}P. This end labelling is achieved by a standard technique using enzymes.

(a) Why is the DNA radiolabelled?

(b) Suggest two techniques that can be used to detect radioactive substances.

One version of the footprinting technique uses a chemical treatment that destroys A residues and breaks the DNA. The DNA is treated with a low concentration of the chemical reagent so that only one out of every eight A residues will be affected.

The following sequence is found around the *lac* gene in *E. coli*.

start site for transcription
↓

ACCCCAGGCTTTACACTTTATGCTTCCGGCTCGTATGTTGTGTGGAATTGTGAGCGG

Consider twenty of the millions of DNA molecules present in the test tube. All are labelled at the 3′ end with ^{32}P. The sites where the A residue will react with the chemical are shown in red. For this example, the sites were selected randomly using a die with eight sides.

ACCCCAGGCTTTACACTTTATGCTTCCGGCTCGT ATGTTGTGTGGAATTGTGAGCGG•
ACCCCAGGCTTTACACTTTATGCTTCCGGCTCGTATGTTGTGTGGAATTGTGAGCGG•
ACCCC AGGCTTTACACTTTATGCTTCCGGCTCGTATGTTGTGTGGAATTGTGAGCGG•
ACCCCAGGCTTTACACTTTATGCTTCCGGCTCGT ATGTTGTGTGGA ATTGTGAGCGG•
ACCCCAGGCTTTACACTTTATGCTTCCGGCTCGTATGTTGTGTGGAATTGTGAGCGG•
ACCCCAGGCTTTAC ACTTT ATGCTTCCGGCTCGTATGTTGTGTGGAATTGTGAGCGG•
ACCCCAGGCTTTACACTTTATGCTTCCGGCTCGTATGTTGTGTGGAATTGTGAGCGG•
ACCCC AGGCTTTACACTTTATGCTTCCGGCTCGTATGTTGTGTGGAATTGTGAGCGG•
ACCCCAGGCTTTACACTTTATGCTTCCGGCTCGTATGTTGTGTGGAATTGTGAGCGG•
ACCCCAGGCTTTACACTTTATGCTTCCGGCTCGTATGTTGTGTGGAATTGTGAGCGG•
ACCCC AGGCTTTACACTTTATGCTTCCGGCTCGTATGTTGTGTGGAATTGTGAGCGG•
ACCCCAGGCTTTACACTTTATGCTTCCGGCTCGTATGTTGTGTGGAATTGTGAGCGG•
ACCCCAGGCTTTACACTTTATGCTTCCGGCTCGTATGTTGTGTGGAATTGTGAGCGG•
ACCCCAGGCTTTACACTTTATGCTTCCGGCTCGTATGTTGTGTGGAATTGTGAGCGG•
ACCCCAGGCTTT ACACTTTATGCTTCCGGCTCGTATGTTGTGTGGAATTGTGAGCGG•
ACCCCAGGCTTTACACTTTATGCTTCCGGCTCGTATGTTGTGTGGAATTGTGAGCGG•
ACCCCAGGCTTTAC ACTTTATGCTTCCGGCTCGTATGTTGTGTGGAATTGTGAGCGG•
ACCCCAGGCTTTACACTTTATGCTTCCGGCTCGTATGTTGTGTGGAATTGTGAGCGG•
ACCCCAGGCTTTACACTTTATGCTTCCGGCTCGTATGTTGTGTGGAATTGTGAGCGG•
ACCCCAGGCTTTACACTTTATGCTTCCGGCTCGTATGTTGTGTGGAATTGTGAGCGG•

• = radiolabel

The breakage sites are randomly distributed across the twenty fragments. When the same thing happens over the millions of DNA molecules in the test tube, every possible fragment is produced in equal quantities.

(c) How many *possible* different radioactive fragments could be produced from the molecules shown above?

(d) How many different radioactive fragments *are* produced from the population of molecules shown above?

The fragments are then analysed by gel electrophoresis which separates the DNA molecules on the basis of their size. The small DNA molecules travel further than the larger molecules. The radioactive fragments are then detected by drying the gel down and putting it against a photographic film.

The whole procedure is then repeated, only this time the protein thought to bind to the DNA is mixed with the DNA before adding the chemical that will break the DNA at A residues. Figure 5.6 shows the pattern of radioactive fragments from the electrophoresis for both experiments, with and without the protein.

(e) Which bands are present in the gel from the experiment without the protein but are absent in the gel from the experiment with the protein?

(f) What does this suggest?

(g) What is significant about the region found around 35 nucleotide residues upstream of bacterial genes?

(h) What protein might have given this result?

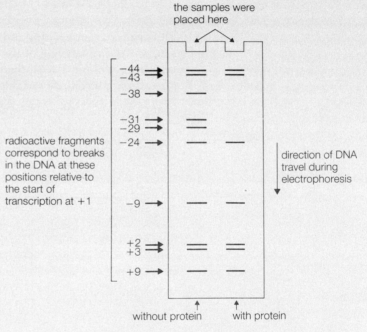

Fig 5.6   Diagram of a DNA footprinting gel.

Cells with the same DNA can produce different proteins

Cells that contain the same DNA do not necessarily produce the same proteins. For example, *E. coli* grown on a solution of glucose do not produce the enzymes needed to feed on lactose. If the bacteria are transferred into a solution containing lactose they immediately begin to produce the enzymes necessary to feed on lactose. This phenomenon is called **enzyme induction** because adding lactose to the solution induces the production of the enzymes. If the bacteria are transferred back to a solution that does not contain lactose the enzymes are no longer produced. The bacteria always contain the genes coding for the proteins but sometimes the proteins are produced and sometimes they are not.

Enzyme induction was investigated using mutant strains of *E. coli*

Francois Jacob and Jacques Monod set out to explain the fact that adding lactose to the solution induced the formation of the three enzymes needed to feed on lactose: β-galactosidase, lactose permease and transacetylase. Their first step was to look for mutants, strains of bacteria that did not behave in the standard fashion. Then they tried to think of a model that would explain both the behaviour of the normal bacteria and the behaviour of the mutant bacteria.

Jacob and Monod isolated mutant strains that could grow on glucose but not on lactose. Studying these mutants led them to identify the genes for the enzymes β-galactosidase, lactose permease and transacetylase. They called these genes **structural genes** because they contained the information for the enzymes.

Jacob and Monod then identified another class of mutants. These mutants always produced the three enzymes whether there was lactose present in the solution or not: such mutant strains are referred to as **constitutive mutants**. They proposed that the bacteria normally contained a gene that stopped the production of the three enzymes: they called this gene an **inhibitory** gene. In normal bacteria the inhibitory gene would stop the production of the enzymes if there was no lactose present. They suggested that constitutive mutant strains, the ones that produced the enzymes all the time, had a fault in the inhibitory gene. These strains were called i-strains.

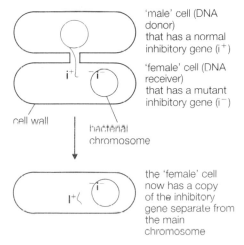

'male' cell (DNA donor) that has a normal inhibitory gene (i$^+$)

'female' cell (DNA receiver) that has a mutant inhibitory gene (i$^-$)

cell wall

bacterial chromosome

the 'female' cell now has a copy of the inhibitory gene separate from the main chromosome

Fig 5.7 Conjugation between bacteria leads to transfer of DNA from one cell to the other.

The inhibitory gene codes for a repressor protein

To investigate what was wrong with these i$^-$ strains, Jacob and Monod used the fact that bacteria reproduce sexually. During bacterial sex, which is called **conjugation**, a tube forms between two bacteria and a small portion of genetic material passes from one bacterium to the other (Fig 5.7). The cell that has received the DNA has two copies of one part of its genome for a short period of time.

If the receiving cell is i$^-$ and the donor cell normal, it is possible to get a cell that has a copy of the normal inhibitory gene separate from the main chromosome (Fig 5.7). The scientists discovered that these bacteria no longer behaved like constitutive mutants: the cells could now turn off the production of the three enzymes when they were not required. They concluded that the normal inhibitory gene did not have to be joined to the genes coding for the enzymes in order to inhibit the production of the enzymes.

To explain this result the scientists suggested that the inhibitory gene produced a substance that could diffuse through the cell and interact with the structural genes coding for the enzymes. The obvious candidate for this substance was a protein, because genes code for proteins. Jacob and Monod proposed that the inhibitory gene coded for a **repressor** protein that repressed the production of the enzymes.

The operator also has a role in enzyme induction

Jacob and Monod then isolated a second type of constitutive mutant. This constitutive mutant could not be corrected by introducing a copy of the inhibitory gene, so the fault was in a different region of the DNA. The scientists called this second region the **operator**. If the operator was normal the enzymes were only produced if lactose was present, but if the operator was faulty the enzymes were produced all the time.

The fault in the operator could not be corrected by introducing any separate piece of DNA from a normal cell. This suggested that there was no diffusible substance involved and that the operator has to be joined to the structural genes to have its effect.

The *lac* operon model explains enzyme induction in *E. coli*

Jacob and Monod, with their co-workers, had been working on this problem for almost fifteen years when all the evidence they had accumulated finally began to fall into a single pattern. At last they had enough pieces of the puzzle to suggest a single, simple model that accounted for everything. They proposed their model, called the *lac* operon, in 1961. They suggested that genes coding for enzymes that worked together, like β-galactosidase, lactose permease and transacetylase, occurred in clusters called **operons**. The structural genes in an operon were transcribed as a single unit, the RNA polymerase producing one long mRNA molecule. Either all the genes were transcribed or none.

In their model Jacob and Monod suggested that the control system for the *lac* operon would work in the following manner (Fig 5.8). There was a **regulatory gen**e, in this case the **inhibitory gene**, situated a long way upstream from the cluster of three structural genes. This regulatory gene was transcribed all the time, producing an RNA that coded for a protein called the **repressor**. When no lactose was present in the solution (Fig 5.8(a)) the repressor protein bound to a region just upstream of the structural genes. This region is called the **operator**. When the repressor was bound to the operator no transcription could occur because the RNA polymerase was unable to bind. However, when lactose was present in the solution (Fig 5.8(b)) the repressor bound a substance called the **inducer**. When bound to the inducer the repressor no longer bound to the operator, RNA polymerase could bind and transcription of the three genes took place.

This model fitted the evidence that Jacob and Monod had at the time: it explained why all three structural genes were switched on or switched off at the same time; it involved the diffusible repressor protein; it accounted for the two types of constitutive mutant.

The first type of constitutive mutant (Fig 5.9(a)) corresponded to faults in the regulatory gene (the inhibitory gene). A fault in the regulatory gene

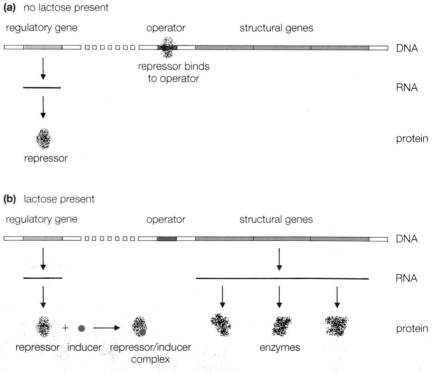

Fig 5.8 The *lac* operon.

would lead to no repressor protein being produced. If no repressor was produced it could not bind to the operator and block the RNA polymerase. A faulty regulatory gene would therefore lead to the structural genes being transcribed all the time and the enzymes being produced all the time: the bacteria would be a constitutive mutant.

The second type of constitutive mutant (Fig 5.9(b)) corresponded to a fault in the operator. A fault in the operator would prevent the repressor protein binding. If the repressor protein could not bind then it could not block the RNA polymerase and transcription of the structural genes would take place all the time. Again the bacterium would be a constitutive mutant.

The *lac* operon model allows predictions to be made and tested

The repressor protein was crucial to the *lac* operon model but Jacob and Monod had no direct evidence that this protein existed. The model predicted that the repressor protein would have to have the following properties:

- it was coded for by the regulatory gene;
- it binds to the operator;
- it binds to the inducer;
- it does not bind to the operator once it is bound to the inducer.

Since Jacob and Monod proposed the *lac* operon model in 1961, hundreds of scientists have studied it using more and more sophisticated techniques. In 1967 the repressor was isolated in a reasonably pure form and was

(a) constitutive mutant (type one)

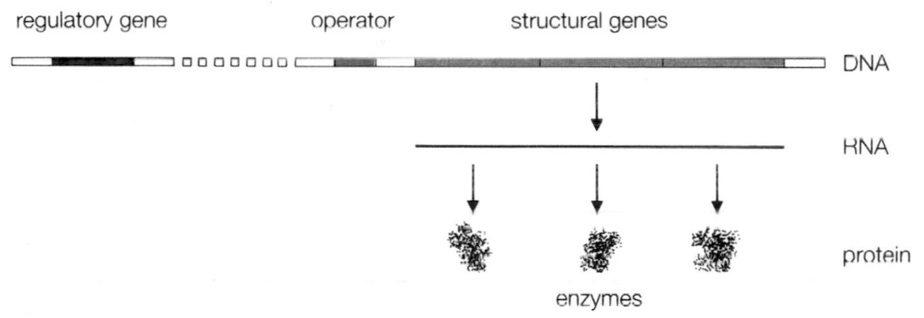

If there is a fault in the regulatory gene no functional repressor protein will be produced. This means that RNA polymerase can bind at all times so the enzymes will be produced all the time.

(b) constitutive mutant (type two)

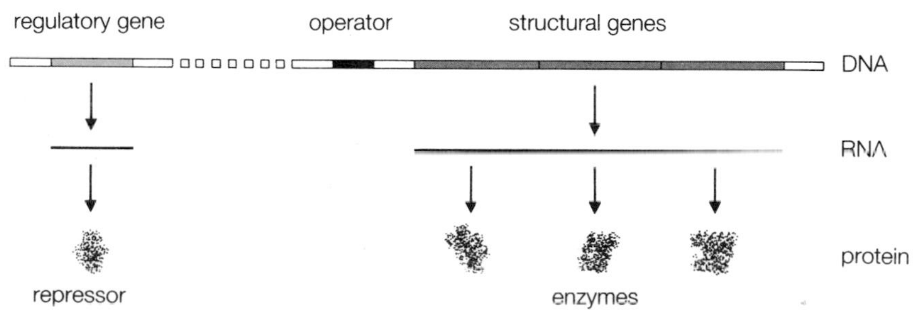

If there is a fault in the operator the repressor protein cannot bind to the DNA. This means that RNA polymerase can bind at all times so the enzymes will be produced all the time.

Fig 5.9 Constitutive mutants in the *lac* operon.

shown to have the characteristics of a protein: it was denatured at high temperatures and it was destroyed by proteases (enzymes that digest proteins).

Later it was shown that the repressor protein bound to the correct fragment of DNA, the one containing the operator, but did not bind to this DNA in the presence of the inducer. The inducer was isolated and identified as allolactose, an isomer of lactose. More recently, the repressor protein has been purified in large amounts, crystallised and studied by X-ray diffraction. Finally, using modern techniques, the relevant region of the *E. coli* chromosome has been sequenced in both the normal and the mutant strains. The evidence supporting the *lac* operon model is now overwhelming.

Other operons are controlled in a similar manner

The simplicity and clarity of the *lac* operon model inspired many scientists to seek out similar transcriptional control mechanisms in bacteria. Only one will be described here and it has been selected because it is subtly different to the *lac* operon in that the protein coded for by the regulatory gene switches on transcription of the structural genes rather than switching transcription off. The *lac* operon is an example of **negative control** while the *ara* operon is an example of **positive control**.

The *ara* operon is arranged in a similar way to the *lac* operon (Fig 5.10). The structural genes are clustered together. These genes code for the enzymes that are necessary for the bacterium to feed on the sugar arabinose. The regulatory gene is again some distance upstream. This regulatory gene codes for a protein called **araC**. Instead of being a repressor, araC is an **activator**. When araC is bound to the operator, again a little upstream from the structural genes, transcription of the structural genes takes place. When araC does not bind to the operator, transcription does not take place.

The *ara* operon appears to work in the following manner. The structural gene is transcribed all the time, producing RNA that codes for the araC protein. The araC protein is therefore always present in the cell. When arabinose is present in the solution (Fig 5.10(a)) an inducer substance is

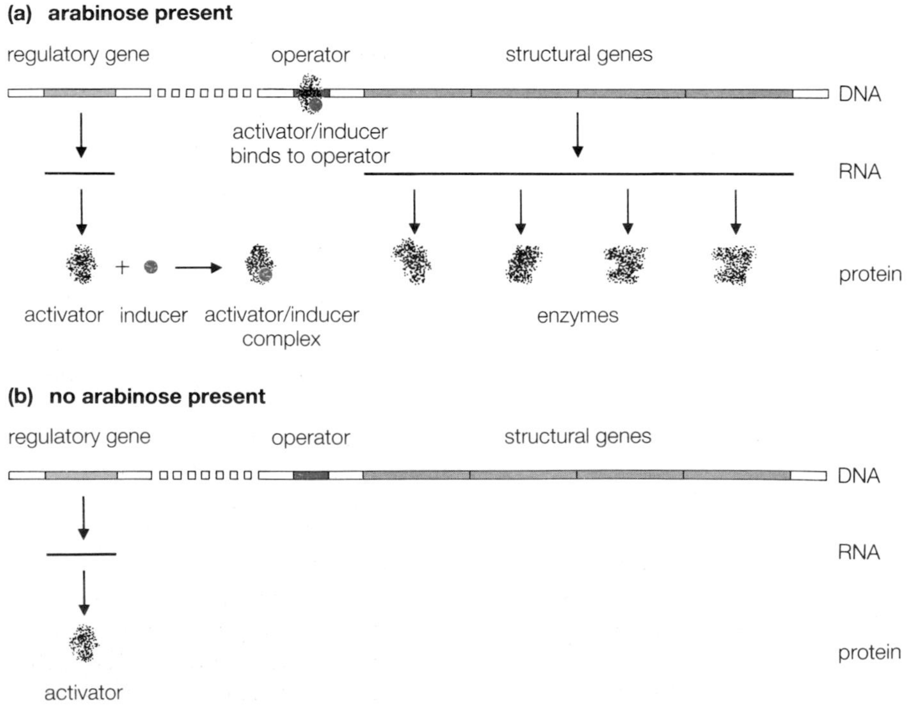

(a) arabinose present

regulatory gene · · · · · · · operator · · · · · · · structural genes

activator/inducer binds to operator

activator inducer activator/inducer complex · · · · · · · enzymes

(b) no arabinose present

regulatory gene · · · · · · · operator · · · · · · · structural genes

activator

Fig 5.10 The *ara* operon.

produced inside the cell. This inducer binds to araC and the araC then binds to the operator. Once the araC is bound to the operator, the RNA polymerase can bind and transcription takes place. When arabinose is not present in the solution (Fig 5.10(b)) no inducer is produced and the araC does not bind to the operator. This means that RNA polymerase cannot bind and no transcription takes place.

Some generalisations about control of transcription in bacteria

The operon model appears to be an accurate representation of the way that bacteria control transcription. A number of general points can be drawn from the many examples of operons that have been studied.

1. Genes occur in clusters with a single mechanism controlling the transcription of the whole group. The RNA polymerase transcribes all the genes at once, producing a single long mRNA molecule.
2. Regions occur upstream of genes, that control the transcription of genes by binding proteins. These are called **control sequences**. Some of these sequences are not specific to particular genes and must be present so that the RNA polymerase will bind: these make up the promoter. In the strictest sense a promoter is not a control sequence, as it is required by all genes. Other control sequences are specific to a particular set of genes and their regulation, for example the operator in the bacterial operon.
3. Proteins exist that control transcription of genes, apparently by affecting RNA polymerase binding. If the protein increases transcription it is called an activator, if it decreases transcription it is called a repressor.
4. In bacteria these proteins are produced constantly, and whether or not they bind to the operator is controlled by an inducer. Production of the inducer depends on the external environment. For example, allolactose is produced only when lactose is present in the external environment. The bacterium's initial response to an environmental change is to produce the appropriate inducer.

Control of transcription in eukaryotes may be very different from that in bacteria

In recent years scientists have started to apply the techniques developed to study transcriptional control in *E. coli* to eukaryotes. The results have been too varied, complex and sometimes confusing to describe in this book, but it is a fascinating field and it is worth picking out a few trends.

Firstly, *E. coli* contains only 1.34 mm of DNA while a human cell contains 2.2 m of DNA. A human cell contains 6×10^9 base pairs (6000 million base pairs) of DNA. An activator protein may bind to one sequence only 10 nucleotide residues long, so it would have to encounter that one particular little sequence out of 600 million possible 10-base-pair lengths. That is like trying to find one particular person out of the population of Europe and North Africa! There is some evidence that this problem is reduced by programmed packing of the DNA in the nucleus. Regions of the DNA that are not needed may be packed down tightly so that the proteins only have to diffuse though part of the genome to find their particular control sequence. The regions that are 'packed away' are thought to vary, depending on the type of cell.

Secondly, eukaryotic genes are arranged differently to bacterial genes. They are arranged singly, each with its own control region. Eukaryotic genes are also broken up: the coding regions, called **exons**, are separated by non-coding regions, called **introns** (Fig 5.11). No one is certain what these introns are for. The eukaryotic genome also contains a vast amount of DNA that appears to have no function and certainly does not code for proteins.

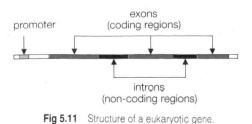

promoter

exons
(coding regions)

introns
(non-coding regions)

Fig 5.11 Structure of a eukaryotic gene.

Another problem is that some genomes are more stable than others. Certain eukaryotic organisms break all the rules and shuffle their genome into different arrangements depending on the circumstances. This even happens in certain human cells. The genomes of lymphocytes, the cells that produce antibodies, are rearranged radically in order to generate the necessary diversity to produce all the different antibodies needed to defend the body against so many potential invaders. To add even more confusion, some organisms, for example wheat, have mobile DNA sequences called **transposons** that skip around the genome of the cell, altering the transcriptional activity of individual genes.

Fourthly, negative control such as demonstrated by the *lac* operon appears to be very rare in eukaryotes. The proteins that have been identified as having a role in transcriptional control all appear to be activators. This is not very surprising, as a eukaryotic cell contains vastly more genes than a bacterium. In a bacterium, keeping unneeded genes switched off is probably as easy as switching necessary genes on. However, in a eukaryote, where thousands of unneeded genes would have to be kept switched off for the whole of the lifetime of the organism, it seems an unlikely mechanism that has too great a chance of developing a fault.

However, some of the elements in bacterial transcriptional control do occur in eukaryotes. Transcriptional control definitely occurs in eukaryotes and it appears to be the major mechanism by which eukaryotic cells control which proteins they produce. Activator proteins do exist, they do bind to control regions that are usually upstream from the gene coding for the protein and this binding does affects RNA polymerase activity. However, no scientist, however optimistic by nature, would say that transcription control in eukaryotes is fully understood.

QUESTIONS

5.11 Study Fig 5.8. What would be the effect of the following:
(a) putting lactose into a solution containing normal *E. coli*;
(b) removing lactose from a solution containing normal *E. coli*?

5.12 Study Fig 5.8. How would the following mutant *E. coli* behave when in (i) a solution without lactose and (ii) a solution containing lactose?
(a) one with a fault in the regulatory gene that prevented that gene being transcribed;
(b) one with a fault in the operator that prevented the repressor protein binding;
(c) one with a fault in the operator that caused it to bind the repressor protein even when the repressor protein was bound to the inducer;
(d) one with a fault in the regulatory gene that allowed the regulatory gene to be transcribed and the repressor protein to be produced but meant that the repressor protein could not bind the inducer;
(e) one with a fault that meant that lactose outside the cell did not produce inducer inside the cell?

5.13 Study Fig 5.10. What would be the effect of the following:
(a) putting arabinose into a solution containing normal *E. coli*;
(b) removing arabinose from a solution containing normal *E. coli*?

5.14 Study Fig 5.10. How would the following mutant *E. coli* behave when in (i) a solution without arabinose and (ii) a solution containing arabinose?
(a) one with a fault in the regulatory gene that prevented that gene being transcribed;

ACCESSING THE GENETIC INFORMATION

(b) one with a fault in the operator that prevented the araC binding;

(c) one with a fault in the operator that caused it to bind araC even when the araC was not bound to the inducer;

(d) one with a fault in the regulatory gene that allowed the regulatory gene to be transcribed and araC to be produced but meant that the araC could not bind the inducer;

(e) one with a fault that meant that arabinose outside the cell did not produce inducer inside the cell?

5.15 (a) What is a repressor protein? How does this affect transcription?
(b) What is an activator protein? How does this affect transcription?

5.16 Consider a prokaryotic cell and a eukaryotic cell. What are the problems with applying the simple operon model to the control of eukaryotic transcription?

DATA HANDLING 5.3

Study Fig 5.12, which shows the *trp* operon. The *trp* operon contains the genes that code for the enzymes that synthesise the amino acid tryptophan. The bacterium must produce tryptophan when required but should 'turn off' tryptophan synthesis when there is enough tryptophan present in the cell.

(a) Which letter represents the regulatory gene?
(b) Which letter represents the operator?
(c) Which letter represents the promoter for the operon?
(d) Which letters represent the genes coding for the enzymes that synthesise tryptophan?
(e) Do you expect transcription of the *trp* operon to be high or low when there is a large amount of tryptophan in the cell?

The protein coded for by the regulator gene only binds to the operator when tryptophan is present. The tryptophan binds to the protein, changing its shape so that it can bind to the operator.

(f) Does the protein act as a repressor or an activator?
(g) Explain what will happen when the amount of tryptophan in the cell falls.
(h) Explain what will happen when the amount of tryptophan in the cell rises.

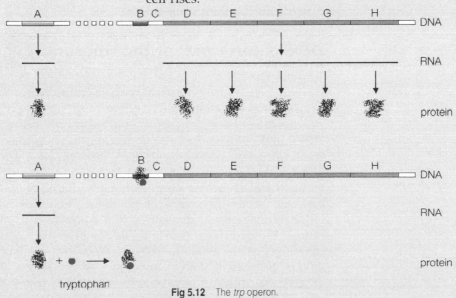

Fig 5.12 The *trp* operon.

5.4 THE DIFFERENT TYPES OF RNA

Not all RNAs carry information for the synthesis of proteins. There are many different types of RNA molecule in the cell, all of which are transcribed from the DNA. The three most studied are **messenger RNA (mRNA) transfer RNA (tRNA)** and **ribosomal RNA (rRNA)**.

mRNAs carry the genetic information for proteins

As mentioned in section 5.3, bacterial genes are often transcribed together, producing a single mRNA that codes for many polypeptides. In contrast, eukaryotic genes are transcribed singly, producing an mRNA that codes for a single polypeptide.

Eukaryotic mRNA synthesis is more complicated that mRNA synthesis in a bacterium. Eukaryotic genes contain **introns**, non-coding regions within the genes. These are transcribed along with the regions of the DNA that do code for proteins, so they are present in the initial transcript (Fig 5.13(a)). Also, the initial transcript is modified as it is produced: a **5′ cap** is added to the 5′ end and a **poly A** tail is added to the 3′ end (Fig 5.13(a)). Without the 5′ cap and the poly A tail the mRNA is not handled properly by the cellular machinery. The poly A tail also makes the mRNA more stable in the cytoplasm.

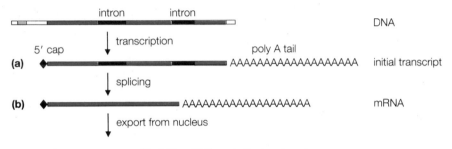

Fig 5.13   mRNA production in eukaryotes.

The non-coding regions then have to be removed from the RNA (Fig 5.13(b)). This is called **splicing** because the unwanted sequence is cut out of the RNA by enzymes and then the two cut ends are rejoined, much like splicing an audio or video tape. Only mRNA molecules that have been spliced properly are exported from the nucleus. In eukaryotic cells the DNA is in the nucleus while protein synthesis occurs in the cytoplasm on the ribosomes. The properly processed mRNAs are exported from the nucleus through the nuclear pores, transferring the genetic information from the nucleus to the cytoplasm.

rRNAs form part of the ribosome

Another form of RNA in the cell is rRNA. rRNA is found in the ribosome, the structure in the cytoplasm which synthesises proteins. Every ribosome in a bacterial cell contains five different rRNA molecules and fifty different polypeptides. Every ribosome in a eukaryotic cell contains four different rRNA molecules and more than eighty polypeptides. rRNA molecules are transcribed by a specialised RNA polymerase from genes called rRNA genes.

A cell that is synthesising a large amount of protein, for example a root cap cell, needs thousands of ribosomes and thousands of molecules of rRNA to make those ribosomes. In a eukaryotic cell, like the root cap cell, there is the additional problem that the proteins for the ribosome are made in the cytoplasm while the rRNA molecules are made in the nucleus. Most eukaryotic cells contain many copies of the rRNA genes, so that enough rRNA molecules can be produced. The rRNA genes are scattered throughout the genome but the different rRNA genes on different chromosomes

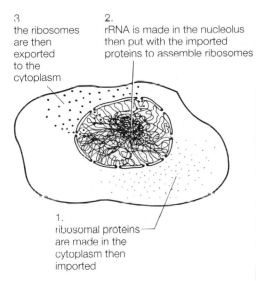

3 the ribosomes are then exported to the cytoplasm

2. rRNA is made in the nucleolus then put with the imported proteins to assemble ribosomes

1. ribosomal proteins are made in the cytoplasm then imported

Fig 5.15 Ribosome synthesis and assembly.

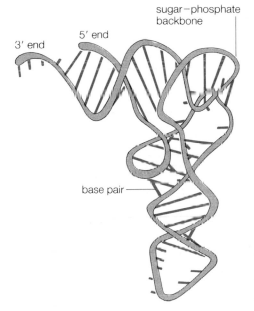

sugar−phosphate backbone

5′ end

3′ end

base pair

Fig 5.16 The 3D structure of a tRNA molecule.

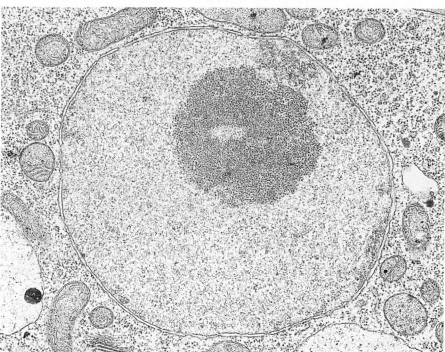

Fig 5.14 The nucleolus as seen using the electron microscope. (Magnification × 22 000)

are brought together between cell divisions in a specialised structure called the **nucleolus** (Fig 5.14).

The proteins needed for the ribosomes are imported into the nucleus and into the nucleolus. The ribosomes are then assembled in the nucleolus itself from the newly transcribed rRNA molecules and the imported proteins. The finished ribosomes are then exported back into the cytoplasm through the nuclear pores (Fig 5.15).

tRNAs have a role in protein synthesis

tRNAs are also transcribed from DNA by an RNA polymerase. tRNAs have an essential role in protein synthesis that is discussed in Chapter 6. In brief, the tRNAs are responsible for bringing the amino acids to the ribosome in the correct order. There are more than twenty different tRNAs, each transcribed from a separate gene. tRNA molecules have been studied thoroughly and the generalised structure shown in Fig 5.16 illustrates that RNA molecules can have precise three-dimensional shapes. The shape of the tRNA molecules is maintained by base pairing between different parts of the polynucleotide chain.

QUESTIONS

5.17 Describe three modifications that have to take place to the initial transcript of a gene to make an mRNA molecule. What would happen to an mRNA molecule that had been processed wrongly?

5.18 (a) What is a nucleolus?
(b) List two functions of the nucleolus.
(c) What would you infer if a cell had more than one nucleolus or if it had a very large nucleolus?

5.19 How does a eukaryotic cell produce ribosomes for use in protein synthesis?

5.20 A gene contains the genetic information for a polypeptide. Why are the terms 'rRNA gene' and 'tRNA gene' inappropriate?

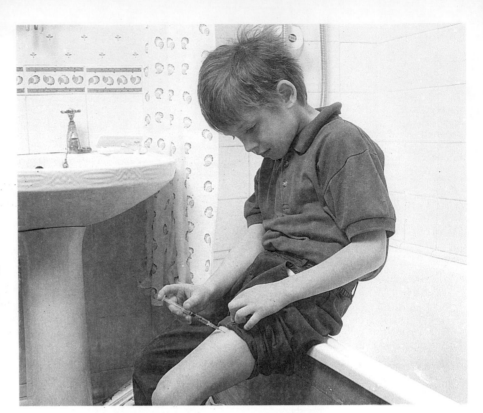

Fig 5.17 A bacterial cell has been persuaded to make the life-saving human insulin which this boy is injecting. A gene coding for human insulin was created from insulin messenger RNA using reverse transcriptase and then linked to a bacterial promoter. This engineered gene was then placed into a bacterial plasmid and forced through the bacterial cell membrane and into the cell. The bacterial transcription and translation mechanism is unable to distinguish between the human gene and its own and makes the insulin protein in large amounts. The foreign gene is replicated by the cell's enzymes and passed on to the next generation of bacteria.

REVIEW OF CRUCIAL POINTS

- The genetic information, the DNA, is arranged as genes. Each gene contains the genetic information for one polypeptide. This is called the one gene–one polypeptide hypothesis.

- The genetic information in the DNA is transferred to RNA molecules by a process called transcription. The RNA molecules are synthesised on the DNA template by RNA polymerase and the RNA produced is complementary to the DNA. The RNA polymerase binds upstream of the beginning of the gene at specific sequences called promoters: these promoters locate the RNA polymerase so that transcription always begins at the correct position. Only one strand of the DNA is transcribed, producing a single-stranded RNA molecule that has been synthesised 5' to 3'.

- RNA molecules can be mRNAs, rRNAs or tRNAs. All three types are transcribed from DNA, each by a different RNA polymerase. mRNAs carry the genetic information for proteins out into the cytoplasm where protein synthesis takes place. rRNAs form part of the ribosome. tRNAs have an essential role in protein synthesis: tRNAs bring the amino acids that will make up a polypeptide into the ribosome in the correct order.

- Although rRNAs and tRNAs are required by all cells, different cells require different mRNAs at different times. The process of transcription is controlled so that genes coding for those proteins that are needed are transcribed while others are not. Control of transcription in bacteria is quite well understood, the best studied example being the *lac* operon. The situation in eukaryotes appears to be a lot more varied and is not well understood. A few basic principles have been established: specific sequences outside the coding region of the gene, usually upstream, bind specific proteins that modify the probability of RNA polymerase binding to the promoter.

ACCESSING THE GENETIC INFORMATION

Chapter 6

IMPLEMENTING THE GENETIC INFORMATION

The cell contains the genetic information within its DNA and the parts of this information that are relevant to a particular cell are transcribed into messenger RNA and used to make proteins. Proteins are the building blocks and the workers of the cell: if the DNA is a book of house plans, and the messenger RNAs in a cell are the plan for a particular house, then the proteins are both the house itself and all the workers required to build it. This chapter addresses the problem of how a linear polynucleotide with only four different ribonucleotides can carry the information for thousands of different proteins, each with a unique three-dimensional structure that determines its function.

LEARNING OBJECTIVES

After studying this chapter you should:

1. understand how the genetic code allows information to flow from DNA to RNA to protein;

2. be able to describe the process of translation;

3. appreciate how the sequence of amino acid residues in a polypeptide determines its unique three-dimensional shape;

4. be able to discuss how the function of a protein depends on its structure using haemoglobin and collagen to illustrate your arguments.

6.1 BREAKING THE CODE

The genetic code is based on triplets of nucleotide residues

Once the structure of the double helix was known, scientists realised that it was probably the order of nucleotide residues in the DNA that contained the information for the polypeptide. However, it was not immediately obvious how the order of nucleotides could code for a polypeptide. One insight came from knowing that each protein has a unique sequence of amino acid residues in the polypeptide. Scientists speculated that the order of nucleotides in the DNA determined the order in which the amino acids were joined to make the polypeptide.

There are twenty common amino acids but only four different nucleotide residues. Obviously one nucleotide residue cannot code for one amino acid because this would cater for only four amino acids (4^1). If two nucleotide residues coded for a single amino acid there would be 16 possible pairs of nucleotide residues (4^2), still not enough to cater for all the amino acids. If three nucleotide residues coded for every one amino acid then there would be 64 possible combinations (4^3), definitely enough to cater for all the amino acids with some to spare. Scientists were therefore predisposed towards a genetic code that had three nucleotide residues coding for each amino acid: a **triplet** code. The triplets were called **codons**.

The discovery of mRNA opened the way to breaking the genetic code

Until the late 1950s it was not clear how the information got from the DNA to the relevant protein. At that time evidence began to accumulate that a special type of RNA molecule interacted with ribosomes and that if these RNA molecules were changed the polypeptide synthesised by the ribosomes changed. Finally, it was shown that when bacteria were infected by a bacteriophage a new version of this type of RNA molecule was produced after the viral DNA entered the cells. Scientists hypothesised that this RNA was a **messenger RNA** that carried the information from the DNA to the ribosomes.

Once the existence of mRNA molecules was established, scientists concentrated on how the genetic code in the DNA was transcribed into the mRNA and then translated during protein synthesis on the ribosome. mRNAs are transcribed from DNA by RNA polymerase (section 5.2) and the sequence of nucleotides in the mRNA is a complementary version of the sequence of nucleotide residues in the DNA. This meant that if they could break the code present in the mRNA, scientists would also break the genetic code itself.

The first real progress in breaking the genetic code came from a scientist realising that an unexpected result was exciting rather than irritating. Marshall Nirenberg had been investigating protein synthesis using extracts from bacterial cells. He was adding different RNAs to the cell extract and seeing whether more protein was produced. He decided to add a man-made RNA to the extract as a control and added polyuridylic acid (..UUUUUUUU..). There was a sudden increase in the amount of phenylalanine being put into polypeptides. It turned out that the extract was making a polypeptide made of only phenylalanine residues, ..Phe-Phe-Phe-Phe-Phe.. .

This was the big break. The codon UUU was tentatively assigned to phenylalanine and scientists rushed to perform similar experiments. The first few were simple: a polyA polynucleotide increased the incorporation of lysine into a polypeptide, so AAA was thought to be the code for lysine; a polyG polynucleotide increased the incorporation of glycine into a polypeptide so GGG was thought to code for glycine; a polyC polynucleotide increased the incorporation of proline into a polypeptide so CCC was thought to code for proline. After that the scientists had to design more devious experiments in order to assign the various codons to the correct amino acids. One approach they used was to make polynucleotides from mixtures of two nucleotides in various ratios. Another even more decisive approach depended on another discovery, that of tRNA molecules.

tRNAs act as 'adaptors' in translation of the genetic code

One hypothesis that came from thinking about a problem rather than an experimental approach was that of an **adaptor molecule** which had been published by Francis Crick in 1955. Crick considered the structure of a polynucleotide and the structure of an amino acid and came to the conclusion that it was very unlikely that the amino acids would interact directly with the polynucleotide. He suggested that there was an adaptor molecule that would 'plug' an amino acid into the polynucleotide. As the adaptor would have to 'read' the sequence of nucleotide residues in the polynucleotide Crick suggested that the adaptor molecule was an RNA so that the bases in the adaptor RNA could hydrogen bond with the bases in the polynucleotide, The adaptor molecule would also have to interact with only one specific amino acid so Crick suggested that it was a relatively large molecule, with a specific shape, so that one adaptor molecule could be distinguished from another.

Soon after Crick made his suggestion, another scientist, Mahlon Hoagland, discovered a population of soluble RNA molecules in the cell that had amino acids covalently attached to them. These seemed the perfect candidates for Crick's adaptor molecules because they were RNAs and because they interacted with amino acids. Similar RNA molecules were also described by two other scientists, Paul Berg and Robert Holley. Later these RNA molecules became known as **transfer RNAs** or tRNAs.

The genetic code is finally solved using aminoacyl-tRNAs

tRNAs were discovered because they were found in the cell covalently bonded to amino acids. A molecule that contains both groups is called an **aminoacyl-tRNA**. These aminoacyl-tRNAs were used to finally solve the genetic code. The final breakthrough was made by Nirenberg, the scientist who had started it all, and his co-workers. They discovered that putting a synthetic trinucleotide into a cell extract stimulated the binding of a specific aminoacyl-tRNA to the ribosomes. For example, the artificial trinucleotide $^{5'}GUG^{3'}$ stimulated valine-tRNA binding to the ribosomes, so it was deduced that GUG was the codon for valine.

With this technique, 61 out of the 64 possible codons were assigned to amino acids (Table 6.1). The final three, UAA, UAG and UGA turned out to be codons that marked the end of the polypeptide chain.

Table 6.1 The genetic code

First position [5' end]	Second position				Third position [3' end]
	U	C	A	G	
U	Phe	Ser	Tyr	Cys	U
	Phe	Ser	Tyr	Cys	C
	Leu	Ser	STOP	STOP	A
	Leu	Ser	STOP	Trp	G
C	Leu	Pro	His	Arg	U
	Leu	Pro	His	Arg	C
	Leu	Pro	Gln	Arg	A
	Leu	Pro	Gln	Arg	G
A	Ile	Thr	Asn	Ser	U
	Ile	Thr	Asn	Ser	C
	Ile	Thr	Lys	Arg	A
	Met	Thr	Lys	Arg	G
G	Val	Ala	Asp	Gly	U
	Val	Ala	Asp	Gly	C
	Val	Ala	Glu	Gly	A
	Val	Ala	Glu	Gly	G

Ala = alanine   Arg = arginine   Asn = asparagine   Asp = aspartic acid
Cys = cysteine   Gln = glutamine   Glu = glutamic acid   Gly = glycine
His = histidine   Ile = isoleucine   Leu = leucine   Lys = lysine
Met = methionine   Phe = phenylalanine   Pro = proline   Ser = serine
Thr = threonine   Trp = tryptophan   Tyr = tyrosine   Val = valine

Breaking the genetic code was one of the most significant advances in molecular biology because it finally established the functional basis of the link between the gene and the protein. Although the code was broken using viruses and bacteria it appears to be universal: every organism, from a virus to a giant sequoia tree, uses the same language. There is little doubt that the genetic code dates from so deep in the evolutionary past that every organism in existence today is descended from the organisms in which it evolved. Perhaps it is older than the cell itself.

QUESTIONS

6.1 (a) How many nucleotide residues would there have to be in a codon in order for there to be enough codons to code for all 20 amino acids if:
   (i) there were 3 bases instead of 4;
   (ii) there were 5 bases instead of 4?
   (b) Suggest a reason why there are 4 different bases rather than 3 or 5.

6.2 A coding strand of a gene reads $^{3'}$AAAAATGAAGGGATGCGA$^{5'}$.
   (a) What would be the sequence in the complementary strand of the DNA?
   (b) What would be the sequence in the mRNA?
   (c) What would be the sequence of amino acid residues in the polypeptide?
   (d) If there was a mutation in the gene that changed the sequence to $^{3'}$AAAAATGAAGGGATTCGA$^{5'}$ what effect would this have on the polypeptide?

6.3 A bacterial polypeptide has the sequence Met-Ala-Ser-His-Gly-Ile. The same polypeptide from a mutant strain has the sequence Met-Ala-Cys-Gln-Gly-Ile. How many point mutations (changes in individual nucleotide residues) would be needed to cause this change in the polypeptide?

6.2 TRANSLATION

Protein synthesis on a ribosome is a very precise and carefully regulated process. The information in the mRNA is used to ensure that the amino acids are inserted in the correct order to make the particular polypeptide for which the gene codes. The process by which this is achieved is called **translation** because information in the mRNA is 'translated' to form a polypeptide. For translation to take place three components are required: the mRNA, ribosomes and aminoacyl-tRNAs.

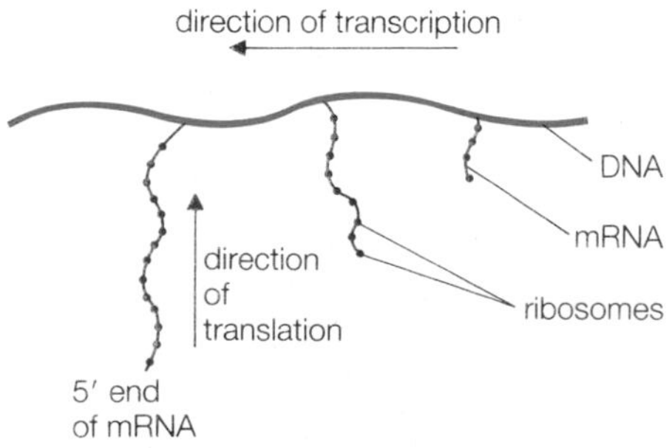

Translation requires mRNA to code for the polypeptide

The mRNA is transcribed from the gene (section 5.2). The sequence of ribonucleotide residues in the mRNA codes for the polypeptide: each triplet of nucleotide residues forms one codon that codes for a single amino acid (section 6.1).

For protein synthesis to take place the mRNA must bind one or more ribosomes. In bacterial cells, where there is no nucleus, the ribosomes bind to the 5' end of the mRNA as soon as it is transcribed (Fig 6.1). However in eukaryotic cells, cells with a nucleus, the mRNA must be processed and exported from the nucleus before it can associate with the ribosomes (section 5.4).

Fig 6.1 Translation in a bacterial cell. In prokaryotic cells translation begins as soon as the mRNA is clear of the DNA. The ribosomes travel along the mRNA one after another and many ribosomes can be on one mRNA molecule at the same time. This information was obtained by studying electron micrographs of DNA from bacteria that had been spread on a grid.

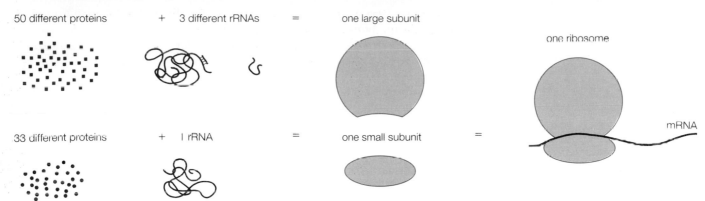

| 50 different proteins | + | 3 different rRNAs | = | one large subunit |
| 33 different proteins | + | 1 rRNA | = | one small subunit |

one ribosome

mRNA

Fig 6.2 The eukaryotic ribosome. Ribosomes are complicated machines made from many different components. The ribosomes exist in the cell as the large and small subunits and only form the complete ribosome on the mRNA.

Ribosomes are complex

The ribosome is a very complicated machine: the ribosomes in a eukaryotic cell contain four different ribosomal RNA molecules and 83 different proteins assembled into two different subunits (Fig 6.2). The structure of the ribosome is very precise, like a complex three-dimensional puzzle.

The ribosome is more than a passive site where protein synthesis takes place. Many of the 83 proteins in the ribosome have an active role in the synthesis of the polypeptide: some are the enzymes that catalyse the polymerisation of the amino acids; others ensure that the ribosome is exactly the right shape to bind the mRNA and the aminoacyl-tRNAs; others move the ribosome along the mRNA molecule in a 5' to 3' direction during the protein synthesis process.

Transfer RNA molecules bring amino acids into the ribosome

Protein synthesis requires a supply of amino acids to be polymerised to make the polypeptide. These are brought to the ribosome by transfer RNA (tRNA) molecules. tRNAs are linear polynucleotides like all RNAs but they

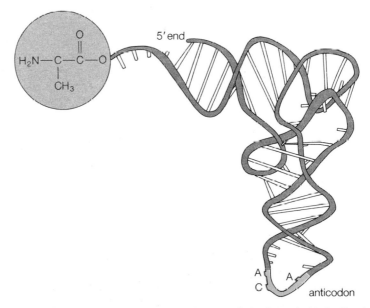

5' end

anticodon

Fig 6.3 Aminoacyl-tRNA molecule. The amino acid, in this case alanine, is attached to the 3' end of the tRNA molecule. In another region of the tRNA molecule there is one of the anticodons for alanine, ACA.

are folded into a precise three-dimensional shape that is maintained by base pairing between the nucleotide residues in different parts of the molecule (Fig 6.3). All tRNAs have a similar shape but there are over twenty distinct tRNAs in the cell: each different tRNA carries a particular amino acid.

The amino acid is attached covalently to the 3′ end of the tRNA molecule, making an aminoacyl-tRNA (Fig 6.3). The amino acid is linked to the correct tRNA molecule by a specific enzyme, an aminoacyl-tRNA synthetase. There are over twenty aminoacyl-tRNA synthetases, one for each aminoacyl-tRNA. Each enzyme binds both tRNA and amino acid and catalyses the linking reaction.

tRNAs are the adaptors that translate the information in the mRNA into the polypeptide

All tRNAs have three unpaired ribonucleotide residues that protrude from one side of the molecule (Fig 6.3). This triplet of unpaired residues has a crucial role in the translation process because it interacts with the codons in the mRNA. The triplet of unpaired ribonucleotide residues in the tRNA is called the **anticodon**. The anticodon varies from one tRNA to another, just as the amino acid the tRNA carries varies from one tRNA to the next.

The mRNA is a string of codons and each codon in the mRNA base pairs in turn with the anticodon of a tRNA molecule. Only the correct tRNA, with the correct anticodon and bearing the correct amino acid, will base pair to that particular codon. In this way the amino acids are brought into the ribosome in the correct order so that the sequence of amino acids in the polypeptide reflects the order of codons in the mRNA and ultimately the information in the DNA.

Translation occurs within the ribosome

The process of translation has been closely studied and is understood in great detail. An outline of the process is shown in Fig 6.4.

The ribosome has two sites: the A-site and the P-site. The mRNA, the ribosome and the aminoacyl-tRNA are brought together in a complicated initiation procedure. Once this is finished the first codon of the mRNA is in the P-site of the ribosome and the appropriate aminoacyl-tRNA is base paired to the first codon (Fig 6.4(a)). The first codon is usually AUG and it codes for methionine. Another aminoacyl-tRNA, the one complementary to the second codon, comes into the A-site and hydrogen bonds form between the codon and the anticodon (Fig 6.4(b)).

There is now one aminoacyl-tRNA opposite the first codon in the A-site and another aminoacyl-tRNA opposite the second codon in the A-site. Four events then happen almost simultaneously:

- a peptide bond forms between the two amino acids, forming a dipeptide (Fig 6.4(c));
- the covalent bond between the amino acid residue and the tRNA in the P-site is broken (Fig 6.4(c));
- the tRNA is released from the P-site;
- the ribosome moves on so that the second tRNA, the one attached to the dipeptide, moves into the P-site (Fig 6.4(d)).

The third codon of the mRNA is now in the A-site. Another aminoacyl-tRNA comes into the A-site, base pairing with the third codon (Fig 6.4(e)). The same four events occur:

- a peptide bond forms between the dipeptide in the P-site and the amino acid in the A-site, forming a tripeptide;

IMPLEMENTING THE GENETIC INFORMATION

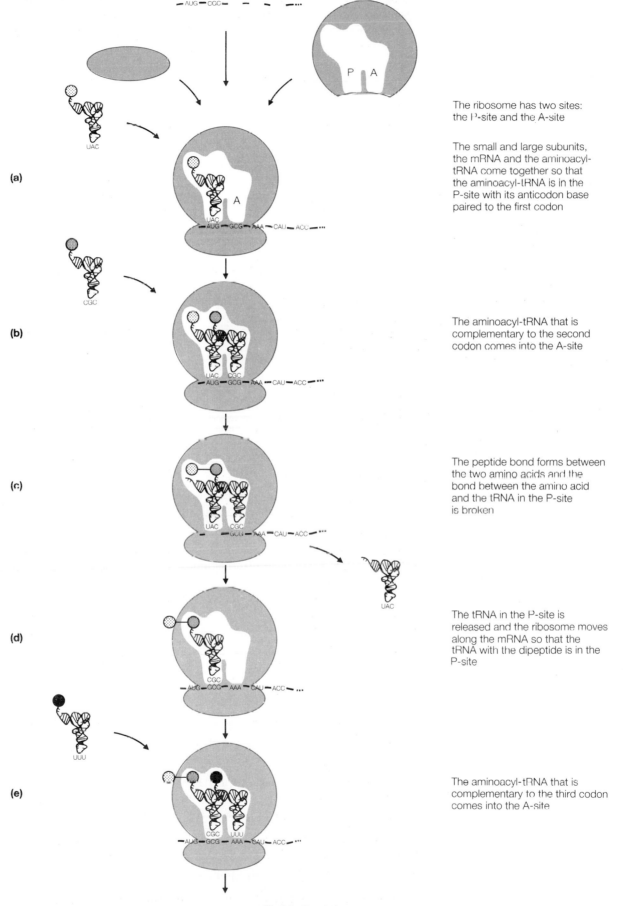

The ribosome has two sites: the P-site and the A-site

The small and large subunits, the mRNA and the aminoacyl-tRNA come together so that the aminoacyl-tRNA is in the P-site with its anticodon base paired to the first codon

The aminoacyl-tRNA that is complementary to the second codon comes into the A-site

The peptide bond forms between the two amino acids and the bond between the amino acid and the tRNA in the P-site is broken

The tRNA in the P-site is released and the ribosome moves along the mRNA so that the tRNA with the dipeptide is in the P-site

The aminoacyl-tRNA that is complementary to the third codon comes into the A-site

Fig 6.4 Translation.

- the covalent bond between the amino acid residue and the tRNA in the P-site is broken;
- the tRNA is released from the P-site;
- the ribosome moves on so that the second tRNA, the one attached to the tripeptide, moves into the P-site.

This process continues until the last codon, a codon for which there is no aminoacyl-tRNA, moves into the A-site. When the covalent bond between the polypeptide and the tRNA in the P-site is broken, the polypeptide and the tRNA are released.

In this way the ribosome moves down the mRNA from the 5' to the 3' end, synthesising the polypeptide. Once the first ribosome is clear of the 5' end of the mRNA another ribosome may bind and begin synthesising another polypeptide. Often many ribosomes will be translating the mRNA at once, forming a structure called a polyribosome or **polysome** (Fig 6.5).

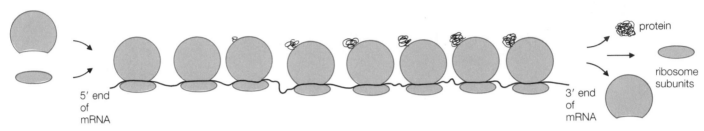

Fig 6.5   A polysome. Many ribosomes can travel one after the other along the mRNA.

QUESTIONS

6.4 **(a)** What codons will base pair to the following anticodons:
$^{3'}AAA^{5'}$;
$^{3'}CCC^{5'}$;
$^{3'}TAC^{5'}$?
(b) What amino acids do these codons code for (see Table 6.1)?
(c) Where would you find an anticodon?
(d) Where would you find a codon?

6.5. A tRNA molecule:
- forms a covalent bond with one particular amino acid;
- has three unpaired nucleotide residues that stick out from the molecule;
- has a very specific three-dimensional shape.
How are these three properties important in protein synthesis?

6.6. **(a)** List three of the functions of the proteins that are found in the ribosome.
(b) What other substance forms part of the ribosome?
(c) What is the name of the structure formed when many ribosomes are translating the same mRNA?

6.7. **(a)** What is the general formula for an amino acid?
(b) What is the formula for glycine?
(c) Write a balanced equation for the formation of a tripeptide with three glycine residues from a dipeptide and an amino acid.
(d) On your diagram label the peptide bond that has formed and label the N-terminal and the C-terminal of the polypeptide.
(e) What type of chemical reaction occurs during the polymerisation process?

IMPLEMENTING THE GENETIC INFORMATION

6.3 A TALE OF TWO PROTEINS

Genes have their effect in organisms through the proteins they code for. Yet all proteins are essentially the same: they are all made from the same twenty amino acids joined by the same peptide bonds in a long, unbranched polymer. How can such a simple polymer give rise to the thousands of different proteins in the cell, proteins as different as haemoglobin and collagen? Haemoglobin is the protein that fills red blood cells: the function of haemoglobin is to carry oxygen around the body. Collagen is the protein that makes up tendons and forms a network in the skin and in bone: the function of collagen is to make a structural material that has great strength when it is pulled. This section deals with how two chemically similar polypeptides can fulfil two such different functions.

Table 6.2 lists some of the properties of haemoglobin and type I collagen. Type I collagen is the collagen that is found in tendons, skin and bone. Other types of collagen are found in other parts of the body and have slightly different properties.

(a)

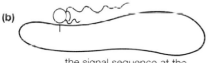

the ribosome begins to translate the mRNA. The signal sequence clears the ribosome

(b)

the signal sequence at the N-terminal end of the polypeptide interacts with the membrane of the endoplasmic reticulum

(c)

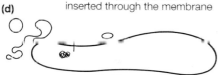

the growing polypeptide is inserted through the membrane

(d)

when all of the polypeptide has been inserted into the lumen of the endoplasmic reticulum the signal sequence is chopped off the polypeptide

(e)

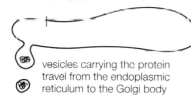

vesicles carrying the protein travel from the endoplasmic reticulum to the Golgi body

(f)

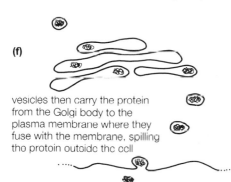

vesicles then carry the protein from the Golgi body to the plasma membrane where they fuse with the membrane, spilling the protein outside the cell

Fig 6.6 Extracellular proteins are synthesised on membrane-bound ribosomes.

The endoplasmic reticulum is a membranous organelle in eukaryotic cells. The Golgi body is a subcellular organelle (see Fig 3.1).

Table 6.2

	Haemoglobin	Type I collagen
function:	oxygen transport	tensile strength
location:	cytoplasmic	extracellular
solubility:	soluble	insoluble
final form:	globular protein	50 nm fibril
precursor:	none	procollagen
subunits:	assembled directly from polypeptides	tropocollagen
different polypeptides:	α-globin, β-globin	α1(I), α2(I)
number of polypeptides:	four per haemoglobin two α-globin, two β-globin	three per tropocollagen precursor two α1(I), one α2(I)
prosthetic groups:	four haem, one per globin	none
sensitivity:	sensitive to its environment	insensitive to its environment

Extracellular proteins are synthesised on membrane-bound ribosomes

Haemoglobin is an intracellular protein, found in the cytoplasm of red blood cells, while type I collagen is a protein that is only found outside cells. There must be a signal that tells the cell where the protein should end up and there must also be a mechanism by which certain proteins are exported from the cell. The signal is in the polypeptide. The N-terminal ends of the polypeptides that make up collagen, α1(I) and α2(I), both have a short sequence of amino acid residues called a **signal sequence**. As soon as the N-terminal end of the polypeptide is synthesised and pokes out of the ribosome this signal sequence interacts with the membrane of the endoplasmic reticulum (Fig 6.6(b)). The ribosome synthesising the protein becomes stuck to the cytoplasmic side of the endoplasmic reticulum membrane (Fig 6.7).

As the rest of the polypeptide is made it is pushed through the membrane and into the lumen of the endoplasmic reticulum, probably through a special protein (Fig 6.6(c)). As the polypeptide comes through the membrane the signal sequence is removed from the N-terminal end by an

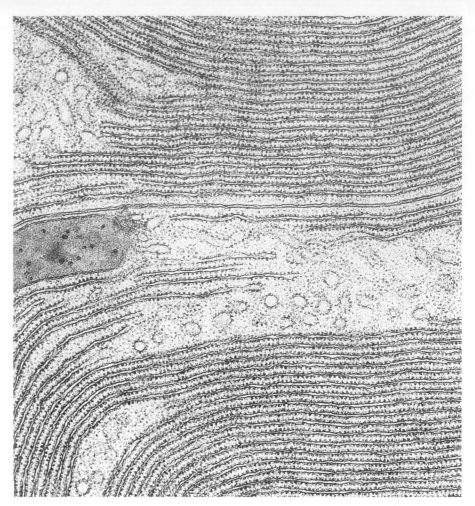

Fig 6.7 Ribosomes (the tiny black dots) bound to the cytoplasmic face of the endoplasmic reticulum as seen using an electron microscope.

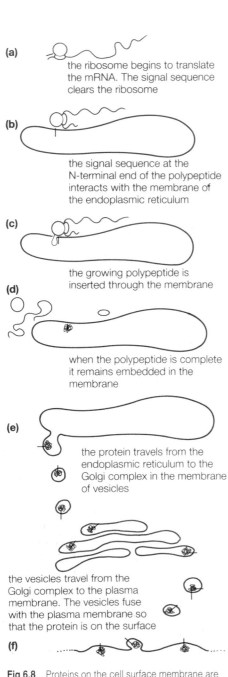

(a)

the ribosome begins to translate the mRNA. The signal sequence clears the ribosome

(b)

the signal sequence at the N-terminal end of the polypeptide interacts with the membrane of the endoplasmic reticulum

(c)

the growing polypeptide is inserted through the membrane

(d)

when the polypeptide is complete it remains embedded in the membrane

(e)

the protein travels from the endoplasmic reticulum to the Golgi complex in the membrane of vesicles

the vesicles travel from the Golgi complex to the plasma membrane. The vesicles fuse with the plasma membrane so that the protein is on the surface

(f)

Fig 6.8 Proteins on the cell surface membrane are synthesised on membrane-bound ribosomes.

enzyme (Fig 6.6(d)). The polypeptides are then carried by a series of vesicles first to the Golgi body and then to the plasma membrane (Fig 6.6(e)). The vesicles then fuse with the plasma membrane, spilling their contents out into the extracellular fluid (Fig 6.6(f)).

All proteins that are going to be exported from the cell have signal sequences and are synthesised on membrane-bound ribosomes. The polypeptides are then carried to the plasma membrane in a similar way to the collagen polypeptides. Proteins that are going to end up in the membrane of the cell are synthesised and transported in a similar fashion, but they remain embedded in the membrane (Fig 6.8).

Haemoglobin is a cytoplasmic protein. This means that the polypeptides, α-globin and β-globin, do not contain signal sequences. As there is no signal sequence at the N-terminal end of the polypeptide the ribosome does not become attached to the endoplasmic reticulum but remains free in the cytoplasm. All cytoplasmic proteins are synthesised on ribosomes that are free in the cytoplasm.

Globular proteins are folded in a different manner to fibrous proteins

As soon as the N-terminal end of a polypeptide is clear of the ribosome it begins to fold. This is because a folded polypeptide is much more stable than an unfolded polypeptide. When a polypeptide folds interactions occur between different parts of the polypeptide and these interactions, usually

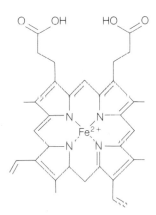

Fig 6.10 The folding pattern of a globin polypeptide. In a globular protein there are regions of secondary structures such as α-helices joined by regions where the polypeptide has a less ordered structure. Sharp kinks are introduced by proline residues.

Fig 6.9 All proteins are similar in that they can be denatured by heat, a change in pH or mechanical stress. Beating egg whites denatures the albumin protein, causing the weak bonds that stabilise its three-dimensional, globular structure to break. The weak bonds then reform randomly between different polypeptide chains, causing the gelatinous solution to change into a stiff froth that traps the air.

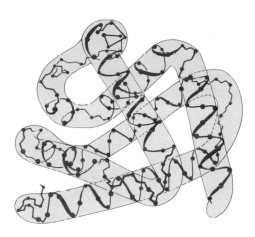

Fig 6.11 Haem, the prosthetic group in haemoglobin.

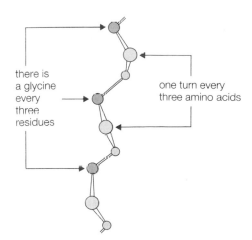

there is a glycine every three residues

one turn every three amino acids

Fig 6.12 A single collagen polypeptide kinks into a helix. The α1(I) and α2(I) polypeptides have a distinctive structure with a glycine residue at every third position in the polypeptide.

weak bonds like hydrogen bonds, release energy so that the polypeptide becomes progressively more stable. The polypeptide will end up in the most stable three-dimensional shape for that particular molecule. The different shapes that polypeptides form when they fold are discussed in section 2.3. In brief, interactions between different parts of the protein backbone are called the secondary structure of the protein. Two common secondary structures are the α-helix and the β-pleated sheet. Interactions between the R groups are called the tertiary structure of the protein.

The α-globin and β-globin polypeptides fold to give globular structures. Globular proteins have short sections of secondary structure, such as short sections of α-helix or β-pleated sheet, joined by bends that fold the polypeptide back on itself. α-globin and β-globin both contain sections of α-helix joined by bends, giving a compact, globular structure (Fig 6.10). The different regions of the folded chain are held in this globular shape by weak bonds between the R groups: this is what is meant by the tertiary structure of the polypeptide.

When the α-globin and β-globin polypeptides fold into their typical, globular shape they each interact with a haem molecule. Haem is a flat, organic ring molecule called a porphin, with an Fe^{2+} ion at its centre (Fig 6.11). The haem is held in place within the folded polypeptide by weak bonds between haem and some of the R groups in the polypeptide.

The polypeptides that make up collagen, α1(I) and α2(I), have a completely different structure. Each polypeptide forms a perfectly regular helix with three amino acid residues per turn (Fig 6.12).

So why do the globin polypeptides fold up to form globular structures while the collagen polypeptides form this regular helix? The reason lies in the sequence of the amino acid residues that make up the polypeptide. Only certain amino acid resides can make a stable α-helix (Table 2.3, p.39). Other amino acid residues make an α-helix less stable and a few amino acid residues, for example proline, cause the polypeptide to kink sharply.

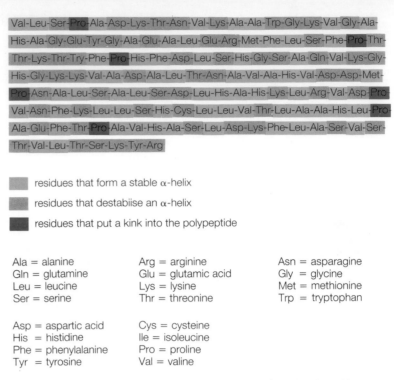

Val-Leu-Ser-Pro-Ala-Asp-Lys-Thr-Asn-Val-Lys-Ala-Ala-Trp-Gly-Lys-Val-Gly-Ala-
His-Ala-Gly-Glu-Tyr-Gly-Ala-Glu-Ala-Leu-Glu-Arg-Met-Phe-Leu-Ser-Phe-Pro-Thr-
Thr-Lys-Thr-Try-Phe-Pro-His-Phe-Asp-Leu-Ser-His-Gly-Ser-Ala-Gln-Val-Lys-Gly-
His-Gly-Lys-Lys-Val-Ala-Asp-Ala-Leu-Thr-Asn-Ala-Val-Ala-His-Val-Asp-Asp-Met-
Pro-Asn-Ala-Leu-Ser-Ala-Leu-Ser-Asp-Leu-His-Ala-His-Lys-Leu-Arg-Val-Asp-Pro-
Val-Asn-Phe-Lys-Leu-Leu-Ser-His-Cys-Leu-Leu-Val-Thr-Leu-Ala-Ala-His-Leu-Pro-
Ala-Glu-Phe-Thr-Pro-Ala-Val-His-Ala-Ser-Leu-Asp-Lys-Phe-Leu-Ala-Ser-Val-Ser-
Thr-Val-Leu-Thr-Ser-Lys-Tyr-Arg

■ residues that form a stable α-helix

■ residues that destabiise an α-helix

■ residues that put a kink into the polypeptide

Ala = alanine	Arg = arginine	Asn = asparagine
Gln = glutamine	Glu = glutamic acid	Gly = glycine
Leu = leucine	Lys = lysine	Met = methionine
Ser = serine	Thr = threonine	Trp = tryptophan

Asp = aspartic acid	Cys = cysteine
His = histidine	Ile = isoleucine
Phe = phenylalanine	Pro = proline
Tyr = tyrosine	Val = valine

Fig 6.13 The sequence of amino acids in the human β-globin polypeptide.

Looking at the sequence of the β-globin polypeptide (Fig 6.13) one can see sections that are rich in those amino acid residues that form stable α-helices. These sections would be more likely to form α-helices than those sections that are mainly amino acid residues that destabilise an α-helix. There are also seven proline residues in the sequence: these proline residues would introduce a sharp kink into the polypeptide, folding it back on itself.

The α1(I) and α2(I) polypeptides have a very unusual sequence of amino acid residues (Fig 6.14). Every third amino acid residue is glycine and there is usually a proline or a hydroxyproline residue adjacent to the glycine residue. Glycine only has a hydrogen atom as its R group so a glycine residue is very small. The small size of the glycine residue means that the polypeptide can be kinked by the proline and hydroxyproline residues into a helix with three amino acid residues per turn (Fig 6.12).

Hydroxyproline is a modified form of proline. The modification is carried out by an enzyme.

-Gly-Pro-Met-Gly-Pro-Ser-Gly-Pro-Arg-Gly-Leu-Hyp-Gly-Pro-Hyp-Gly-Ala-Hyp-
Gly-Pro-Gln-Gly-Phe-Gln-Gly-Pro-Hyp-Gly-Glu-Hyp-Gly-Glu-Hyp-Gly-Ala-Ser-
Gly-Pro-Met-Gly-Pro-Arg-Gly-Pro-Hyp-Gly-Pro-Hyp-Gly-Lys-Asn-Gly-Asp-Asp-

■ glycine residues

Fig 6.14 The sequence of amino acids in part of the α1(I) polypeptide of collagen.

So haemoglobin and collagen form very different shaped polypeptides because of the sequence of their amino acid residues. The shape of the polypeptide is therefore fixed by the gene, because it is the sequence of nucleotides in the gene that determines the sequence of the amino acid residues in the polypeptide through the processes of transcription and translation.

Another question is why does each globin polypeptide interact with a haem group while the α1(I) and α2(I) polypeptides do not? The answer to this has two parts: firstly, the haem group is present in the cytoplasm of a red blood cell rather than the endoplasmic reticulum of a collagen-producing cell; secondly, each globin polypeptide folds into exactly the correct shape to interact with the flat, ring shaped haem molecule and the folded globin molecule has all the right R groups in exactly the right places to hold the haem molecule in place. In this way the ability of a globin polypeptide to bind a haem molecule is dependent on the nature of the R groups and their position in the polypeptide: in other words, it is dependent on the sequence of amino acid residues of the polypeptide and ultimately on the sequence of nucleotides in the gene coding for the globin polypeptide.

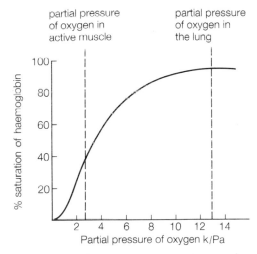

Fig 6.15 The oxygen dissociation curve for haemoglobin. The percentage of haemoglobin that is saturated with oxygen increases with increasing oxygen concentration. The curve is 'S' shaped, showing that there is a co-operative effect.

Redox reactions are reactions involving oxidation and reduction.

Some proteins react to their environment while others do not

Haemoglobin is an oxygen carrier. This means that it must react with oxygen at one location, move to another location and then give up that oxygen. The oxygen molecules are carried on the haem groups that are found associated with each of the polypeptides.

The haem is a **prosthetic group**, an organic molecule that is closely associated with a protein and essential for that protein to be able to carry out its function. In haemoglobin the haem group is needed for haemoglobin to be able to carry oxygen molecules. Collagen contains no such prosthetic group. Prosthetic groups are usually found in proteins that are involved in the chemical reactions that occur in the cell, particularly in redox reactions. Collagen is a structural protein and its role is to be stable rather than to react. It is therefore not very surprising that collagen does not contain a prosthetic group.

Haemoglobin is sensitive to oxygen concentration. At high oxygen concentrations haemoglobin binds oxygen molecules and at low oxygen concentrations it dissociates to release those oxygen molecules. The **oxygen dissociation curve** for haemoglobin is shown in Fig 6.15.

As well as being sensitive to oxygen concentration haemoglobin is also sensitive to carbon dioxide concentration and to pH. At high carbon dioxide concentrations or low pH the oxygen dissociation curve shifts to the right (Fig 6.16). This shift is because the haemoglobin is more inclined to release the oxygen molecules it is carrying at high carbon dioxide concentrations or low pH. This is called the **Bohr effect** and it is important for the efficient functioning of haemoglobin in the body. Cells need oxygen most

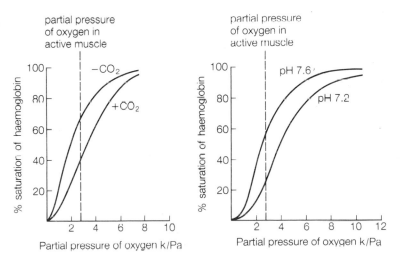

Fig 6.16 The Bohr shift. The oxygen dissociation curve for haemoglobin is altered in the presence of carbon dioxide or if the pH is reduced. This means that haemoglobin is more likely to give up its oxygen when the concentration of carbon dioxide is high or when the pH is reduced.

IMPLEMENTING THE GENETIC INFORMATION

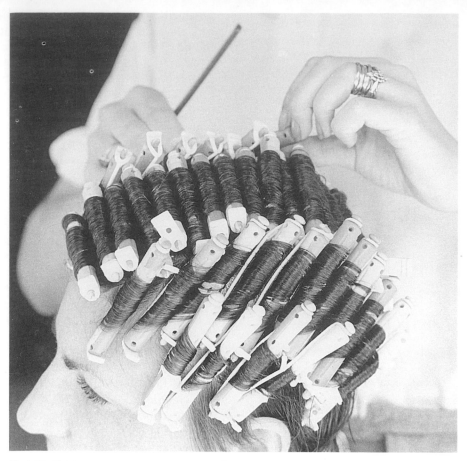

Fig 6.17 Hair is permed by treating it chemically. Changing the pH causes the weak bonds that stabilise the three-dimensional structure of the α-keratin to break. The hair is then stretched into the desired pattern, usually curls for someone with straight hair. The pH is then neutralised and the weak bonds reform, fixing the hair into its new structure. Most perms are done using an alkaline perming solution but acidic treatments also are used and have a similar effect.

when they are respiring and respiring cells excrete carbon dioxide and sometimes lactic acid as waste products. If the haemoglobin is more likely to release its oxygen molecules at high carbon dioxide concentrations and in acidic conditions then it will be likely to release the oxygen close to cells that are respiring and need the oxygen badly.

Haemoglobin is therefore very sensitive to its environment: it reacts to the oxygen concentration, the carbon dioxide concentration and small changes in the cellular pH. In contrast, collagen is very, very unreactive: it remains in place year after year providing the strength needed for a tendon or a bone to function correctly. The sensitivity of haemoglobin to its environment is due to the way in which the globin polypeptides interact with each other within the haemoglobin macromolecule. The stability of collagen is also due to the way in which the α1(I) and α2(I) polypeptides are built up to make a fibre of collagen. The properties of both proteins are therefore dependent on the quaternary structure of the protein.

Quaternary structure can be essential for a protein's function

A macromolecule of haemoglobin contains two α-globin polypeptides and two β-globin polypeptides: each polypeptide is called a **subunit** of the overall haemoglobin structure (Fig 6.18). The way that the four subunits interact is referred to as the quaternary structure of the haemoglobin protein (section 2.3). Having four subunits interacting gives haemoglobin certain properties that are essential to its role as an oxygen carrier.

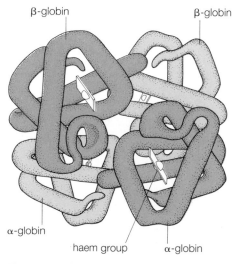

β-globin   β-globin

α-globin

haem group   α-globin

Fig 6.18 A model of haemoglobin showing the four subunits.

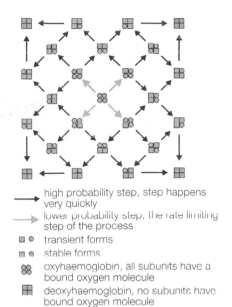

→ high probability step, step happens very quickly

→ lower probability step, the rate limiting step of the process

▫ ◦ transient forms

▪ ● stable forms

88 oxyhaemoglobin, all subunits have a bound oxygen molecule

⊞ deoxyhaemoglobin, no subunits have bound oxygen molecule

Fig 6.19 Haemoglobin shows a positive co-operative effect. Once one of the subunits has lost its oxygen molecule the other three subunits lose their oxygen molecules almost simultaneously, giving rise to the deoxygenated form. The process works similarly in the opposite direction; once one of the subunits binds an oxygen molecule the other three also become oxygenated.

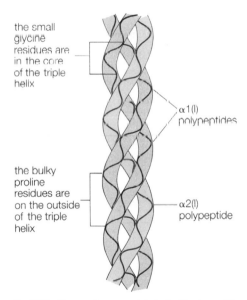

the small glycine residues are in the core of the triple helix

α1(I) polypeptides

the bulky proline residues are on the outside of the triple helix

α2(I) polypeptide

Fig 6.20 Tropocollagen: a triple helix. The two α1(I) helices and the one α2(I) helix are wound around each other to make a triple helix.

Being an oxygen carrier means that the haemoglobin must bind oxygen at one place and give that oxygen up at another place. This process is more efficient if the haemoglobin travels fully charged, with all four subunits each carrying an oxygen molecule, and then dumps all its oxygen molecules at a single location. If the four subunits acted independently then the oxygen molecules would bind gradually, one at a time, and be lost gradually. However, this is not the case; either all four subunits carry an oxygen molecule on their haem or none. This can be seen from the oxygen dissociation curve for haemoglobin (Fig 6.15). If the subunits gave up their oxygen molecules gradually the dissociation would give a simple curve; instead the curve is 'S' shaped, or **sigmoid**.

This means that the subunits do not act independently, instead they co-operate. If one subunit binds an oxygen molecule then the probability of the other three subunits binding an oxygen molecule increases, in fact the probability becomes so high that it happens at once. In the same way, if one of the subunits loses its oxygen molecule the probability of the other three subunits losing their oxygen molecules increases and so all four subunits lose their oxygen molecules almost simultaneously. This all-or-nothing behaviour is called a **positive co-operative effect** (Fig 6.19).

The haemoglobin molecule achieves this positive co-operative effect by a change in the three-dimensional shape of the protein. Scientists have used X-ray diffraction to compare the structure of deoxyhaemoglobin, haemoglobin carrying no oxygen, with the structure of oxyhaemoglobin, haemoglobin carrying four oxygen molecules. They have detected a change in the tertiary structure of a subunit that occurs when it binds an oxygen molecule. This change in shape in a single subunit appears to force a change in the quaternary structure of the whole protein, making the other three subunits much more likely to bind an oxygen molecule.

Collagen has two levels of quaternary structure. Two helical α1(I) polypeptides and one helical α2(I) polypeptide are wound around each other to form a right-handed triple helix (Fig 6.20). This triple helix is only possible because of the small size of the glycine residue. The three helices are coiled together so that all the glycine residues lie on the inside of the triple helix while the more bulky proline residues lie on the outside. The triple helix is stabilised by hydrogen bonds that form between the hydroxy-proline residues in the different polypeptides.

This triple helix is the basic subunit of collagen structure and a protein with this structure, called **tropocollagen**, can be isolated from cells that are making collagen. Once outside the cell the tropocollagen subunits come to lie side by side and overlapping, building up a collagen fibril (Fig 6.21). These **collagen fibrils** are stabilised by covalent bonds between the tropocollagen subunits. Finally the collagen fibrils aggregate to form **collagen fibres** (Fig 6.21).

The significance of the quaternary structure of collagen is that it builds up a structure that is very strong when pulled: it has a very high tensile strength. Winding the polypeptides together to form a triple helix increases the tensile strength of the structure because three polypeptides require more force to break them than one. The tensile strength is increased still further when the tropocollagen subunits pack together to form a fibril and any slipping between subunits is prevented by the strong, covalent bonds. Finally the overall tensile strength of a structure like a tendon is increased by having many fibrils side by side (Fig 6.22).

Quaternary structure is dependent on the primary structure of the polypeptide

Sickle cell anaemia is an inherited disease. If a person has sickle cell anaemia their red blood cells sometimes change shape, forming 'sickle' shape crescents (Fig 6.23). The spleen removes the 'sickle' shaped red blood

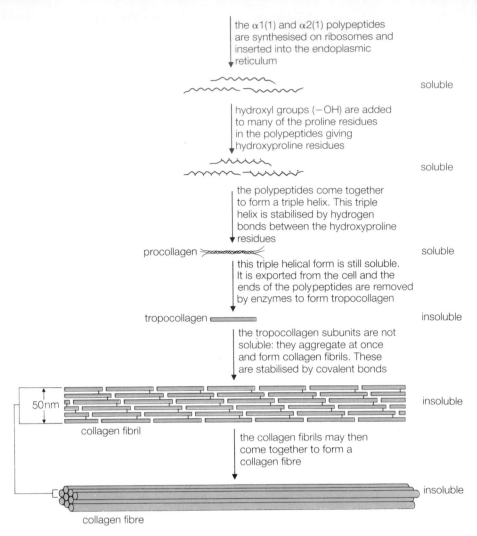

the α1(1) and α2(1) polypeptides are synthesised on ribosomes and inserted into the endoplasmic reticulum

soluble

hydroxyl groups (−OH) are added to many of the proline residues in the polypeptides giving hydroxyproline residues

soluble

the polypeptides come together to form a triple helix. This triple helix is stabilised by hydrogen bonds between the hydroxyproline residues

procollagen

soluble

this triple helical form is still soluble. It is exported from the cell and the ends of the polypeptides are removed by enzymes to form tropocollagen

tropocollagen

insoluble

the tropocollagen subunits are not soluble: they aggregate at once and form collagen fibrils. These are stabilised by covalent bonds

50nm

collagen fibril

insoluble

the collagen fibrils may then come together to form a collagen fibre

collagen fibre

insoluble

Fig 6.21 Assembly of a collagen fibre.

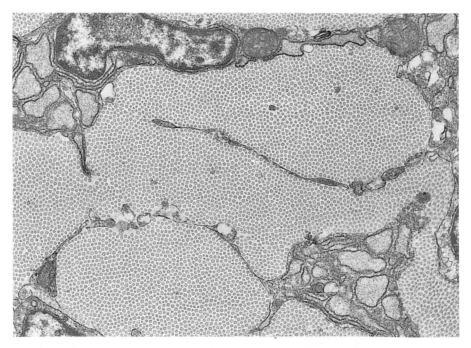

Fig 6.22 Cross section through a tendon, showing collagen fibres. When a tendon is cut through in cross section the collagen fibres can be seen to be made up of closely packed collagen microfibrils. This image was obtained using an electron microscope.

IMPLEMENTING THE GENETIC INFORMATION

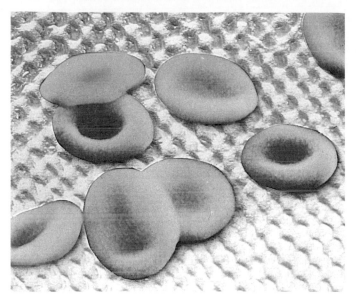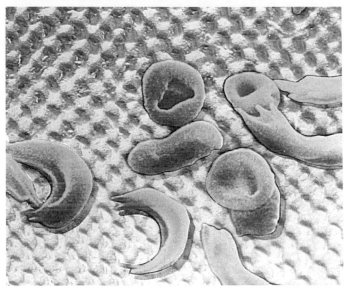

Fig 0.23 (Left) Normal red blood cells and (right) abnormal red blood cells from a sickle cell patient. When an individual with sickle cell goes into crisis, the red blood cells deform because the abnormal haemoglobin aggregates within the cells.

cells from the blood, resulting in anaemia. This tendency to form abnormally shaped red blood cells can be traced to the haemoglobin and specifically to the β-globin polypeptide. Haemoglobin containing the abnormal β-globin has an altered quaternary structure that can cause the haemoglobin molecules to aggregate together at low oxygen concentrations. It is this aggregation that causes the red blood cells to change shape.

Scientists investigating sickle cell anaemia sequenced the β-globin polypeptide and discovered that only one amino acid residue was different in the abnormal β-globin: one glutamic acid had been replaced by a valine. This one tiny alteration in the primary structure of the β-globin polypeptide alters the entire structure of the haemoglobin protein, making it incapable of fulfilling its function. This illustrates that it is the sequence of amino acid residues, and ultimately the sequence of nucleotides in the gene, that determine the shape and therefore the function of the protein.

Brittle bone disease, or osteogenesis imperfecta, is a genetic disease in which the bones are very weak and break under the least strain. There are many different forms of this disease but all can be traced to small faults in either the α1(I) or the α2(I) polypeptides. These small faults mean that the triple helix cannot form properly, so the collagen fibrils are irregular and weak. As type I collagen fibrils give bone much of its strength this means that the bone breaks easily.

Even a single amino acid substitution in the α1(I) or α2(I) polypeptide can have drastic effects. This is because the structure of the triple helix is dependent on there being a glycine residue at every third position in the polypeptide. Any other amino acid residue will have a larger R group and will disrupt the triple helix. If the mutation is in the gene coding for α1(I) the disease is much more severe than it would be if α2(I) was affected. This is because there are two α1(I) polypeptides and only one α2(I) polypeptide in each triple helix.

The solubility of a protein depends on its size

It is essential for the function of collagen that it should be insoluble, otherwise it could not form a structure like a tendon. Insoluble proteins cannot be produced inside the cell because once they are insoluble they cannot be exported. To solve this problem collagen is produced inside the cell as soluble procollagen and then exported.

The procollagen has 'untidy' ends that do not form an ordered triple helix. This means that the procollagen cannot aggregate to form a collagen fibril, so it remains soluble. Once the procollagen is outside the cell it is modified by enzymes that cut off the 'untidy' N-terminal ends and the C-terminal ends of the polypeptides (Fig 6.21). This forms tropocollagen subunits that promptly assemble to make a fibril. Other enzymes then modify some of the amino acid residues in the tropocollagen subunits so that they can make the strong covalent bonds that stabilise the structure of the fibril.

The cytosol is the intracellular solution.

Haemoglobin is a cytoplasmic protein and as such is small and compact enough to remain soluble in the cytosol. However, in sickle cell anaemia the different haemoglobin molecules aggregate, much as the tropocollagen subunits aggregate once they are outside the cell. The aggregation of the haemoglobin molecules creates a structure that is too large to be soluble so the haemoglobin precipitates out of the cytosol. Inside the cell the insoluble haemoglobin has a disastrous effect, altering the shape of the whole cell and ultimately leading to its destruction.

DATA HANDLING 6.1

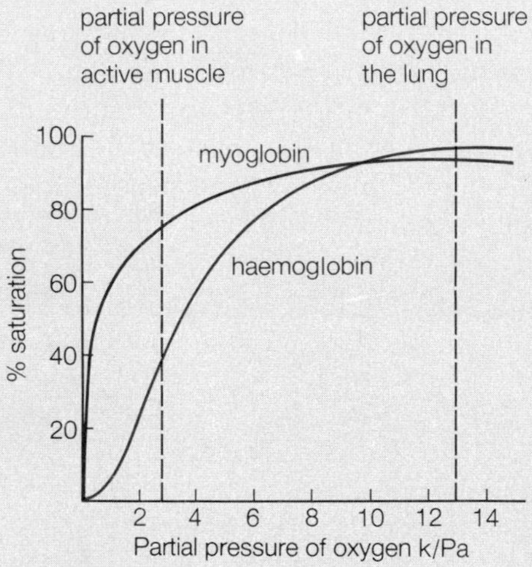

Fig 6.24 The oxygen dissociation curves for myoglobin and haemoglobin.

Myoglobin is an oxygen storage protein found in muscle while haemoglobin is an oxygen-carrying protein. Myoglobin has a similar structure to haemoglobin except that it contains only one globin polypeptide and one haem. The oxygen dissociation curves for haemoglobin and myoglobin are shown in Fig 6.24.

(a) At what oxygen concentration is 50% of the myoglobin bound to oxygen molecules? At what oxygen concentration is 50% of the haemoglobin bound to oxygen?

(b) As muscle respires the oxygen concentration in the muscle falls. Which will release its oxygen first, a haemoglobin molecule or a myoglobin molecule?

(c) Using your answer to (b), when is the oxygen stored in the myoglobin used by the muscle cells?

The oxygen dissociation curves for myoglobin and haemoglobin are very different shapes. The myoglobin oxygen dissociation curve is a simple curve while the haemoglobin dissociation curve is a sigmoid curve.

(d) Why is the oxygen dissociation curve for haemoglobin sigmoid while the oxygen dissociation curve for myoglobin is not sigmoid?

The very steep portion of the haemoglobin oxygen dissociation curve shows that haemoglobin is almost fully saturated with oxygen at the oxygen concentration in the lungs but is only about 34% saturated with oxygen at the oxygen concentration in the capillaries of active muscle.

(e) Explain why this is essential for the function of haemoglobin in the body.

(f) When we say that the haemoglobin is 34% saturated, how would the oxygen molecules be distributed among 100 haemoglobin molecules each with four subunits? Explain why you chose this particular distribution of oxygen.

(g) What effect would increasing the carbon dioxide concentration have on the oxygen dissociation curve of haemoglobin? Relate your answer to the situation in the body.

(h) What effect would lowering the pH slightly have on the oxygen dissociation curve of haemoglobin? Relate your answer to the situation in the body.

IMPLEMENTING THE GENETIC INFORMATION

DATA HANDLING 6.2

The α1(I) and α2(I) polypeptides that make up type I collagen contain many hydroxyproline residues. Hydroxyproline is not an amino acid that is coded for by a particular codon. Instead hydroxyproline residues are produced from proline residues by an enzyme in the endoplasmic reticulum (Fig 6.25).

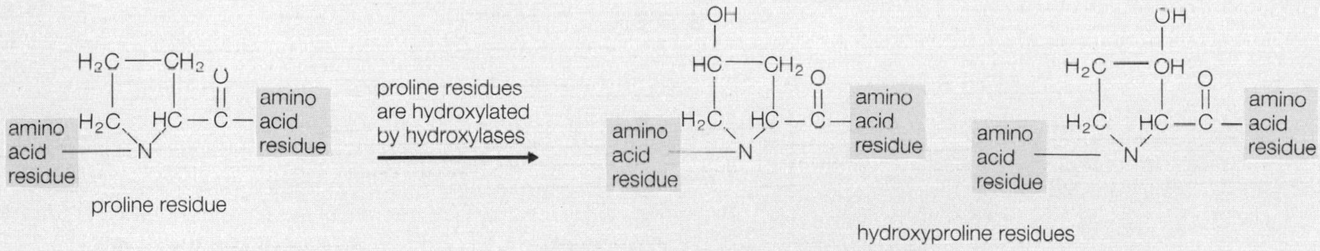

proline residues are hydroxylated by hydroxylases

proline residue

hydroxyproline residues

Fig 6.25

proline residue

hydroxyproline residue

glycine residue

Fig 6.26

The three most common amino acid residues in α1(I) and α2(I) are glycine, proline and hydroxyproline (Fig 6.26).

(a) Describe the quaternary structure produced when α1(I) and α2(I) polypeptides associate.

(b) This structure is stabilised by hydrogen bonds between the R groups of the polypeptides. Using Fig 6.26, which of the amino acid residues are likely to form hydrogen bonds?

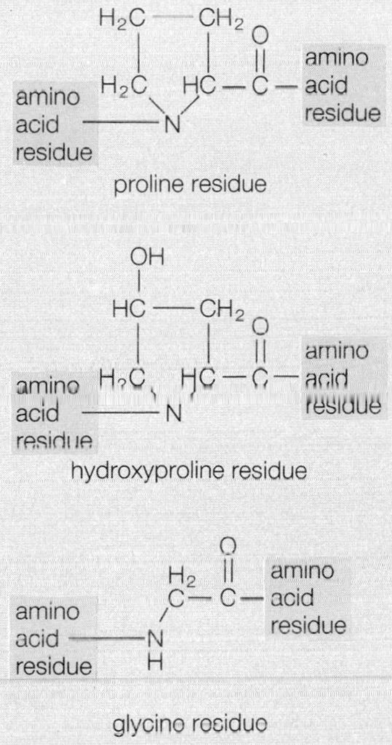

Vitamin C is an essential cofactor for the hydroxylase enzymes that convert proline residues to hydroxyproline residues. A cofactor is a non-protein molecule needed for an enzyme to function. Collagen taken from mammals suffering from vitamin C deficiency shows abnormal behaviour when heated (Fig 6.27).

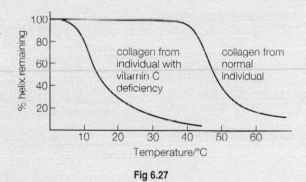

Fig 6.27

(c) At what temperature is 50% of the normal collagen denatured?

(d) At what temperature is 50% of the collagen from the individual suffering from vitamin C deficiency denatured?

(e) Which protein is the more stable, the collagen from the healthy individual or the collagen from the individual suffering from vitamin C deficiency?

(f) Explain why vitamin C deficiency should lead to the collagen being less stable.

(g) Collagen that is less stable when heated also has less tensile strength. Explain this in terms of the structure of a collagen fibril.

(h) What is the common name given to vitamin C deficiency and what are its symptoms?

(i) Explain these symptoms in terms of abnormal formation of collagen.

6.8 What is the role of the following in translation:
- the ribosome;
- the mRNA;
- the tRNAs;
- the aminoacyl-tRNA synthetases?

6.9 (a) Describe how a collagen fibre is built up from α1(I) and α2(I) polypeptides.
(b) What is the function of collagen in the body? How does the structure of the collagen fibre adapt it to this function?

6.10 Haemoglobin and collagen are two of the most closely studied proteins.
(a) Why have haemoglobin and collagen been studied so thoroughly when important proteins such as gene activators in eukaryotes have been much less thoroughly investigated?
(b) In the past scientists sequenced proteins, but this technique has been replaced in most situations by DNA sequencing of the gene coding for the protein. Explain why sequencing the gene makes sequencing the protein unnecessary.
(c) Name one technique that has been used to study the three-dimensional shape of proteins.

6.11 The amino acid sequences of the N-terminal end of the β-globin polypeptides found in the haemoglobin of three different individuals are shown below. Individual 1 has normal haemoglobin while the other two people have abnormal haemoglobin. Individual 2 has sickle cell anaemia.

Individual 1 Val-His-Leu-Thr-Pro-Glu-Glu-Lys....
Individual 2 Val-His-Leu-Thr-Pro-Val-Glu-Lys....
Individual 3 Val-His-Leu-Thr-Pro-Lys-Glu-Lys....

Neutral amino acid residues: Val Leu Thr Pro
Acidic amino acid residues (negatively charged at pH 7): Glu
Basic amino acid residues (positively charged at pH 7): Lys His

(a) What is the difference shown between the sickle cell haemoglobin and the normal haemoglobin? What difference will this produce in the charge on this part of the polypeptide?
(b) What is the difference shown between the haemoglobin of Individual 3 and the normal haemoglobin? What difference will this produce in the charge on this part of the polypeptide?
(c) Using Table 6.1, the genetic code, work out how many changes in the DNA sequence are needed to produce each of the two abnormal polypeptides.

6.4 PROTEIN ENGINEERING

Protein structure can be deduced from the primary structure

Protein structure can be investigated directly using the technique of X-ray diffraction. However, studies of this type are very time consuming and require a large amount of expensive equipment. By comparing the X-ray diffraction data with the amino acid sequence of the protein scientists were able to associate specific structures, like the α-helix, with a certain amino acid residue sequence (Table 2.3). Sequencing a protein is a much simpler technique than X-ray diffraction and DNA sequencing is an even easier technique that can be automated. The amino acid sequence can then be worked out from the DNA sequence using the genetic code (Table 6.1).

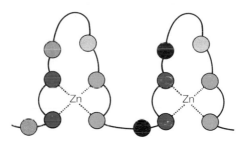

Fig 6.28 Zinc fingers are a structure found in a number of proteins that regulate transcription. It is possible to predict the presence of zinc fingers from a DNA sequence, so proteins that regulate transcription can be identified by DNA sequencing.

Protein function can be deduced from the secondary and tertiary structures in the protein

The amino acid sequence of the protein being studied is stored in a computer file and then compared with sequences that are known to form distinctive secondary or tertiary structures. If the protein contains one of these distinctive amino acid sequences scientists gain an insight into the protein's function.

For example, a string of hydrophobic amino acid residues in the sequence implies that the protein may be a membrane protein. The hydrophobic amino acid residues are thought to be embedded in the phospholipid bilayer. Membrane proteins are discussed more thoroughly in Chapter 3. Many DNA binding proteins that regulate transcription have a distinct structure called **zinc fingers** (Fig 6.28). A protein with the necessary amino acid sequence to form a zinc finger structure would be worth investigating as a regulator of transcription. Another common sequence is the **nuclear transport sequence**. Only proteins with this short sequence of amino acid residues in one of their polypeptides are allowed through the nuclear pores into the nucleus. If the gene is sequenced rather than the final protein, a **signal sequence** may be identified (section 6.3). This tells the scientist that the protein produced will be located in the membrane or secreted from the cell.

Future research may lead to designer proteins

As computer models of protein structure become more and more sophisticated, scientists will be able to load the DNA into a sequencing machine that will automatically read the sequence of nucleotide residues and feed it to the computer. The computer will locate the parts of the sequence that code for protein and translate the DNA sequence into the protein sequence using the genetic code. Finally, the computer will apply all the rules about protein folding and deduce the final stable form of the protein. This structure will be displayed as a 3-D graphic image that we could study.

Perhaps, in time, we will be able to go still further. In the future we may be able to design a protein to carry out a particular function. The computer would design a polypeptide with the necessary primary structure to form a protein with all the required characteristics. A gene could then be designed to code for such a polypeptide, synthesised on a polynucleotide synthesiser and put into a bacterium that would transcribe the DNA and make the protein. Even now each step in this process is possible, so this futuristic scenario may not be far away!

QUESTION

6.12 Here is the DNA sequence of a very short, imaginary prokaryotic gene.

TACCTTCTCCTACTTGAACGGCAACAGGAAGACGATACAAA
ATTCGCAGCTGTAACGCGGCCGACT

(a) Write out the sequence of mRNA transcribed from this gene.
(b) How many codons are present in the mRNA?
(c) How many amino acid residues are coded for by this mRNA?
(d) Use Table 6.1 to write out the amino acid sequence of the polypeptide formed. Number the amino acid residues.
(e) One section of the polypeptide would be negatively charged at pH 7 and another section would be positively charged at pH 7. Identify these sections. (Table 1.6, p. 18.)
(f) The polypeptide can form one disulphide bond. Between which two residues would this disulphide bond form?

REVIEW OF CRUCIAL POINTS

- The genetic information is used by the cell to make proteins. The information in a gene is transcribed to make an mRNA which is then translated to make a polypeptide. The polypeptide folds and may interact with other molecules to form the finished protein.

- The translation process has evolved so that the sequence of nucleotide residues in the gene strictly determines the sequence of amino acid residues in the polypeptide. The sequence of nucleotides in the gene is accurately transcribed into an mRNA molecule and this mRNA molecule is used for protein synthesis. Every three nucleotide residues in the mRNA code for one amino acid residue in the polypeptide: the triplet of nucleotide residues in the mRNA is called a codon. As there are four different nucleotide residues and each codon has three of them there are 64 different codons, more than one for each of the twenty amino acids. This means that the code is degenerate, it has more than one codon for each amino acid.

- Matching the correct amino acid with the correct codon requires an adaptor molecule. This role is fulfilled by tRNA molecules. There are over twenty different tRNA molecules, one to match each codon except for the three codons that do not code for amino acids. The tRNA molecule has an anticodon that is complementary to a specific codon. Linked to another part of the tRNA is the amino acid that matches that specific codon.

- Synthesis of the polypeptide occurs in a ribosome. Ribosomes are complicated assemblies of structural proteins, enzymes and rRNA molecules. The mechanism of protein synthesis is known in great detail but essentially it is as follows. The mRNA binds to the ribosome at its 5' end and then the tRNAs bring the correct amino acids into position by base pairing with the codons of the mRNA. The ribosome moves along the mRNA in a 5' to 3' direction, catalysing the polymerisation of the amino acids as the tRNAs bring them into position. When the polypeptide chain is complete it is released and the ribosome comes away from the mRNA.

- The polypeptide begins to interact with its environment as soon as the N-terminal end is clear of the ribosome. A large number of different interactions can occur, all depending on the sequence of amino acid residues in the polypeptide. The location of the protein with respect to the cell, the pattern of folding and the association of the polypeptide with any prosthetic group are all determined by the sequence of the protein and therefore, ultimately, by the sequence of nucleotide residues in the gene.

- The factors that influence the folding patterns of polypeptides have been studied in detail by many scientists and much is known about what makes a protein assume a specific three-dimensional structure. It is this three-dimensional structure that allows each particular protein to fulfil its specific role in the cell and any alteration in the shape of the protein can lead to loss of function.

- It has been shown that the three-dimensional structure of a protein is determined by the sequence of amino acid residues in the polypeptide although some modifications of protein structure are carried out by enzymes. The dependency of the overall structure of a protein on the sequence of amino acid residues can be shown by studying the abnormal proteins produced by individuals suffering from genetic diseases: a mutation in the DNA leading to a single amino acid substitution can lead to a gross alteration in the structure of the protein and a subsequent loss of function.

Theme **3**

THE MOLECULAR MACHINE

Organisms are made of trillions of molecules interacting with trillions of other molecules like a fascinatingly complex machine. Many of these interactions are molecules coming together to make structures as discussed in Chapter 3, but other interactions are the chemical reactions that synthesise new molecules inside the cell or provide the apparatus by which energy is transferred within the cell, making life possible.

PREREQUISITES

To appreciate this theme you will need:

- an understanding that energy can be stored (potential energy) or be on the move (kinetic energy);
- an understanding that energy can be stored or moved in a variety of ways and that it is transferred from one carrier to another every time that it is moved;
- a knowledge of protein structure (sections 2.3 and 6.3).
- a basic understanding of cellular structure (Fig 3.1, p. 59).

This field of sunflowers is like a vast factory, in which each plant cell is a complex machine that uses the sun's energy to turn simple molecules from the soil and the air into an enormous variety of complex molecules.

Chapter 7

CHEMICAL REACTIONS IN CELLS

Life is a series of chemical reactions that occur within cells. Some of these reactions have been discussed in earlier chapters, for example the polymerisation of nucleotides to make RNA or DNA and the polymerisation of amino acids to make proteins. Others will be discussed in this chapter and the next. To reproduce many of these chemical reactions in a laboratory would require high or low pH, long times at high temperature and toxic solvents, yet these reactions occur within a cell at neutral pH and moderate temperatures with all the reagents dissolved in water. This remarkable achievement is possible due to one group of molecules within the cell: the enzymes.

LEARNING OBJECTIVES

After studying this chapter you should:

1. have an appreciation of the chemical environments in a cell;

2. know that enzymes are biological catalysts;

3. be able to describe the properties of enzymes that are typical of catalysts;

4. be able to describe the properties of enzymes that are typical of proteins;

5. understand the standard terminology of enzyme kinetics, including simple Michaelis–Menton kinetics;

6. be able to discuss models for the mechanism of enzyme action;

7. appreciate that enzymes cooperate to form biochemical pathways;

8. be familiar with a range of enzyme activators and inhibitors;

9. know examples to illustrate all the above points.

7.1 THE CHEMICAL ENVIRONMENTS WITHIN THE CELL

Cells are complicated

It is all too easy to think of a cell as a miniature plastic bag of watery solution with a nucleus in the middle, when in reality the cell is a tiny, complicated factory. Electron microscopy has shown that animal and plant cells contain **organelles** (Fig 3.1, p. 59). Each of these organelles is surrounded by its own membrane and each contains its own different environment with its own assortment of molecules. Even the **cytosol** between these organelles is complex: it is crossed by microtubules and microfilaments, liberally sprinkled with ribosomes and thick with proteins. Many of these proteins are not actually dissolved in the water but form colloids. Colloids are particles, in this case single molecules, that are so large that they are suspended in the water rather than dissolved.

Some scientists have speculated that the cell is too crowded for there to be any liquid water there at all! They think that all the water is hydrogen bonded to the surface of membranes or proteins, or attracted and held by ions. This view is probably a little extreme but it helps to focus the mind on the fact that all parts of the cell are highly organised, even the cytosol, and that chemical reactions within cells take place in a very different environment to that within a test tube.

Colloids are discussed in section 2.1.

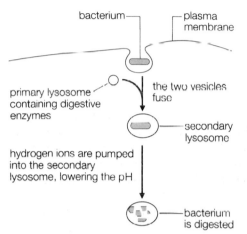

Fig 7.1 Lysosomes. Primary lysosomes containing digestive enzymes bud off the Golgi body and fuse with the vesicle containing the material to be digested to form a secondary lysosome. The pH inside the secondary lysosome is reduced, denaturing the proteins and making digestion more effective.

Cell membranes can maintain different environments

The cellular environment is very different from the environment outside the cell (Table 1.9, p. 30). This difference is possible because every cell is surrounded by a plasma membrane that is selectively permeable, allowing some molecules to pass freely and restricting or preventing the passage of others (section 3.2, p. 61). This allows molecules to be present at different concentrations on either side of the membrane.

This is also true of the cell organelles. All the cell organelles are surrounded by selectively permeable membranes. This means that a different environment can be maintained inside an organelle than in the cytosol. This is illustrated by the cell's disposal system, the **lysosomes** (Fig 7.1). Once the material to be broken down is within the lysosome, the lysosomal membrane allows the passage of hydrogen ions to lower the pH. This denatures the proteins within the lysosome and they can then be digested by pH-resistant enzymes.

The cellular environment is mild

There are a few general statements that can be made about the environment within cells. Firstly, the solvent is water: cells are about 65% water although, as discussed above, a lot of this water is fixed in place rather than free moving within the cell. Secondly, the pH within a cell is near neutral, about pH 7.2, although acid environments can occur within particular organelles. Thirdly, the temperature of a cell lies within the range 0 °C to 50 °C.

Few chemical reactions occur spontaneously under these mild conditions. Most carbon-containing molecules are stable when dissolved in water at pH 7 and 35 °C: they remain as they are and do not react to form other molecules. This stability allows life to exist because if these molecules were not stable our genetic material would fall apart more quickly than it could be repaired, our RNA would degenerate before it could be translated and our proteins would denature. However, if all the molecules within cells were so stable that they never reacted, life would not exist at all: DNA would not replicate, RNA and proteins would not be made, muscles would not contract and chloroplasts would not fix the sun's energy.

This apparent paradox does not exist because cells are not restricted to chemical reactions that would occur in a test tube of water at neutral pH and low temperatures. Chemical reactions within cells are **catalysed**. Every chemical reaction that occurs in a cell is catalysed by a specific catalyst, a protein molecule called an **enzyme**.

An introduction to catalysis is given in Tutorial 7.2.

7.2 ENZYMES AS PROTEINS

All enzymes are proteins and as such they have the properties of proteins:

- they are polymers of amino acid residues (section 2.3);
- they are denatured by high temperatures and extremes of pH (section 2.3);
- their final shape is determined by the sequence of the amino acid residues and ultimately by the sequence of nucleotide residues in the DNA (section 6.3);
- their three-dimensional structure is unique to that particular protein, a product of its unique primary structure (section 6.3);
- some enzymes require non-protein groups to function efficiently (section 6.3).

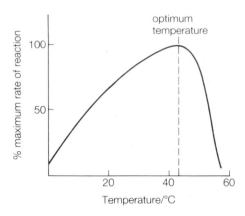

Fig 7.2 Rate of reaction and temperature. When the temperature is varied the rate of a reaction catalysed by an enzyme varies in a characteristic manner. The temperature at which the maximum rate of reaction occurs is called the optimum temperature.

An introduction to rates of reaction is given in Tutorial 7.2, p. 163.

Fig 7.3 Proteases and lipases extracted from bacteria have revolutionised washing detergents. These enzymes hydrolyse the protein and fat in stains, creating soluble fragments that are easy to wash away. As enzymes work most effectively at relatively low temperatures, 40 °C or under, energy can be saved by heating the water to a lower temperature.

Enzymes are denatured by heating

Almost all enzymes are globular proteins: the polypeptide is folded into a compact, almost spherical, shape that is stabilised by weak bonds between the R groups and the polypeptide backbone. When a protein is heated these weak bonds break and the protein loses its typical three-dimensional structure. In the case of an enzyme molecule this means that the molecule loses its typical globular shape.

Enzyme denaturation by heat can be investigated by measuring the rate of the reaction catalysed by the enzyme. Figure 7.2 shows the rate of reaction of an enzyme-catalysed reaction at different temperatures. Between the temperatures of 0 °C and approximately 40 °C the effect of heating on an enzyme-catalysed reaction is very similar to the effect of heating on an uncatalysed reaction, but between 40 °C and 60 °C the rate of reaction starts to decrease. This sudden decrease is typical of a reaction that is being catalysed by an enzyme.

At low temperatures the molecules have little kinetic energy and collisions are few, so the rate of reaction is low. At very low temperatures there is no detectable reaction and the enzyme is said to be **deactivated**. As the temperature rises the molecules have more energy, move faster, and more collisions occur: the reaction rate increases. This is similar to the effect of temperature on most reactions and the graph shows a typical straight line over this temperature range: the rate of reaction is proportional to the temperature. The relationship between the rate of a reaction and temperature can be expressed as the **temperature coefficient**, Q_{10}. An enzyme-catalysed reaction usually has a Q_{10} of 2 between the temperatures of 0–40 °C, indicating that it doubles for each 10 °C rise in temperature.

$$Q_{10} = \frac{\text{rate of reaction at } (x + 10)\ °C}{\text{rate of reaction at } x\ °C}$$

However, at a certain temperature the increase in rate stops and the rate of reaction reaches a maximum. This is the **optimum temperature** for the enzyme because this is the temperature at which the enzyme works 'best'. Above the optimum temperature the rate of the reaction decreases sharply in a manner that is typical of an enzyme-catalysed reaction.

The sharp decrease in the rate of the reaction above the optimum temperature is because the enzyme molecules are being denatured. The weak bonds stabilising the tertiary structure of the enzyme are breaking and as the temperature increases more and more of the enzyme molecules are losing their three-dimensional shape. Experiments like this show that when an enzyme molecule is denatured and loses its three-dimensional shape it no longer works as a catalyst. As the temperature increases there are less and less functional enzyme molecules in the solution so the overall rate of reaction slows. At very high temperature, above about 65 °C, all the enzyme molecules have been denatured and there is no longer any catalyst present. The rate of reaction at this high temperature is the same as for the uncatalysed reaction.

Enzymes are affected by changes in pH

Figure 7.4 compares the rates of some enzyme-catalysed reactions in solutions of varying acidity. The graph obtained by plotting the results of such an experiment is typical of a reaction catalysed by an enzyme. It shows that there is a maximum rate of reaction and the pH at which this maximum occurs is called the **optimum pH** for that particular enzyme. Below and above the optimum pH the graph falls away, showing a decrease in the rate of reaction at both low and high pH.

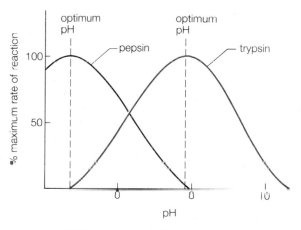

Fig 7.4 Rate of reaction and pH. When the pH is varied the rate of reaction catalysed by an enzyme also varies. The maximum rate of reaction is at the optimum pH and the optimum pH is typical of that particular enzyme.

Both high and low pH affect the enzyme molecules in a similar way. An alteration in the concentration of hydrogen ions (the pH) can change the charges of the R groups of the amino acid residues in the enzyme polypeptide. The precise globular shape of the enzyme molecule is maintained by weak bonds between these R groups and when the charges on the R groups are altered the weak bonds can break and the three-dimensional shape of the molecule is changed. Once the three-dimensional shape of an enzyme molecule is altered that molecule is ineffective as a catalyst and the overall rate of reaction decreases. At very high or very low pH it is likely that all the enzyme molecules will have been denatured, no catalysis will occur and the rate of the reaction will be the same as that of an uncatalysed reaction.

Cofactors are non-protein groups needed by many enzymes

Many enzymes require a non-protein group that is necessary for them to function as catalysts. A non-protein group that is necessary for an enzyme to function is called a **cofactor**. Cofactors come in many different forms, ranging from inorganic ions to complex organic molecules.

Some cofactors are actually integrated into the enzyme itself, remaining as part of the enzyme molecule at all times. Zn^{2+} is a cofactor for the enzyme carboxypeptidase and the zinc ion is part of the structure of the enzyme molecule, held in place by the R groups of the amino acid residues. Haem is a cofactor for a number of different enzymes, including cytochrome oxidase, an enzyme involved in respiration.

Some cofactors are separate from the enzyme itself but still necessary for the enzyme to function as a catalyst. Cofactors that are separate from the enzyme molecule are called **coenzymes**. Coenzymes are often responsible for carrying small groups of atoms into or out of an enzyme-catalysed reaction, for example the coenzyme nicotinamide adenine dinucleotide (NAD) brings hydrogen atoms into a reaction or takes them away from a reaction: it is called a **hydrogen carrier**. NAD and many other coenzymes are discussed in more detail in Chapter 8.

QUESTIONS

7.1 (a) Describe briefly the way in which the rate of a reaction that was catalysed by an inorganic catalyst would be expected to vary with temperature.

(b) Describe briefly the way in which the rate of a reaction that was catalysed by an enzyme would be expected to vary with temperature.

(c) A certain species of bacteria, *Thermus aquaticus*, lives in hot springs where the temperature can be as high as 98 °C. Suggest how the rate of a reaction that was catalysed by an enzyme from *Thermus aquaticus* would vary with temperature.

7.2 Figure 7.2 shows how the rate of a reaction that is catalysed by an enzyme varies with temperature.

(a) Explain why the rate of reaction increases between 0 °C and 40 °C.

(b) Explain why the rate of reaction decreases between 40 °C and 60 °C.

(c) Explain the meaning of the following terms when used to describe an enzyme-catalysed reaction:

- denaturation;
- deactivation;
- optimum temperature.

7.3 Figure 7.1 illustrates the function of lysosomes in the cell.

(a) How do lysosomes dispose of unwanted material in the cell?

(b) Why do the enzymes inside the lysosome have to be pH resistant?

(c) Why does the environment inside the lysosome make proteins easier to digest?

7.4 Figure 7.4 shows the way in which the rate of a reaction that is catalysed by an enzyme varies with the acidity of the solution.

(a) Explain why there is an optimum pH for the reaction.

(b) Explain why the rate of reaction is so low at high or low pH.

(c) The digestion of proteins in the stomach is catalysed by the enzyme pepsin. The hydrochloric acid in the stomach means that the pH of the stomach contents is 1–2. Describe briefly the results you would expect to obtain if you investigated the digestion of protein by pepsin over a range of pH.

7.5 (a) What is a cofactor?

(b) What types of substances function as cofactors in the cell?

(c) What is the difference between a cofactor like NAD and a cofactor like haem?

CHEMICAL REACTIONS IN CELLS

An investigation was carried out into the effect of temperature on a reaction. All factors except temperature were kept constant.

Temperature (°C)	Rate of reaction (mg per minute)
0	0.3
5	0.7
10	1.0
15	1.7
20	2.9
25	3.9
30	5.4
35	6.5
40	7.3
45	7.2
50	4.6
55	1.7
60	0.0

(a) Plot a graph of the rate of reaction against temperature.
(b) Describe the results between 0 °C and 30 °C.
(c) Describe the results between 45 °C and 60 °C.
(d) Use your graph to calculate the optimum temperature of the reaction.
(e) Use your graph to calculate the Q_{10} for this reaction over the temperature range below 40 °C.
(f) What evidence do these data give that this is an enzyme-catalysed reaction?
(g) Can you think of a simple experiment that would confirm that this is indeed an enzyme-catalysed reaction?

TUTORIAL 7.1
NAMING ENZYMES

Most enzymes are named according to a system of rules:

- enzyme names end in -ase, e.g. amylase, hydrolase;
- the **second** part of the name, the one that ends in -ase, describes the **type** of reaction that the enzyme catalyses, e.g. **hydrol**ases hydrolyse the substrate, **hydroxyl**ases add hydroxyl groups and **oxid**ases oxidise the substrate;
- the **first** part of the name is the name of the **substrate**, e.g. **cytochrome** oxidase oxidises a substrate called a cytochrome and **glucose phosphate** isomerase rearranges the atoms in a glucose phosphate molecule.

Like all naming systems there are exceptions to the rules. Some enzymes were discovered and studied long before the naming system was agreed upon and the names of these enzymes have stayed the same, for example pepsin, trypsin and lysozyme. Other enzymes have abbreviated names that are used by so many scientists that no-one bothers to use the right one, for example ATPase and DNase. In order to eliminate this confusion a scientist writing about an enzyme in a scientific journal will also use an internationally agreed name and number for each enzyme.

However, understanding the way in which enzymes are named can be useful when trying to understand a biochemical reaction or process. Table 7.1 summarises the common terms used when naming enzymes.

Table 7.1

- the first part of the name is the substrate for that particular enzyme;
- the second part of the name describes the type of reaction the enzyme catalyses;
- the name should end in -ase.

Class name	Specific types	Reaction catalysed
oxido-reductases		**oxidation–reduction reactions**
	oxidase	oxidation
	dehydrogenase	oxidation by removing hydrogen atoms
	reductase	reduction
	hydrogenase	reduction by adding hydrogen atoms
transferases		**transfer of a reactive group**
	kinase	adding a phosphate group
	phosphorylase	removing a phosphate group
	hydroxylase	adding a hydroxyl group
hydrolases		**hydrolysis**
	protease	hydrolyse proteins
	peptidase	hydrolyse peptides
	DNase	hydrolyse DNA
	RNase	hydrolyse RNA
	amylase	hydrolyse amylose (starch)
lyases		**addition to double bonds**
isomerases		**isomerisation**
	racemase	isomerisation
	mutase	isomerisation
ligases		**formation of a bond with ATP → ADP + phosphate ion**

What types of reactions are catalysed by the following enzymes:

- phosphoglucomutase;
- glycogen phosphorylase;
- pyruvate kinase;
- succinate dehydrogenase;
- hexokinase?

7.3 ENZYMES HAVE THE PROPERTIES OF A CATALYST

All enzymes are catalysts and as such they have the properties of a catalyst:

- they increase the rate of a reaction;
- they do not alter the outcome of the reaction;
- the enzyme itself emerges unchanged from the reaction.

So if a catalysed reaction was compared to an uncatalysed reaction, the same reagents would have been used, the same products would have been made but many more reactions would have occurred during the time in which the reaction was taking place. Enzymes are biological catalysts: they are the catalysts found in organisms.

CHEMICAL REACTIONS IN CELLS

Enzymes, like all catalysts, lower the activation energy

The rate of a reaction can be measured by monitoring how the concentration of the reagents decreases with time or how the concentration of the product increases with time (Tutorial 7.2). To understand how a catalyst works, it is important to relate the overall rate of the reaction to what is happening at the molecular level.

A simple reaction in which a reacting molecule A gives a product molecule B can be modelled by the graph shown in Fig 7.5. In the reaction shown, molecule A has a certain amount of energy stored in it while molecule B has less energy stored in it. If a molecule of A reacts to give a molecule of B it will be an **exergonic** reaction, one in which energy is given out. Even though molecule A has more energy than molecule B it does not automatically react to give B because in order to start reacting it needs extra energy. This is shown in Fig 7.5 as a peak on the graph. We say that there is an **energy barrier** between molecule A and molecule B that must be crossed before molecule A can react. Because of this energy barrier, molecule A is stable: it will stay as it is.

The energy that is needed to overcome the energy barrier is called the **activation energy**. Once molecule A has the activation energy, it will react to form molecule B. As molecule B has less energy than molecule A the overall reaction will have released energy into the surroundings. This extra energy may then be absorbed by another molecule of A, giving it the necessary activation energy to climb the energy barrier and form B.

The rate of the reaction is dependent on the number of molecules of A that form B in a given time. This is dependent on the activation energy. If the activation energy is low many molecules of A will have enough energy to cross the energy barrier and the rate of the reaction will be high. If the activation energy is high very few molecules of A will have the necessary energy to cross the energy barrier and the rate of the reaction will be low. This is why heating a reaction mixture usually speeds up the rate of a reaction.

However, cells cannot be heated up to speed up the rate of a reaction, so the rate is increased by enzymes. Enzymes, like all catalysts, work by decreasing the activation energy of the reaction (Fig 7.5). Once the energy barrier has been lowered the molecules of A will need less energy in order to react to form B. This means that more molecules of A will react, so rate of reaction is increased.

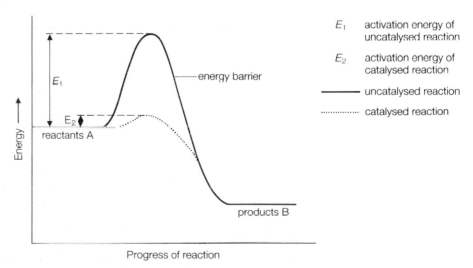

E_1 activation energy of uncatalysed reaction

E_2 activation energy of catalysed reaction

——— uncatalysed reaction

············ catalysed reaction

Fig 7.5 A molecule needs a certain amount of energy to react. This energy is called the activation energy. Catalysts reduce the activation energy of the reaction.

Enzymes are different from other catalysts

Most inorganic catalysts catalyse a series of reactions that involve similar substances. Enzymes, however, are very specific: they catalyse only one particular reaction. An enzyme can distinguish one hexose sugar from another, one amino acid from another or one nucleotide from another. This **specificity** is essential, as many of the molecules within a cell are chemically very similar, often differing from each other only by the position of one small group of atoms. Each enzyme has a specific **substrate**. The substrate is the substance that interacts with the enzyme and then reacts. For example, the enzyme succinate dehydrogenase only catalyses one specific reaction, the dehydrogenation of succinate. The substrate of this reaction is succinate.

Enzymes are very effective catalysts: they have a larger effect on the rate of reaction than do most inorganic catalysts. Many enzymes increase the rate of the reaction that they catalyse from practically zero molecules reacting in every minute to thousands, or even millions, of molecules reacting per minute. However, different enzymes accelerate the reactions they catalyse by differing amounts. We compare the efficiency of different enzymes by comparing the number of molecules of substrate that one enzyme molecule turns into product within one minute. This quantity is called the **turnover number** or **molecular activity** of the enzyme. The turnover numbers of various enzymes are listed in Table 7.2.

Table 7.2

Enzyme	Turnover number (number of substrate molecules transformed per enzyme molecule per minute)
carbonic anhydrase C	36 000 000
catalase	5 600 000
β-amylase	1 100 000
β-galactosidase	12 500
phosphoglucoisomerase	1240
succinate dehydrogenase	1150

7.6 **(a)** What is a catalyst?
   (b) How do enzymes resemble inorganic catalysts?
   (c) How do enzymes differ from inorganic catalysts?

7.7 **(a)** Define the following terms:

   • enzyme;
   • substrate;
   • turnover number.

   (b) β-galactosidase catalyses the breakdown of lactose into glucose and galactose.
   (i) Name the enzyme and the substrate in this reaction.
   (ii) Using Table 7.2 calculate the number of molecules of substrate that will be converted into product by one enzyme molecule in five minutes.
   (iii) What is the total number of product molecules produced during this five minute period?

TUTORIAL 7.2
RATES OF REACTION

The rate of a reaction is the amount of product made in a certain time or the amount of a reactant used up in a certain time.

$$\text{Rate of reaction} = \frac{\text{amount of product produced}}{\text{time taken}}$$

or

$$\text{Rate of reaction} = \frac{\text{amount of reactant used}}{\text{time taken}}$$

The units of a rate are the amount per unit time. For example, if the amount of product produced was being measured in grams the rate would be:

- 'grams per second' written g/s or $g\ s^{-1}$;
- 'grams per minute' written g/min or $g\ min^{-1}$;
- 'grams per hour' written g/h or $g\ h^{-1}$.

Which of these units refer to a rate of reaction: s^{-1}, g/s, mg products produced, millimoles of product made in a minute?

A scientist is investigating the enzyme catalase that converts hydrogen peroxide to oxygen. The time taken for 15 cm^3 of oxygen gas to be produced is recorded. For one reaction mixture this was 5.6 minutes. Use these results to calculate a rate.

The rate of reaction in a solution can be increased in a number of ways including:

- increasing the temperature: this gives each molecule more energy and makes it more likely to react;
- increasing the concentration, because if there are more molecules in a certain volume they will be more likely to meet and therefore to react;
- using a catalyst, a substance that accelerates the reaction.

A catalyst is a substance that increases the rate of a reaction without affecting the final outcome of the reaction and without being used up in the reaction. A catalyst works by allowing the reaction to proceed along a different reaction pathway with a lower activation energy (Fig 7.5). The activation energy is the amount of energy that the molecules have to have before they can react. Not all the molecules present in a solution have the same energy, only a proportion of the molecules will have the activation energy needed to react. If the activation energy is made smaller by using a catalyst more of the molecules will have the necessary energy to react.

Organisms could increase the rate of their cellular reactions by increasing their body temperature. Why is there an upper limit to the body temperature of an organism?

What would happen if the activation energy for a reaction was very low all the time, rather than being low only when the catalyst was present?

7.4 DEFINING AN ENZYME-CATALYSED REACTION

Certain terms are used to describe reactions that are catalysed by enzymes

Thousands of scientists specialise in the study of enzymes and their properties. When many scientists study the same subject they need a language that helps them communicate, so that when one scientist uses a certain word the other scientists interpret it in the right way.

CHEMICAL REACTIONS IN CELLS

The reactants in an enzyme-catalysed reaction are called the **substrates** while the products are still referred to as the **products**. Abbreviations are used: **E** for enzyme, **S** for substrates and **P** for products. Square brackets are used for concentrations: [**S**] means concentration of substrate and [**P**] means concentration of products.

The rate of the reaction can be calculated by measuring the decrease in the concentration of substrate with time or the increase in the concentration of the product with time. The study of the rates of reaction is called **kinetics**. Often, studying the rate of an enzyme-catalysed reaction can tell us a lot about the enzyme and give us some insight into how the enzyme acts within the cell.

The rate of the reaction is usually given the symbol v (for velocity). To keep matters simple, all the rates of reaction mentioned here are **initial rates**, the rate of the reaction immediately after the enzyme and the substrate(s) have been mixed together. This is because the concentration of substrate is altered as soon as the reaction is underway and the rate of reaction will change accordingly. By sticking to the initial rate it can be assumed that the concentration of the substrate is the concentration that was added at the start.

Enzymes show saturation kinetics

Scientists investigating the rate of a reaction usually measure the way that the initial rate of the reaction varies with the initial concentration of the substrate and plot a graph of rate of reaction, v, against concentration of substrate, [S]. For a simple reaction, involving only one substrate, one might expect the rate of the reaction to be proportional to the concentration of the substrate. As can be seen from Fig 7.6 this is true for low substrate concentrations; the first part of the graph is a straight line with a positive gradient, confirming that the rate of reaction is proportional to the substrate concentration. However, at high substrate concentrations this is no longer the case: the graph flattens out and the rate of reaction becomes independent of the substrate concentration; increasing the substrate concentration no longer increases the rate of the reaction.

There appears to a maximum rate of reaction, or V_{max}, for the enzyme-catalysed reaction. Once the V_{max} has been reached, increasing the substrate concentration no longer increases the rate of the reaction. However, adding a little more enzyme increases the V_{max} (Fig 7.6): this implies that the rate

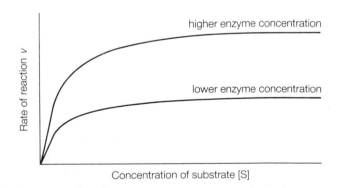

Fig 7.6 When the initial rate of reaction is measured at different substrate concentrations, it can be shown that the rate of reaction is proportional to the concentration of substrate at low substrate concentrations but independent of substrate concentration at high substrate concentrations. This phenomenon is typical of enzymes and the maximum rate of reaction can only be increased by increasing the concentration of the enzyme.

CHEMICAL REACTIONS IN CELLS

limiting factor at high substrate concentrations is the concentration of the enzyme.

As enzymes are catalysts, and as such are not used up in the reaction, it seems a little odd that the rate limiting factor, the thing stopping the reaction from going faster, should be the concentration of the enzyme. Scientists deduced that at some point during the reaction the substrate molecule must bind to the enzyme molecule in a one-to-one manner. This would mean that it was possible to **saturate** the enzyme molecules with substrate molecules. If every enzyme molecule has a substrate molecule bound to it, then adding more substrate molecules could not possibly make any difference to the overall rate of the reaction, only adding more enzyme molecules would allow the reaction to go faster. Scientists called this phenomenon **saturation** and the shape of the graph shown in Fig 7.6 is typical of a reaction that is catalysed by an enzyme. The fact that all reactions catalysed by enzymes showed saturation led scientists in the early part of this century to suggest that the substrate molecules must actually bind to the enzyme molecule, forming an **enzyme–substrate complex**.

$$E + S \rightleftharpoons ES \rightleftharpoons E + P$$

An enzyme's kinetics reflect its role in the cell

The kinetics of enzyme-catalysed reactions were studied in detail by Leonor Michaelis and L.M. Menten. Their analysis, first published in 1913, is rather mathematical but some of their conclusions can be used to compare different enzymes without understanding how these conclusions were reached.

Michaelis and Menten identified two important measurements of enzyme activity: V_{max}, the maximum rate of reaction when the enzyme is saturated (Fig 7.7), and K_m, the Michaelis Menten constant. The K_m of a reaction is the substrate concentration when the rate of reaction is $\frac{1}{2}V_{max}$ (Fig 7.7).

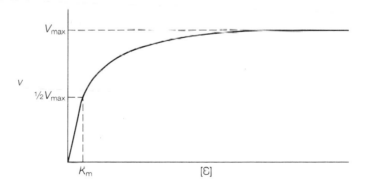

Fig 7.7 Michaelis–Menten kinetics identified two important parameters: the V_{max}, the maximum rate of reaction, and K_m the substrate concentration that gave $\frac{1}{2}V_{max}$

Michaelis–Menten kinetics say that the K_m of a particular enzyme with a particular substrate should always be the same. Alterations in the K_m of an enzyme point to the presence of certain types of **inhibitors**, substances that slow the reaction, or **activators**, substances that accelerate the reaction. This is discussed in section 7.7.

The K_m of an enzyme indicates whether the enzyme functions efficiently at low substrate concentrations or whether it requires a high substrate concentration in order to catalyse the reaction effectively. If the K_m is low this

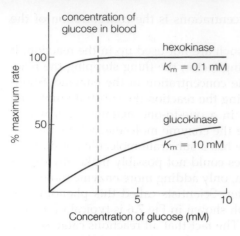

Fig 7.8 Hexokinase and glucokinase catalyse the same reaction but each has a very different K_m. This means that hexokinase works efficiently at a low glucose concentration while glucokinase only functions when there is an excess of glucose to be removed from the blood.

indicates that half the maximum rate, $\frac{1}{2}V_{max}$, is achieved at low substrate concentrations so the enzyme should function efficiently at all substrate concentrations. If the K_m is high this indicates that half the maximum rate, $\frac{1}{2}V_{max}$, is achieved only at high substrate concentrations and that the enzyme is ineffective at low substrate concentrations.

This is illustrated by two enzymes: **hexokinase** and **glucokinase**. Both enzymes catalyse the same reaction, the phosphorylation of α-glucose.

$$\alpha\text{-glucose} + \text{ATP} \xrightarrow{\text{Mg}^{2+}} \alpha\text{-glucose 6-phosphate} + \text{ADP}$$

Hexokinase has a low K_m, 0.1 mM glucose, while glucokinase has a high K_m, 10 mM glucose (Fig 7.8). This reflects the different roles that the two enzymes have in the mammalian body.

All cells produce small amounts of glucose 6-phosphate from glucose as the first step in respiration, the process by which all cells produce their energy. Only a small amount of glucose 6-phosphate is required, but that amount is essential and it must be produced even if the glucose concentration is low. In order to produce this glucose 6-phosphate from glucose all cells contain the enzyme hexokinase. Hexokinase has a low K_m, so it catalyses the reaction efficiently even when the glucose concentration is low. This ensures that the necessary amount of glucose 6-phosphate is maintained in the cell at all times.

Liver cells also covert glucose into glucose 6-phosphate so that the glucose 6-phosphate can be polymerised to make glycogen. Liver cells contain the enzyme glucokinase as well as the enzyme hexokinase. When the glucose level in the blood rises, for example after a meal, a lot of glucose is transported into the liver cells in order to control the blood glucose level. Glucokinase has a high K_m which means that it only functions efficiently when the glucose concentration is high, so the glucokinase only comes into operation when it is required, for example after a meal.

Studies of the kinetics of hexokinase have shown that it is regulated by the product of the reaction that it catalyses, glucose 6-phosphate. Glucose 6-phosphate inhibits hexokinase, slowing down the rate of the reaction. This means that the required amount of glucose 6-phosphate is produced in the cell by hexokinase and after this amount is produced the enzyme is inactive. This ensures that exactly the correct amount of glucose 6-phosphate is always present in the cell so that respiration can proceed: enough is produced because hexokinase has a low K_m and therefore works even if the glucose concentration is very low but too high a level of glucose 6-phosphate is prevented because hexokinase is inhibited by glucose 6-phosphate.

In contrast, glucokinase is not inhibited by glucose 6-phosphate. This means that glucokinase will continue working as an efficient catalyst even when the concentration of glucose 6-phosphate is high. Glucokinase is ideally suited to its role in liver cells: it has a high K_m so it only works when the concentration of glucose is high and it is not inhibited by glucose 6-phosphate so a large amount of glucose 6-phosphate can be produced to make glycogen.

By studying the kinetics of an enzyme-catalysed reaction and defining an enzyme's K_m and V_{max}, we can make deductions about the way in which the enzyme will function within the cell: for example, knowing the K_m of hexokinase and glucokinase gave us important clues as to their separate roles in liver cells. We can also investigate the effect that other substances have on the rate of the reaction and from their results we can infer how the enzyme is regulated within the cell: for example, demonstrating that glucose 6-phosphate inhibits hexokinase suggests an explanation of why only a limited amount of glucose 6-phosphate is produced in a cell unless glucokinase is present.

7.8 What is meant by the following terms when applied to the study of reactions that are catalysed by enzymes:

- [S];
- enzyme–substrate complex;
- V_{max};
- K_m?

7.9 Study Fig 7.9.

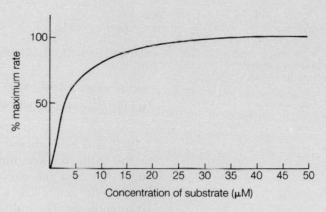

Fig 7.9

(a) Describe the relationship between the rate of the reaction and substrate concentration between 0 mM substrate and 2.5 mM substrate.

(b) Describe the relationship between the rate of the reaction and the substrate concentration between 25mM substrate and 50 mM substrate.

(c) Estimate the K_m for the enzyme.

7.10 (a) What reaction is catalysed by both hexokinase and glucokinase?

(b) Why does a liver cell contain both hexokinase and glucokinase when both enzymes catalyse the same reaction?

7.5 MODELS OF ENZYME ACTION

There are two main models of enzyme action

The overall rate of a reaction depends on the whole population of molecules, millions of enzyme molecules binding with millions of substrate molecules to give millions of product molecules. However, to understand how enzymes work we must also consider what is happening at the molecular level, how an individual enzyme molecule binds the substrate and how that substrate reacts to form the product. After over a hundred years of studying enzymes, scientists talk of two main models for the way that enzymes work: the lock and key hypothesis and the induced fit hypothesis.

The **lock and key hypothesis** is a very powerful model that has helped generations of scientists to think clearly about enzyme-catalysed reactions. It originated with Emil Fischer who suggested in 1894 that the enzyme was a 'lock' that could only be opened by a certain 'key', the specific substrate for that enzyme. The lock and key hypothesis has gone through many modifications and elaborations over the last century but central to the model is the idea that there is a 'keyhole' in the enzyme that is a specific, fixed shape. This 'keyhole' is called the **active site**. The active site is where the substrate binds to the enzyme and where the reaction occurs. The active site is exactly the right shape to bind the substrate molecule: the substrate binds to the enzyme like a key fitting into a lock. Once the substrate has bound to the active site the reaction occurs and the product is released. The lock and key hypothesis is outlined in Fig 7.10.

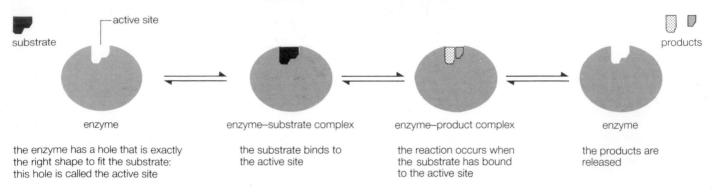

the enzyme has a hole that is exactly the right shape to fit the substrate: this hole is called the active site

the substrate binds to the active site

the reaction occurs when the substrate has bound to the active site

the products are released

Fig 7.10 The lock and key hypothesis.

In 1959 D.E. Koshland proposed an alternative model of enzyme action to the lock and key model. Central to this alternative model was the suggestion that the enzyme changes shape when the substrate molecule binds to the active site. Koshland called his alternative model the **induced fit hypothesis**. The induced fit hypothesis also includes an active site, but this active site is the wrong shape to catalyse the reaction when there is no substrate bound. Koshland proposed that the active site changes shape when the substrate binds and that the change in shape is essential: the reaction would not take place without it. Once the product is released the enzyme falls back into its original shape. The induced fit hypothesis is outlined in Fig 7.11.

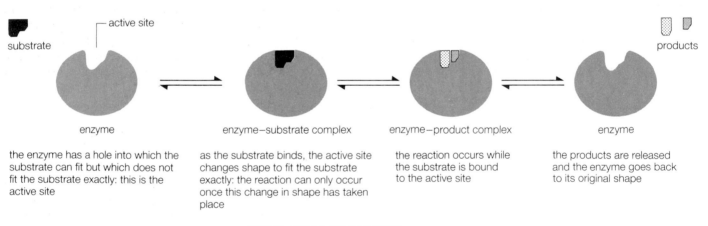

the enzyme has a hole into which the substrate can fit but which does not fit the substrate exactly: this is the active site

as the substrate binds, the active site changes shape to fit the substrate exactly: the reaction can only occur once this change in shape has taken place

the reaction occurs while the substrate is bound to the active site

the products are released and the enzyme goes back to its original shape

Fig 7.11 The induced fit hypothesis.

Both models explain the specificity of enzymes

Enzymes are specific: they only catalyse a single reaction or occasionally a series of very closely related reactions. The lock and key model explains the specificity of enzymes because it postulates that the active site has a precise shape that will bind only the substrate molecule; no other molecule will fit. In the terminology of the lock and key hypothesis the active site is the 'lock' and only the correct 'key', the substrate, will fit within it.

The induced fit hypothesis explains the specificity of enzymes even better than the lock and key hypothesis. In the induced fit hypothesis there has to be a change in shape before the reaction can occur and this change in shape can only happen if the correct substrate binds. In the induced fit hypothesis the whole of the structure of the substrate molecule is important, not just the reactive group, because the whole molecule is needed to make the active site change shape.

Both models explain why enzymes display saturation kinetics

Reactions catalysed by enzymes show saturation kinetics (Fig 7.7); there is a maximum rate of reaction, V_{max}, for a given concentration of enzyme. Both the lock and key hypothesis and the induced fit hypothesis state that every substrate molecule must bind to an active site in order for the reaction to take place. This means that the number of active sites is the limiting factor at high concentrations of substrate: the maximum rate of reaction will occur when all the active sites are occupied. Once all the active sites are occupied by substrate molecules, increasing the substrate concentration further will make no difference to the rate as there are no more active sites available.

There is evidence for an active site

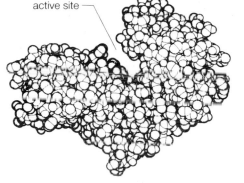

active site

Fig 7.12 There is a groove or pocket in the enzyme where the substrate will bind: this is the active site.

Both the lock and key hypothesis and the induced fit hypothesis depend on the existence of an active site, a place on the enzyme molecule where the substrate binds and where the reaction occurs. The existence of the active site has been confirmed by X-ray diffraction studies that have given accurate three-dimensional structures for a number of enzymes. Grooves or pockets can be seen in these structures and the substrate can be shown to occupy these grooves or pockets (Fig 7.12). This confirms that there is a site in the enzyme molecule where the substrate binds and presumably where the reaction occurs.

There is also a lot of evidence to suggest that altering the active site destroys the catalytic activity of the enzyme. Treatments that are known to make a protein lose its three-dimensional shape, like heating the protein or exposing it to extremes of pH, wipe out enzyme activity. Also, modifying the R groups that are known to be in the active site wipes out catalytic activity in many enzymes. These results imply that the active site is where the substrate binds and the reaction occurs.

There is evidence that the active site changes shape when the substrate binds

The crucial difference between the lock and key hypothesis and the induced fit hypothesis is that in the lock and key hypothesis the active site has a rigid shape that exactly fits the substrate while in the induced fit hypothesis the active site changes shape as the substrate binds. Koshland suggested that the lock and key hypothesis did not explain why enzymes did not catalyse reactions when the substrate was replaced by a smaller but chemically similar molecule. If the active site was precisely the correct shape to catalyse the reaction, as the lock and key hypothesis suggested, these small molecules should be able to slip into the site and undergo the reaction. This does not happen: only the substrate itself reacts.

Koshland suggested that an extra step that had to happen before the reaction could take place and that this extra step required the correct substrate. He suggested that the R groups necessary for the reaction were not in the right positions for the reaction to occur when the enzyme had no substrate bound. When the small molecules enter the active site they do not fit the active site and the R groups stay in the wrong positions. However, when the correct substrate enters the active site of the shape, the whole protein changes to bring the R groups into the correct positions and the reaction goes ahead.

X-ray diffraction studies of the enzyme carboxypeptidase have provided evidence that a change in shape does occur when the substrate binds. Scientists have compared the shape of the enzyme carboxypeptidase with the shape of carboxypeptidase with a bound substrate molecule and shown that the enzyme does indeed have a different structure to the enzyme part of the enzyme–substrate complex.

These X-ray diffraction data support the idea that there is a change in the three-dimensional structure of the enzyme, what is called a **conformational** change, when the substrate binds. This indicates that the induced fit hypothesis may be more accurate than the lock and key hypothesis; but it should be kept in mind that the induced fit hypothesis grew out of the lock and key hypothesis and in many ways is merely a modification of the lock and key model.

QUESTIONS

7.11 Two hypotheses have been suggested to explain the mechanism of enzyme action: the lock and key hypothesis and the induced fit hypothesis.
(a) What features do these two models have in common?
(b) In which ways do these models differ?

7.12 Enzymes are specific catalysts.
(a) What is meant by 'specific'?
(b) How far do the lock and key hypothesis and the induced fit hypothesis go to explain the fact that enzymes are specific catalysts?

7.13 (a) How does the lock and key hypothesis depend on the fact that enzymes are proteins?
(b) In what additional way is the induced fit hypothesis dependent on the fact that enzymes are proteins?

7.14 The following two observations have been made by scientists:

- molecules having the same reactive groups as glucose but smaller in size do not react when bound to the active site of hexokinase;
- X-ray diffraction studies of carboxypeptidase show that the free enzyme has a different structure to the enzyme portion of the enzyme–substrate complex.

(a) Why do these two observations imply that the lock and key hypothesis does not reflect the true molecular situation?
(b) How does the induced fit hypothesis account for these observations?

7.6 THE CATALYTIC ACTIVITY OF ENZYMES

Models of enzyme action do not explain catalysis

Both the lock and key hypothesis and the induced fit hypothesis explain the specificity of enzymes and explain why enzymes display saturation kinetics, but they do not explain how enzymes actually catalyse reactions. Several mechanisms by which enzymes accelerate the rate of the reaction they catalyse have been suggested. The main suggestions are as follows:

- that enzymes increase the effective concentration of the substrate;
- that enzymes ensure that the reacting groups are always exactly in the correct positions for the reaction to occur;
- that enzymes allow the reaction to proceed by a different reaction pathway, therefore lowering the activation energy required;

- that enzymes impose a strain on the substrate molecule, forcing it into a shape in which it is more likely to react;
- that enzymes stabilise the transition state of the reaction, so decreasing the activation energy.

Some of these suggestions are consistent with the lock and key hypothesis, while others suggest that the lock and key model may be a little simple and that a more complex model, such as the induced fit hypothesis, may be needed to explain an enzyme's catalytic activity.

Enzymes increase the effective concentration of the substrate

One suggestion is that the enzyme increases the effective concentration of the substrate. The substrate molecules are physically brought together in the active site of the enzyme instead of having to collide randomly. This increases the probability of the reaction occurring and therefore increases the rate of the reaction. This bringing together of substrate molecules is included in both the lock and key and the induced fit models of enzyme action. However, it cannot explain all catalysis because many reactions catalysed by enzymes involve only one substrate molecule, so bringing the substrate molecules together is irrelevant.

Enzymes bind the substrate in the correct orientation

Another suggestion is that the enzyme molecule holds the substrate molecules in exactly the right position, so that the reacting groups are adjacent to each other. Holding the reactive groups in exactly the correct orientation would increase the probability of the molecules reacting and thus increase the rate of reaction. This suggestion is consistent with both models, as they both propose that the active site has a precise three-dimensional shape which would be ideal for ensuring that the molecules were in the correct orientation. It is not important to this argument whether the exact shape of the active site is fixed before the substrate binds, as the lock and key hypothesis suggests, or whether the active site changes shape when the correct substrate binds, as proposed in the induced fit hypothesis: either way the substrate molecules would be orientated correctly. It is even possible to imagine that orientation is important in a one-molecule reaction, because the molecule must be bound so that the reacting groups within the same molecule are close together. However, it is doubtful that orientating the substrate molecule(s) correctly accounts for catalysis by all enzymes.

Enzymes provide alternative reaction pathways with lower activation energies

One idea is that the enzyme could provide an alternative reaction pathway in which the highest energy barrier was much lower than that of the uncatalysed reaction. The reaction still starts at the substrate and ends at the product but it would go through a number of intermediate steps involving the enzyme (Fig 7.13). Each step would have a much lower activation energy than the uncatalysed, one-step reaction. There would be a lower energy barrier, more molecules would have the necessary energy to react and the rate of reaction would increase.

If the reaction in the active site did follow an alternative pathway, we might expect to see reaction intermediates that involved the enzyme itself. The active site of the enzyme is lined with the R groups of amino acid residues, so an R group could react with the substrate, producing a reaction intermediate. This reaction intermediate could then react to produce the product and regenerate the R group, leaving the enzyme in its original state. Such reaction intermediates have been found for various enzymes, for example phosphoglucoisomerase.

The suggestion that enzymes catalyse reactions by creating an alternative reaction pathway with a lower activation energy is compatible with both

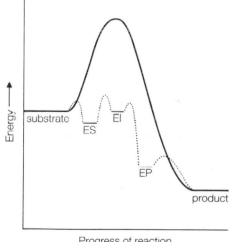

----- catalysed reaction

―――― uncatalysed reaction

ES   enzyme–substrate complex

EI   enzyme–intermediate complex

EP   enzyme–product complex

Fig 7.13 The enzyme allows an alternative reaction mechanism to occur. The maximum activation energy of the alternative pathway is smaller than that of the uncatalysed reaction.

the lock and key hypothesis and the induced fit hypothesis. None of the events suggested in either model conflict with the idea that the reaction itself occurs by a different mechanism from the uncatalysed reaction.

The enzyme may bend the substrate, forcing it to react

When a molecule reacts it changes into a different molecule and there is a very unstable intermediate form that is called the **transition state**. As the transition state molecule is very unstable it has a lot of energy; in fact, it is at the top of the energy barrier (Fig 7.14). Scientists have suggested that enzymes catalyse reactions by bending the substrate, forcing it into the transition state. In a way, the enzyme molecule is giving the substrate molecule the energy it needs to climb to the top of the energy barrier by bending and twisting it into the transition state. In other words, the enzyme catalyses the reaction by providing the activation energy necessary.

This proposed bending of the substrate molecule could take place in one of two ways: the active site could fit the transition state rather than the substrate, forcing the substrate into the transition state as it entered the active site, or the enzyme could change change shape, bending the substrate molecule once it had bound. Neither of these suggestions are compatible with the lock and key hypothesis. The idea that the active site is the correct shape to bind the transition state rather than the substrate is in direct conflict with the lock and key model that states that the active site is exactly the correct shape to bind the substrate molecule. The idea that the active site might actually change shape is even more in conflict with the lock and key hypothesis which treats the enzyme like a solid 'lock' that fits its individual 'key', the substrate, precisely. Unlike the lock and key model, the induced fit hypothesis is compatible with the suggestion that the substrate molecule is bent into the transition state, making the reaction more likely. A change in shape of the active site is essential to the induced fit hypothesis, so the suggestion that the change of shape goes a little further, bending the substrate molecule out of shape, would fit with the induced fit hypothesis quite well.

The enzyme may stabilise the transition state

It has also been suggested that enzymes might stabilise the transition state of the reaction. If the transition state is stabilised its energy will be decreased and this would decrease the overall activation energy of the reaction (Fig 7.14). If the activation energy was decreased more of the substrate molecules would have the necessary energy to cross the energy barrier and the overall rate of reaction would increase. The stabilisation would occur because of interactions between the transition state and the R groups in the active site. The suggestion that R groups in the active site may stabilise the transition state does not fit very well into the lock and key model of enzyme action. In the lock and key hypothesis the active site fits the substrate exactly, and it is difficult to imagine an active site that both fits the substrate exactly and forms stabilising weak bonds with the transition state. The induced fit model would accommodate stabilisation of the transition site more easily than the lock and key model. The induced fit hypothesis suggests that the active site is a dynamic structure that changes shape. It is possible to imagine the active site changing shape as the substrate bound, bending the substrate and then stabilising the transition state. The reaction would then be completed, the product released and the enzyme would revert to its resting state.

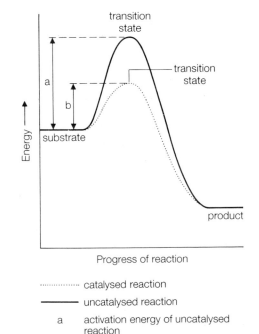

catalysed reaction
uncatalysed reaction

a   activation energy of uncatalysed reaction

b   activation energy of catalysed reaction

Fig 7.14   The enzyme might stabilise the transition state, thus reducing the activation energy of the catalysed reaction.

A variety of mechanisms probably occurs

It is likely that all the mechanisms suggested above play some role in catalysis in some enzymes. It it even possible to imagine that a single enzyme

CHEMICAL REACTIONS IN CELLS

could achieve the necessary increase in the rate of reaction using a variety of these mechanisms. Section 7.8 examines a single enzyme, lysozyme, and discusses how that particular enzyme achieves catalysis.

QUESTIONS

7.15 (a) How would the following increase the rate of a reaction
A + B → C:
    (i) bringing a molecule of A and a molecule of B physically together;
    (ii) ensuring that the molecules of A and B are correctly orientated?
(b) How do enzymes:
    (i) bring molecules of substrate physically together;
    (ii) ensure that the molecules of substrate are correctly orientated?

7.16 (a) What is meant by activation energy?
(b) Explain why lowering the activation energy will increase the rate of a reaction.
(c) Suggest two ways in which an enzyme can lower the activation energy of a reaction.

7.17 (a) What is a transition state?
(b) Explain how bending a substrate molecule so that it resembled the transition state could increase the rate of a reaction.
(c) How is this bending dependent on the catalyst being an enzyme?

7.7 THE CONTROL OF ENZYME ACTION

The cell does not need every enzyme working at full rate at all times. Some enzymes are needed one millisecond but not the next and must be kept on standby in an inactive form; others must produce a certain amount of product and then stop. Enzyme activity must be controlled or **regulated** in the cell.

Inhibitors give an insight into how enzymes are regulated

Scientists studying enzyme kinetics discovered that certain substances slowed the rate of reaction when they were added to the reaction mixture. These substances are called **enzyme inhibitors**. Further studies showed that there were two common types of enzyme inhibitors that had different effects on the kinetics of the inhibited reaction. These were called **competitive inhibitors** and **noncompetitive inhibitors** because of the way in which they are thought to inhibit the reaction.

Competitive inhibitors resemble the substrate in shape but they cannot react. The similarity in shape means that the competitive inhibitor can bind to the active site, but as it cannot react it comes away again without producing any product (Fig 7.15). The active site is therefore occupied by the competitive inhibitor for some of the time and during this time no substrate molecule can bind. This decreases the number of reactions occurring in the active sites and slows the overall rate of reaction. The classic example of competitive inhibition is the inhibition of succinate dehydrogenase by various substances that resemble the substrate, succinate. Figure 7.16 shows succinate with three of the competitive inhibitors.

The competitive inhibitor and the substrate are competing for a limited number of active sites, so increasing the substrate concentration reduces the amount of inhibition that occurs. If there is one molecule of competitive inhibitor for every one molecule of substrate, the reaction will be slower

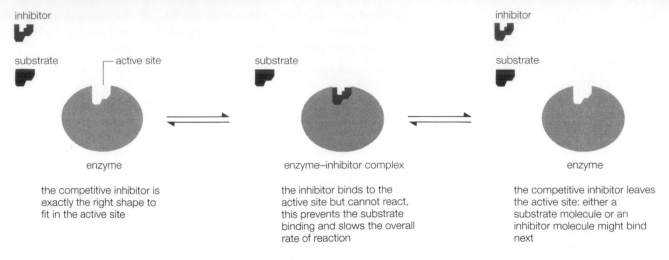

the competitive inhibitor is exactly the right shape to fit in the active site

the inhibitor binds to the active site but cannot react, this prevents the substrate binding and slows the overall rate of reaction

the competitive inhibitor leaves the active site: either a substrate molecule or an inhibitor molecule might bind next

Fig 7.15 Competitive inhibition.

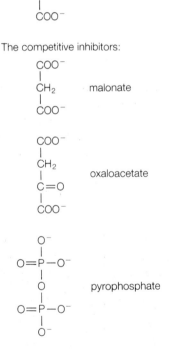

The substrate:

$$\begin{array}{c} COO^- \\ | \\ CH_2 \\ | \\ CH_2 \\ | \\ COO^- \end{array} \quad \text{succinate}$$

The competitive inhibitors:

$$\begin{array}{c} COO^- \\ | \\ CH_2 \\ | \\ COO^- \end{array} \quad \text{malonate}$$

$$\begin{array}{c} COO^- \\ | \\ CH_2 \\ | \\ C=O \\ | \\ COO^- \end{array} \quad \text{oxaloacetate}$$

$$\begin{array}{c} O^- \\ | \\ O=P-O^- \\ | \\ O \\ | \\ O=P-O^- \\ | \\ O^- \end{array} \quad \text{pyrophosphate}$$

Fig 7.16 The competitive inhibitors of the enzyme succinate dehydrogenase all resemble the substrate, succinate. Each inhibitor has two anionic groups, one at each end of the molecule.

than if there are ten molecules of substrate for every one molecule of competitive inhibitor. Therefore, if there is a competitive inhibitor present and the substrate concentration is increased to a very high level the effect of the competitive inhibitor will be swamped and the rate of the reaction will be the same as it would be if no competitive inhibitor was present.

Comparing the graph of rate of reaction, v, against substrate concentration, [S], with and without a competitive inhibitor present (Fig 7.17, red graph) shows this quite clearly. The maximum rate of the reaction, V_{max}, is the same with and without the competitive inhibitor but when the inhibitor is present a much higher substrate concentration is needed to achieve this maximum rate. As a consequence, K_m, the substrate concentration at which $\frac{1}{2}V_{max}$ is achieved, is higher when the competitive inhibitor is present.

Noncompetitive inhibition occurs when the inhibitor binds to the enzyme and prevents the reaction from occurring. A noncompetitive inhibitor binds to a site on the enzyme other than the active site and it is thought that the inhibitor causes a change in the shape of the enzyme, preventing it from binding the substrate, or changes the shape of the enzyme–substrate complex so it cannot react (Fig 7.18).

Noncompetitive inhibition can be distinguished from competitive inhibition by increasing the substrate concentration. This does not reverse inhibition by a noncompetitive inhibitor, because the inhibitor and the substrate are not binding to the same site on the enzyme. As the inhibitor cannot be

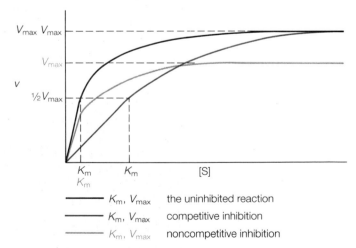

Fig 7.17 Inhibition of an enzyme can be detected by studying the kinetics of the reaction. Competitive inhibition does not change the V_{max}, but increases the K_m. Noncompetitive inhibition does not change the K_m but reduces the V_{max}.

CHEMICAL REACTIONS IN CELLS

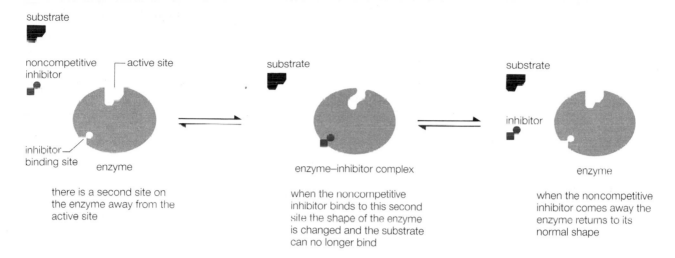

substrate

noncompetitive inhibitor — active site

inhibitor binding site   enzyme

there is a second site on the enzyme away from the active site

substrate

enzyme–inhibitor complex

when the noncompetitive inhibitor binds to this second site the shape of the enzyme is changed and the substrate can no longer bind

substrate

inhibitor

enzyme

when the noncompetitive inhibitor comes away the enzyme returns to its normal shape

Fig 7.18 Noncompetitive inhibition.

competed out, a noncompetitive inhibitor does affect the maximum rate of the reaction because some of the enzyme molecules are out of action, even at high substrate concentrations.

Comparing the graph of rate of reaction, v, against substrate concentration, $[S]$, with and without a noncompetitive inhibitor present (Fig 7.17, grey graph) shows this quite clearly. The maximum rate of the reaction, V_{max}, is lower when the noncompetitive inhibitor is present. However the K_m, the substrate concentration at which $\frac{1}{2}V_{max}$ is achieved, is the same whether the noncompetitive inhibitor is present or not. This is because adding a noncompetitive inhibitor has the same effect as lowering the concentration of enzyme but does not affect the way the substrate interacts with those enzyme molecules that are uninhibited.

By definition, noncompetitive inhibitors must act reversibly. Many enzymes contain -SH R-groups and these enzymes are noncompetitively inhibited by heavy metal ions. These heavy metal ions react reversibly with one or more -SH groups, replacing the hydrogen atom with a heavy metal atom. Although the -SH group is away from the active site, the modification changes the shape of the enzyme, preventing the reaction. The inhibition is reversible: if the concentration of heavy metal ions is reduced, the -SH groups revert to their original structure and the reaction can proceed.

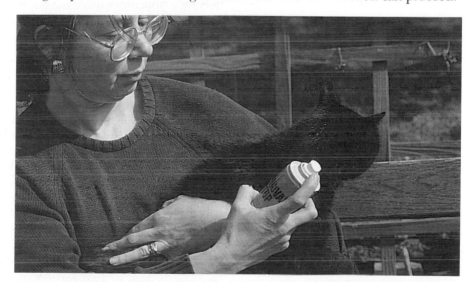

Fig 7.19 Fighting the fleas has been helped by the creation of insecticides that are irreversible inhibitors of the insect enzyme cholinesterase. This causes the malfunction of the nerve impulses in the insect and immediate death but does not affect the cat, which does not have the same cholinesterase enzyme.

Certain inhibitors totally inactivate the enzyme, making it incapable of ever catalysing another reaction. These inhibitors are called **irreversible inhibitors**. Irreversible inhibitors affect the rate of reaction slowly but the inhibition then increases. This is because the inhibitor is reacting with each enzyme molecule, chemically modifying it so that it is permanently inactivated. The longer the time, the more reactions that have occurred and the more enzyme molecules that are inactivated. One example of irreversible inhibition is the nerve poison diisopropylphosphofluoridate. This permanently inactivates the enzyme acetylcholinesterase, which is necessary for nerves to function.

Enzyme inhibitors are studied by scientists in test tubes but also affect enzymes in organisms. Many poisons, such as the nerve poison mentioned above, inhibit important enzymes in humans and cause death. Even more inhibitors occur naturally in cells and are used to regulate the rate of the reaction in the cell.

Some enzymes in cells are regulated by enzyme modulators

The most important type of inhibition in cells is a form of noncompetitive inhibition. **Allosteric enzymes** have two sites (Fig 7.20): they have the active site that binds the substrate and another site that binds another molecule. This other molecule can inhibit the enzyme, and as it is binding to the enzyme away from the active site this is a form of noncompetitive inhibition.

One example of an allosteric enzyme has already been mentioned in section 7.4. The enzyme hexokinase is inhibited by glucose 6-phosphate, the product of the reaction it catalyses. The glucose 6-phosphate inhibits the enzyme by binding to a site away from the active site, changing the shape of the enzyme and preventing the reaction. This inhibition has the effect of regulating the amount of glucose 6-phosphate produced, because once enough glucose 6-phosphate is produced there is enough present to bind to the enzyme at the second site, inhibiting the enzyme so that no more glucose 6-phosphate will be produced. However, if the concentration of glucose 6-phosphate falls the glucose 6-phosphate will come away from the second binding site, the enzyme will become active again, and more glucose 6-phosphate will be produced.

Series of linked reactions occur in cells, each catalysed by its own enzyme. These series of reactions are called **biochemical pathways** because they are the pathway by which a certain substance is produced. These pathways are usually regulated so that the amount of the final product can be controlled. The first enzyme in the pathway is usually an allosteric enzyme that is inhibited by the final product of the pathway. This phenomenon is called **end product inhibition**. It is a form of negative feedback, because if too much of the end product is produced the first enzyme in the pathway will be inhibited and production will stop. However, if the concentration of the end product then falls the inhibition will be reversed and more of the end product will be produced.

It is also possible for an enzyme to be *stimulated* by a molecule binding to another site separate from the active site. Substances that bind to the enzyme at a site other than the active site and that regulate enzyme activity are called **modulators** (Fig 7.20).

Some enzymes have both negative modulators (inhibitors) and positive modulators (stimulators). One well studied example is aspartate carbamoyltransferase (ATCase), an enzyme in the bacterium *E. coli*. This enzyme occurs in two forms, an active form when ATP is bound to the enzyme and an inactive form when CTP is bound to the enzyme. ATP is a positive modulator of ATCase and and CTP is a negative modulator of ATCase.

CHEMICAL REACTIONS IN CELLS

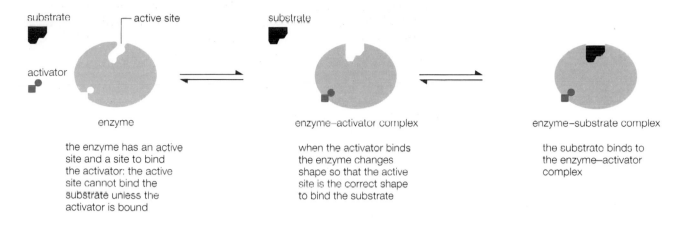

the enzyme has an active site and a site to bind the activator: the active site cannot bind the substrate unless the activator is bound

when the activator binds the enzyme changes shape so that the active site is the correct shape to bind the substrate

the substrate binds to the enzyme–activator complex

Negative modulation

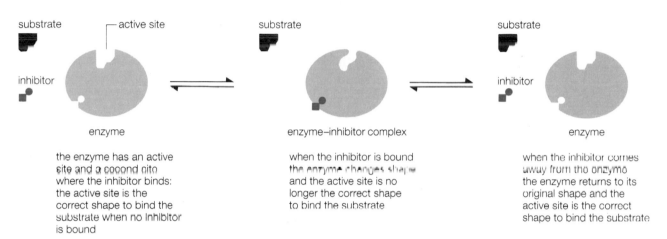

the enzyme has an active site and a second site where the inhibitor binds: the active site is the correct shape to bind the substrate when no inhibitor is bound

when the inhibitor is bound the enzyme changes shape and the active site is no longer the correct shape to bind the substrate

when the inhibitor comes away from the enzyme the enzyme returns to its original shape and the active site is the correct shape to bind the substrate

Some enzymes in cells are regulated by covalent modifications

Binding a second molecule away from the active site is not the only way of regulating an enzyme. Some enzymes also exist in an inactive form and an active form but the difference between the two is a covalent modification. The most common of these modifications is phosphorylation, where a phosphate group is covalently bonded to a serine residue.

One example of this is the enzyme glycogen phosphorylase that occurs in mammals. Glycogen phosphorylase exists in two forms, phosphorylase a, which catalyses the reaction, and phosphorylase b, which is inactive. The active form, phosphorylase a, is phosphorylated while the inactive form, phosphorylase b, is not. The two forms of the enzyme are interconverted by another pair of enzymes, phosphorylase kinase and phosphorylase phosphatase (Fig 7.21).

Phosphorylation is an example of a reversible covalent modification, but other covalent modifications are permanent. One example is the conversion of an inactive enzyme to an active enzyme by cutting the polypeptide chain. This cutting (a hydrolysis reaction) is done by an enzyme. This occurs for many of the proteases present in the mammalian digestive system. Pepsin, trypsin and chymotrypsin are all secreted into the gut in an inactive form: pepsinogen (the inactive form of pepsin), trypsinogen (the inactive form of trypsin) and chymotrypsinogen (the inactive form of

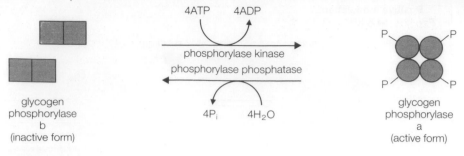

Fig 7.21 The enzyme glycogen phosphorylase is regulated by covalently modifying one of the amino acid residues.

chymotrypsin). Pepsinogen is converted into pepsin by pepsin that has already been produced, trypsinogen into trypsin by enterokinase and chymotrypsinogen into chymotrypsin by trypsin. This ensures that the enzymes are activated only when they are required and not when they are still inside cells, where they would cause great damage.

Enzymes do not work in isolation

There are thousands of enzymes in a cell, each catalysing one specific reaction. Some of the different types of enzymes and the reactions they catalyse are summarised in Table 7.1. These reactions may form pathways, converting one molecule through many intermediates to another, or cycles that continuously turn within cells, producing substances that the cell always needs.

All these processes must be balanced; each pathway must be regulated so that the correct amount of a substance will be produced at the correct time. The whole enzymatic machinery must work as one integrated and regulated machine. The examples of enzyme regulation mentioned above give only a glimpse of the possible mechanisms and a hint of the sophisticated regulatory mechanisms that occur.

QUESTIONS

7.18 (a) Which type of inhibition alters the K_m but not the V_{max}?
(b) Which type of inhibition alters the V_{max} but not the K_m?
(c) Which type of inhibition eventually reduces the rate of the reaction to zero?

7.19 (a) List three different types of enzyme inhibition.
(b) Nerve gases exist that inhibit essential enzyme-catalysed reactions in cells. What type of enzyme inhibitors have been used as nerve gases? Why is this type of inhibitor used for this purpose?
(c) A scientist used an inhibitor to investigate the interaction between an enzyme and its substrate using X-ray diffraction. What type of enzyme inhibitor would the scientist have used? Why is this type of inhibitor appropriate?
(d) Another scientist was investigating an allosteric enzyme. What type of enzyme inhibition would the scientist expect to observe? Explain your choice.

7.20 Figure 7.22 shows a hypothetical biochemical pathway in a cell. There are three allosteric enzymes in this pathway, a, d and g. a is inhibited by substance T, d by substance W and g by substance Z.
(a) What will happen if the concentration of substance Z rises?
(b) What will happen if the concentration of substance W rises?
(c) What will happen if the concentration of substance T rises?
(d) What form of control does this type of mechanism illustrate?

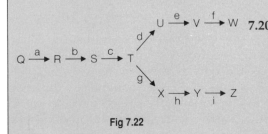

Fig 7.22

DATA HANDLING 7.2

An experiment was performed on the enzyme glutamate dehydrogenase to investigate whether the substance salicylate affected the activity of the enzyme. The following results were obtained.

Substrate concentration (mM)	Product per minute (mg)	
	0 mM salicylate	40 mM salicylate
1.5	0.21	0.08
2.0	0.25	0.10
3.0	0.28	0.12
4.0	0.33	0.13
6.0	0.39	0.15
8.0	0.44	0.16
10.0	0.45	0.17
12.0	0.44	0.18
14.0	0.45	0.17

(a) What is the substrate of this reaction?

(b) What general class of enzyme does glutamate dehydrogenase belong to? What type of reaction does this general type of enzyme catalyse? What can you deduce about the specific reaction that this enzyme catalyses?

(c) Plot a graph of the rate of the reaction against substrate concentration for both sets of results.

(d) Comment on the shape of the 0 mM salicylate graph. What does this indicate about the mechanism of enzyme action?

(e) Use your graph to estimate the V_{max} for the reaction with and without salicylate. What effect does salicylate have on the rate of the reaction?

(f) Use your graph to estimate the K_m for the reaction with and without salicylate. What can you deduce about the mechanism by which salicylate affects the rate of the reaction?

7.8 A SINGLE ENZYME IN DETAIL: LYSOZYME

Lysozyme is an enzyme found in human tears and saliva. It is an antibacterial agent, catalysing the hydrolysis of one of the types of polysaccharide chain found in the bacterial cell wall. Lysozyme is one of the best studied enzymes, its structure is known and the mechanism by which it catalyses the hydrolysis is well understood.

The structure of lysozyme

The primary structure of lysozyme was worked out in the 1950s using the technique of protein sequencing (section 2.3). It consists of a single polypeptide chain of 129 amino acid residues (Fig 7.23) and it has an unusually high proportion of basic amino acid residues that form positive R groups at pH 7.

This polypeptide chain is folded into a compact, globular structure and the final structure is stabilised in part by four disulphide bonds, each between two cysteine residues. The exact three-dimensional structure of lysozyme was obtained by high resolution X-ray diffraction studies in 1965 and the structure is known to be accurate to 0.2 nm.

The main structural features of lysozyme can be summarised:

• the charged and polar residues are mainly found on the outside of the folded structure and the hydrophobic residues on the inside;

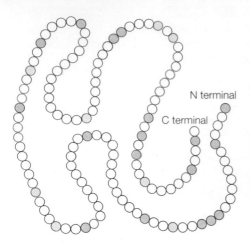

Fig 7.23 The primary structure of lysozyme. The acidic amino acid residues are shown in pink and the basic amino acid residues are shown in grey. Those residues with a red rim form the active site when the polypeptide is folded into its final three-dimensional structure.

N terminal

C terminal

- only 25% of the residues are involved in α-helical structures;
- there is a region of antiparallel β-pleated sheet;
- there is a cleft running down the middle of the molecule.

The cleft seemed the perfect candidate for the active site of the molecule. This was proved to be true by crystallising a complex of the enzyme with a competitive inhibitor that resembled the substrate very closely and then studying the crystals by X-ray diffraction. The competitive inhibitor was shown to occupy the cleft, implying that this was the site where the substrate would bind and the reaction would take place. It would have been impossible to do the same experiment with the real substrate because the reaction would have occurred and the product would have been released before the solution could crystallize.

The active site of lysozyme is lined with amino acids that had been shown to be far apart in the sequence of amino acid residues that formed the polypeptide (Fig 7.23). These widely spaced amino acid residues come together to form the active site when the polypeptide chain is folded. This is typical of the active site of enzymes and explains why disruption of the tertiary structure of the enzyme destroys the active site and removes the catalytic activity of the protein.

The enzyme mechanism for lysozyme is well understood

Knowing the structure of lysozyme so accurately, scientists were able to determine the manner in which it functioned with a similar degree of accuracy. The mechanism of the reaction catalysed by lysozyme has been reconstructed from X-ray diffraction studies and various other investigations and can be summarised in the following eight steps.

1. A length of the polysaccharide substrate binds to the active site, the cleft that runs along the entire width of the enzyme. This binding is known to involve the formation of six hydrogen bonds and some hydrophobic interactions.
2. A change in the three-dimensional shape of the enzyme occurs as the substrate binds; this deepens and narrows the cleft.
3. The active site bends the substrate. This makes the transition state more likely to form.
4. The transition state of the reaction forms. A glutamic acid residue, Glu 35, gives a hydrogen ion to carbon 1 of one of the sugar residues in the polysaccharide, making the carbon 1 of this sugar residue positively charged (a carbonium ion) (Fig 7.24(a)). A water molecule in the active site breaks down to give a hydrogen ion that replaces the hydrogen ion donated by the glutamic acid residue and a hydroxyl ion (Fig 7.24(a)).
5. This transition state is stabilised by the closely positioned negative charge on one of the aspartic acid residues, Asp 52 (Fig 7.24(b)).
6. The hydroxyl ion produced in step 4 then neutralises the positive ion on the sugar residue (Fig 7.24(b)). Hydrolysis of the polysaccharide is now complete (Fig 7.24(c)) and the product molecules are released.

The reaction mechanism of lysozyme supports the induced fit model

It has been shown by X-ray diffraction studies that lysozyme changes shape when the substrate binds. The cleft becomes narrower and deeper as the substrate binds due to a conformational change in the protein. This was the first direct evidence for the induced fit hypothesis, which suggests that substrate binding causes a change in shape that must occur before the reaction can proceed (section 7.6).

CHEMICAL REACTIONS IN CELLS

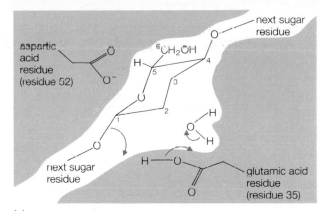

The polysaccharide binds to the active site. Two amino acid residues in the active site play an important part in the reaction mechanism: a glutamic acid residue and an aspartic acid residue. A water molecule in the active site also has an important role in the reaction.

(a)

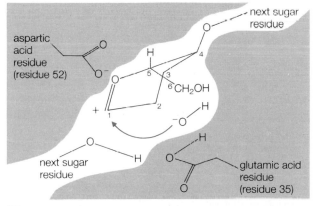

The bond between one sugar residue and the next is broken and an unstable, positively charged ion is formed (a carbonium ion). This unstable reaction intermediate is stabilised by the aspartic acid residue.

(b)

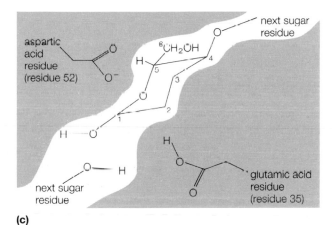

The hydroxide ion that had been formed from the water molecule earlier in the reaction reacts with the positively charged ion.

Key:

→ Movement of electrons

(c)

Fig 7.24 The reaction mechanism for lysozyme.

The reaction mechanism for lysozyme includes many steps that accelerate the reaction

If the overall rate of reaction is to be increased, then the probability of each individual molecular reaction must be increased. This will mean that more molecules of the substrate will react per second, increasing the overall rate of the reaction. Whether an individual molecule of substrate reacts depends on whether that molecule has the necessary energy to overcome the energy barrier. There are two ways of ensuring that the molecule has the necessary energy: either the molecule of substrate can be given more energy, or the necessary activation energy can be decreased by lowering the energy barrier.

When the substrate binds, the conformational change in the enzyme means that the protein exerts a force on the polysaccharide, bending the molecule. This destabilises the substrate, giving it more energy and making it more likely to react: some of the necessary activation energy is supplied by the protein. This means that the substrate is more likely to have the necessary energy to react so the probability of an individual substrate molecule reacting is increased and the overall rate of reaction will go up.

Once the transition state is formed, it is stabilised by some of the R groups present in the active site. This reduces the energy of the transition state, reducing the energy barrier of the overall reaction. This means that the substrate is more likely to have the necessary activation energy and the reaction is more likely to occur. This also increases the overall rate of reaction.

Finally, the actual chemistry of the reaction is very unlikely to occur in the solution making up the tears or the saliva. The positively charged ion, the carbonium ion, is formed because a glutamic acid residue donates a hydrogen ion to the sugar residue, an event that is very unlikely to occur in tears or saliva, both of which have a slightly alkaline pH. The active site is acting as tiny low-pH environment in which the reaction can occur. This means that the enzyme is allowing a reaction to occur that would be highly unlikely in the surrounding solution: the probability of an individual substrate molecule reacting is increased and the overall reaction rate rises.

QUESTIONS

7.21 The large proportion of charged amino acid residues means that lysozyme is soluble in water.
(a) Why does a large proportion of charged amino acid residues make a protein more soluble?
(b) Why must lysozyme be soluble to fulfil its function in the human body?

7.22 In what ways does the reaction mechanism for lysozyme described in section 7.8 support the induced fit hypothesis rather than the lock and key hypothesis?

7.23 Briefly discuss how the following events account for an increase in the rate of the reaction:

* the bending of the substrate molecule;
* the stabilisation of the transition state;
* the presence of an acidic amino acid residue in the active site.

7.9 ENZYMES IN BIOTECHNOLOGY

Biotechnology was an ancient craft before it was a modern science. People have used the enzymes present in micro-organisms to make beer, wine, cheese and bread for many thousands of years. In this century scientists have started to isolate enzymes from these micro-organisms so that they can be used to catalyse reactions in industrial processes. Some of these many enzymes are summed up in Table 7.3.

Immobilised enzymes can be recycled

As they are catalysts, enzymes remain unaltered by the reaction they catalyse, which means that it should be possible to use expensive enzymes again and again. However, this is only possible if they can be removed from the reaction mixture, not an easy task given that they are soluble. This problem has been overcome by the technique of **enzyme immobilisation** in which the enzyme molecules are stuck on the outside of a solid carrier, or encased in a gel-like substance that is permeable to small molecules. Either

Table 7.3

Application	Enzyme	Uses
dairy industry	renin (from stomachs of young ruminants)	cheese making
fruit juices	cellulases, pectinases	clarify the juice
baking industry	fungal amylase	hydrolyse starch to give sugars so that yeast makes CO_2
baby foods	proteases	to predigest protein
brewing industry	amylases	hydrolyse starch to feed yeast
	proteases	hydrolyse proteins to feed yeast
	amyloglucosidase	removes sugar to make low calorie beer
rubber industry	catalase	produces oxygen from peroxide to make latex into foam rubber
biological detergents	proteases	digest protein stains

way, the enzyme can be easily removed from the reaction mixture or the reaction mixture from the enzyme.

Protein engineering may lead to tailor made enzymes

Modern genetic engineering techniques mean that it is possible to design and manufacture an enzyme with a specific function. A gene can be removed from an organism, linked to a bacterial gene control sequence and put into bacteria. The bacteria will then transcribe and translate the gene, producing the protein. By altering the nucleotide sequence of the gene before inserting it into the bacteria, we can alter the protein produced, modifying its properties. In this way a 'designer enzyme' can be produced. In the near future it may be possible to design enzymes to catalyse the formation of essential drugs, or to 'crack' long chain hydrocarbons, or to act as biosensors.

Enzymes may be used in biosensors

Enzymes are specific: each enzyme will react only with its particular substrate. This specificity is typical of proteins and is very rare in any other branch of science. Scientists are trying to take advantage of this specificity by incorporating enzymes into sensors, creating a hybrid of biological molecules and electronics, a **biosensor**.

A biosensor would consist of an immobilised enzyme that would detect the presence of the substrate molecule, even if thousands of other substances were present. The enzyme would react, producing a product that would be detected by a **transducer**. A transducer is an electronic device that would only produce an electrical signal if the product was present. This electrical signal would then be amplified and processed, giving information about the amount of the substrate present.

Biosensors have already been developed that can detect and measure the amount of glucose present in blood, using an immobilised version of the enzyme glucose oxidase. If the biosensor can be miniaturised it may be

Fig 7.25 Rennet is an enzyme used in cheesemaking that promotes the curdling of milk. The traditional source of rennet is the stomachs of calves that are still young enough to require the enzyme in order to live on their diet of milk. Faced with the fact that vegetarians find such an enzyme unacceptable, cheese manufacturers have changed to using rennet made by bacteria from genes that have been engineered by modern DNA manipulation techniques.

A person suffering from diabetes does not make enough insulin and therefore cannot control their blood sugar level.

possible to implant it in patients suffering from diabetes. If the output of such a biosensor could be linked to a miniature pump delivering insulin, the level of insulin in the blood could be finely controlled, eliminating many of the side effects caused by infrequent insulin injections.

QUESTIONS

7.24 (a) What advantages do enzymes have over conventional catalysts?
(b) What disadvantages are there in using enzymes rather than conventional catalysts?

7.25 (a) When an immobilised enzyme is made, the enzyme molecules are often encased in a gel-like substance. Why must this gel-like substance be permeable to small molecules?
(b) What is the advantage of being able to reuse the enzyme?

7.26 Genetic engineering often involves transferring a gene from a eukaryotic cell, for example a human or a flowering plant, into a bacterium.
(a) Why is the bacterial transcription control sequence added to the gene before it is placed in the bacteria?
(b) Some enzymes are covalently modified after synthesis. What problems would you anticipate if you were producing such an enzyme in a bacterial cell?

REVIEW OF CRUCIAL POINTS

- The environment inside the cell is mild: the pH is near neutral, the temperature is low and the solvent is water. Under these conditions the organic compounds that make up the cell are very stable and very unlikely to react. The reactions that occur in the cell are all catalysed by enzymes.

- Enzymes are catalysts and proteins. Like all catalysts they increase the rate of a reaction but unlike inorganic catalysts they are very specific, only catalysing a single reaction or a series of very closely related reactions. This specificity is due to the fact that enzymes are proteins: they have a specific three-dimensional shape that means that the enzyme molecule only binds the correctly shaped substrate molecule.

- There are two scientific models that have been proposed to explain the action of enzymes. The lock and key hypothesis proposes that there is a hole or groove in the enzyme which is precisely the correct shape to fit the substrate molecule. Once the substrate molecule has bound to the enzyme, the reaction occurs and the product molecules are released. The lock and key model explains enzyme specificity but it does not accommodate some other observations about enzymes, particularly X-ray diffraction data that indicate that the enzyme changes shape when the substrate binds.

- The induced fit hypothesis proposes that the protein changes shape when the substrate binds, altering the shape of the active site. In the induced fit hypothesis this change in shape is essential; without it the reaction will not occur. The induced fit hypothesis is consistent with the X-ray diffraction data and may be a more accurate representation of the true situation than the rather simple lock and key model.

CHEMICAL REACTIONS IN CELLS

- Some indication of how enzymes work within cells can be obtained from studying the kinetics of enzyme-catalysed reactions. Michaelis–Menten kinetics identify two important parameters, V_{max}, the maximum rate of the reaction for a given enzyme concentration and K_m the concentration of substrate that gives half the maximum rate. A low K_m, indicates that the enzyme works efficiently even when there is very little of the substrate present, while a high K_m indicates that the enzyme requires a large concentration of the substrate before being active. Enzyme inhibitors, particularly noncompetitive inhibitors, give scientists an insight into how enzymes are regulated in the cell. Allosteric enzymes are regulated by substances that bind to the enzyme away from the active site yet modify the manner in which the substrate binds.

Chapter 8

ENERGY

Without energy every molecule would be absolutely still, nothing would ever happen and life would be impossible. Cells are packed with energy: chemical energy, potential energy and kinetic energy. Every chemical reaction, every tiny movement of a molecule involves a transfer of energy: organisms need a constant supply of energy to stay alive. This chapter deals with how the energy supplied by the sun is transferred to every living cell.

LEARNING OBJECTIVES

After studying this chapter you should:

1. understand how the energy in light is transferred to the chemical energy of carbohydrate by photosynthesis;

2. understand how the energy in carbohydrates is converted to the chemical energy in ATP by anaerobic and aerobic respiration;

3. have an appreciation of the relative efficiency of aerobic and anaerobic respiration;

4. understand that fats and proteins can be used as respiratory substrates;

5. know a range of energy storage molecules;

6. appreciate that the Krebs cycle is used as a metabolic hub.

8.1 ENERGY IN ORGANISMS

Organisms contain a lot of energy. If you wanted to know how much energy was in an organism you could kill the organism, place it in a piece of apparatus called a calorimeter and burn the organism under controlled conditions. The amount of heat energy given off would be a measure of the amount of energy that had been stored in the organism. This experiment, although it conjures up gruesome images of incinerating bodies, is very similar to the way that the energy content of various foods is calculated. The food is placed in the calorimeter and burnt, and we can calculate the amount of energy stored in that particular type of food.

Molecules contain energy

The experiment with the calorimeter would give us an idea of how much energy was stored in an organism. That energy is stored in the molecules making up the organism: in the sugars and polysaccharides, the amino acids and proteins, the nucleotides and the nucleic acids, the glycerol, fatty acids, triglycerides and phospholipids. If we consider an organism as big as an oak tree there are tonnes of cellulose alone, without considering all the other organic molecules present, and that cellulose represents a huge energy store – imagine how much heat energy would be given off if a whole mature oak tree was burnt.

Complex organic molecules contain more energy than simple inorganic molecules

The synthesis of complex organic molecules, like cellulose, from simple molecules, like carbon dioxide and water, is called **metabolism**. Metabolic processes require energy because the end products, the complex organic molecules, contain more energy than the starting molecules, the simple inorganic molecules. For example, glucose yields 2802.5 kJ mol^{-1} when it is burnt to form carbon dioxide and water, so one can assume that the minimum amount of energy needed to form glucose from carbon dioxide and water is 2802.5 kJ mol^{-1}. In fact, more energy than this is needed because no process is 100% efficient and some of the energy will end up elsewhere rather than in the glucose molecules.

So organisms need energy to build up complex organic molecules from simpler starting materials or, in other words, to grow. Many organisms also need energy for other processes, for example movement, transporting substances around the organism, detecting changes in their environment and communication both within and between organisms. Energy is therefore crucial to life, and the study of how energy is transferred within and between organisms is one of the most important branches of biochemistry.

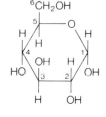

Fig 8.1 Glucose.

Certain molecules act as energy stores

Energy is stored within organisms in two main forms, chemical energy and potential energy. The store of chemical energy has already been discussed: it is the amount of energy stored within a molecule because of the particular bonds between the atoms of that molecule. For example glucose, Fig 8.1, contains five C—C bonds, seven C—O bonds, seven C—H bonds and five O—H bonds. Each of these bonds contributes towards the energy content of the molecule.

Most molecules in organisms are built to fulfil a particular function, for example cellulose is synthesised to form strong walls around plant cells, haemoglobin is synthesised in red blood cells to carry oxygen and lysozyme is synthesised to act as an antibacterial agent in tears. A few molecules are synthesised to act as energy storage molecules. These molecules are synthesised when energy is freely available and broken down to release energy when energy is required. Different molecules are used to store energy in different circumstances. Macromolecules such as triglycerides (section 1.6) and starch (section 2.2) act as long term energy stores, while sugars such as sucrose and glucose act as short term energy storage molecules. The type of energy storage molecule employed often varies from organism to organism, for example starch is the energy storage polysaccharide in plants while glycogen fulfils a similar role in animals.

All cells use ATP as an energy store for immediate use

However, even though energy storage molecules vary from organism to organism, all cells, no matter which organism they are in, use the same molecule to store energy for immediate use – **adenosine triphosphate** or **ATP**. When energy is required within a cell ATP is broken down to give ADP, adenosine diphosphate, and P_i, an inorganic phosphate ion (Fig 8.2). During this reaction the terminal phosphate group is separated from the ATP molecule by breaking the bond between this group and the rest of the nucleotide. When this bond is broken a large amount of energy is released, and therefore this bond is often referred to as a **high energy phosphate bond**.

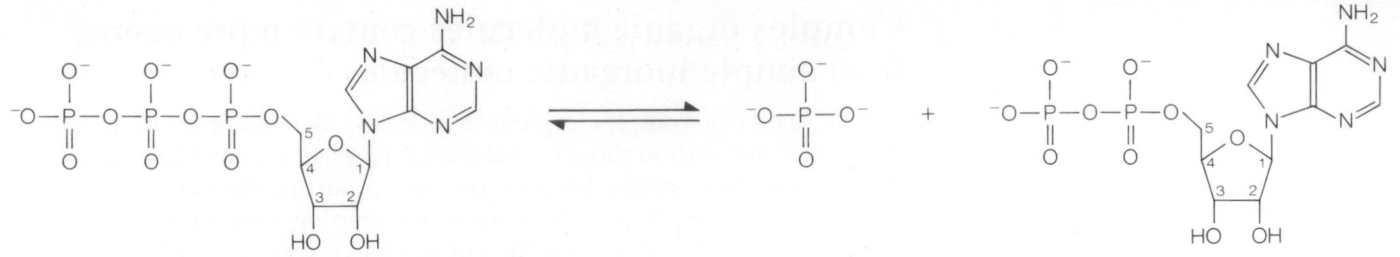

Fig 8.2 The end phosphate group of the ATP molecule can be separated from the rest of the molecule, making ADP and an inorganic phosphate ion. Energy is released when this reaction occurs: it is an exergonic reaction.

The energy stored in ATP is used for many cellular processes. For example, the energy released by breaking down ATP can be used to power endergonic reactions. Endergonic reactions take in energy and such reactions cannot happen unless there is energy available. All metabolic reactions, those in which complex organic molecules are synthesised from simpler molecules, require energy and this energy is usually supplied by breaking down ATP to make ADP and P_i.

ATP is also used to provide the energy for many other processes in organisms. It is used to generate movement: for example, the energy stored in ATP is used to make a muscle contract (section 3.3), to make flagella and cilia move and to transport vesicles around large cells such as nerve cells. ATP is also used to supply the energy for processes involving **active transport**, the movement of molecules or ions against a concentration gradient.

QUESTIONS

8.1 Look up the structures of amylose (Fig 2.4, p. 35), amylopectin (Fig 2.5, p. 36) and cellulose (Fig 2.7, p. 37).
   (a) Compare the way the polymer is arranged in amylose and amylopectin to the way in which it is arranged in cellulose.
   (b) What properties of amylose and amylopectin make them good energy storage polysaccharides?
   (c) What properties of cellulose make it a good structural polysaccharide?

8.2 ATP is soluble in water, insoluble in lipids and small enough to diffuse easily. Why are these properties useful in an energy storage molecule that powers many cellular processes?

8.3 A 70 kg human male contains 15 kg of fat stored as triglycerides in his fatty tissue but only 0.225 kg of glycogen stored in his liver and muscle. Triglycerides contain about 592 000 kJ kg^{-1} while glycogen contains about 3800 kJ kg^{-1}.
   (a) If all the energy had to be stored as glycogen how much would the man weigh?

   Triglycerides are insoluble in water while glycogen binds water molecules, forming a shell of water molecules around each molecule of glycogen.

   (b) Suggest two reasons why humans use triglycerides as long term energy stores rather than glycogen.

   (c) Why is glycogen rather than triglycerides used for energy storage in muscle cells?

   Starch has a similar energy content per kilogram to glycogen.

ENERGY

(d) Why is starch used as a long term energy storage molecule in many plants when animals use triglycerides rather than glycogen, a very similar energy storage molecule?

DATA HANDLING 8.1

$$6CO_2 + 6H_2O \longrightarrow C_6H_{12}O_6 + 6O_2$$

Bond type	Energy (kJ mol^{-1})
C—C	347
C—H	413
C—O	358
O—H	464
C=O	805
O=O	498.3

(a) Copy and complete the table below and use it to calculate the amount of energy that would have to be put in in order to synthesise glucose from carbon dioxide and water, producing oxygen as a waste product.

Bonds present before reaction	Bonds present at end of reaction
$6 \times 2 \times$ C=O – _____ kJ mol^{-1}	$5 \times$ C—C = _____ kJ mol^{-1}
$6 \times 2 \times$ O—H = _____ kJ mol^{-1}	$7 \times$ C—O = _____ kJ mol^{-1}
	$7 \times$ C—H = _____ kJ mol^{-1}
	$5 \times$ O—H = _____ kJ mol^{-1}
	$6 \times$ O=O = _____ kJ mol^{-1}
Total before _____ kJ mol^{-1}	Total after _____ kJ mol^{-1}

(b) The energy released when glucose is burnt is 2802.5 kJ mol^{-1}. Compare this to your answer to (a). What does this tell you about using bond energies to calculate the amount of energy stored in a molecule?

(c) What naturally occurring process can be summarised in the equation given in (a)?

8.2 ATP PRODUCTION

ATP is used continually in the cell to synthesise molecules and to generate concentration gradients of ions by active transport. If it runs out, these processes will come to a halt and the cell will die. This means that ATP must be constantly produced within the cell to replace the ATP that is being used.

ATP is produced from ADP and P

ATP is produced by reversing the reaction described in section 8.1. As the breakdown of ATP to give ADP and P_i is an exergonic reaction, releasing 30.6 kJ mol^{-1} of energy, the reverse reaction, converting ADP and P_i to ATP, is an endergonic reaction requiring 30.6 kJ mol^{-1} of energy to be put in. The energy needed to power the conversion of ADP and P_i to ATP must come from somewhere else within the cell.

ATP production can be powered directly by enzyme-catalysed reactions

Any chemical reaction that releases 30.6 kJ mol^{-1} could theoretically provide the energy needed to convert ADP and P_i to ATP. In reality it is more complicated, because there must also be a reaction mechanism that joins the phosphate group to the ADP molecule. Both elements are needed: enough energy must be released to power the reaction and a phosphate group must be transferred to the ADP molecule.

Examples of such a reaction form part of the glycolysis pathway found in almost all cells. The glycolysis pathway will be discussed in more detail later in this chapter but it contains two reactions in which ATP is made. In the first, ATP is formed when 1,3-bisphosphoglycerate is converted into 3-phosphoglycerate by the enzyme phosphoglycerate kinase (Fig 8.3(a)). In the second, ATP is formed when phosphoenolpyruvate is converted to pyruvate by the enzyme pyruvate kinase (Fig 8.3(b)).

Another reaction where ATP is made from ADP forms part of the tricarboxylic acid cycle (Krebs cycle) (section 8.3). The ATP is made when succinyl CoA is converted into succinate in a reaction catalysed by the enzyme succinyl CoA synthetase (Fig 8.3(c)). This reaction is more complex than the simple reactions described above. The energy released in the reaction is used to join GDP and P_i to make GTP. This GTP is then used to convert ADP to ATP.

ATP formation can be powered by an ion gradient

Most of the ATP in cells is formed using potential energy stores within the cell. These potential energy stores can be used to make ATP in a similar way to that in which water behind a dam can be used to make electricity in a hydroelectric power station. In a hydroelectric power station there is a difference in the level of water on either side of the dam and this is a store of potential energy. A gate in the dam is opened and the water flows through, turning turbines that turn generators.

In the cells membranes act like the dam and instead of the difference in the level of water on either side of the dam there is a difference in the concentration of hydrogen ions on either side of the membrane. A protein in the membrane acts as a gate: the protein can act as a pore to let the hydrogen ions flow through. Another protein attached to the pore protein

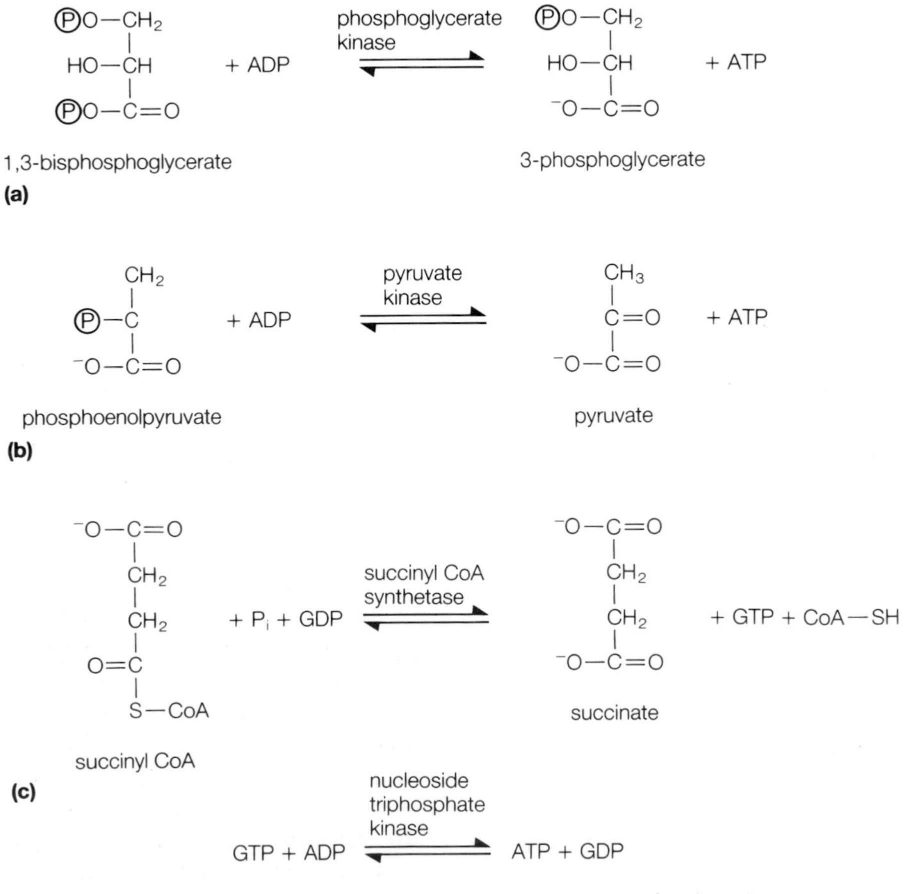

(a) 1,3-bisphosphoglycerate → 3-phosphoglycerate (phosphoglycerate kinase, + ADP → + ATP)

(b) phosphoenolpyruvate → pyruvate (pyruvate kinase, + ADP → + ATP)

(c) succinyl CoA → succinate (succinyl CoA synthetase, + P_i + GDP → + GTP + CoA—SH)

GTP + ADP ⇌ ATP + GDP (nucleoside triphosphate kinase)

Fig 8.3 ATP can be made as part of an ordinary, enzyme-catalysed reaction.

acts as the 'turbine' and as the hydrogen ions flow through the energy is transferred from the hydrogen ions to the protein. This protein uses the energy from the hydrogen ions to power the reaction that turns ADP and P_i to ATP and is called an **ATPase**.

This process by which energy is transferred from a potential energy store across a membrane into ATP occurs in all cells. In bacterial cells the membrane used is the cell membrane itself while in eukaryotic cells the inner membrane of the mitochondrion is used (Fig 8.4(a)). Some plant cells, those containing chloroplasts, have membranes in the chloroplast that work in a similar way (Fig 8.4(b)). In order for the energy transfer process to work there need to be three components:

- a closed membrane that does not leak hydrogen ions;
- a difference in hydrogen ion concentration across the membrane;
- a protein structure that acts as a pore, linked to a protein that acts as an ATPase.

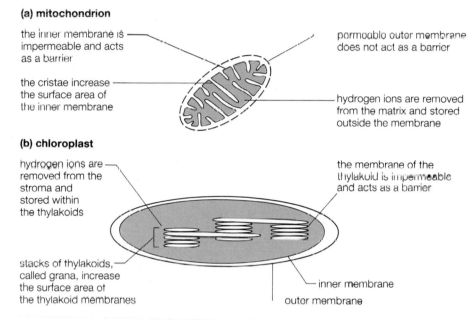

(a) mitochondrion

the inner membrane is impermeable and acts as a barrier

the cristae increase the surface area of the inner membrane

permeable outer membrane does not act as a barrier

hydrogen ions are removed from the matrix and stored outside the membrane

(b) chloroplast

hydrogen ions are removed from the stroma and stored within the thylakoids

stacks of thylakoids, called grana, increase the surface area of the thylakoid membranes

the membrane of the thylakoid is impermeable and acts as a barrier

inner membrane

outer membrane

Fig 8.4 Both mitochondria and chloroplasts store hydrogen ions.

The inner membrane of a mitochondrion forms a closed barrier between the matrix of the mitochondrion and the intermembrane space (Fig 8.4(a)). Experimental measurements show that there is a difference in hydrogen ion concentration between the matrix and the intermembrane space: the matrix has a higher pH, showing that the concentration of hydrogen ions is lower in the matrix than in the intermembrane space. Examination of mitochondria using electron microscopy shows the presence of stalked particles that protrude into the matrix from the inner membrane. These stalked particles consist of two parts, F_0 and F_1 (Fig 8.5). The F_0 portion is a protein pore in the membrane while the F_1 portion is an ATPase.

Chloroplasts contain flattened membrane bags called **thylakoids** within a solution called the **stroma** (Fig 8.4(b)). The membrane of these thylakoids is a closed structure which is impermeable to hydrogen ions. In chloroplasts there is a pH difference between the solution inside the thylakoid and the stroma: this time there is a higher concentration of hydrogen ions inside the thylakoid than outside the thylakoid. Electron microscopy has shown that there are stalked particles that protrude from the thylakoid membrane into the stroma. Again, this stalked particle is in two parts, CF_0 which forms a pore within the membrane and CF_1 that functions as the ATPase.

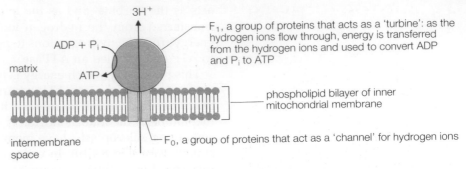

Fig 8.5 The F_0F_1 ATPase.

The cell membrane of a bacterial cell is also closed and does not leak hydrogen ions. The pH inside the bacterium is lower than that outside the cell. Stalked particles protrude from the plasma membrane into the cytoplasm. These are very similar to the stalked particles in mitochondria, consisting of a protein pore (F_0) and an ATPase (F_1).

These three ATPases all work in a very similar way. Each synthesises one ATP molecule for every three hydrogen ions travelling through the pore down the gradient (Fig 8.5).

The idea that it was a hydrogen ion concentration gradient that powered ATP synthesis was a novel concept proposed by Peter Mitchell in 1961 in his **chemiosmotic theory**. A series of reactions was known to occur in mitochondria and it was assumed that the energy released in these reactions was used to synthesise ATP. However, the link between the two processes, the process by which the energy was transferred between the two, was obscure. Mitchell's idea of potential energy stored in a gradient across a membrane was revolutionary and it took decades for it to become accepted by the majority of scientists studying the subject.

The energy for ATP synthesis originates in the sun

So ATP can be synthesised in two different ways: using the energy released in a chemical reaction and using the energy stored in a difference in ion concentration across a membrane. However, the energy in the substrates of the enzyme-catalysed reaction, or in the ion concentration gradient, must have come from somewhere. Ultimately this energy must have come from the sun, the source of energy for all life, and the rest of this chapter discusses the manner in which the energy from the sun is transferred into ATP.

QUESTIONS

8.4 (a) What substances are used to make ATP?
   (b) What is the name of an enzyme used to make ATP?
   (c) ATP can be produced in a cell by two different types of process. What are they?

8.5 ATP can be synthesised using a potential energy store in the cell.
   (a) What is this potential energy store made of and where would such a store be found in a plant cell?
   (b) How is the energy in the potential energy store transferred into ATP?

8.6 Compare the potential energy store across the inner membrane of the mitochondrion, the thylakoid membrane in a chloroplast and in a bacterial cell. Which way across the membrane would the hydrogen ions have to move to transfer the energy to ATP?

8.3 PHOTOSYNTHESIS

Fig 8.6 Most photosynthesis occurs in the upper layers of the oceans. Tiny organisms, collectively called phytoplankton, occupy the photic zone of the sea, the first 250 metres through which light can penetrate. The light intensity falls ten-fold for every 85 metres depth, and only the shortest wavelengths of blue light penetrate the full 250 metres. Photosynthetic organisms living at these depths have specialised pigments that are very efficient at absorbing blue light.

The energy from the sun is used directly by organisms that photosynthesise. Photosynthesis transfers the energy in light into the chemical energy of carbohydrates. The process of photosynthesis is complicated, involving many pathways, but it is often summarised in this simple equation.

$$6CO_2 + 6H_2O + ENERGY \longrightarrow C_6H_{12}O_6 + 6O_2$$

Photosynthesis occurs in two major stages. As the name suggests, the **light-dependent** stage requires light energy and it uses this energy to produce ATP and **reduced nicotinamide adenine dinucleotide phosphate, NADPH.** The NADPH is then used to reduce carbon dioxide to carbohydrates, a process that also requires an input of energy from ATP. This conversion of carbon dioxide to carbohydrates is the **light-independent** stage of photosynthesis.

The main events of photosynthesis are summed up in Table 8.1.

Table 8.1   Photosynthesis

The light-dependent stage

Location:	the thylakoid membranes in the chloroplast
Substances in:	H_2O, $NADP^+$, ADP, P_i
Useful products:	NADPH, ATP
Waste products:	O_2
Energy transferred from:	light
Energy transferred to:	ATP, NADPH

1. Light energy excites electrons in chlorophyll molecules.
2. The excited electrons are emitted from the chlorophyll molecules.
3. The energy carried by these electrons is used:
   * to reduce $NADP^+$ to NADPH;
   * to move hydrogen ions across the thylakoid membrane to create a potential energy store;
   * to split water into hydrogen ions, electrons and oxygen.
4. The electrons from the water are used to replace the electrons emitted by the chlorophyll molecules.
5. The potential energy store is used to make ATP from ADP and P_i.

The light-independent stage

Location:	the stroma of the chloroplast
Substances in:	CO_2, ATP, NADPH
Useful products:	carbohydrate (3-carbon sugar)
Other products:	$NADP^+$, ADP, P_i
Energy transferred from:	ATP, NADPH
Energy transferred to:	carbohydrate

1. The enzyme ribulose 1,3-bisphosphate carboxylase fixes carbon dioxide by converting one carbon dioxide molecule and one 5C molecule (ribulose 1,3-bisphosphate) into two 3C molecules.
2. The 3C molecules are then phosphorylated using ATP. This increases the energy of the molecules.
3. The 3C molecules are then reduced using NADPH to give 3C sugar molecules.
4. One out of every six 3C sugar molecules produced is used to make other carbohydrates, including glucose.
5. Five out of every six 3C sugar molecules produced are recycled to make more 5C molecules to fix more carbon dioxide.

THE LIGHT-DEPENDENT STAGE

The main purpose of the light-dependent stage of photosynthesis is to transfer energy from light into ATP and to produce the reduced form of the coenzyme nicotinamide adenine dinucleotide phosphate, NADPH.

A coenzyme is a non-protein group needed by an enzyme for a reaction, that exists separately from the enzyme and often transfers groups of atoms between enzymes.

There is a hydrogen ion concentration gradient across the thylakoid membrane

In the light-dependent stage, ATP is formed using the potential energy stored in the hydrogen ion concentration difference across the thylakoid membrane (section 8.2). The difference in hydrogen ion concentration across the membrane is produced in three ways (Fig 8.7).

1. A reaction occurs that produces hydrogen ions within the lumen of the thylakoid membrane ($2H_2O \longrightarrow 4H^+ + 4e^- + O_2$).

2. A reaction occurs that removes hydrogen ions from the stroma ($NADP^+ + H^+ + 2e^- \longrightarrow NADPH$).

3. Hydrogen ions are moved from the stroma to the lumen by the Q cycle ($2H^+_{stroma} + PQ \longrightarrow PQH_2 \longrightarrow PQ + 2H^+_{lumen}$).

PQ is plastoquinone – see p. 194.

These three reactions transfer hydrogen ions across the membrane from a region of low concentration of hydrogen ions to a region of high concentration, against the gradient down which the ions would normally diffuse. This transport against the concentration gradient requires energy and is therefore a form of active transport. The energy for this active transport is supplied by light.

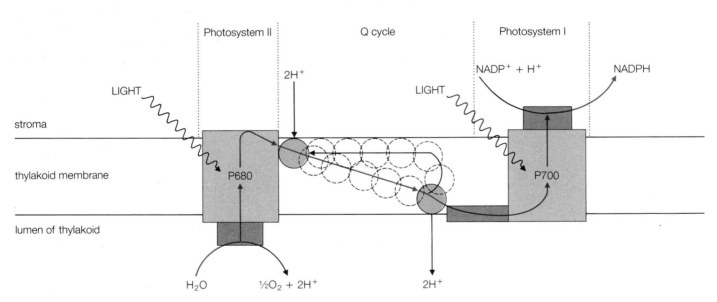

Fig 8.7 The flow of electrons in non-cyclic photophosphorylation. Energy is transferred from light to electrons in photosystem II. This energy is used to split water, producing hydrogen ions in the lumen of the thylakoids, and to power the Q cycle that transfers hydrogen ions from the stroma to the lumen. More energy is transferred from light to electrons in photosystem I and this energy is used to reduce NADP$^+$, with a further removal of hydrogen ions from the stroma. The red arrows show the flow of the electrons.

Energy is harvested from light by chlorophyll molecules

All types of chlorophyll have essentially the same structure: a haem group with a Mg^{2+} ion at its centre on the end of a long hydrocarbon chain (Fig 8.8). This hydrocarbon chain anchors the chlorophyll molecule in the

Fig 8.8 Chlorophyll a

membrane with the haem group on the outer face of the thylakoid membrane. There are various types of chlorophyll each with small variations in the side groups attached to the haem group. The most common forms of chlorophyll are called chlorophyll a and chlorophyll b but there are many more forms, each of which absorbs light of a slightly different wavelength.

A chlorophyll molecule contains an electron that is excited by light energy. This electron absorbs energy from light and becomes a **high energy electron**. This high energy electron can leave the chlorophyll molecule and enter another molecule, carrying the energy with it. Molecules that accept high energy electrons and then pass them on to another molecule are called **electron carriers**.

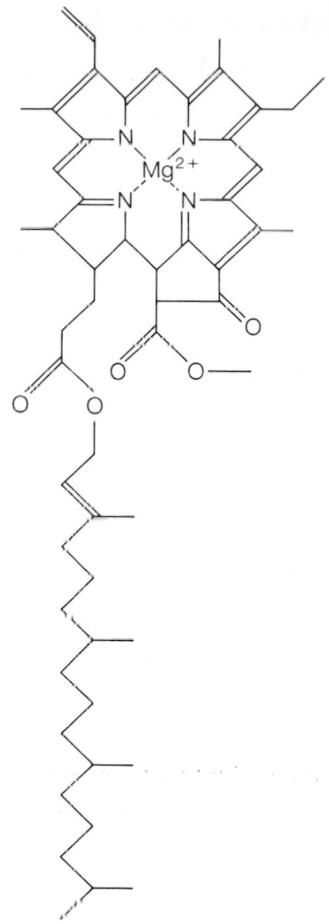

Chlorophyll molecules and electron carriers are arranged in photosystems

The high energy electrons emitted by the chlorophyll molecules are transferred to the first of these electron carriers in a complex of proteins called a **photosystem**. There are two photosystems in the thylakoid membrane, called simply photosystem I and photosystem II. Light is collected by many different chlorophyll molecules and transferred to the P680 chlorophyll a molecules which sit at the base of photosystem II (Fig 8.7). P680 can be identified because it absorbs light of 680 nm wavelength. The P680 molecules absorb energy and emit electrons that are used to reduce the first electron carrier of the **Q cycle**.

The two electrons that leave photosystem II to enter the Q cycle have to be replaced, or the chlorophyll molecules will not be able to absorb any more light energy. Photosystem II contains a water-splitting protein on the inner face of the membrane. This water-splitting protein is an enzyme that catalyses the breakdown of water into hydrogen ions, oxygen and electrons.

$$H_2O \longrightarrow 2H^+ + O_2 + 2e^-$$

The electrons released are used to replace the electrons in the chlorophyll molecules, the hydrogen ions are released into the lumen of the thylakoid, increasing the difference in hydrogen ion concentration across the membrane, and the oxygen is released as a waste product.

Photosystem I also contains chlorophyll molecules, this time **P700** chlorophyll molecules (chlorophyll molecules that absorb energy from light of wavelength 700 nm). The light energy is absorbed by many chlorophyll molecules and transferred to the P700 molecules that sit at the base of photosystem I. The P700 molecules absorb the energy and then emit electrons which are passed to an electron carrier in photosystem I, then to two other electron carriers on the outer face of the membrane. Finally the pair of high energy electrons is used to reduce NADP$^+$ in the stroma. This reaction removes hydrogen ions from the stroma (Fig 8.7).

$$NADP^+ + H^+ + 2e^- \longrightarrow NADPH$$

The electrons emitted from the P700 chlorophyll molecules must be replaced so that the chlorophyll molecules can absorb more light energy. The electrons in the chlorophyll molecules are replaced by electrons entering photosystem I from the Q cycle via electron carriers (Fig 8.7).

The Q cycle moves hydrogen ions across the thylakoid membrane

The electrons emerging from photosystem II are transferred by a lipid soluble molecule called **plastoquinone** or **PQ**. The PQ reacts with two hydrogen ions from the stroma and the two electrons from photosystem II to make reduced plastoquinone, PQH_2.

$$PQ + 2H^+_{stroma} + 2e^- \longrightarrow PQH_2$$

The PQH_2 diffuses across the phospholipid bilayer and then passes two electrons to the next electron carrier which is in the lumen of the thylakoid (Fig 8.7). As part of the redox reaction that passes on the electrons, two hydrogen ions are released into the lumen and the PQ molecule is regenerated.

$$PQH_2 \longrightarrow PQ + 2H^+_{lumen} + 2e^-$$

The net result of the Q cycle is to move two hydrogen ions across the membrane using some of the energy carried by the electrons.

Photophosphorylation

Photophosphorylation is the phosphorylation of ADP that is powered by light energy. Figure 8.7 shows the net flow of electrons from water through photosystem II, the Q cycle and photosystem I to NADPH. Energy is injected into the electrons when they are in the chlorophyll molecules, and is released from the electrons as they pass from electron carrier to electron carrier. Some of the energy released from the electrons is used to set up the difference in hydrogen ion concentration across the membrane, creating a store of potential energy from which ATP can be synthesised using the ATPase in the thylakoid membrane (section 8.2).

ATP synthesis can be separated from NADPH synthesis

The linear flow of electrons from photosystem II through photosystem I and finally into NADPH has two consequences: it causes $NADP^+$ to be reduced to NADPH and it causes an increase in the pH gradient across the thylakoid membrane that can be used to make ATP. Scientists call this series of reactions **non-cyclic photophosphorylation** because the light energy is used to phosphorylate ADP to make ATP using a linear series of reactions.

However, the pathway can be short-circuited so that only photosystem I is used and no NADPH is produced (Fig 8.9). This short-circuited pathway is a closed ring of reactions, called a **cycle**, and its net effect is to use the energy from light to move hydrogen ions across the thylakoid membrane. This pH gradient is then used to make ATP in the usual manner. As the series of reactions is a cycle and the overall effect is to produce ATP, this alternative pathway is called **cyclic photophosphorylation**.

The alternative pathway is shown in Fig 8.9. The high energy electrons from photosystem I are not passed to $NADP^+$ as they are in the linear pathway. Instead they are passed to a different electron carrier which then passes them into the Q cycle. The Q cycle uses the energy in the electrons to move hydrogen ions across the membrane and then passes electrons, now carrying less energy, into photosystem I to replace the electrons that were emitted at the start of the cycle.

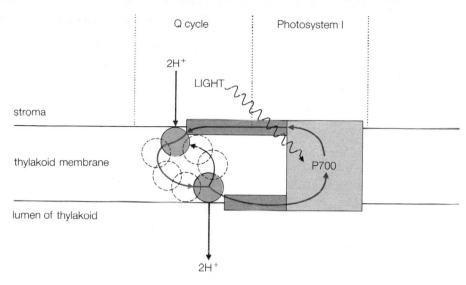

Fig 8.9 The flow of electrons in cyclic photophosphorylation. Energy is transferred from light to electrons in photosystem I. This energy is used to power the Q cycle that transfers hydrogen ions from the stroma to the lumen of the thylakoid. The red arrows show the flow of electrons.

THE LIGHT-INDEPENDENT STAGE

The light-independent stage consists of a series of enzyme-catalysed reactions in the stroma of the chloroplasts that convert carbon dioxide into glyceraldehyde 3-phosphate (Fig 8.10). The glyceraldehyde 3 phosphate is then converted into a range of carbohydrates by various enzymes.

The light-independent stage uses carbon dioxide, ATP and NADPH

The light-independent stage of photosynthesis uses the ATP and NADPH produced in the light-dependent stage. The ATP provides the energy needed to convert carbon dioxide into carbohydrate that contains very much more chemical energy. The NADPH reduces carbon dioxide to carbohydrate compounds that contain hydrogen as well as carbon and oxygen. The light-independent stage also requires carbon dioxide, which is the source of the carbon and the oxygen present in the carbohydrate.

Carbon dioxide diffuses into the cell and then into the chloroplasts, where it is reduced to glyceraldehyde 3-phosphate by the addition of hydrogen. The hydrogen atoms needed for this reduction are supplied by the NADPH. Glyceraldehyde 3-phosphate contains a lot more energy than carbon dioxide because it is a larger molecule containing many more bonds. This energy is supplied by breaking down the ATP that was made during the light-dependent stage.

The light-independent stage is a cyclical process

The series of enzyme-catalysed reactions that make up the light-independent stage form a cycle (Fig 8.10). This particular cycle is called the **Calvin cycle** after the scientist who headed the research group that worked out which enzyme-catalysed reactions were involved. For the cycle of reactions to keep turning, the material entering and leaving the cycle must be balanced. Carbon dioxide, a 1C molecule, is the only carbon-containing material entering the cycle, while glyceraldehyde 3-phosphate, a 3C molecule, is the only carbon-containing material that leaves the cycle. This means that the cycle must turn three times in order for enough carbon to enter so that one glyceraldehyde 3-phosphate molecule can leave.

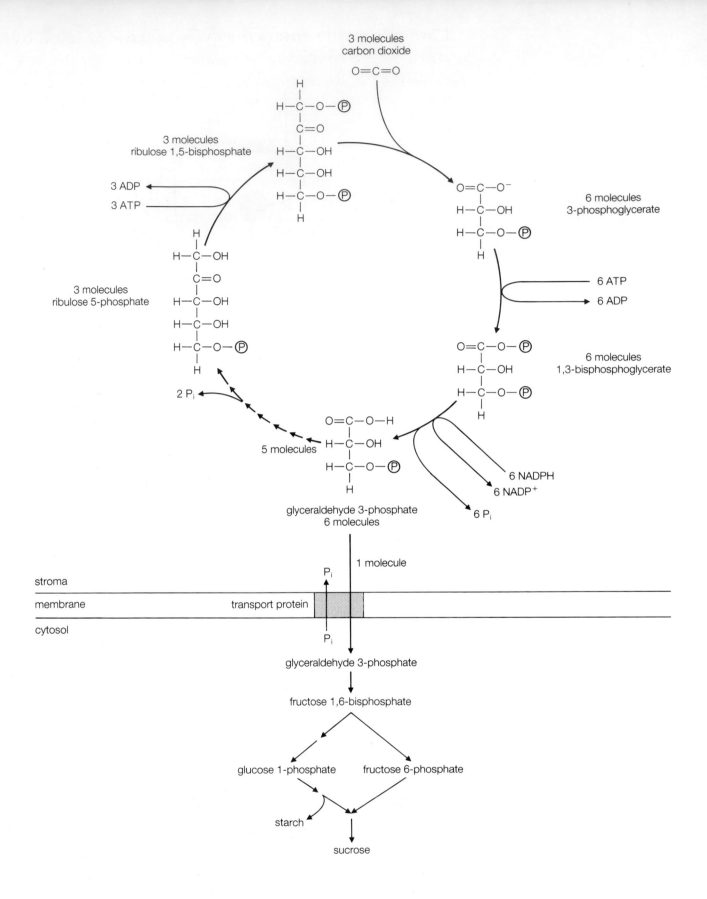

Fig 8.10 The light-independant stage of photosynthesis.

Carbon dioxide enters the cycle when it is fixed by ribulose 1,3-bisphosphate carboxylase

The carbon dioxide enters the cycle by reacting with ribulose 1,3-bisphosphate in a reaction catalysed by the enzyme ribulose 1,3-bisphosphate carboxylase.

$$\text{ribulose 1,3-bisphosphate} + \text{carbon dioxide} \longrightarrow \text{3-phosphoglycerate}$$

(a 5C molecule)   (a 1C molecule)   (two 3C molecules)

The 3-phosphoglycerate is then phosphorylated to produce 1,3-bisphosphoglycerate using the energy and the phosphate group from an ATP molecule (Fig 8.10). 1,3-bisphosphoglycerate is then reduced to give glyceraldehyde 3-phosphate using the reduced coenzyme NADPH to provide the necessary hydrogen (Fig 8.10).

For every three turns of the cycle one glyceraldehyde 3-phosphate leaves the cycle and is used to make other carbohydrates. Two glyceraldehyde 3-phosphate molecules are made from one ribulose 1,3-bisphosphate molecule every time the cycle turns. In three turns of the cycle six glyceraldehyde 3-phosphate molecules are produced, five of which remain in the cycle and one of which leaves.

The five molecules of glyceraldehyde 3-phosphate then go through seven enzyme-catalysed reactions that have the summed effect of converting them into three ribulose 5-phosphate molecules. The ribulose 5-phosphate is then phosphorylated to produce ribulose 1,3-bisphosphate using ATP (Fig 8.10). The cycle is complete and the ribulose 1,3-bisphosphate reacts with another molecule of carbon dioxide.

Glyceraldehyde 3-phosphate is exported from the chloroplast and used to synthesise other carbohydrates

For every five molecules of glyceraldehyde 3-phosphate that re-enter the cycle, one molecule of glyceraldehyde 3-phosphate leaves the cycle. This molecule of glyceraldehyde 3-phosphate leaves the chloroplast through a specific transport protein in the inner chloroplast membrane. This protein exchanges glyceraldehyde 3-phosphate for phosphate ions (Fig 8.10) and then the phosphate ions are used to make ATP.

Once in the cytosol, glyceraldehyde 3-phosphate is used to synthesise other carbohydrates. Figure 8.10 shows how glyceraldehyde 3-phosphate is converted to glucose, fructose and sucrose. The glucose molecules are also used to make starch and cellulose.

QUESTIONS

8.7   (a) Give a simple chemical equation that sums up photosynthesis.
     (b) Photosynthesis occurs in two stages.
       (i) What are these two stages called?
       (ii) Where do these stages occur in the cell?
       (iii) What substances are required for the first stage?
       (iv) What substances are produced by the first stage?
       (v) What substances are required for the second stage?
       (vi) What substances are produced by the second stage?

8.8   What energy transfers occur to move the energy from light into the chemical energy of a sugar molecule?

8.9   (a) Give one oxidation reaction that occurs during photosynthesis.
     (b) Give one reduction reaction that occurs in photosynthesis.
     (c) Which enzyme 'fixes' carbon dioxide during photosynthesis?

8.10 Divide this list of events into three: those that occur in photosystem I, those that occur in photosystem II and those that occur in the Q cycle. Arrange the events in order to show the flow of electrons during non-cyclic photophosphorylation.

(a) High energy electrons are emitted from P680 chlorophyll molecules.

(b) Energy is absorbed from light by P700 chlorophyll molecules.

(c) Electrons from the P680 chlorophyll molecules react with PQ and two hydrogen ions from the stroma producing PQH_2.

(d) Water is split into hydrogen ions, electrons and oxygen.

(e) High energy electrons are emitted from the P700 chlorophyll molecules.

(f) PQH_2 diffuses across the phospholipid bilayer.

(g) Electrons from the splitting of water are used to replace the electrons emitted by the P700 chlorophyll molecules.

(h) PQH_2 reacts to give PQ, releasing two hydrogen ions into the lumen of the thylakoid and passing two electrons to an electron carrier which then passes the electrons on to replace the electrons emitted by the P700 chlorophyll molecules.

(i) High energy electrons from the P700 chlorophyll molecules are used to reduce an electron carrier and then to reduce $NADP^+$ to give NADPH, removing hydrogen ions from the stroma.

(j) Energy is absorbed from light by P680 chlorophyll molecules.

8.11 Using the list (a)–(j) in question 4, select those events that occur during cyclic phosphorylation and place them in order to show the net flow of electrons.

DATA HANDLING 8.2

Chlorophyll a is found in all plants. The structure of chlorophyll a is shown in Fig 8.8. The chlorophyll molecules are arranged in the membrane of the thylakoids so that the haem group projects from the outer surface. The chlorophyll molecules are arranged in groups called light harvesting complexes. The structure of a light harvesting complex is shown in Fig 8.11. At the base of the funnel-like structure is a photosystem. The chlorophyll molecules in the light harvesting complex collect light energy and feed it to the chlorophyll molecules in the photosystem.

(a) Look at the structure of a chlorophyll molecule (Fig 8.8). What part of the chlorophyll molecule anchors the molecule in the membrane and why?

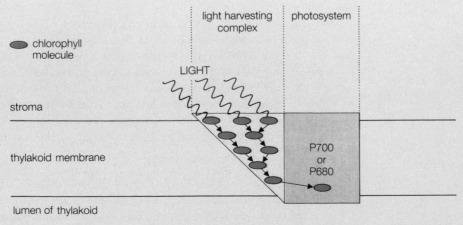

Fig 8.11 The light harvesting complex.

(b) The projecting chlorophyll molecules lie with the plane of the haem group at right angles to the direction of the light. Why is this desirable?

(c) Light energy is absorbed by the chlorophyll molecules. How do chlorophyll molecules give out the energy they have absorbed?

(d) What are the names of the two photosystems that are found at the base of the light harvesting complexes? Which specific forms of chlorophyll do these photosystems contain?

(e) Suggest why the many chlorophyll molecules found in a light harvesting complex all feed into a single photosystem.

Figure 8.12 shows the absorption spectrum of chlorophyll a and chlorophyll b (two common forms of chlorophyll). An absorption spectrum shows which wavelengths of light are absorbed by the chlorophyll pigments. Figure 8.12 also shows the efficiency of photosynthesis at different wavelengths of light.

(f) Which wavelengths of light are absorbed most strongly by chlorophylls a and b?

(g) Which wavelengths of light give the most efficient photosynthesis?

(h) Comment on your answer to (f) and (g).

(i) Why are leaves green?

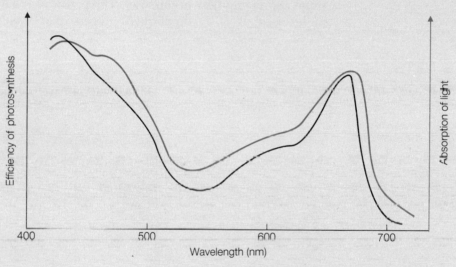

Fig 8.12 Graph comparing the absorption spectrum of chlorophyll with the efficiency of photosynthesis for different wavelengths of light.

8.4 FINE TUNING PHOTOSYNTHESIS

All plants photosynthesise but not all plants live in the same environment. Some plants live in tropical climates where the temperature is high and the light intensity is very great. Other plants grow in arid environments where the ability to conserve water is essential for survival. The biochemistry of these plants is adapted to their environments just as the shape of their leaves or their flowers is adapted to the environment.

At high light intensities photosynthesis is inhibited

Oxygen is made as a waste product during the light-dependent stage of photosynthesis (section 8.3). A high level of photosynthesis gives rise to a high oxygen concentration in the leaf and under these conditions a strange phenomenon occurs in most plants. The plants begin to produce less oxygen than expected and consume less carbon dioxide than expected even though the light intensity is high and there is adequate carbon dioxide. The scientists who first observed this phenomenon suggested that it was due to a respiration-like process that only took place in the light and they called the process **photorespiration**. In fact, it has nothing to do with respiration at all: it occurs because photosynthesis is inhibited at high oxygen concentrations. The cause of this phenomenon lies with the enzyme ribulose 1,3-bisphosphate carboxylase. Oxygen is a competitive inhibitor of the enzyme, competing with carbon dioxide for the active site of the enzyme. This inhibition only becomes significant at high oxygen concentrations.

This inhibition makes the light-independent stage of photosynthesis less efficient because the ribulose 1,3-bisphosphate carboxylase fixes less carbon dioxide. The ribulose 1,3-bisphosphate carboxylase binds one molecule of ribulose 1,3-bisphosphate and a molecule of oxygen instead of a molecule of carbon dioxide. A faulty reaction mechanism occurs in which the 5C molecule is broken into one 3C molecule, 3-phosphoglycerate, and one 2C molecule, phosphoglycolate (Fig 8.13). This means that some of the carbon and energy is being removed from the cycle in a very unproductive manner. Plants which are photorespiring can lose 30–40% of the carbohydrate that they should be producing under those conditions.

Normal plants recycle the phosphoglycolate in an inefficient manner

Plants have evolved a 'recycling' pathway to try and recover some of the carbon and energy lost in this way. The pathway is shown in Fig 8.13. As can be seen, it is a complicated process that involves three separate

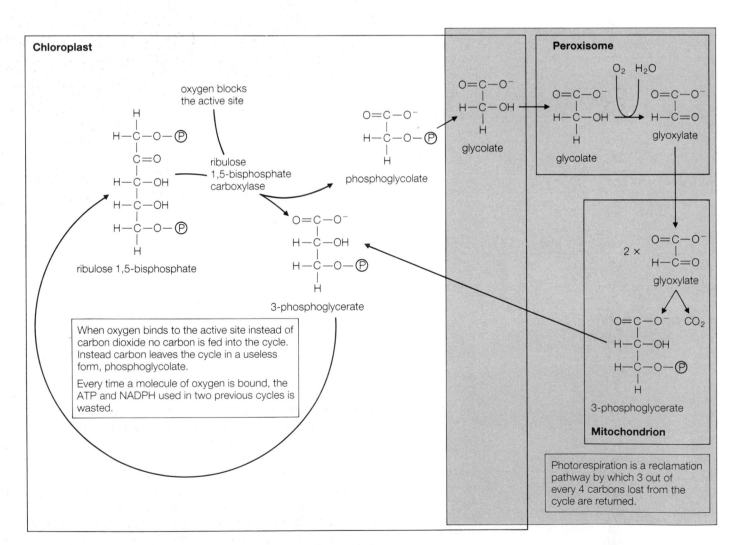

Fig 8.13 Photorespiration.

organelles in the cell. This recovery pathway involves the intake of more oxygen and the production of carbon dioxide, and gives rise to the phenomenon of photorespiration.

C$_4$ plants avoid photorespiration

The photorespiration pathway is not perfect. It only recovers some of the carbon and it involves the expenditure of some energy. In hot climates with high light levels the rate of photosynthesis is high and the oxygen concentration increases within the leaf, causing a high rate of photorespiration. So plants which can avoid photorespiration have an advantage over those that cannot. In such climates plants have evolved that have an alternative method of fixing carbon dioxide which is not affected by a high oxygen concentration. Sugar cane and maize are examples of such plants.

Fig 8.14 About half the sugar Britons consume comes from the sugar cane (shown here growing in Barbados). Sugar cane is a C$_4$ plant that is adapted to the high intensity light that occurs in tropical regions. The ribulose 1,5-bisphosphate carboxylase enzyme in normal plants is inhibited by oxygen, so carbon dioxide fixation is reduced. Photosynthesis in normal plants is therefore inefficient at high light intensities which cause a lot of oxygen to be produced by the light-dependent stage. C$_4$ plants have evolved so that the carbon dioxide fixation is catalysed by an alternative enzyme that is not inhibited by high oxygen concentrations. The fixed carbon dioxide is then exported to another cell where the oxygen concentration is low and released so that the light-independent stage of photosynthesis can proceed.

In C$_4$ plants the light-dependent and light-independent stages of photosynthesis are separated

In these plants the carbon dioxide reacts with phosphoenolpyruvate instead of ribulose 1,3-bisphosphate (Fig 8.15). The enzyme phosphoenolpyruvate carboxylase catalyses the reaction between phosphoenolpyruvate and carbon dioxide, producing oxaloacetate (Fig 8.15). Phosphoenolpyruvate carboxylase is not inhibited by oxygen and therefore photorespiration is avoided. Oxaloacetate is a 4C molecule so these plants are called C$_4$ plants. (Normal plants are called C$_3$ plants because 3-phosphoglycerate, a 3C molecule, is formed when carbon dioxide is fixed.)

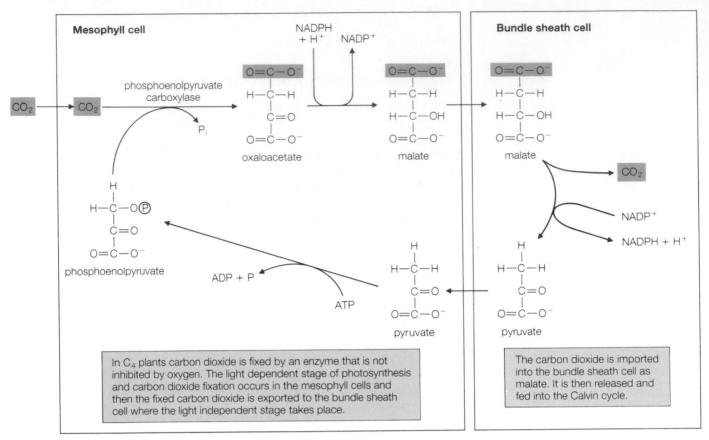

Fig 8.15 The C$_4$ pathway.

In C$_4$ plants carbon dioxide is fixed by an enzyme that is not inhibited by oxygen. The light dependent stage of photosynthesis and carbon dioxide fixation occurs in the mesophyll cells and then the fixed carbon dioxide is exported to the bundle sheath cell where the light independent stage takes place.

The carbon dioxide is imported into the bundle sheath cell as malate. It is then released and fed into the Calvin cycle.

However, this fixes the carbon into oxaloacetate rather than feeding it into the Calvin cycle. If the carbon dioxide is then released in the same cell the ribulose 1,3-bisphosphate carboxylase will still be acting in a high oxygen environment. Instead, the oxaloacetate is converted into malate and exported from the mesophyll cell, where the light-dependent stage of photosynthesis occurs, into a neighbouring bundle sheath cell (Fig 8.15). Once within the bundle sheath cell the malate reacts to release the carbon dioxide which then enters the Calvin cycle. The light-independent stage of photosynthesis therefore occurs in the bundle sheath cell (Fig 8.15). As no oxygen is being produced in the bundle sheath cell the ribulose 1,3-bisphosphate carboxylase is not inhibited.

When the malate reacts in the bundle sheath cell to produce carbon dioxide, pyruvate is produced (Fig 8.15). This pyruvate is transported back into the mesophyll cell where it is used to generate phosphoenolpyruvate. This closes the pathway and ensures that no useful carbon-containing compounds are lost.

However, the light-independent stage needs more than just carbon dioxide, it also needs the ATP and NADPH that is produced in the light-dependent stage. The pathway that exports malate from the mesophyll cell and imports pyruvate back also leads to the net transfer of NADPH from the mesophyll cell to the bundle sheath cell (Fig 8.15), where it is used in the light-independent stage. However, the C$_4$ pathway does not export the ATP needed from the mesophyll cell to the bundle sheath cell. The ATP needed for the light-independent stage has to be provided by other means so the C$_4$ pathway is a rather energy expensive process.

Nevertheless, the C$_4$ or Hatch–Slack pathway still gives the plants an advantage in tropical climates. This is because the rate of photosynthesis can be much higher in C$_4$ plants than in C$_3$ plants.

CAM plants conserve water by closing their stomata in daylight

For plants living in arid environments water conservation is of paramount importance. Plants lose most of their water through their stomata, the small holes through which gases diffuse in and out of the leaves. From the water conservation point of view the stomata should be closed during the day-time when the temperature is high but from a photosynthesis point of view this is when the stomata need to be open so that the maximum amount of carbon dioxide can enter the leaf.

Some plants solve this dilemma by separating carbon dioxide fixation and the light-dependent stage of photosynthesis. The plants only open their stomata at night and they fix the carbon dioxide in a mechanism similar to that found in C_4 plants. The plants 'store' the carbon dioxide as a 4C organic acid, then the 4C organic acid is broken down during the daytime to release the carbon dioxide as it is required during the day. This means that the stomata can remain closed during the day, reducing water loss. This separation of carbon fixation from the other parts of photosynthesis is called **crassulacean acid metabolism** or **CAM** because many members of the Crassulaceae family of plants use this mechanism to conserve water. However, it also occurs in many other plants, including cacti, orchids and members of the pineapple family.

QUESTIONS

8.12 (a) Under what conditions does a C_4 plant have an advantage over a C_3 plant?
(b) Where does carbon dioxide fixation occur in a C_4 plant?
(c) Where does the light-dependent stage of photosynthesis occur in a C_4 plant?
(d) Where does the light-independent stage of photosynthesis occur in C_4 plants?
(e) Give one example of a C_4 plant.

8.13 (a) Under what conditions does a CAM plant have an advantage over a C_3 plant?
(b) When does carbon dioxide fixation occur in a CAM plant?
(c) When does the light-dependent stage of photosynthesis occur in a CAM plant?
(d) When does the light-independent stage of photosynthesis occur in a CAM plant?
(e) Give one example of a CAM plant.

8.14 A C_3 crop like tobacco grows, on average, at only half the rate of a C_4 crop like sugar cane. Explain.

8.15 A scientist was investigating a CAM plant, a C_4 plant and a C_3 plant with a similar leaf surface area. The scientist measured:
(a) carbon dioxide uptake at high light intensity and in the dark;
(b) carbohydrate production at high light intensity and in the dark.

Predict which plants would give the highest and the lowest measurements under each of the two conditions.

8.5 RESPIRATION

Plants make a range of carbohydrates from the glyceraldehyde 3-phosphate made during photosynthesis. These carbohydrates are structural poly-saccharides such as cellulose or energy storage molecules like glucose, sucrose and starch which will be oxidised to release energy in the process called **respiration**. This oxidation process may occur in the plant where the carbohydrates were made, or in an animal that has eaten the plant!

Respiration occurs in two stages

The process of respiration is often summarised in this simple equation.

$$C_6H_{12}O_6 + 6O_2 \longrightarrow 6CO_2 + 6H_2O + ENERGY$$

In reality the process is much more complicated than this simple equation implies. Respiration occurs in two major stages (Fig 8.16), **glycolysis** and **oxidative phosphorylation**, each of which is comprised of many separate chemical reactions.

Glycolysis occurs in the cytosol of the cell and it has two main roles: the first is to produce a small amount of ATP and the second is to produce a suitable substrate for oxidative phosphorylation. Glycolysis itself does not require oxygen, unlike the later stages of respiration, so when no oxygen is available glycolysis occurs in isolation, providing the cell with a small amount of energy. In brief, glycolysis involves the oxidation of glucose to

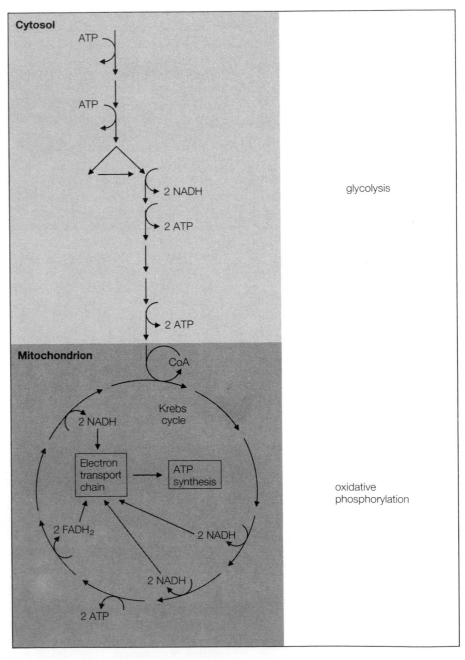

Fig 8.16 Respiration.

make a 3C compound called **pyruvate**. For every molecule of glucose oxidised, two molecules of ATP are produced from ADP and P_i and two molecules of reduced nicotinamide adenine dinucleotide, NADH, are produced from the coenzyme nicotinamide adenine dinucleotide, NAD^+. Glycolysis is summarised in Table 8.2.

The overall effect of the second stage of respiration is to oxidise pyruvate to give carbon dioxide and water and to phosphorylate ADP to make ATP: scientists named the second stage of photosynthesis oxidative phosphorylation because it had these two overall effects. In fact, oxidative phosphorylation occurs in two stages: the **Krebs cycle** and the **electron transport chain**. These two stages are closely linked, in that one cannot occur without the other, and they require the presence of oxygen.

The Krebs cycle is referred to by many names, including the TCA cycle and the citric acid cycle.

The Krebs cycle occurs in the matrix of the mitochondrion and its main role is to oxidise pyruvate by the removal of hydrogen atoms to give carbon dioxide and NADH. The NADH produced in the Krebs cycle then reduces the first electron carrier in the electron transport chain. The electron transport chain is in the inner membrane of the mitochondrion and its main role is to use the energy in the NADH to move hydrogen ions across the inner mitochondrial membrane. This translocation of hydrogen ions causes a pH gradient which is then used to make ATP from ADP and P_i (section 8.2). The Krebs cycle and the electron transport chain are summarised in Table 8.3.

GLYCOLYSIS

The simplest pathway for the oxidation of carbohydrates is the series of enzyme-catalysed reactions called glycolysis, or the **Embden–Myerhoff** pathway after two of the scientists who described it. The glycolysis pathway occurs in the cytoplasm of the cell and does not require oxygen. The overall characteristics of the glycolysis pathway are summed up in Table 8.2 while more detail of the individual reactions involved is given in the rest of this section.

Table 8.2 Glycolysis.

Location:	the cytosol
Substances in:	glucose, NAD^+, ADP, P_i
Useful products:	pyruvate, NADH, ATP
Waste products:	H_2O
Energy transferred from:	glucose
Energy transferred to:	ATP, pyruvate, NADH
Amount ATP produced:	2 molecules ATP per glucose molecule
Amount NADH produced:	2 molecules NADH per glucose molecule

1. The glucose molecule is first phosphorylated using two molecules of ATP so that they have enough energy to undergo the oxidation reaction.
2. The 6C glucose molecule is then split into two 3C sugars.
3. Each 3C sugar is then oxidised using NAD^+ and producing NADH.
4. Each of the 3C molecules is converted into pyruvate and in this process a total of four ATP molecules are produced from ADP and P_i.

The conversion of glucose to pyruvate does not occur in one, or even a small number of, enzyme-catalysed reactions; it requires nine separate reactions (Fig 8.17). These nine separate reactions are needed because the

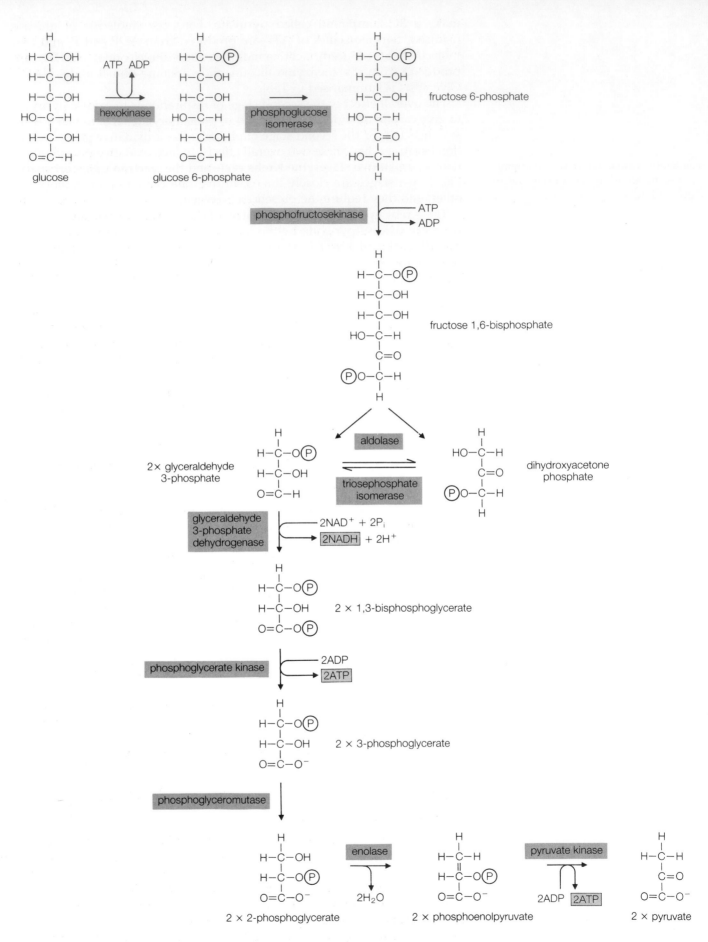

Fig 8.17 Glycolysis.

molecule has to be rearranged and 'primed' so that when it reacts it will phosphorylate an ADP molecule to give ATP. Similarly, the molecule has to be rearranged to contain the correct reactive group so that it can reduce nicotinamide adenine dinucleotide, NAD^+, the molecule itself being oxidised in the process.

Energy is injected into the sugar molecule

The first stage of glycolysis begins with the conversion of various carbohydrates, including glucose, to glucose 6-phosphate. Two of the enzymes that convert glucose to glucose 6-phosphate, glucokinase and hexokinase, are discussed in section 7.4. The glucose 6-phosphate then undergoes an enzyme-catalysed molecular rearrangement to produce fructose 6-phosphate. The fructose 6-phosphate is then phosphorylated again, producing fructose 1,6-bisphosphate and this fructose 1,6-bisphosphate then splits to form two 3C molecules, dihydroxyacetone phosphate and glyceraldehyde 3-phosphate. The dihydroxyacetone phosphate then undergoes a molecular rearrangement to produce a second molecule of glyceraldehyde 3-phosphate.

The first stage of glycolysis, the conversion of glucose to glyceraldehyde 3-phosphate, seems non-productive at first glance. Glycolysis is meant to be an energy-producing process, yet two molecules of ATP are consumed in the conversion of glucose to glyceraldehyde 3-phosphate. This breakdown of ATP is necessary because it is only by injecting this extra energy that the two molecules of glyceraldehyde 3-phosphate will have enough energy to enter the next phase of the glycolysis pathway.

Glyceraldehyde 3-phosphate is reduced, and then reacts to produce ATP

The glyceraldehyde 3-phosphate molecules react to form two molecules of 1,3-bisphosphoglycerate (Fig 8.17). This is an oxidation reaction in which NAD^+ is converted to $NADH + H^+$.

The two molecules of 1,3-bisphosphoglycerate then react to produce two molecules of 3-phosphoglycerate with the production of ATP from ADP. The 3-phosphoglycerate is then rearranged to form 2-phosphoglycerate which reacts to form phosphoenolpyruvate and water. The two molecules of phosphoenolpyruvate then react to form two molecules of pyruvate, again with the production of ATP from ADP. These two ATP-producing reactions are discussed in section 8.2.

Four molecules of ATP are produced in this second stage in glycolysis for every two molecules of glyceraldehyde 3-phosphate that enter, but two molecules of ATP were used in the production of these two glyceraldehyde 3-phosphate molecules. As the two glyceraldehyde 3-phosphate molecules were formed from one glucose molecule, the net production of ATP is two molecules for every glucose molecule entering the glycolysis pathway.

Pyruvate is converted to ethanol or lactate if there is no oxygen available

If oxygen is available in the cell the pyruvate produced in glycolysis enters the Krebs cycle and is oxidised to generate more energy. However, if oxygen is not available the Krebs cycle does not occur and the pyruvate must be converted into a molecule than can be excreted from the cell. When glycolysis occurs in isolation the process is referred to as **anaerobic respiration**, because ATP is produced but no oxygen is used.

In plants and fungi the pyruvate is converted into ethanol ($C_3H_3O_3 \rightarrow C_2H_6O$) (Fig 8.18). This is achieved by a decarboxylation reaction (pro-

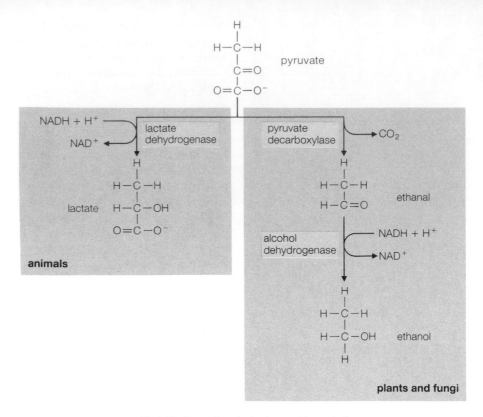

Fig 8.18 The end products of anaerobic respiration.

ducing carbon dioxide) and a reduction reaction using NADH as a source of hydrogen.

In animals the pyruvate is converted into lactate ($C_3H_3O_3 \rightarrow C_3H_5O_3$) (Fig 8.18) in an enzyme-catalysed reduction reaction using NADH as a source of hydrogen. Various cells in the human body rely on glycolysis for ATP production, including red blood cells, which make all their ATP by glycolysis, and muscle cells, which are often deprived of oxygen during

Fig 8.19 Athletes often suffer from cramp. When muscle cells are deprived of oxygen they resort to anaerobic respiration in order to make enough ATP for the muscles to contract. Anaerobic respiration is inefficient, converting only a small amount of the energy trapped in the glucose into ATP, but even a limited amount of ATP produced at a cost would have provided a survival advantage when fleeing a predator. Glycolysis proceeds as normal, except that the pyruvate produced is reduced to make lactate. This lactate is harmful to the muscle cells and if it accumulates it will lead to cramp. The blood takes the lactate away from the muscles and to the liver where it is oxidised back into pyruvate when oxygen is again available.

ENERGY

exercise. The lactate produced by anaerobic respiration diffuses into the blood plasma and is carried to the liver, where it is converted back into pyruvate and used for energy production.

OXIDATIVE PHOSPHORYLATION

Table 8.3

The Krebs cycle

Location:	the matrix of the mitochondrion
Substances in:	pyruvate, NAD^+, FAD, ADP, P_i
Useful products:	NADH, $FADH_2$, ATP
Waste products:	CO_2
Energy transferred from:	pyruvate
Energy transferred to:	NADH, $FADH_2$, ATP
ATP produced:	1 molecule ATP per pyruvate molecule
Hydrogen carriers produced:	1 NADH per pyruvate molecule
	1 $FADH_2$ per pyruvate molecule

1. Pyruvate is decarboxylated and reduced in a reaction with coenzyme A that produces acetyl CoA, NADH and CO_2.

2. The acetyl CoA enters the cycle by reacting with oxaloacetate, a 4C molecule, to make a 6C molecule called citrate.

3. The 6C molecule undergoes a series of reactions including a number of molecular rearrangements, two decarboxylation reactions and four reduction reactions.

4. These reactions regenerate the 4C oxaloacetate and produce:
   - 3 molecules NADH from NAD^+;
   - 1 molecule $FADH_2$ from FAD;
   - 1 molecule ATP from ADP and P_i;
   - 2 molecules of CO_2.

The electron transport chain and ATPase

Location:	the inner mitochondrial membrane
Substances in:	NADH, $FADH_2$, O_2, ADP, P_i
Useful products:	ATP
Waste products:	H_2O
Energy transferred from:	NADH, $FADH_2$
Energy transferred to:	ATP
ATP produced:	2.5 ATP for every NADH entering chain
	1.5 ATP for every $FADH_2$ entering chain

1. NADH reduces the first electron carrier in the electron transport chain by donating two high energy electrons to the electron carrier: $FADH_2$ reduces an electron carrier further down the chain.

2. These high energy electrons are 'passed along' the electron transport chain in a series of redox reactions.

3. During these redox reactions energy is removed from the electrons and used to move hydrogen ions from the matrix into the inter-mitochondrial space, creating a potential energy store.

4. Finally, the electrons are used to reduce oxygen and hydrogen ions to make water. The potential energy store is used to make ATP from ADP and P_i: the hydrogen ions flow back into the matrix through the ATPase and the energy stored in the gradient is used to power the reaction.

There is still a lot of energy in the pyruvate molecule at the end of glycolysis. If oxygen is available this pyruvate is oxidised further in a cyclic pathway of enzyme-catalysed reactions referred to as the **tricarboxylic acid cycle** or **citric acid cycle** or **Krebs cycle** (Fig 8.20). The reactions of the Krebs cycle occur in the matrix of the mitochondrion.

The main function of the Krebs cycle is to produce hydrogen attached to hydrogen carrier, nicotinamide adenine dinucleotide, NADH. The NADH

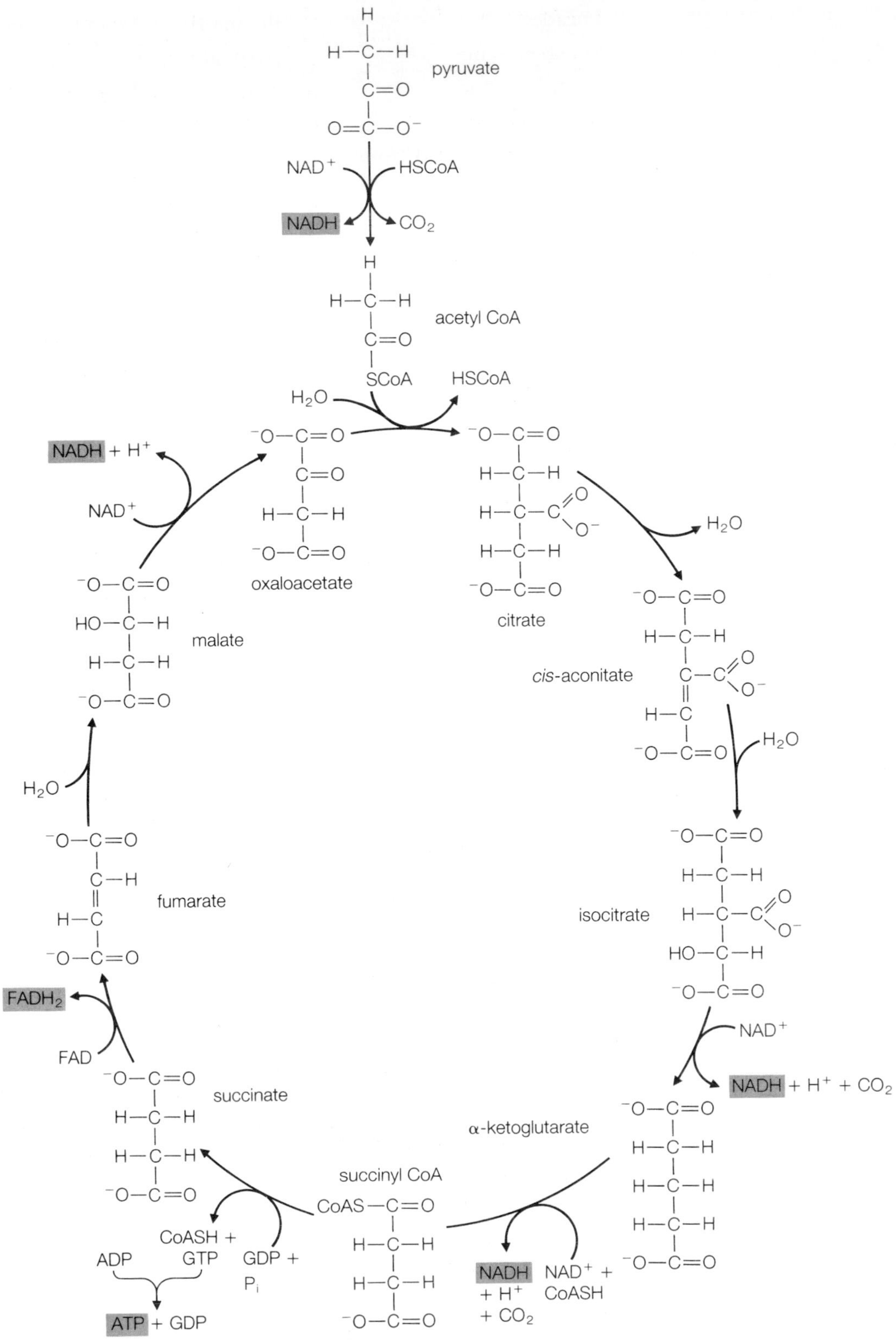

Fig 8.20 The Krebs cycle.

is then used used in the electron transport chain to generate a pH gradient across the inner mitochondrial membrane. The Krebs cycle also produces a small amount of ATP directly, in the course of an enzyme-catalysed reaction.

Pyruvate from glycolysis enters the mitochondrion and reacts to form acetyl coenzyme A

The outer membrane of the mitochondrion contains many, permanently open protein channels and is therefore permeable to small molecules. Pyruvate passes freely through this outer membrane and it then crosses the inner membrane via a specific protein, a **permease**, that allows only pyruvate to diffuse into the matrix. Once in the matrix pyruvate reacts with **coenzyme A (CoA)** to make acetyl coenzyme A (acetyl CoA) and carbon dioxide (Fig 8.20). This reaction is an oxidation and the hydrogen released is transferred to NAD^+ to make NADH. Acetyl CoA is the form in which material can be injected into the Krebs cycle.

The oxidation of pyruvate to give acetyl CoA is a highly exergonic reaction, giving out a lot of energy. As a lot of energy is given out during the reaction the reverse reaction, converting acetyl CoA to pyruvate, is impossible under the conditions within the cell: it would need too much energy. This means that the pyruvate is removed as soon as it enters the matrix of the mitochondrion, maintaining an extremely low concentration of pyruvate in the matrix. This ensures that pyruvate enters the matrix at a steady rate by diffusing down the concentration gradient.

The Krebs cycle produces reduced hydrogen carriers and a small amount of ATP

The Krebs cycle is a closed path of enzyme-catalysed reactions. The acetyl CoA (a 2C molecule) produced from the pyruvate reacts with oxaloacetate (a 4C molecule) to form citrate (a 6C molecule) (Fig 8.20). When the citrate is formed the coenzyme A is regenerated; this coenzyme A is then free to react with another pyruvate molecule.

The citrate (6C) is then reorganised via two enzyme-catalysed reactions to form isocitrate (6C). Once isocitrate is formed the molecule is in the correct form to undergo the first of four oxidations, producing α-ketoglutarate (Fig 8.20). The α-ketoglutarate is then oxidised to form succinyl CoA, a reaction that also produces carbon dioxide.

The succinyl CoA is then converted into succinate. This is the step in the Krebs cycle that produces ATP from ADP and the reaction is discussed in section 8.2. Succinate is then oxidised to form fumarate and the hydrogen atoms removed are transferred to the coenzyme **flavin adenine dinucleotide, FAD**, forming $FADH_2$. The fumarate reacts to produce malate which is oxidised to regenerate the oxaloacetate. NADH is produced during this final oxidation.

The net result of one turn of the Krebs cycle is the production of three molecules of NADH, one molecule of $FADH_2$ and one molecule of ATP, with two molecules of carbon dioxide produced as a waste product. One additional molecule of NADH and one more carbon dioxide molecule are produced when pyruvate is oxidised to acetyl CoA: the net total of useful products is four NADH, one $FADH_2$ and one ATP.

The electron transport chain

In the electron transport chain, NADH and $FADH_2$ produce a pH gradient across the inner mitochondrial membrane. The purpose of respiration is to produce ATP that can then be used for a variety of cellular processes (section 8.1). The molecules of NADH and $FADH_2$ produced during the Krebs cycle set up a potential energy store in the form of a difference of hydrogen ion concentration across the inner membrane of the mitochondrion. This potential energy store is then used to generate ATP from ADP (section 8.2).

The NADH and $FADH_2$ generate the difference in hydrogen ion concentration across the membrane by reducing electron carriers in the inner membrane of the mitochondrion. These electron carriers make up the electron transport chain (Fig 8.21).

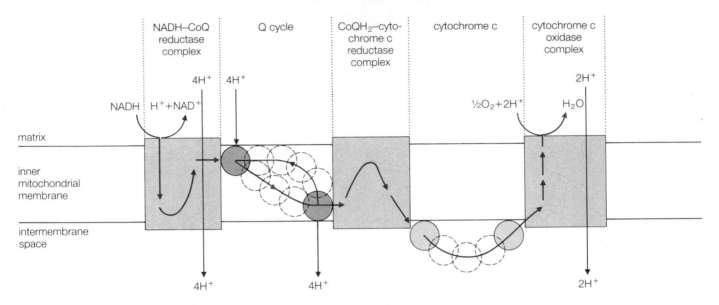

Fig 8.21   The electron transport chain.

Hydrogen ions are moved across the inner membrane of the mitochondrion at three points:
- a hydrogen ion pump powered by the energy released when NADPH is oxidised and the electrons released are passed through three electron carriers;
- a Q cycle where **quinone**, **Q**, is reduced to **reduced quinone**, **QH_2**, taking hydrogen ions from the matrix. The reduced quinone then diffuses across the membrane and is oxidised to quinone, releasing the hydrogen ions into the intermembrane space;
- a hydrogen ion pump powered by the energy released when the electrons from the Q cycle are passed through six electron carriers and used to reduce oxygen, producing water.

The NADH from the oxidation of pyruvate reacts with the first electron carrier in the electron transport chain, reducing it by adding two electrons (Fig 8.21). This electron carrier is part of the first complex that can move hydrogen ions across the membrane. Every time the electrons move from carrier to carrier some of the energy they carry is transferred to the protein complex. This energy is used to transport four hydrogen ions across the membrane against the concentration gradient.

The electrons leave the first complex and reduce coenzyme Q, removing two hydrogen ions from the matrix ($Q + 2H^+_{matrix} + 2e \rightarrow QH_2$). The reduced coenzyme Q diffuses across the bilayer and reduces another electron carrier, releasing the two hydrogen ions into the intermembrane space ($QH_2 \rightarrow Q + 2H^+_{intermembrane\ space} + 2e$). The pair of electrons from the first

Redox is a word used for an oxidation or a reduction reaction. When a molecule is oxidised, another molecule must be reduced and vice versa, so both reactions occur together, a redox reaction.

protein complex actually travels around the Q cycle twice, so four hydrogen ions are transported across the membrane for every two electrons travelling through the electron transport chain.

The electrons then pass along the chain in a series of redox reactions until they reach another protein complex that can pump hydrogen ions. The first electron carrier in this complex is reduced by the addition of the two electrons from the Q cycle. These electrons are finally used to reduce oxygen, producing water. Energy is released each time the electrons are used to reduce the next electron carrier in the chain and this energy is used to transport two hydrogen ions from the matrix into the intermembrane space against the concentration gradient.

For every two electrons passing along the electron transport chain, four hydrogen ions are transported across the membrane in the first protein complex, four in the Q cycle and two in the final protein complex, making a total of ten hydrogen ions translocated for every NADH molecule.

The $FADH_2$ produced during the Krebs cycle also contributes a pair of electrons to the electron transport chain. However, these electrons do not have enough energy to reduce the first electron carrier so instead they reduce an electron carrier further down the chain, entering the chain at the Q cycle. This means that only six electrons are translocated across the membrane for every $FADH_2$ molecule, four in the Q cycle and two in the final protein complex.

The hydrogen ion concentration gradient powers the ATP synthase

The energy stored in the hydrogen ion concentration gradient is used to synthesise ATP. The hydrogen ions travel through the ATP synthase complex in the inner mitochondrial membrane, down the concentration gradient, and the energy transferred to the protein is used to convert ADP to ATP (see section 8.2).

Three hydrogen ions passing through the ATP synthase complex give out enough energy to convert one ADP molecule to ATP. Another hydrogen ion from the matrix is used up to exchange an ATP in the matrix with an ADP from the cytoplasm so that the mitochondrion does not run short of ADP. This means that four hydrogen ions from the matrix give one ATP molecule in the cytoplasm. Every NADH molecule processed by the electron transport chain produces ten hydrogen ions in the matrix and four hydrogen ions from the matrix are needed to generate one ATP molecule in the cytoplasm, so one would expect 2.5 molecules of ATP to be produced for every NADH molecule processed. Careful measurements indicate that this theoretical ratio is very close to that actually observed, supporting the mechanism outlined above.

ATP production is maximised by shuttling other NADH molecules into the mitochondrion

The electron transport chain converts the energy stored in NADH into a potential energy store across the inner mitochondrial membrane which is then used to generate ATP. Any molecule of NADH can be used for this purpose, for example the NADH that is produced during glycolysis. NADH from the cytoplasm can be transferred into the mitochondrial matrix and used to generate ATP.

The efficiency of aerobic respiration can be calculated

The complete oxidation of glucose to give carbon dioxide and water would yield 2802.5 kJ mol^{-1}. The maximum number of ATP molecules that can theoretically be produced from one glucose molecule is calculated thus:

NADH produced during glycolysis per glucose	2
NADH produced during acetyl CoA production	2
NADH produced in Krebs cycle	6
Total NADH	10
Number ATP produced per NADH	2.5
ATP produced from NADH	25
FADH$_2$ produced in Krebs cycle	2
ATP produced per FADH$_2$	1.5
ATP produced from FADH$_2$	3
ATP produced in glycolysis	2
ATP produced in Krebs cycle	2
Total ATP produced per glucose	**32**

ATP converted to ADP releases 30.6 kJ mol^{-1}. 979.2 kJ mol^{-1} (30.6 × 32) therefore represents the energy that has ended up in the ATP. This makes the process 35% efficient (979.2/2802.5 × 100). The generators in a modern power station are only 20–30% efficient: we have yet to build a power station that can rival the (not so) humble cell!

If the complete oxidation of glucose would yield so much energy, why not just burn the glucose in the cells? The answer is that very little of the energy released in this single, explosive event could be harnessed to do useful work in the cell, most of it would end up as heat energy. Instead the energy is released in small steps that allow a large proportion of the energy to be transferred, ultimately, to ATP.

QUESTIONS

8.16 Arrange these statements about glycolysis in the correct order.
   (a) The phosphorylated 3C sugar is oxidised and NAD$^+$ is reduced to NADH.
   (b) The phosphorylated 6C sugar is split into two phosphorylated 3C sugars.
   (c) The 6C sugar is phosphorylated twice, converting two ATP molecules to ADP.
   (d) The 3C molecule is converted to pyruvate in a series of reactions that also convert two ADP molecules to ATP.

8.17 (a) Where in the cell does glycolysis occur?
   (b) Where in the cell does the Krebs cycle occur?
   (c) Where in the cell is the electron transport chain found?

8.18 What are the products of glycolysis:
   (a) when oxygen is present;
   (b) in plant cells when oxygen is not present;
   (c) in animal cells when oxygen is not present?

8.19 Study Fig 8.17.
   (a) Which two reactions are isomerisation reactions?
   (b) Which reaction is an oxidation reaction?
   (c) Which three reactions are phosphorylation reactions?
   (d) Which two reactions are dephosphorylation reactions?
   (e) Is the conversion of phosphoenolpyruvate to pyruvate an exergonic or an endergonic reaction? Explain your answer.

8.20 Arrange these statements about oxidative phosphorylation in the correct order.

(a) The Q cycle moves four hydrogen ions from the matrix to the intermembrane space.

(b) Pyruvate is decarboxylated and reacts with coenzyme A to make acetyl CoA.

(c) The succinate is then oxidised to make fumarate, with the production of $FADH_2$ from FAD.

(d) Electrons from the Q cycle are used to reduce the first in a series of electron carriers and some of the energy in the electrons is used to move two hydrogen ions across the inner mitochondrial membrane.

(e) Citrate is reorganised to give isocitrate which is then oxidised over two reactions and decarboxylated to give succinyl CoA, producing NADH from NAD^+.

(f) Two hydrogen ions from the matrix and two electrons from the electron transport chain react with 'half' an oxygen molecule to make a molecule of water.

(g) Succinyl CoA reacts to give succinate and an ATP molecule is produced from ADP.

(h) The potential energy stored in the hydrogen ion concentration gradient across the inner mitochondrial membrane is used to convert ADP and P_i to ATP.

(i) Acetyl CoA reacts with oxaloacetate to make citrate.

(j) Fumarate is rearranged to give oxaloacetate, closing the cycle.

(k) NADH reduces the first in a series of electron carriers and some of the energy in the electrons is used to move four hydrogen ions across the inner mitochondrial membrane.

8.21 The complete oxidation of glucose would yield 2802.5 kJ mol^{-1}. 30.6 kJ mol^{-1} is yielded by the breakdown of ATP.

(a) What percentage of the energy in the glucose is transferred into ATP during anaerobic respiration? Where does the rest of the energy end up?

(b) What percentage of the energy in glucose is transferred into ATP during aerobic respiration, assuming that the process is occurring under the ideal conditions?

8.22 (a) What is a coenzyme?

(b) Name three coenzymes that play a role in respiration.

(c) Outline the role of each of the coenzymes that you have named.

8.23 The outer mitochondrial membrane is permeable to most small organic molecules but the inner mitochondrial membrane is much more selectively permeable.

(a) Pyruvate enters the mitochondrion though a protein channel that allows only pyruvate through. Does transport of pyruvate into the mitochondrion require energy? Explain your answer.

(b) How does oxygen enter the mitochondrion?

(c) A protein channel in the inner mitochondrial membrane exchanges ATP for ADP. Why is this protein channel important?

(d) How are hydrogen ions moved from the matrix into the intermembrane space?

(e) How are hydrogen ions moved from the intermembrane space into the matrix?

DATA HANDLING 8.3

Many different substances can be fed into the Krebs cycle at various points while other substances can be fed into the glycolysis pathway. Alternatively, the intermediates in glycolysis or the Krebs cycle can be used to synthesise many substances of biological importance, indeed the Krebs cycle is sometimes referred to as a metabolic hub.

Under ideal conditions:

Every molecule of NADH entering the electron transport chain yields 2.5 molecules of ATP.

Every molecule of $FADH_2$ entering the electron transport chain yields 1.5 molecules of ATP.

	per glucose molecule processed		
	ATP directly	ATP via NADH	ATP via $FADH_2$
glycolysis	2	5	0
pyruvate → acetyl CoA	0	5	0
Krebs cycle	2	15	3

(a) Glycogen is a short term energy storage substance in humans.
   (i) What class of substance is glycogen?
   (ii) Where is glycogen fed into the respiration process?
   (iii) If a glycogen macromolecule was 500 residues long, how much ATP would be produced by the complete oxidation of the molecule under ideal conditions?

(b) Triglycerides are long term energy storage substances in humans. Imagine a triglyceride with three fatty acid side chains, each with sixteen carbons. The fatty acids are fed into the Krebs cycle via acetyl CoA by a process called β-oxidation. β-oxidation changes every 2C from a fatty acid into a molecule of acetyl CoA, producing one molecule of $FADH_2$ and one molecule of NADH in the process.
   (i) What class of substance is a triglyceride?
   (ii) Where are triglycerides fed into the respiratory process?
   (iii) How many molecules of ATP will be produced from one glycerol molecule?
   (iv) How many molecules of $FADH_2$ will be produced from one molecule of the triglyceride described above by the β-oxidation process?
   (v) How many molecules of NADH will be produced from one molecule of the triglyceride described above by the β-oxidation process?
   (vi) How many molecules of ATP will be produced from the $FADH_2$ and NADH produced during the β-oxidation process?
   (vii) How many molecules of ATP will be produced per acetyl CoA molecule?
   (viii) How many molecules of acetyl CoA are produced by the complete β-oxidation of the triglyceride described above?
   (ix) How many molecules of ATP are produced by the complete oxidation of the triglyceride molecule described above?

(c) Proteins in the body are broken down and used as a substrate for respiration only when a human is starving.
   (i) What is the name of the reaction by which proteins are broken down into amino acids?
   (ii) Amino acids have to be deaminated before they can be fed into the respiratory pathway. What is meant by deamination?

ENERGY

8.6 EXPERIMENTAL EVIDENCE FOR BIOCHEMICAL PATHWAYS

Every neat little diagram of a biochemical pathway represents years of many scientists' lives. Some have their names enshrined in textbooks: the Krebs cycle, the Embden–Myerhoff pathway, the Calvin cycle, the Hill reaction, the Hatch–Slack pathway, Mitchell's chemiosmotic theory. Others fade into obscurity, their years of labour reduced to a forgotten paper in a dusty journal on a library shelf. To have made their way into the textbooks those biochemical pathways have to be accepted by a large proportion of the scientific community. This is a long, and usually slow, process. Careful measurements have to be made of what enters and what emerges from the pathway, intermediates have to be isolated and identified, models have to be proposed and evidence collected to support them.

Weighty volumes have been written about the biochemical pathways involved in energy production and utilisation and it is impossible to discuss all the evidence supporting those pathways here. Instead, a very limited number of experiments will be discussed, to give the reader the flavour of the nature of the research.

Isotopes can allow an atom to be traced through a pathway

Isotopes are one of the most useful tools a biochemist or molecular biologist has at their disposal. Indeed they are so useful that companies have been set up that specialise in providing isotopically labelled molecules of all types. Molecules with a heavier or lighter atom behave exactly the same way as their unlabelled version in all chemical reactions. However, they make the molecule unusually heavy or may give out radiation, allowing the scientist to follow the atom's progress from molecule to molecule along the pathway.

When scientists were trying to describe the reactions that occurred during photosynthesis, one of the important questions was the origin of the oxygen that was produced as a waste product. Oxygen enters photosynthesis in two forms, water (H_2O) and carbon dioxide (CO_2). Knowing whether water or carbon dioxide gave rise to the excreted oxygen gas would give scientists an insight into the biochemical processes.

Normal oxygen is ^{16}O but a stable isotope occurs, ^{18}O. Isotopically labelled water, $H_2^{18}O$, was supplied to a plant in one experiment and isotopically labelled carbon dioxide, $C^{18}O_2$ was supplied to an identical plant in another. The oxygen given off was then collected and analysed using a mass spectrometer. This instrument would distinguish between $^{16}O_2$ and $^{18}O_2$. $^{18}O_2$ was given off when $H_2^{18}O$ was supplied to the plant. This made scientists speculate that the water was acting as a reducing agent. This was one of the first steps in describing the mechanism of the light-dependent stage of photosynthesis.

Radioactive isotopes are even more useful, because they can be followed using a radiation detector such as a Geiger counter. The reactions that make up the Calvin cycle in the light-independent stage of photosynthesis were investigated by providing a photosynthetic unicell, the alga *Chlorella*, with radiolabelled carbon dioxide, $^{14}CO_2$ (Fig 8.22). The progress of the radioactive carbon atom through the various molecules was followed by the technique of paper chromatography. The radioactive 'spots' were identified by comparing them with chromatograms of all the likely candidates. (See Data handling 8.4.)

Subcellular fractionation allows scientists to locate reactions within cells

Cells can be broken open and divided into their various organelles by centrifugation. Each type of organelle has a different density and can be separated according to how fast it travels down the centrifuge tube.

This allows the mitochondria to be separated from the cytosol of the cell. The different fractions can then be tested for the presence of certain enzyme-catalysed reactions. By this technique glycolysis was located in the cytosol and the Krebs cycle (TCA cycle) was located in the mitochondrion. Isolated mitochondria can also be broken open and separated into a membranous fraction and the soluble, matrix fraction. This allowed scientists to locate the electron transport chain and the ATP synthase in the membrane of the mitochondrion and the Krebs cycle in the matrix.

Chloroplasts can be broken open carefully and separated into the stroma and the thylakoids. This allowed the light-dependent reactions to be located in the thylakoids and the light-independent reactions in the stroma. Breaking open the thylakoids tells us which of the molecules are actually anchored in the thylakoid membrane.

The chemiosmotic hypothesis, the idea that a concentration gradient across a membrane can be used to synthesise ATP, has been supported by investigations using isolated mitochondria and chloroplasts. Small closed spheres of membrane called vesicles, formed from isolated inner mitochondrial membranes or from isolated thylakoid membranes, have been used to confirm that a pH gradient exists across the membrane. The structure and function of the ATP synthase has been investigated using such membrane vesicles.

Inhibitors can be used to investigate pathways

Many well known poisons, including cyanide, inhibit the electron transport chain in mitochondria. This allows scientists to block the electron transport chain at different points and decide which reactions occur downstream or upstream from the block. This helped scientists to sequence the events in the electron transport chain. One of these inhibitors, rotenone, is a plant-derived toxin used as a commercial insecticide and fish poison.

Other substances inhibit electron transport in the thylakoid membrane. One of these substances, DCMU, blocks electron flow from photosystem II and allows scientists to study photosystem I in isolation. There is a whole class of substances, referred to as S-triazines, that inhibit photosystem II. These are used widely as commercial herbicides.

QUESTIONS

8.24 How do scientists know that the oxygen given off as a waste product of photosynthesis comes from the oxygen in the water and not the oxygen in carbon dioxide?

8.25 If isolated thylakoids were treated with DCMU and then illuminated would they produce (i) ATP and NADPH, (ii) ATP alone or (iii) NADPH alone? Explain your answer.

8.26 **(a)** Name two inhibitors of the electron transport chain in mitochondria. What effect do these inhibitors have on an organism?
(b) Name two inhibitors of the light-dependent stage of photosynthesis. What effect do these inhibitors have on plants?

DATA HANDLING 8.4

The light-independent stage of photosynthesis converts carbon dioxide to glyceraldehyde 3-phosphate. The formula for carbon dioxide is CO_2 and the formula for glyceraldehyde 3-phosphate is

$$O{=}CH{-}CHOH{-}CH_2OPO_3{}^{2-}$$

(a) How many carbon dioxide molecules would be needed to provide enough carbon for one molecule of glyceraldehyde 3-phosphate?

(b) Where might the phosphate group in glyceraldehyde 3-phosphate come from? What type of reaction is the addition of a phosphate group?

(c) How many hydrogens are present in glyceraldehyde 3-phosphate as compared to the appropriate number of carbon dioxides? Where do these hydrogens come from? What type of reaction is the addition of hydrogen?

The reactions of the Calvin cycle were first described by Melvin Calvin and his co-workers. They conducted a series of experiments where radiolabelled carbon dioxide, $^{14}CO_2$, was given to algae (unicellular photosynthetic organisms) growing in nutrient medium within a peculiar apparatus called the lollipop apparatus because of its shape (Fig 8.22). Samples of the algae were removed rapidly at short intervals after the $^{14}CO_2$ was injected into the nutrient medium and the radiolabelled molecules present were analysed by paper chromatography. In this way the path of the radiolabelled carbon was followed through the molecules in the cycle.

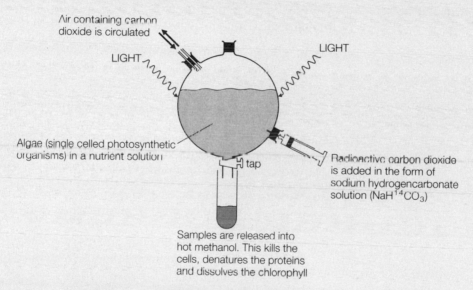

Air containing carbon dioxide is circulated

LIGHT

LIGHT

Algae (single celled photosynthetic organisms) in a nutrient solution

tap

Radioactive carbon dioxide is added in the form of sodium hydrogencarbonate solution ($NaH^{14}CO_3$)

Samples are released into hot methanol. This kills the cells, denatures the proteins and dissolves the chlorophyll

Fig 8.22 The lollipop apparatus.

(d) Why was the lollipop apparatus made of glass?

(e) Why is it important that the valve at the bottom of the apparatus can be opened and closed rapidly?

(f) What effect will the hot methanol have on the sample of algae removed from the apparatus? Why is pouring the algae directly into the hot methanol a good way of taking a sample?

(g) The scientists analysed the radiolabelled molecules by paper chromatography. What effect will paper chromatography have on the mixture of organic molecules from the cells?

(h) How could the scientists detect the radiolabelled molecules on the paper?

(i) The radiolabelled carbon atoms start in carbon dioxide and then pass from molecule to molecule. Put these molecules in order, starting with the one that would be radiolabelled first and ending with the one you would expect to be radiolabelled last: starch, glyceraldehyde 3-phosphate, 3-phosphoglycerate, ribulose 1,3-bisphosphate, glucose.

DATA HANDLING 8.5

Centrifugation is a method of separating objects according to density. A simple bench centrifuge can separate a precipitate from a solution, or cells from solution. The centrifuge spins the tubes and this spinning forces the contents of the tube outwards. The tubes are horizontal when the centrifuge is spinning, so the dense objects end up at the bottom of the tube.

An ultracentrifuge is a centrifuge that can spin very fast. Modern ultracentrifuges can spin at up to 100 000 revolutions per minute. The forces acting on the contents of a tube in such a centrifuge can be 500 000 times the force of gravity. This huge force is used to exploit tiny differences in density between cell organelles or between macromolecules, allowing them to be separated. It is possible to obtain a sample of pure cytoplasm and a sample of pure mitochondria by ultracentrifuging cells that have been broken open.

(a) In which of these two samples would you expect to find the enzymes responsible for:
  • glycolysis;
  • the Krebs cycle;
  • the electron transport chain?

The mitochondria can then be broken open and the membranes separated from the soluble fraction by ultracentrifugation. The membranes form small, closed vesicles as shown in Fig 8.23.

(b) Would you expect the enzymes involved in the Krebs cycle to be found in the membranous fraction or the soluble fraction of the mitochondria?
(c) Would you expect the enzymes involved in the electron transport chain to be found in the membranous fraction or the soluble fraction of the mitochondria?

Under carefully controlled conditions, glycolysis, the Krebs cycle and the electron transport chain can be made to work in isolation.

(d) Investigations were carried out on three subcellular fractions from plant cells: cytosol fraction, soluble mitochondrial fraction and membranous mitochondrial fraction. Which fraction(s) would:
  • produce ethanol;
  • produce NADH;
  • produce FADH;
  • produce carbon dioxide;
  • use oxygen;
  • decrease the pH of the sample;
  • produce ATP?

DATA HANDLING 8.6

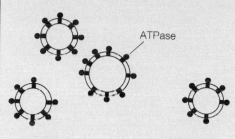

Fig 8.23 Submitochondrial vesicles.

The structure of a mitochondrion is shown in Fig 8.4. The outer mitochondrial membrane is permeable to all small soluble molecules, including ions. The inner mitochondrial membrane is selectively permeable and forms a barrier to large and/or charged molecules. The pH of the cytoplasm of most cells is neutral, pH 7.

Mitochondria can be isolated from cells by breaking open the cells and then centrifuging (spinning) the mixture so that the dense mitochondria are separated from the less dense cytoplasm. The isolated mitochondria can then be broken apart by sonication (vibrating the mitochondria with ultrasound waves). Small vesicles are formed that can be studied in the electron microscope. Figure 8.23 shows the structure of the vesicles as deduced by the electron microscopic study.

(a) What will be the pH inside the vesicles?
(b) What would happen if the vesicles are placed in a solution containing ADP and P_i with a pH above 7?
(c) What would happen if the vesicles are placed in a solution containing ADP and P_i with a pH below 7?
(d) What would happen if the vesicles were treated with a chemical that made the membrane permeable to ions and the vesicles were then placed in a solution with a pH above 7 containing ADP and P_i?

TUTORIAL 8.1

Oxidation and reduction

Oxidation can occur in three ways:
- the addition of oxygen
  e.g. $C + O_2 \rightarrow CO_2$ (oxidising agent is oxygen)

- the removal of hydrogen
  e.g. $H_2S + Cl_2 \rightarrow S + 2HCl$ (oxidising agent is chlorine)

- the removal of electrons
  e.g. $Zn + Fe^{2+} \rightarrow Zn^{2+} + Fe$ (oxidising agent is iron(II) ions)

When an oxidation occurs the oxidising agent itself is reduced.

Reduction can occur by:

- removal of oxygen
  e.g. $2CuO + C \rightarrow 2Cu + CO_2$ (reducing agent is carbon)

- addition of hydrogen
  e.g. $2Na + H_2 \rightarrow 2NaH$ (reducing agent is hydrogen)

- addition of electrons
  e.g. $Cu^{2+} + Zn \rightarrow Cu + Zn^{2+}$ (reducing agent is zinc)

When a reduction occurs the reducing agent itself is oxidised.

As an oxidation is always accompanied by a reduction and a reduction is always accompanied by an oxidation these reactions are called **redox** reactions.

REVIEW OF CRUCIAL POINTS

- Energy cannot be created or destroyed but only transferred. Plants transfer the energy in light into the chemical energy of carbohydrates by the process of photosynthesis. Plants and other organisms then transfer the chemical energy stored in carbohydrates and other organic compounds into ATP by the process of respiration. ATP is the immediate source of energy in all cells but energy is stored for longer periods of time in energy storage compounds such as starch, glycogen and triglycerides.

- Photosynthesis is a complex process involving many reactions. It occurs in two main stages: the light-dependent stage that occurs in the membrane of the thylakoids of the chloroplast and the light-independent stage that occurs in the stroma of the chloroplasts. In the light-dependent stage the energy in light is trapped by chlorophyll molecules and then transferred into ATP and NADPH. In the light-independent stage the energy stored in the ATP and NADH is used to reduce carbon dioxide to build carbohydrates.

- Respiration is also a complex process and it also occurs in two main stages. The first stage, glycolysis, does not require oxygen and occurs in the cytosol of the cell. During glycolysis glucose is oxidised to give pyruvate and the chemical energy stored in the glucose is transferred into pyruvate, a small amount of ATP and NADH. If oxygen is not present the NADH is used to reduce the pyruvate to either lactate or ethanol which can be excreted from the cell.

- The second stage, oxidative phosphorylation, does require oxygen. The pyruvate enters the matrix of the mitochondrion where it is decarboxylated and reduced to give acetyl CoA which is then injected into the Krebs cycle. During this cycle the 2C group that has been injected into the cycle is oxidised to carbon dioxide, producing NADH, $FADH_2$ and a little ATP. The NADH and $FADH_2$ is then used to reduce electron carriers in the electron transport chain that is present in the inner mitochondrial membrane. The energy carried by the electrons passed into the electron transport chain is used to move hydrogen ions across the membrane to create a potential energy store. This potential energy store is then transferred to ATP through an ATPase in the membrane. Oxidative phosphorylation is a very energy efficient process that transfers a large amount of the energy stored in the pyruvate into ATP.

Appendix A

ANSWERS TO DATA HANDLING EXERCISES

Data handling 1.1

(a) Maltose contains a reducing group, so reduces the silver ions, $Ag^+(aq)$, to silver, $Ag(s)$. Sucrose does not contain a reducing group, as the reducing groups on both the glucose and the fructose are destroyed when the 1,2-glycosidic bond is made. This means that the sucrose cannot reduce the silver ions, so the silver mirror test is negative.

(b) Test a sample of the solution with Benedict's reagent, then hydrolyse a second sample and retest. If the second test shows a greater amount of the red-brown precipitate than the first then sucrose was probably present.

(c) Non-reducing.

(d) C = sucrose. A = glucose. B = lactose

Data handling 1.2

(a) (i) +1, (ii) 0, (iii) −1.

(b) (i) +1, (ii) −1, (iii) −2.

(c) (i) +2, (ii) +1, (iii) −1.

(d) All three towards the negative electrode.

(e) All three towards the positive electrode.

(f) Alanine will not move, glutamic acid will go towards the positive electrode and lysine will go towards the negative electrode.

(g) pH 6.

Data handling 1.3

(a) B, D, E.

(b) A, G.

(c) C.

(d) F.

(e) 4.

(f) The melting points of unsaturated fats are lower than those of saturated fats.

(g) B, D and E would be solids. All others are liquids.

(h) F and H.

Data handling 2.1

(a) Glucose forms hydrogen bonds with the water molecules, therefore the glucose molecules mix with the water molecules and the glucose dissolves.

(b) Fructose

(c) A condensation polymerisation reaction.

(d) Colloidal suspension. There are enough hydroxyl groups on the outside of the starch macromolecule to form bonds with the water and keep the macromolecule suspended in the solvent. However, the water molecules will not penetrate the macromolecule itself.

(e) The starch is too large a macromolecule to be transported around the plant, and far too big to be transported across a cell membrane. Sucrose is a much smaller molecule.

(f) A hydrolysis reaction.

(g) Cellulose microfibrils are insoluble in water because the hydroxyl groups projecting from one cellulose polymer hydrogen bond with the next polymer, rather than hydrogen bonding with water molecules. Once the microfibril has been made there are too few hydroxyl groups on the surface for such a large structure to be suspended in water.

Data handling 2.2

(a) 124.

(b) Serine.

(c) Positive. 18 positively charged residues but only 10 negatively charged residues.

(d) C. Scientists showed that the C-terminal residue was valine.

(e) A or D. Scientists showed that the N-terminal residue was lysine.

(f) Methionine. As the treatment cuts after a methionine residue, then if there were two consecutive methionine residues, a large amount of free methionine would be produced. This was detected.

(g) First peptide from cyanogen bromide treatment runs from end of A into C. The second runs from the end of D, through B and into A. Therefore the order is D, B, A, C.

Data handling 2.3

(a) Control 1 is included to give the maximum expected counts, and to indicate the expected level if no insulin is present in the blood. Control 2 is included to give the minimum expected result, the level if there is insulin in the blood. Control 3 is included to show that the radiation was due to the binding of the radiolabelled antibody to the anti-insulin antibody, and not to the plastic.

(b) Patient B, 20 minutes after a meal.

(c) Patient A. No insulin was secreted into the blood, even after a meal (when it would be expected).

Data handling 2.4

(a) The assay could be whether the sample hydrolysed RNA.

(b) Net positive. It stuck to the negatively charged CM-cellulose.

(c) Increase the pH. This will mean that the positively charged residues in the protein will lose a hydrogen ion, becoming neutral, so the protein will no longer stick to the column.

(d) Increase the concentration of positive ions in the solution (e.g. increase the concentration of salt). These positive ions will compete with the protein for the negatively charged groups on the CM-cellulose.

(e) Biuret test.

(f) Any protein used in the biuret test will be lost.

(g) 80 mg (20% lost in the two tests).

(h) To give more accurate assay, to do immunofluorescence studies.

Data handling 3.1

(a) (i) 59%, (ii) 29%, (iii) 12%.

(b) (i) 26%, (ii) 44%, (iii) 30%.

(c) (i) 39%, (ii) 28%, (iii) 33%.

(d) The part of the polypeptide in the bilayer is richer in hydrophobic residues than the parts of the polypeptide that are exposed to the aqueous environments inside and outside the membrane. In contrast, the parts of the polypeptide exposed to the intracellular or extracellular solution are richer in charged residues than the part in the bilayer.

(e) This is an electrostatic attraction between the positively charged residue and the negatively charged phosphate-containing head group.

(f) This is an electrostatic attraction between positively charged and negatively charged residues.

(g) α-helix, stabilised by hydrogen bonds between different parts of the backbone.

(h) (i) The part of the polypeptide that was on the outside of the membrane.

    (ii) The parts of the polypeptide that were on the outside or the inside of the membrane.

    (iii) The whole polypeptide.

Data handling 3.2

1 (a) Diffusion.

(b) K^+ cannot pass through the phospholipid bilayer because it is charged.

(c) A concentration gradient occurs where there is a region where the concentration of a substance is higher adjacent to a region where the concentration of the same substance is lower.

(d) Transport across a membrane that requires an input of energy.

(e) The hydrolysis of ATP.

(f) Between step 2 and step 3.

(g) Phosphorylated is when a phosphate group is covalently linked to the R group of one of the amino acid residues in the protein.

Dephosphorylated is when such a phosphate group is removed.

2 (a) The three-dimensional shape of a protein is determined by weak interaction between different parts of the polypeptide backbone, between the R groups and the backbone and between the R groups themselves.

(b) (i) It changes the R group from being neutral to being negatively charged.

    (ii) It could change the nature of the weak interactions between this R group and the backbone or this R group and another.

(c) Dephosphorylase.

3 (a) The sides of the protein that are adjacent to the bilayer would be neutral and non-polar. The sides of the protein that are adjacent to the external or internal solution would be mainly polar or charged.

(b) It would move in the plane of the membrane (horizontally), not up or down at right angles to the membrane.

4 (a) A reaction that can occur backwards or forwards.

(b) ATP from ADP and P_i.

Comprehension 3.3

1 (a) To get a significant decrease in the length of the whole myofibril.

(b) So that when the Ca^{2+} is released it reaches all parts of the myofibril at the same time, so that all the sarcomeres will contract at the same time.

(c) Ca^{2+} is charged and therefore will not pass through the sarcoplasmic membrane. When it is released it must pass through the 'pore' of a membrane protein that is opened as a 'gate'.

2 (a) The myofibrils would always be contracted if ATP was present.

(b) The tropomyosin and troponins decrease the rate of ATP hydrolysis. The tropomyosin binds to the actin and stops the actin interacting with the myosin.

(c) The myosin heads can only hydrolyse the ATP if they can interact with the actin. If the tropomyosin and the troponins bind to the actin, then no ATP hydrolysis will occur and the myofibril will not contract.

(d) The rate of ATP hydrolysis increases in the presence of Ca^{2+}. The Ca^{2+} binds to troponin C. This alters the shape of the troponin C and the tropomyosin so that the tropomyosin no longer binds to the actin filaments. This means that the actin filaments can interact with the myosin head and ATP hydrolysis will happen.

(e) (i) The Ca^{2+} binds to troponin C.

    (ii) The shape of the troponin C protein changes.

    (iii) This causes a change in shape of the tropomyosin protein.

(iv) This exposes the myosin head binding site on the actin filament.

(v) The myosin head binds to the actin filament and the ADP that was bound to the myosin head is released.

(vi) ATP binds to the myosin head, causing the myosin head to detach from the actin filament.

(vii) The ATP is hydrolysed, causing the myosin head to pivot and then rebind to the actin filament at a site that is further along, causing the filaments to slide relative to each other.

(viii) As these actions are co-ordinated throughout the sarcomere, and the Ca^{2+} release occurs in every sarcomere at the same time, the whole muscle decreases in length.

Data handling 4.1

(a) The phosphate group nearest to the sugar group should be radiolabelled, as this is the only phosphate group that ends up in the polynucleotide.

(b) ddATP has no oxygen atom on carbon 3 of the sugar group in the nucleotide, there is a hydrogen instead of a hydroxyl group.

(c) The ddATP will be joined to the growing polynucleotide in the normal manner, as the reactive group that forms the phosphodiester bond (the phosphate group attached to the carbon 5 of the ddATP) is normal.

(d) The next nucleotide would be joined to the growing polynucleotide by a phosphodiester bond through the oxygen atom on carbon 3. As there is no oxygen atom on carbon 3, the polymerisation reaction cannot take place.

(e) 1 in 100, i.e. 100 000 (10^5).

(f) The hydrogen bonds are much weaker than the covalent bonds, so less energy is needed to break them.

(g) The phosphate groups in the DNA each carry a negative charge.

(h) 6.

(i) CGATTA
GCTAATGCTTAGCATGCTCATC

CGATTACGA
GCTAATGCTTAGCATGCTCATC

CGATTACGAA
GCTAATGCTTAGCATGCTCATC

CGATTACGAATCGTA
GCTAATGCTTAGCATGCTCATC

CGATTACGAATCGTACGA
GCTAATGCTTAGCATGCTCATC

CGATTACGAATCGTACGAGTA
GCTAATGCTTAGCATGCTCATC

CGATTACGAATCGTACGAGTAG
GCTAATGCTTAGCATGCTCATC

(j) CGATTA

CGATTACGA

CGATTACGAA

CGATTACGAATCGTA

CGATTACGAATCGTACGA

CGATTACGAATCGTACGAGTA

CGATTACGAATCGTACGAGTAG

(k) X = CGATTACGAATCGTACGAGTAG (the longest)

Y = CGATTACGAATCGTA (4th longest)

Z = CGATTA (the shortest)

(l) XXXXXXTACGGTATATCGGTAAATGCCT where XXXXXX stands for the primer.

Data handling 4.2

(a) The input of energy breaks the weak hydrogen bonds between the bases that hold the polynucleotides together in the double helix.

(b) Because DNA polymerase will not start to copy single-stranded DNA without a primer.

(c) 2^{20} = 1 048 576.

(d) Because a primer will be needed for every polynucleotide that is synthesised during the whole process.

(e) Nucleotides (ATP, TTP, GTP, CTP).

(f) Because it is not denatured by the high temperatures used to separate the two strands of the DNA double helix.

(g) It would be denatured and would lose enzymatic activity.

(h) ^{3}TCCATTGGATATACG^5

Data handling 5.1

(a) An amino acid that the organism cannot make.

(b) A fungus (a mould).

(c) They cannot synthesise valine, and valine is essential for survival.

(d) They lack one or more of the enzymes needed to make valine.

(e) A wild type strain shows the normal phenotype: in this case a strain that can make valine.

(f) As a control.

(g) No, because each strain shows a different pattern of growth.

(h) Z would only grow if valine was added.

(i) Z is missing the enzyme for step 5.

(j) X will grow on valine and 2-keto-3-methyl-3-hydroxy-butanoic acid.

(k) X is missing the enzyme for step 4.

(l) W will grow on valine, 2-keto-3-methyl-3-hydroxy-butanoic acid and 2,3-dihydroxy-3-methyl-butanoic acid.

(m) X is missing the enzyme for step 3.

(n) V will grow on valine, 2-keto-3-methyl-3-hydroxy-butanoic acid, 2,3-dihydroxy-3-methyl-butanoic acid and 2-keto-3-methyl-butanoic acid.

(o) V is missing the enzyme for step 2.

(p) Y will grow on valine, 2-keto-3-methyl-3-hydroxy-butanoic acid, 2,3-dihydroxy-3-methyl-butanoic acid, 2-keto-3-methyl-butanoic acid and 2-methyl-2-hydroxy-3-keto-butanoic acid.

(q) Y is missing the enzyme for step 1.

(r) Pyruvic acid → 2-methyl-2-hydroxy-3-keto-butanoic acid → 2-keto-3-methyl-butanoic acid → 2,3-dihydroxy-3-methyl-butanoic acid → 2-keto-3-methyl-3-hydroxy-butanoic acid → valine.

Data handling 5.2

(a) The DNA is radiolabelled so that it can be detected.

(b) A radiation counter or photographic film.

(c) 10.

(d) 10.

(e) The bands at −38, −31 and −29.

(f) That the protein is binding to the DNA in this region, preventing breakage of the DNA.

(g) This is one of the two sites that must have a certain sequence for the RNA polymerase to bind to the gene and start transcribing: it is part of the bacterial promoter.

(h) RNA polymerase.

Data handling 5.3

(a) A is the regulatory gene.

(b) B is the operator.

(c) C is the promoter for the operon.

(d) D, E, F, G and H code for the enzymes that make tryptophan.

(e) Transcription of the *trp* operon should be low when there is lots of tryptophan in the cell.

(f) The protein is a repressor.

(g) If the level of tryptophan in the cell is low there will be no tryptophan to bind to the regulatory protein (coded by A). When no tryptophan is bound to the regulatory protein then the regulatory protein does not bind to the operator (B). This means that RNA polymerase can bind to the promoter (C) and transcription will occur. The enzymes will be made, and more tryptophan will be synthesised.

(h) If the level of tryptophan in the cell is high then all the regulatory protein will bind tryptophan. The regulatory protein will then bind to the operator (B). This means that RNA polymerase cannot bind to the promoter (C), so no transcription will occur, no enzymes will be produced and no tryptophan will be made.

Data handling 6.1

(a) 50% of the myoglobin is saturated at approximately 0.5 kPa. 50% of the haemoglobin is saturated at approximately 3.5 kPa.

(b) Haemoglobin will release its oxygen at a higher oxygen concentration than myoglobin, so the haemoglobin will release its oxygen first as the oxygen concentration falls.

(c) The oxygen stored in the myoglobin is used when oxygen is being used so quickly that the haemoglobin cannot deliver it fast enough, i.e. when the muscle is respiring at a high rate during exercise.

(d) Haemoglobin has four subunits while myoglobin has only one. This means that myoglobin cannot show co-operative effects, so does not have a sigmoid curve.

(e) The steep curve shows that the oxygen will be fully loaded with oxygen as the blood is pumped through the lungs but will release the majority of its oxygen as it passes through the tissues of the body. Haemoglobin releases the majority of its oxygen at quite high oxygen concentrations compared to myoglobin, so the cells do not have to be running out of oxygen before more will be delivered.

(f) 34 out the 100 molecules would have oxygen molecules carried by all four of the subunits while 66 of the 100 molecules would be carrying no oxygen at all. Haemoglobin shows a positive co-operative effect: either all the four subunits carry oxygen or none.

(g) The dissociation curve would shift to the right. This would mean that the haemoglobin would give up its oxygen at higher oxygen concentrations. An increase in respiration rate would cause more oxygen to be delivered even before the oxygen concentration started to fall.

(h) Lowering the pH also shifts the oxygen dissociation curve to the right. This means that haemoglobin gives up its oxygen more easily (at a higher oxygen concentration) when the pH drops. This means that more oxygen will be delivered in a region where lactic acid is being produced (i.e. anaerobic respiration is occurring).

Data handling 6.2

(a) The quaternary structure is a triple helix.

(b) Hydroxyproline is likely to form hydrogen bonds.

(c) Approximately 48 °C.

(d) Approximately 14 °C.

(e) The collagen from the healthy individual.

(f) Without the vitamin C the enzyme that converts proline to hydroxyproline cannot function because it lacks its cofactor. This means that there are few or no hydroxyproline residues in the collagen, so there are few, if any, hydrogen bonds between the polypeptides. This means that the triple helix is less stable and so it denatures at a lower temperature.

(g) A collagen fibril is made up of many overlapping triple helical subunits. When there are no hydrogen bonds within the triple helix, each subunit will stretch easily, causing the subunits to move relative to each other and reducing the tensile strength of the collagen fibril.

(h) Scurvy. Bleeding gums, slow wound healing, ulcers.

(i) There is a network of collagen fibres in the skin. If this network is weak, the skin will break easily, making bleeding gums and ulcers more likely. Collagen fibres also have an important role in scar formation and skin growth, so wound healing is affected.

Data handling 7.1

(a) (graph)

(b) The rate of reaction increases, first slowly and then at a steady rate.

(c) The rate of reaction decreases sharply.

(d) The optimum temperature for the reaction is about 42 °C.

(e) Rate at 35 °C = 6.6, rate at 25 °C = 4.0, Q_{10} = 1.65.

(f) Reaches a maximum rate, then slows until no reaction. This indicates that the enzyme is being denatured by the increasing temperature.

(g) Measure the rate of the reaction at a set temperature with increasing concentration of substrate – saturation kinetics should be shown; or repeat the experiment across a pH range – an optimum pH should be found.

Data handling 7.2

(a) Glutamate is the substrate.

(b) Oxido-reductases. This enzyme oxidises glutamate by removing hydrogen.

(c) (graph)

(d) The rate increases with substrate concentration until it reaches a maximum, after which the reaction continues at this maximum rate. This is saturation kinetics and indicates that there are a limited number of active sites (one per enzyme molecule).

(e) V_{max} is approximately 4.5 mg min^{-1} for 0 mM salicylate, V_{max} is approximately 1.7 mg min^{-1} for 40 mM salicylate. Salicylate is an inhibitor of the reaction.

(f) K_m at 0 mM salicylate is approximately 1.8 mM, K_m at 40 mM is approximately 1.7 mM. Salicylate affects the V_{max} of the reaction but not the K_m: this is typical of a non-competitive enzyme inhibitor.

Data handling 8.1

(a) Bonds before = 9660 + 5568 = 15 228 kJ mol^{-1}
Bonds after = 1735 + 2506 + 2891 + 2320 + 2989.8 = 12 441.8 kJ mol^{-1}
Therefore, energy put in to break bonds is 15 228 kJ mol^{-1} and energy got out when bonds form is 12 441.8 kJ mol^{-1}, total energy in = 2786.2 kJ mol^{-1}.

(b) Energy out when reaction is reversed is actually 2802.5 kJ mol^{-1}, so using the bond energies gives a good estimate of the energy change, but it is not absolutely accurate.

(c) Photosynthesis.

Data handling 8.2

(a) The long hydrocarbon tail, as this will be soluble in the phospholipid bilayer.

(b) So that the maximum amount of light energy can be harvested.

(c) The chlorophyll molecules emit an electron that carries the energy to another molecule.

(d) Photosystem I contains P700, photosystem II contains P680.

(e) Each chlorophyll molecule in the light harvesting complex absorbs light energy and all the energy is fed into a single photosystem: this provides enough energy for the photosystem to operate at its maximum rate.

(f) The chlorophyll molecules absorb 430–490 nm and 660–680 nm wavelength light most strongly.

(g) The most efficient photosynthesis occurs at approximately 430 nm and 670 nm.

(h) This implies that the light energy needed for photosynthesis is absorbed by the chlorophyll molecules.

(i) Green light has a wavelength of 510–540 nm, and this is the wavelength of light that the chlorophyll does not absorb. Therefore green light is reflected or transmitted, and leaves look green.

Data handling 8.3

(a) (i) Carbohydrate, polysaccharide.

(ii) It is hydrolysed to form glucose that is fed into the glycolysis process.

(iii) Glycogen → 500 glucose molecules. Each glucose molecule gives
2 + 5 + 5 + 2 + 15 + 3 = 32 molecules ATP, therefore the total will be 16 000 molecules of ATP.

(b) (i) Lipid.

(ii) The fatty acid chains are broken into 2C units and fed into the Krebs cycle via acetyl CoA. The glycerol molecule will probably not be fed into the respiration process.

(iii) Probably none.

(iv) (16/2) × 3 = 24 FADH$_2$ molecules.

(v) (16/2) × 3 = 24 NADH molecules.

(vi) 24 × 1.5 = 36 ATP molecules from the FADH$_2$. 24 × 2.5 = 60 molecules of ATP. Total = 96 molecules.

(vii) Every acetyl CoA molecule produces 1 ATP directly, 7.5 ATP via NADH and 1.5 ATP via FADH$_2$ for every turn of the Krebs cycle. Total = 10 ATP.

(viii) (16/2) × 3 = 24 molecules of acetyl CoA are produced.

(ix) Acetyl CoA oxidation produces 24 × 10 = 240 molecules of ATP.
β-oxidation produces 96 molecules ATP.
Total for complete oxidation = 336 molecules of ATP.

(c) (i) Hydrolysis (depolymerisation).

(ii) The amino group is removed.

(iii) Because proteins are needed as building materials and for enzymes, etc.

(iv) The nitrogen-containing part is converted into urea.

Data handling 8.4

(a) 3.
(b) Likely to be from ATP. This is a phosphorylation reaction.
(c) There are no hydrogens in carbon dioxide and there are five in each glyceraldehyde 3-phosphate molecule. These hydrogens come from water. Addition of hydrogen is a reduction reaction.
(d) So that the light would pass through it.
(e) So that samples of the reaction mixture could be removed at frequent intervals to monitor the progress of the reaction.
(f) The hot methanol will stop all reactions because it will denature all the proteins present immediately. This should stop all enzyme-catalysed reactions in the cells, giving a 'snapshot' of the situation when the sample was taken.
(g) The mixture of organic molecules will be separated.
(h) They could put the paper against a photographic film, or pass a radiation counter across the paper.
(i) ribulose 1,3-bisphosphate, 3-phosphoglycerate, glyceraldehyde 3-phosphate, glucose, starch.

Data handling 8.5

(a) Glycolysis in the cytoplasm. The Krebs cycle and the electron transport chain in the mitochondria.
(b) In the soluble fraction of the mitochondria.
(c) In the membranous fraction of the mitochondria.
(d) The cytosol would produce ethanol. The cytosol and the
soluble fraction of the mitochondria would produce NADH.
The soluble fraction of the mitochondria would produce FADH.
The soluble fraction of the mitochondria would produce carbon dioxide. The membranous fraction of the mitochondria would use oxygen. The cytosol would decrease the pH (due to lactic acid production). All fractions would make ATP, although the membranous fraction of the mitochondria would make the most.

Data handling 8.6

(a) pH 7.
(b) ATP would be made. The concentration of H^+ ions would be higher inside the vesicles than outside, so H^+ ions would flow out through the ATPase, making ATP from the ADP and P_i.
(c) Nothing. The H^+ concentration gradient would be the wrong way.
(d) Nothing, no concentration gradient could occur across the membrane.

Appendix B
ANSWERS TO IN-TEXT QUESTIONS

Only numerical or short answers are given.

Chapter 1

1.1 (a) Soluble: sodium chloride, ethanol, glycerol. Insoluble: hexane, 2,2-dimethylbutane.
    (b) Soluble: hexane, 2,2-dimethylbutane. Insoluble: sodium chloride, ethanol, glycerol.

1.8 (a) C,H,O. (b) Carbohydrates.
    (c) —C=O, —OH.

1.11 (a) C,H,O,N. (b) —NH$_2$, —COOH.
    (c) H$_2$NCHRCOOH.

1.12 (c) (i) Neutral. (ii) Positive. (iii) Negative.

1.14 (a) Ribose, deoxyribose. (b) Adenine, guanine, cytosine, thymine, uracil. (c) Phosphate.

1.15 (a) RNA. (b) DNA. (c) ATP (energy storage).

1.16 (a)/(b)/(c) Hydrocarbon chain, neutral, hydrophobic; carboxylic group, negative, hydrophilic.

1.20 (a) K^+, Mg^{2+}. (b) Organic anions.
    (c) Selectively permeable.

Chapter 2

2.2 (a) 300 $C_6H_{12}O_6 \rightarrow C_{1800}H_{3002}O_{1501} + 299H_2O$.
    (b) $C_{200}H_{302}O_{101}N_{100} + 99H_2O \rightarrow 100C_2H_5O_2N$.

2.4 (a) α-glucose. (b) Condensation polymerisation. (c) 1,4-glycosidic.

2.7 (a) Condensation. (c) Hydrolysis.

2.13 (b) (i) Benedict's reagent. (ii) Biuret test. (iii) Iodine solution.

2.14 (b) CM-cellulose: lysozyme, cytochrome c, silk fibroin (just), alcohol dehydrogenase. DEAE-cellulose: α-casein. (c) Silk fibroin.

Chapter 3

3.1 (a) Ribosomes. (b) Nucleus. (c) Mitochondria. (d) Lysosomes. (e) Golgi complex.

3.3 (c) Monosaccharide in the water, triglyceride in the oil, phospholipid at the interface.

3.5 (a) Extracellular surface. Protein. Glycoprotein. (b) Bilayer: soluble in phospholipid. (c) Peripheral, integral, pores. (d) To transport substances. (e) Control transport.

Chapter 4

4.2 (b) Cysteine, methionine. (c) Nucleotides.

4.3 B and C are essential.

4.4 (a) C,H,O,N,P. (b) Ribose, deoxyribose, pentoses. (c) Adenine and guanine (purines); thymine, cytosine and uracil (pyrimidines).

4.5 Organic bases are 'bases'; phosphate groups are 'acidic'.

4.13 Have no DNA repair mechanism to repair u.v. damage to DNA.

4.14 It now resembles thymine.

4.15 (a) By spermine and spermidine. (b) By histones.

4.16 $-NH_2$. Positively charged in cell, neutralise negatively charged phosphate groups.

4.17 $-NH_2$ (as **4.16**).

Chapter 5

5.1 Approximately 87 000.

5.2 $4^{10} = 1\,048\,576$.

5.3 (a) To make protein. (b) To make proteins and structural polysaccharides. (c) For energy.

5.6 UUAAGCGCAACCGAUAAUGC.

5.7 (a) Deoxyribonucleotide. (b) Ribonucleotide. (c) DNA polymerase. (d) RNA polymerase. (e) Condensation polymerisation.

5.10 (a) A → B. (b) The end furthest from the RNA polymerase. (c) Lower. (d) W.

5.11 *E. coli* start transcribing structural genes if lactose present, stop if it is absent.

5.12 First mutant: transcribes structural genes all the time.
Second mutant: transcribes structural genes all the time.

Third mutant: never transcribes structural genes.
Fourth mutant: never transcribes structural genes.
Fifth mutant: never transcribes structural genes.

5.13 *E. coli* only transcribes structural genes if arabinose present.

5.14 First mutant: never transcribes structural genes.
Second mutant: never transcribes structural genes.
Third mutant: always transcribes structural genes.
Fourth mutant: never transcribes structural genes.
Fifth mutant: never transcribes structural genes.

Chapter 6

6.1 (a) (i) 3. (ii) 2. (b) with 3 or 5 base pairing would be impossible, and base pairing is the basis of replication and repair.

6.2 (a) ^{5}'TTTTTACTTCCCTACGCT$^{3'}$. (b) ^{5}'UUUUUACUUCCCUACGCU$^{3'}$. (c) Phe-Leu-Leu-Pro-Tyr-Ala. (d) The polypeptide would be terminated two residues short.

6.3 Two point mutations.

6.4 (a) ^{5}'UUU$^{3'}$, ^{5}'GGG$^{3'}$, there is no anticodon TAC. (b) Phe, Gly, none. (c) tRNA. (d) mRNA.

6.11 (a) A glutamic acid residue has been replaced by a valine residue in the sickle cell individual. This will remove a negative charge.
(b) A glutamic acid residue has been replaced by a lysine residue. This will replace a negative charge with a positive charge.
(c) One base change for Glu → Val; one base change for Glu → Lys.

6.12 (a) AUG GAA GAG GAU GAA CUU GCC GUU GUC CUU CUG CUA UGU UUU AAG CGU CGA CAU UGC GCC GGC UGA.
(b) 22. (c) 21.
(d) (1)Met (2)Glu (3)Glu (4)Asp (5)Glu (6)Leu (7)Ala (8)Val (9)Val (10)Leu (11)Leu (12)Leu (13)Cys (14)Phe (15)Lys (16)Arg (17)Arg (18)His (19)Cys (20)Ala (21)Gly end.
(e) Residues 2–5 are negatively charged. Residues 15–18 are positively charged.
(f) The two cysteine residues.

Chapter 7

7.9 (a) Rate increases proportionally with increasing concentration (straight line). (b) Rate independent of concentration. (c) K_m is approximately 3 mM.

7.18 (a) Competitive inhibition. (b) Non-competitive inhibition. (c) Irreversible inhibition.

7.19 (a) Competitive, non-competitive, irreversible.
(b) Irreversible (ensure death). **(c)** Competitive (binds to active site). **(d)** Non-competitive (binds away from the active site).

7.20 (a) Inhibit g, branch $T \rightarrow X \rightarrow Y \rightarrow Z$ slow, concentration Z decrease, inhibition cease.
(b) Inhibit d, branch $T \rightarrow U \rightarrow V \rightarrow W$ slow, concentration W slow, inhibition cease.
(c) Inhibit a, pathway $Q \rightarrow R \rightarrow S \rightarrow T$ slow, concentration T fall, inhibition cease.
(d) Negative feedback.

7.24 (a) Very specific. **(b)** Can be denatured.

7.25 (a) So the substrate can reach the active site.
(b) Cheaper.

7.26 (a) So that the bacteria can transcribe the gene.
(b) Bacteria lack the enzymes that make the modifications: protein may not function.

Chapter 8

8.3 (a) 2337 kg of glycogen + (70 − 15) = 2392 kg.
(b) Less mass, does not diffuse in tissue fluid as insoluble in water. **(c)** Quickly converted to glucose for use as energy.
(d) Mass does not matter to plant, as not mobile; starch less soluble in water than glycogen.

8.4 (a) ADP, P_i. **(b)** ATPase. **(c)** Enzyme-catalysed reactions, using energy stored in a H^+ concentration gradient.

8.7 (a) $6CO_2 + 6H_2O \rightarrow C_6H_{12}O_6 + 6O_2$. **(b)**(i) light-dependent and light-independent stages. (ii) Light-dependent in the thylakoid membrane. Light-independent in the stroma. (iii) H_2O, $NADP^+$, ADP, P_i. (iv) NADPH, ATP, O_2. (v) CO_2, ATP, NADPH. (vi) Carbohydrate (3C sugar), $NADP^+$, ADP, P_i.

8.10 Photosystem II: a, d, g, j.
Q cycle: c, f, h.
Photosystem I: b, e, i.
Net flow of electrons: d, g, a, c, f, h, i.

8.11 h, e, c (but using photosystem I instead of II), f.

8.12 (a) High light intensities. **(b)** Mesophyll cell.
(c) Mesophyll cell. **(d)** Bundle sheath cell.
(e) Sugar cane/maize.

8.13 (a) Arid environments. **(b)** At night. **(c)** Day.
(d) Day. **(e)** Pineapple.

8.15 (a) Carbon dioxide uptake: at high light intensity, highest = C_4, lowest = CAM; in dark, highest = CAM, lowest = other two.
(b) Carbohydrate production: at high light intensity, highest = C_4, lowest = C_3/CAM; in dark, all three would be very low.

8.16 c, b, a, d.

8.17 (a) Cytosol. **(b)** Matrix of mitochondria.
(c) Inner membrane of mitochondria.

8.18 (a) ATP, NADH, pyruvate. **(b)** ATP and ethanol. **(c)** ATP and lactate.

8.19 (a) Glucose 6-phosphate → fructose 6-phosphate, 3-phosphoglycerate → 2-phosphoglycerate.
(b) Glyceraldehyde 3-phosphate → 1,3-bisphosphoglycerate.
(c) Glucose → glucose 6-phosphate, fructose 6-phosphate → fructose 1,6-bisphosphate, glyceraldehyde 3-phosphate → 1,3-bisphosphoglycerate.
(d) 1,3-bisphosphoglycerate → 3-phosphoglycerate, phosphoenolpyruvate → pyruvate.
(e) Converting phosphoenolpyruvate to pyruvate must be exergonic as enough energy is produced to convert ADP and P_i to ATP.

8.20 b, i, e, g, c, j, k, d, f, h.

8.21 (a) 2.2%, lactate/ethanol/heat energy.
(b) 37.2%.

8.23 (a) No (produced in cytoplasm, used in matrix, concentration gradient correct way).
(b) Diffuses through bilayer. **(c)** So mitochondrion does not run out of ADP.
(d) By the electron transport chain. **(e)** Via ATPase.

8.24 Giving plant $H_2{}^{18}O$ leads to radiolabelled oxygen, giving plant $C^{18}O_2$ does not.

8.25 (a) (ii) ATP alone (just cyclic phosphorylation).

8.26 (a) Cyanide, rotenone: deadly poisons.
(b) DCMU, S-triazines: herbicides.

Index

INDEX